UNITED KINGDOM

IMMIGRATION LAWS AND REGULATIONS HANDBOOK

VOLUME 1

STRATEGIC INFORMATION AND REGULATIONS

International Business Publications, USA
Washington DC, USA – United Kingdom

UNITED KINGDOM

IMMIGRATION LAWS AND REGULATIONS HANDBOOK

VOLUME 1 STRATEGIC INFORMATION AND REGULATIONS

United Kingdom Country Study Guide. Vol. 1 History, Political System, Government
United Kingdom Country Study Guide. Vol. 2 Economy, Industry and Business Development
United Kingdom Country Study Guide. Vol. 3 Foreign Policy and British Commonwealth of Nations
United Kingdom Country Study Guide. Vol. 4 Defense, Security, Army, Intelligence
United Kingdom Country Study Guide. Vol. 5 Culture, Art, Society

UPDATED ANNUALLY

UK express our sincere appreciation to all government agencies and international organizations which provided information and other materials for this handbook

Cover Design: International Business Publications, USA

2016 Edition Updated Reprint International Business Publications, USA
ISBN 1-4387-8370-1

For customer service and information, please contact:
in the USA: **International Business Publications, USA**
P.O.Box 15343, Washington, DC 20003
Phone: (202) 546-2103, Fax: (202) 546-3275.
E-mail: rusric@erols.com

Printed in the USA

UNITED KINGDOM

IMMIGRATION LAWS AND REGULATIONS HANDBOOK

VOLUME 1

STRATEGIC INFORMATION AND REGULATIONS

TABLE OF CONTENTS

STRATEGIC AND BUSINESS PROFILES **9**

STRATEGIC PROFILE 9
COUNTRY OVERVIEW *11*
ECONOMIC OVERVIEW *11*
Geography *11*
People *13*
Government *14*
Economy *19*
Energy *25*
Communications *27*
Transportation *28*
Military *30*
Transnational Issues *30*
IMPORTANT INFORMATION FOR UNDERSTANDING UK 32
BASIC PROFILE *32*
PEOPLE *33*
HISTORY *34*
GOVERNMENT *35*
U.S.-U.K. RELATIONS *39*
ECONOMY 41
NORTH SEA OIL EXPLORATION 43
Reserves and production *45*
Licensing *47*
Carbon dioxide sequestration *47*
DEFENSE AND FOREIGN RELATIONS *48*
TRAVEL AND BUSINESS INFORMATION *48*

IMMIGRATION POLICY FUNDUMENTALS **50**

MODERN HISTORY OF IMMIGRATION TO THE UNITED KINGDOM 50
BRITISH EMPIRE & THE COMMONUKALTH 51
WORLD WAR II 52
POST-WAR IMMIGRATION (1945-1983) 52
CONTEMPORARY IMMIGRATION (1983 ONWARDS) 53
European Union *54*

Managed migration ... 55
Refugees and asylum seekers ... 56
Illegal immigration ... 57
Rivers of Blood speech ... 58

IMPORTANT OFFICES AND PROGRAMS MANAGING IMMIGRATION ... 59

ASYLUM AND IMMIGRATION TRIBUNAL ... 59
BORDER AND IMMIGRATION AGENCY ... 60
BRITISH NATIONAL IDENTITY CARD ... 61
EEA FAMILY PERMIT ... 63
FRESH TALENT INITIATIVE ... 66
LIFE IN THE UNITED KINGDOM TEST ... 66
PURPOSE OF THE TEST ... 66
Content of the test ... 66
Speculation about the test ... 67
Test Errors and Inaccuracies ... 67

LIFE IN THE UK TEST TERMS AND CONDITIONS ... 68

LIST OF COUNTRIES BY BRITISH IMMIGRANTS ... 71
REFUGEE COUNCIL ... 71
UK POINTS-BASED IMMIGRATION SYSTEM ... 71
Structure ... 71
Tier 1 ... 71
Tier 2 ... 72
Tier 3 ... 72
Tier 4 ... 72
Tier 5 ... 72
Public reception ... 73
A POINTS BASED SYSTEM: FIVE TIERS ... 73
Tier 1 ... 73
Tier 2 ... 74
Tier 3 ... 74
Tier 4 ... 74
Tier 5 ... 74
Points-based assessment ... 75
Sponsorship duties ... 75
POINTS BASED SYSTEM TIER 1, INVESTOR (INF 23) ... 75

UK IMMIGRATION RULES: STRATEGIC AND PRACTICAL INFORMATION ... 87

IMMIGRATION, ASYLUM AND NATIONALITY ACT 2006 ... 87
Commencement Orders ... 87
Summary of changes ... 87
Citizenship and Right of Abode ... 88
Notable applications of the Act ... 88
UK IMMIGRATION RULES FOR ASYLUM ... 88
Asylum ... 88
Claiming asylum ... 89
Who can claim asylum? ... 89
Applying within the United Kingdom ... 89
The asylum process ... 89
Human rights applications ... 90
Gateway Protection Programme ... 90

Asylum support ... *90*
Who to contact with questions about support ... *91*
INQUIRY INTO ASYLUM AND IMMIGRATION APPEALS ... 91
Delay in the determination of appeals ... *91*
Administration of the appeals process ... *92*
Family visitor appeals ... *94*
The availability of legal advice and representation ... *96*
HELP AND ADVICE WITH IMMIGRATION ... 97
Legal advice ... *97*
One Stop Services ... *98*
Voluntary return ... *99*
Disability or special care ... *100*
Victims of torture ... *101*
Racial harassment ... *101*
Domestic violence ... *102*
Reporting a crime ... *102*
Emergencies ... *102*
GENERAL RILES TO ENTER OR REMAIN IN THE UNITED KINGDOM ... 103
Leave to enter the United Kingdom ... *103*
Common Travel Area ... *105*
Admission of certain British passport holders ... *105*
Persons outside the United Kingdom ... *105*
Returning Residents ... *106*
Non-lapsing leave ... *106*
Holders of restricted travel documents and passports ... *106*
Leave to enter granted on arrival in the United Kingdom ... *107*
Entry clearance ... *107*
Variation of leave to enter or remain in the United Kingdom ... *109*
Knowledge of language and life in the United Kingdom ... *110*
Specified forms and procedures for applications or claims in connection with immigration ... *110*
Variation of Applications or Claims for Leave to Remain ... *113*
Determination of the date of an application or claim (or variation of an application or claim) in connection with immigration ... *113*
Withdrawn applications or claims for leave to remain in the United Kingdom ... *114*
Undertakings ... *114*
Medical ... *114*
Students ... *115*

IMPORTANT LAWS AND REGULATIONS RELATED TO IMMIGRATION ... 116

REFORM OF IMMIGRATION LAW ... 116
Immigration Case Work Programme ... *117*
BORDERS, CITIZENSHIP AND IMMIGRATION BILL ... 117
Summary of the Bill ... *118*
BRITISH NATIONALITY LAW AND CITIZENSHIP FUNDAMENTAL ... 118
History ... *118*
WHO HAS THE RIGHT TO LIVE IN THE UNITED KINGDOM? ... 119
How to apply for a replacement registration/naturalisation certificate ... *119*
Applying for settlement in the United Kingdom ... *119*
CLASSES OF BRITISH NATIONALITY ... 120
Who is a British subject? ... *121*
Who is a British overseas citizen? ... *122*
Who is a British overseas territories citizen? ... *123*

Who is a British national (overseas)? ... 123
Who is a British protected person? ... 124
What does the term mean? ... 124
Am I a British protected person? ... 124
What rights does a British protected person have? ... 125
Acquisition of British citizenship ... 125
British citizenship by birth in the United Kingdom ... 126
British Citizenship by descent ... 126
British citizenship by adoption ... 127
British citizenship by naturalisation ... 128
Citizens of EEA States and Switzerland ... 129
Ten year rule ... 130
Registration as a British citizen ... 130
ACQUISITION OF BRITISH OVERSEAS TERRITORIES CITIZENSHIP ... 130
Acquisition of other categories of British nationality ... 131
Persons connected with former British colonies ... 131
British National (Overseas) and Hong Kong ... 131
Persons born in the Republic of Ireland ... 131
Descendants of the Electress Sophia of Hanover ... 131
LOSS OF BRITISH NATIONALITY ... 132
Renunciation and resumption of British nationality ... 132
Automatic loss of British nationality ... 132
Deprivation of British nationality ... 132
DUAL NATIONALITY, DUAL AND EU CITIZENSHIP ... 133
British citizenship ceremonies ... 133
European citizenship ... 134
BRITISH NATIONALITY ACT 1981 CHAPTER 61 ... 134
PART I BRITISH CITIZENSHIP ACQUISITION AFTER COMMENCEMENT ... 134
PART II BRITISH DEPENDENT TERRITORIES CITIZENSHIP ... 143
PART III BRITISH OVERSEAS CITIZENSHIP ... 148
PART IV BRITISH SUBJECTS ... 149
PART V MISCELLANEOUS AND SUPPLEMENTARY ... 150
IMMIGRATION, ASYLUM AND NATIONALITY ACT 2006 ... 173
Appeals ... 173
Employment ... 178
Information ... 182
Claimants and applicants ... 191
Miscellaneous ... 195
General ... 198
SCHEDULE 1 Immigration and Asylum Appeals: Consequential Amendments ... 199
SCHEDULE 2 Fees: Consequential Amendments ... 200
UK BORDERS ACT 2007 ... 200
Detention at ports ... 201
Biometric registration ... 202
Treatment of claimants ... 208
Enforcement ... 211
Deportation of criminals ... 214
Information ... 217
Border and Immigration Inspectorate ... 221
General ... 224

TRAVEL TO THE UK ... 226

US STATE DEPARTMENT SUGGESTIONS 226
BUSINESS TRAVEL 229
Business Customs 229
Travel Advisory and Visas 229
Holidays 230
Safety and Security 231
Crime 231
Medical Facilities and Insurance 231
Traffic Safety and Road Conditions 232
Aviation Safety and Oversight 232
Accommodation 232
Food 233

SUPPLEMENTS 233

HIGHLY SKILLED MIGRANT PROGRAMME (HSMP), ... 233
Overview of Points System 233
1. Age Assessment - 20 points (maximum) 233
2) Qualifications. You will gain points as follows: 233
4) Earning poUKr 233
UK Experience - 5 Points (Maximum) 236
English Language Ability 237
8) Other Requirements 237
FEE SCHEDULE FOR UK IMMIGRATION 237
Tier 1 – (General) – Highly Skilled Migrant 237
Tier 1 (Post study work) 238
Tier 1 (Investor; £1m 'passive' investment) 238
Tier 2 – Skilled Migration 238
Work Permit Applications & related work 239
Tier 4 (Student visa) 240
Tier 5 (Youth Mobility Scheme) 240
Indefinite Leave to Remain: 240
Naturalization: 240
Fiancée visa 240
Marriage Visa 240
ECAA – Visa to run a business un the UK under the European Community Accession Agreements . 241
Sole representative 241
Visitor Visa 241
VISA FEES 241
FOREIGN-BORN POPULATION OF THE UNITED KINGDOM 244
VISA FEES 244
SELECTED IMMIGRATION INFORMATION AND STATISTICS 253
IMPORTANT INFORMATION 253
PROVISIONAL 2009 ANNUAL COMPARISONS ON CONTROL OF IMMIGRATION 254
UK entry clearance visas issued 255
Passenger arrivals 256
Non-asylum passengers initially refused entry 257
Initial asylum decisions 257
Timeliness of case processing to a conclusion 258
Resettlement scheme 259
Asylum support applications 259
Issues of entry clearance visas to the United Kingdom, by country of nationality, ... 259
Applications received for asylum in the UK, excluding dependants, and initial decisions by country of nationality 263

Outcome of Asylum Appeals determined at the Asylum and Immigration Tribunal, excluding dependants,by country of nationality *264*
Persons entering detention (1)(2) held solely under Immigration Act powers, by country of nationality, ... *266*
STRATEGIC AND BUSINESS CONTACTS IN UK 268
1. UK Government Agencies *268*
2. UK Trade Associations/Chambers of Commerce *269*
3. U.S. Embassy Contacts *270*
4. Washington DC-based USG Contacts (UK-specific) *270*
5. Relevant U.S.-based Multipliers *271*
CONTACT DIRECTORY 271
Immigration enquiry bureau *271*
Calling UK BORDER AGENCY *271*
Nationality contact centre *272*
EEA residency enquiries *272*
Sponsorship and employers' helpline *273*
Work permits customer contact centre *273*
Asylum support customer contact centre *274*
GLOSSARY 275
A *275*
B *276*
C *279*
D *283*
E *284*
F *286*
G *287*
H *288*
I *289*
K *291*
L *291*
M *292*
N *293*
O *294*
P *295*
Q *296*
R *297*
S *298*
T *301*
U *303*
V *304*
W *304*
BASIC TITLES FOR THE UNITED KINGDOM 306

STRATEGIC AND BUSINESS PROFILES

STRATEGIC PROFILE

Capital and largest city	London 51°30′N 0°7′W51.500°N 0.117°W
Official language and national language	English
Recognised regional languages	Cornish, Irish, Scots, Scottish Gaelic, Ulster-Scots, Welsh
Ethnic groups (2011)	87.1% White 7.0% Asian 3.0% Black 2.0% Mixed 0.9% Other
Demonym	British, Briton
Government	Unitary parliamentary constitutional monarchy
- Monarch	Elizabeth II
- Prime Minister	David Cameron
Legislature	Parliament
- Upper house	House of Lords
- Lower house	House of Commons
	Formation
- Acts of Union 1707	1 May 1707
- Acts of Union 1800	1 January 1801
- Irish Free State Constitution Act	5 December 1922
	Area
- Total	243,610 km^2 (80th) 94,060 sq mi
- Water (%)	1.34
	Population
- 2013 estimate	64,100,000 (22nd)
- 2011 census	63,181,775 (22nd)
- Density	255.6/km^2 (51st) 661.9/sq mi
GDP (PPP)	2014 estimate
- Total	$2.435 trillion (10th)
- Per capita	$37,744 (27th)
GDP (nominal)	2014 estimate
- Total	$2.848 trillion (6th)
- Per capita	$44,141 (22nd)
Gini (2012)	▼32.8 medium · 33rd
HDI (2013)	▬0.892 very high · 14th
Currency	Pound sterling (GBP)

Time zone	GMT (UTC)
- Summer (DST)	BST (UTC+1)
Date format	dd/mm/yyyy (AD)
Drives on the	left
Calling code	+44
ISO 3166 code	GB
Internet TLD	.uk

The **United Kingdom of Great Britain and Northern Ireland** known as the **United Kingdom** (**UK**) or **Britain**, is a sovereign state in Europe. Lying off the north-western coast of the European mainland, the country includes the island of Great Britain (a term also applied loosely to refer to the whole country) , the north-eastern part of the island of Ireland, and many smaller islands. Northern Ireland is the only part of the UK that shares a land border with another state: the Republic of Ireland. Apart from this land border, the UK is surrounded by the Atlantic Ocean, with the North Sea in the east and the English Channel in the south. The Irish Sea lies between Great Britain and Ireland. The UK has an area of 243,610 square kilometres (94,060 sq mi) , making it the 78th-largest sovereign state in the world and the 11th-largest in Europe.

The United Kingdom is the 22nd-most populous country, with an estimated 64.1 million inhabitants. It is a constitutional monarchy with a parliamentary system of governance. Its capital city is London, an important global city and financial centre with the second-largest urban area in Europe, and its metropolitan area is the largest in European Union, with a population of about 14 million according Eurostat. The current monarch—since 6 February 1952—is Queen Elizabeth II. The UK consists of four countries: England, Scotland, Wales, and Northern Ireland. The latter three have devolved administrations, each with varying powers, based in their capitals, Edinburgh, Cardiff, and Belfast, respectively. Guernsey, Jersey, and the Isle of Man are not part of the United Kingdom, being Crown dependencies with the British Government responsible for defence and international representation. The UK has fourteen Overseas Territories, including the disputed Falkland Islands, Gibraltar, and Indian Ocean Territory.

The relationships among the countries of the United Kingdom have changed over time. Wales was annexed by the Kingdom of England under the Acts of Union of 1536 and 1543. A treaty between England and Scotland resulted in a unified Kingdom of Great Britain in 1707, which in 1801, merged with the Kingdom of Ireland to form the United Kingdom of Great Britain and Ireland. In 1922, five-sixths of Ireland seceded from the country, leaving the present formulation of the United Kingdom of Great Britain and Northern Ireland. British Overseas Territories, formerly colonies, are the remnants of the British Empire which, at its height in the late 19th and early 20th centuries, encompassed almost a quarter of the world's land mass and was the largest empire in history. British influence can be observed in the language, culture, and legal systems of many of its former colonies.

The United Kingdom is a developed country and has the world's sixth-largest economy by nominal GDP and tenth-largest by purchasing power parity. The country is considered to have a high-income economy and is categorised as very high in the Human Development Index, currently ranking 14th in the world. It was the world's first industrialised country and the world's foremost power during the 19th and early 20th centuries. The UK remains a great power with considerable economic, cultural, military, scientific, and political influence internationally. It is a recognised nuclear weapons state and its military expenditure ranks fifth or sixth in the world. The UK has been a permanent member of the United Nations Security Council since its first session in 1946. It has been a member state of the European Union (EU) and its predecessor, the European Economic Community (EEC) , since 1973; it is also a member of the Commonwealth of

Nations, the Council of Europe, the G7, the G8, the G20, NATO, the Organisation for Economic Co-operation and Development (OECD) , and the World Trade Organization (WTO) .

COUNTRY OVERVIEW

Head of State: Queen Elizabeth II
Prime Minister: Anthony (Tony) Blair, elected May 1997
Population : 59.1 million
Location/Size: Western Europe, islands including the northern one-sixth of the island of Ireland between the North Atlantic Ocean and the North Sea, northwest of France/244,820 sq km (slightly smaller than Oregon)
Capital City: London
Language: English
Ethnic groups: English 81.5%, Scottish 9.6%, Irish 2.4%, Welsh 1.9%, Ulster 1.8%, West Indian, Indian, Pakistani, and other 2.8%
Religions: Anglican 27 million, Roman Catholic 9 million, Muslim 1 million, Presbyterian 800,000, Methodist 760,000, Sikh 400,000, Hindu 350,000, Jewish 300,000 (1991 est.)
Defense: Army, 113,900; Navy, 44,500; Air Force, 52,540

ECONOMIC OVERVIEW

Chancellor of the Exchequer: Gordon Brown
Currency: Pound sterling
Exchange Rate: 1 US Dollar = 0.67 pounds
Gross Domestic Product (GDP) : $591.8 billion
Real GDP Growth Rate : 1.8% **:** 2.9%
Inflation Rate (consumer prices) : 1.6% **:** 2.9%
Unemployment Rate : 4.3% **: 4.2**%
Merchandise Exports : $110.8 billion
Merchandise Imports : $128.6 billion
Major Trading Partners: United States, Germany, France, Netherlands
Major Exports: Food, beverages, and tobacco; crude materials, fuels, chemicals, machinery, transport equipment
Major Imports: Food, beverages, and tobacco; crude materials, fuels, chemicals, machinery, transport equipment

Background: Great Britain, the dominant industrial and maritime power of the 19th century, played a leading role in developing parliamentary democracy and in advancing literature and science. At its zenith, the British Empire stretched over one-fourth of the earth's surface. The first half of the 20th century saw the UK's strength seriously depleted in two World Wars. The second half witnessed the dismantling of the Empire and the UK rebuilding itself into a modern and prosperous European nation. The UK currently is weighing the degree of its integration with continental Europe. A member of the EU, it chose to remain outside of the EMU for the time being. Constitutional reform is also a significant issue in the UK. Regional assemblies with varying degrees of power opened in Scotland, Wales, and Northern Ireland in 1999.

GEOGRAPHY

Location: Western Europe, islands including the northern one-sixth of the island of Ireland between the North Atlantic Ocean and the North Sea, northwest of France
Geographic coordinates: 54 00 N, 2 00 W

Map references: Europe

Base 800565 (B00425) 6-88

Area:
total: 244,820 sq km
land: 241,590 sq km
water: 3,230 sq km
note: includes Rockall and Shetland Islands

Area - comparative: slightly smaller than Oregon
Land boundaries:
total: 360 km
border countries: Ireland 360 km
Coastline: 12,429 km
Maritime claims:
continental shelf: as defined in continental shelf orders or in accordance with agreed upon boundaries
exclusive fishing zone: 200 nm
territorial sea: 12 nm
Climate: temperate; moderated by prevailing southwest winds over the North Atlantic Current; more than one-half of the days are overcast
Terrain: mostly rugged hills and low mountains; level to rolling plains in east and southeast

Elevation extremes:
lowest point: Fenland -4 m
highest point: Ben Nevis 1,343 m

Natural resources: coal, petroleum, natural gas, tin, limestone, iron ore, salt, clay, chalk, gypsum, lead, silica, arable land

Land use:
arable land: 25% *permanent crops:* 0%
permanent pastures: 46% *forests and woodland:* 10% *other:* 19%

Irrigated land: 1,080 sq km

Natural hazards: NA

Environment - current issues: sulfur dioxide emissions from power plants contribute to air pollution; some rivers polluted by agricultural wastes; and coastal waters polluted because of large-scale disposal of sewage at sea

Environment - international agreements:
party to: Air Pollution, Air Pollution-Nitrogen Oxides, Air Pollution-Sulphur 94, Air Pollution-Volatile Organic Compounds, Antarctic-Environmental Protocol, Antarctic Treaty, Biodiversity, Climate Change, Desertification, Endangered Species, Environmental Modification, Hazardous Wastes, Law of the Sea, Marine Dumping, Marine Life Conservation, Nuclear Test Ban, Ozone Layer Protection, Ship Pollution, Tropical Timber 83, Tropical Timber 94, Wetlands, Whaling
signed, but not ratified: Air Pollution-Persistent Organic Pollutants, Climate Change-Kyoto Protocol

Geography - note: lies near vital North Atlantic sea lanes; only 35 km from France and now linked by tunnel under the English Channel; because of heavily indented coastline, no location is more than 125 km from tidal waters

PEOPLE

Population: 59,511,464

Age structure:
0-14 years: 19% (male 5,816,313; female 5,519,479)
15-64 years: 65% (male 19,622,152; female 19,228,938)
65 years and over: 16% (male 3,864,612; female 5,459,970)
Population growth rate: 0.25%
Birth rate: 11.76 births/1,000 population
Death rate: 10.38 deaths/1,000 population
Net migration rate: 1.07 migrant(s) /1,000 population

Sex ratio:
at birth: 1.05 male(s) /female
under 15 years: 1.05 male(s) /female
15-64 years: 1.02 male(s) /female
65 years and over: 0.71 male(s) /female
total population: 0.97 male(s) /female

Infant mortality rate: 5.63 deaths/1,000 live births

Life expectancy at birth:
total population: 77.66 years
male: 74.97 years
female: 80.49 years

Total fertility rate: 1.74 children born/woman
Nationality:
noun: Briton(s) , British (collective plural)
adjective: British
Ethnic groups: English 81.5%, Scottish 9.6%, Irish 2.4%, Welsh 1.9%, Ulster 1.8%, West Indian, Indian, Pakistani, and other 2.8%
Religions: Anglican 27 million, Roman Catholic 9 million, Muslim 1 million, Presbyterian 800,000, Methodist 760,000, Sikh 400,000, Hindu 350,000, Jewish 300,000 (1991 est.)
Languages: English, Welsh (about 26% of the population of Wales) , Scottish form of Gaelic (about 60,000 in Scotland)

Literacy:
definition: age 15 and over has completed five or more years of schooling
total population: 99%

GOVERNMENT

Country name:

conventional long form: United Kingdom of Great Britain and Northern Ireland; note - Great Britain includes England, Scotland, and Wales
conventional short form: United Kingdom
abbreviation: UK

Government type:

constitutional monarchy and Commonwealth realm

Capital:

name: London
geographic coordinates: 51 30 N, 0 05 W
time difference: UTC 0 (5 hours ahead of Washington, DC, during Standard Time)
daylight saving time: +1hr, begins last Sunday in March; ends last Sunday in October
note: applies to the United Kingdom proper, not to its overseas dependencies or territories

Administrative divisions:

England: 27 two-tier counties, 32 London boroughs and 1 City of London or Greater London, 36 metropolitan districts, 56 unitary authorities (including 4 single-tier counties*)
two-tier counties: Buckinghamshire, Cambridgeshire, Cumbria, Derbyshire, Devon, Dorset, East Sussex, Essex, Gloucestershire, Hampshire, Hertfordshire, Kent, Lancashire, Leicestershire, Lincolnshire, Norfolk, North Yorkshire, Northamptonshire, Nottinghamshire, Oxfordshire, Somerset, Staffordshire, Suffolk, Surrey, Warwickshire, West Sussex, Worcestershire
London boroughs and City of London or Greater London: Barking and Dagenham, Barnet, Bexley, Brent, Bromley, Camden, Croydon, Ealing, Enfield, Greenwich, Hackney, Hammersmith and Fulham, Haringey, Harrow, Havering, Hillingdon, Hounslow, Islington, Kensington and Chelsea, Kingston upon Thames, Lambeth, Lewisham, City of London, Merton, Newham, Redbridge, Richmond upon Thames, Southwark, Sutton, Tower Hamlets, Waltham Forest, Wandsworth, Westminster
metropolitan districts: Barnsley, Birmingham, Bolton, Bradford, Bury, Calderdale, Coventry, Doncaster, Dudley, Gateshead, Kirklees, Knowlsey, Leeds, Liverpool, Manchester, Newcastle upon Tyne, North Tyneside, Oldham, Rochdale, Rotherham, Salford, Sandwell, Sefton, Sheffield, Solihull, South Tyneside, St. Helens, Stockport, Sunderland, Tameside, Trafford, Wakefield, Walsall, Wigan, Wirral, Wolverhampton
unitary authorities: Bath and North East Somerset, Blackburn with Darwen, Bedford, Blackpool, Bournemouth, Bracknell Forest, Brighton and Hove, City of Bristol, Central Bedfordshire, Cheshire East, Cheshire West and Chester, Cornwall, Darlington, Derby, Durham County*, East Riding of Yorkshire, Halton, Hartlepool, Herefordshire*, Isle of Wight*, Isles of Scilly, City of Kingston upon Hull, Leicester, Luton, Medway, Middlesbrough, Milton Keynes, North East Lincolnshire, North Lincolnshire, North Somerset, Northumberland*, Nottingham, Peterborough, Plymouth, Poole, Portsmouth, Reading, Redcar and Cleveland, Rutland, Shropshire, Slough, South Gloucestershire, Southampton, Southend-on-Sea, Stockton-on-Tees, Stoke-on-Trent, Swindon, Telford and Wrekin, Thurrock, Torbay, Warrington, West Berkshire, Wiltshire, Windsor and Maidenhead, Wokingham, York
Northern Ireland: 13 borough councils, 11 district council areas, 1 city and district council, 1 city council
borough councils: Antrim, Ards, Ballymena, Ballymoney, Carrickfergus, Castlereagh, Coleraine, Craigavon, Dungannon and South Tyrone, Larne, Limavady, Newtownabbey, North Down
city and district councils: Armagh
city councils: Lisburn
district council areas: Belfast, Banbridge, Cookstown, Derry, Down, Fermanagh, Magherafelt, Moyle, Newry and Mourne, Omagh, Strabane
Scotland: 32 council areas
council areas: Aberdeen City, Aberdeenshire, Angus, Argyll and Bute, Clackmannanshire, Dumfries and Galloway, Dundee City, East Ayrshire, East Dunbartonshire, East Lothian, East Renfrewshire, City of Edinburgh, Eilean Siar (Western Isles) , Falkirk, Fife, Glasgow

City, Highland, Inverclyde, Midlothian, Moray, North Ayrshire, North Lanarkshire, Orkney Islands, Perth and Kinross, Renfrewshire, Shetland Islands, South Ayrshire, South Lanarkshire, Stirling, The Scottish Borders, West Dunbartonshire, West Lothian
Wales: 22 unitary authorities
unitary authorities: Blaenau Gwent, Bridgend, Caerphilly, Cardiff, Carmarthenshire, Ceredigion, Conwy, Denbighshire, Flintshire, Gwynedd, Isle of Anglesey, Merthyr Tydfil, Monmouthshire, Neath Port Talbot, Newport, Pembrokeshire, Powys, Rhondda Cynon Taff, Swansea, The Vale of Glamorgan, Torfaen, Wrexham

Dependent areas:

Anguilla, Bermuda, British Indian Ocean Territory, British Virgin Islands, Cayman Islands, Falkland Islands, Gibraltar, Montserrat, Pitcairn Islands, Saint Helena, Ascension, and Tristan da Cunha, South Georgia and the South Sandwich Islands, Turks and Caicos Islands

Independence:

12 April 1927 (Royal and Parliamentary Titles Act establishes current name of the United Kingdom of Great Britain and Northern Ireland) ; notable earlier dates: 927 (minor English kingdoms united) ; 3 March 1284 (enactment of the Statute of Rhuddlan uniting England and Wales) ; 1536 (Act of Union formally incorporates England and Wales) ; 1 May 1707 (Acts of Union formally unite England and Scotland as Great Britain) ; 1 January 1801 (Acts of Union formally unite Great Britain and Ireland as the United Kingdom of Great Britain and Ireland) ; 6 December 1921 (Anglo-Irish Treaty formalizes partition of Ireland; six counties remain part of the United Kingdom and Northern Ireland)

National holiday:

the UK does not celebrate one particular national holiday

Constitution:

unwritten; partly statutes, partly common law and practice; note - recent additions include the Human Rights Act of 1998, the Constitutional Reform and Governance Act 2010, the Parliamentary Voting System and Constituencies Act 2011, and the Fixed-term Parliaments Act 2011 (2011)

Legal system:

common law system; has nonbinding judicial review of Acts of Parliament under the Human Rights Act of 1998

International law organization participation:

accepts compulsory ICJ jurisdiction with reservations; accepts ICCt jurisdiction

Suffrage:

18 years of age; universal

Executive branch:

chief of state: Queen ELIZABETH II (since 6 February 1952) ; Heir Apparent Prince CHARLES (son of the queen, born 14 November 1948)
head of government: Prime Minister David CAMERON (since 11 May 2010)
cabinet: Cabinet of Ministers appointed by the prime minister
elections: the monarchy is hereditary; following legislative elections, the leader of the majority party or the leader of the majority coalition usually becomes the prime minister

Legislative branch:

bicameral Parliament consists of House of Lords; note - membership is not fixed (780 seats; consisting of approximately 667 life peers, 88 hereditary peers, and 25 clergy - as of 13 January 2014) and House of Commons (650 seats since 2010 elections; members elected by popular vote to serve five-year terms unless the House is dissolved earlier)
elections: House of Lords - no elections (note - in 1999, as provided by the House of Lords Act, elections were held in the House of Lords to determine the 92 hereditary peers who would remain there; elections are held only as vacancies in the hereditary peerage arise) ; House of Commons - last held on 6 May 2010 (next to be held by June 2015)
election results: House of Commons - percent of vote by party - Conservative 36.1%, Labor 29%, Liberal Democrats 23%, other 11.9%; seats by party - Conservative 305, Labor 258, Liberal Democrat 57, other 30
note: in 1998 elections were held for a Northern Ireland Assembly (because of unresolved disputes among existing parties, the transfer of power from London to Northern Ireland came only at the end of 1999 and has been suspended four times, the latest occurring in October 2002 and lasting until 8 May 2007) ; in 1999, the UK held the first elections for a Scottish Parliament and a Welsh Assembly; the most recent elections for the Northern Ireland Assembly, the Scottish Parliament, and the Welsh Assembly took place in May 2011

Judicial branch:

highest court(s) : Supreme Court (consists of 12 justices including the court president and deputy president)
note - the Supreme Court was established by the Constitutional Reform Act 2005 and implemented in October 2009, replacing the Appellate Committee of the House of Lords as the highest court in the United Kingdom
judge selection and term of office: judge candidates selected by an independent committee of several judicial commissions, followed by their recommendations to the prime minister, and appointed by Her Majesty The Queen; justices appointed during period of good behavior
subordinate courts: England and Wales - Court of Appeal (civil and criminal divisions) ; High Court; Crown Court; County Courts; Magistrates' Courts; Scotland - Court of Sessions; Sherrif Courts; High Court of Justiciary; tribunals; Northern Ireland - Court of Appeal in Northern Ireland; High Court; county courts; magistrates' courts; specialized tribunals

Political parties and leaders:

Conservative [David CAMERON]
Alliance Party (Northerm Ireland) [David FORD]
Democratic Unionist Party or DUP (Northern Ireland) [Peter ROBINSON]
Labor Party [Ed MILIBAND]
Liberal Democrats (Lib Dems) [Nick CLEGG]
Party of Wales (Plaid Cymru) [Leanne WOOD]
Scottish National Party or SNP [Alex SALMOND]
Sinn Fein (Northern Ireland) [Gerry ADAMS]
Social Democratic and Labor Party or SDLP (Northern Ireland) [Alasdair MCDONNELL]
Ulster Unionist Party (Northern Ireland) [Mike NESBITT]
United Kingdom Independent Party or UKIP [Nigel FARAGE]

Political pressure groups and leaders:

Campaign for Nuclear Disarmament
Confederation of British Industry
National Farmers' Union
Trades Union Congress

International organization participation:

ADB (nonregional member) , AfDB (nonregional member) , Arctic Council (observer) , Australia Group, BIS, C, CBSS (observer) , CD, CDB, CE, CERN, EAPC, EBRD, EIB, EITI (implementing country) , ESA, EU, FAO, FATF, G-20, G-5, G-7, G-8, G-10, IADB, IAEA, IBRD, ICAO, ICC (national committees) , ICRM, IDA, IEA, IFAD, IFC, IFRCS, IGAD (partners) , IHO, ILO, IMF, IMO, IMSO, Interpol, IOC, IOM, IPU, ISO, ITSO, ITU, ITUC (NGOs) , MIGA, MINUSMA, MONUSCO, NATO, NEA, NSG, OAS (observer) , OECD, OPCW, OSCE, Pacific Alliance (observer) , Paris Club, PCA, PIF (partner) , SELEC (observer) , UN, UNCTAD, UNESCO, UNFICYP, UNHCR, UNIDO, UNISFA, UNMISS, UNRWA, UNSC (permanent) , UPU, WCO, WHO, WIPO, WMO, WTO, ZC

Diplomatic representation in the US:

chief of mission: Ambassador Peter John WESTMACOTT (since 17 January 2012)
chancery: 3100 Massachusetts Avenue NW, Washington, DC 20008
telephone: (202) 588-6500
FAX: (202) 588-7850
consulate(s) general: Atlanta, Boston, Chicago, Denver, Houston, Los Angeles, Miami, New York, San Francisco
consulate(s) : Dallas, Orlando (FL)

Diplomatic representation from the US:

chief of mission: Ambassador Matthew W. BARZUN (since 15 August 2013)
embassy: 24 Grosvenor Square, London, W1K 6AH note - a new embassy is scheduled to open by the end of 2017 in the Nine Elms area of Wandsworth
mailing address: PSC 801, Box 40, FPO AE 09498-4040
telephone: [44] (0) 20 7499-9000
FAX: [44] (0) 20 7629-9124
consulate(s) general: Belfast, Edinburgh

Flag description:

blue field with the red cross of Saint George (patron saint of England) edged in white superimposed on the diagonal red cross of Saint Patrick (patron saint of Ireland) , which is superimposed on the diagonal white cross of Saint Andrew (patron saint of Scotland) ; properly known as the Union Flag, but commonly called the Union Jack; the design and colors (especially the Blue Ensign) have been the basis for a number of other flags including other Commonwealth countries and their constituent states or provinces, and British overseas territories

National symbol(s) :

lion (Britain in general) ; lion, Tudor rose (England) ; lion, unicorn, thistle (Scotland) ; dragon, daffodil, leek (Wales) ; harp, flax (Northern Ireland)

National anthem:

name: "God Save the Queen"

ECONOMY

Economy - overview:

The UK, a leading trading power and financial center, is the third largest economy in Europe after Germany and France. Over the past two decades, the government has greatly reduced public ownership. Agriculture is intensive, highly mechanized, and efficient by European standards, producing about 60% of food needs with less than 2% of the labor force. The UK has large coal, natural gas, and oil resources, but its oil and natural gas reserves are declining and the UK became a net importer of energy in 2005. Services, particularly banking, insurance, and business services, are key drivers of British GDP growth. Manufacturing, meanwhile, has declined in importance but still accounts for about 10% of economic output. After emerging from recession in 1992, Britain's economy enjoyed the longest period of expansion on record during which time growth outpaced most of Western Europe. In 2008, however, the global financial crisis hit the economy particularly hard, due to the importance of its financial sector.

Falling home prices, high consumer debt, and the global economic slowdown compounded Britain's economic problems, pushing the economy into recession in the latter half of 2008 and prompting the then BROWN (Labour) government to implement a number of measures to stimulate the economy and stabilize the financial markets; these included nationalizing parts of the banking system, temporarily cutting taxes, suspending public sector borrowing rules, and moving forward public spending on capital projects. Facing burgeoning public deficits and debt levels, in 2010 the CAMERON-led coalition government (between Conservatives and Liberal Democrats) initiated a five-year austerity program, which aimed to lower London's budget deficit from about 11% of GDP in 2010 to nearly 1% by 2015.

In November 2011, Chancellor of the Exchequer George OSBORNE announced additional austerity measures through 2017 largely due to the euro-zone debt crisis. The CAMERON government raised the value added tax from 17.5% to 20% in 2011. It has pledged to reduce the corporation tax rate to 21% by 2014. The Bank of England (BoE) implemented an asset purchase program of £375 billion (approximately $605 billion) as of December 2013. During times of economic crisis, the BoE coordinates interest rate moves with the European Central Bank, but Britain remains outside the European Economic and Monetary Union (EMU) . In 2012, weak consumer spending and subdued business investment weighed on the economy, however, in 2013 GDP grew 1.4%, accelerating unexpectedly in the second half of the year because of greater consumer spending and a recovering housing market. The budget deficit is falling but remains high at nearly 7% and public debt has continued to increase.

GDP (purchasing power parity) :

$2.387 trillion
country comparison to the world: 9
$2.343 trillion (2012 est.)
$2.341 trillion (2011 est.)
note: data are in 2013 US dollars

GDP (official exchange rate) :

$2.49 trillion

GDP - real growth rate:

1.8%
country comparison to the world: 152
0.1% (2012 est.)
0.9% (2011 est.)

GDP - per capita (PPP) :

$37,300
country comparison to the world: 34
$37,100 (2012 est.)
$37,300 (2011 est.)
note: data are in 2013 US dollars

Gross national saving:

10.5% of GDP
country comparison to the world: 132
11% of GDP (2012 est.)
13.7% of GDP (2011 est.)

GDP - composition, by end use:

household consumption: 66.5%
government consumption: 21.4%
investment in fixed capital: 13.8%
investment in inventories: 0.4%
exports of goods and services: 31.1%

imports of goods and services: -33.2%

GDP - composition, by sector of origin:

agriculture: 0.7%
industry: 20.5%
services: 78.9%

Agriculture - products:

cereals, oilseed, potatoes, vegetables; cattle, sheep, poultry; fish

Industries:

machine tools, electric power equipment, automation equipment, railroad equipment, shipbuilding, aircraft, motor vehicles and parts, electronics and communications equipment, metals, chemicals, coal, petroleum, paper and paper products, food processing, textiles, clothing, other consumer goods

Industrial production growth rate:

-0.3%
country comparison to the world: 169

Labor force:

30.15 million
country comparison to the world: 20

Labor force - by occupation:

agriculture: 1.4%
industry: 18.2%
services: 80.4% (2006 est.)

Unemployment rate:

7.2%
country comparison to the world: 76
7.8% (2012 est.)

Population below poverty line:

16.2% (2011 est.)

Household income or consumption by percentage share:

lowest 10%: 1.7%
highest 10%: 31.1% (2012)

Distribution of family income - Gini index:

32.3 (2012)
country comparison to the world: 104
34 (2005)

Budget:

revenues: $1.023 trillion
expenditures: $1.112 trillion

Taxes and other revenues:

41.1% of GDP
country comparison to the world: 33

Budget surplus (+) or deficit (-) :

-3.6% of GDP
country comparison to the world: 138

Public debt:

91.1% of GDP
country comparison to the world: 20
88.7% of GDP (2012 est.)
note: data cover general government debt, and include debt instruments issued (or owned) by government entities other than the treasury; the data include treasury debt held by foreign entities; the data include debt issued by subnational entities, as well as intra-governmental debt; intra-governmental debt consists of treasury borrowings from surpluses in the social funds, such as for retirement, medical care, and unemployment; debt instruments for the social funds are not sold at public auctions

Fiscal year:

6 April - 5 April

Inflation rate (consumer prices) :

2%
country comparison to the world: 71
2.7% (2012 est.)

Central bank discount rate:

0.5% (31 December 2013 est.)

country comparison to the world: 134
0.5% (2012 est.)

Commercial bank prime lending rate:

4.4% (31 December 2013 est.)
country comparison to the world: 157
4.22% (31 December 2012 est.)

Stock of narrow money:

$111.6 billion (28 February 2014 est.)
country comparison to the world: 33
$101.8 billion (31 December 2012 est.)

Stock of broad money:

$2.881 trillion (28 February 2014 est.)
country comparison to the world: 6
$3.401 trillion (31 December 2012 est.)

Stock of domestic credit:

$3.636 trillion (31 December 2013 est.)
country comparison to the world: 7
$3.756 trillion (31 December 2012 est.)

Market value of publicly traded shares:

$3.019 trillion
country comparison to the world: 4
$2.903 trillion (31 December 2011)
$3.107 trillion (31 December 2010 est.)

Current account balance:

-$93.6 billion
country comparison to the world: 192
-$93.6 billion (2012 est.)

Exports:

$813.2 billion
country comparison to the world: 5
$801.7 billion (2012 est.)

Exports - commodities:

manufactured goods, fuels, chemicals; food, beverages, tobacco

Exports - partners:

Germany 11.3%, US 10.5%, Netherlands 8.8%, France 7.4%, Ireland 6.2%, Belgium 5.1% (2012)

Imports:

$782.5 billion
country comparison to the world: 5
$777.6 billion (2012 est.)

Imports - commodities:

manufactured goods, machinery, fuels; foodstuffs

Imports - partners:

Germany 12.6%, China 8%, Netherlands 7.5%, US 6.7%, France 5.4%, Belgium 4.4%, Norway 4% (2012)

Reserves of foreign exchange and gold:

$87.48 billion (31 December 2013 est.)
country comparison to the world: 25
$105.1 billion (31 December 2012 est.)

Debt - external:

$9.577 trillion (31 December 2013 est.)
country comparison to the world: 3
$9.457 trillion (31 December 2012 est.)

Stock of direct foreign investment - at home:

$1.557 trillion (31 December 2013 est.)
country comparison to the world: 2
$1.321 trillion (31 December 2012 est.)

Stock of direct foreign investment - abroad:

$1.884 trillion (31 December 2013 est.)
country comparison to the world: 2
$1.81 trillion (31 December 2012 est.)

Exchange rates:

British pounds (GBP) per US dollar -

0.6391
0.6307 (2012 est.)
0.6472 (2010 est.)
0.6175 (2009)
0.5302 (2008)

ENERGY

Electricity - production:

365.7 billion kWh
country comparison to the world: 12

Electricity - consumption:

323.3 billion kWh
country comparison to the world: 12

Electricity - exports:

3.103 billion kWh
country comparison to the world: 34

Electricity - imports:

17.53 billion kWh
country comparison to the world: 10

Electricity - installed generating capacity:

89.24 million kW (31 December 2012)
country comparison to the world: 13

Electricity - from fossil fuels:

76% of total installed capacity (2012 est.)
country comparison to the world: 99

Electricity - from nuclear fuels:

11.2% of total installed capacity (2012 est.)
country comparison to the world: 15

Electricity - from hydroelectric plants:

4.8% of total installed capacity (2012 est.)
country comparison to the world: 126

Electricity - from other renewable sources:

8% of total installed capacity (2012 est.)
country comparison to the world: 31

Crude oil - production:

771,800 bbl/day
country comparison to the world: 26

Crude oil - exports:

637,800 bbl/day
country comparison to the world: 20

Crude oil - imports:

1.053 million bbl/day
country comparison to the world: 12

Crude oil - proved reserves:

3.122 billion bbl (1 January 2013 est.)
country comparison to the world: 30

Refined petroleum products - production:

1.343 million bbl/day
country comparison to the world: 16

Refined petroleum products - consumption:

1.217 million bbl/day
country comparison to the world: 19

Refined petroleum products - exports:

526,400 bbl/day
country comparison to the world: 13

Refined petroleum products - imports:

566,700 bbl/day
country comparison to the world: 11

Natural gas - production:

38.48 billion cu m

country comparison to the world: 25

Natural gas - consumption:

51.63 billion cu m
country comparison to the world: 15

Natural gas - exports:

8.949 billion cu m
country comparison to the world: 27

Natural gas - imports:

48.26 billion cu m
country comparison to the world: 8

Natural gas - proved reserves:

244 billion cu m (1 January 2013 est.)
country comparison to the world: 44

Carbon dioxide emissions from consumption of energy:

178.5 million Mt

COMMUNICATIONS

Telephones - main lines in use:

33.01 million
country comparison to the world: 9

Telephones - mobile cellular:

82.109 million
country comparison to the world: 18

Telephone system:

general assessment: technologically advanced domestic and international system
domestic: equal mix of buried cables, microwave radio relay, and fiber-optic systems
international: country code - 44; numerous submarine cables provide links throughout Europe, Asia, Australia, the Middle East, and US; satellite earth stations - 10 Intelsat (7 Atlantic Ocean and 3 Indian Ocean) , 1 Inmarsat (Atlantic Ocean region) , and 1 Eutelsat; at least 8 large international switching centers

Broadcast media:

public service broadcaster, British Broadcasting Corporation (BBC) , is the largest broadcasting corporation in the world; BBC operates multiple TV networks with regional and local TV service; a mixed system of public and commercial TV broadcasters along with satellite and cable systems provide access to hundreds of TV stations throughout the world; BBC operates multiple national, regional, and local radio networks with multiple transmission sites; a large number of commercial radio stations as well as satellite radio services are available

Internet country code:

.uk

Internet hosts:

8.107 million
country comparison to the world: 15

Internet users:

51.444 million (2009)
country comparison to the world: 7

TRANSPORTATION

Airports:

460
country comparison to the world: 18

Airports - with paved runways:

total: 271
over 3,047 m: 7
2,438 to 3,047 m: 29
1,524 to 2,437 m: 89
914 to 1,523 m: 80
under 914 m: 66

Airports - with unpaved runways:

total: 189
1,524 to 2,437 m: 3
914 to 1,523 m: 26
under 914 m:
160

Heliports:

9

Pipelines:

condensate 502 km; condensate/gas 9 km; gas 28,603 km; liquid petroleum gas 59 km; oil 5,256 km; oil/gas/water 175 km; refined products 4,919 km; water 255 km

Railways:

total: 16,454 km
country comparison to the world: 17
broad gauge: 303 km 1.600-m gauge (in Northern Ireland)
standard gauge: 16,151 km 1.435-m gauge (5,248 km electrified)

Roadways:

total: 394,428 km
country comparison to the world: 16
paved: 394,428 km (includes 3,519 km of expressways)

Waterways:

3,200 km (620 km used for commerce)
country comparison to the world: 32

Merchant marine:

total: 504
country comparison to the world: 22
by type: bulk carrier 33, cargo 76, carrier 4, chemical tanker 58, container 178, liquefied gas 6, passenger 7, passenger/cargo 66, petroleum tanker 18, refrigerated cargo 2, roll on/roll off 31, vehicle carrier 25
foreign-owned: 271 (Australia 1, Bermuda 6, China 7, Denmark 43, France 39, Germany 59, Hong Kong 12, Ireland 1, Italy 3, Japan 5, Netherlands 1, Norway 32, Sweden 28, Taiwan 11, Tanzania 1, UAE 8, US 14)
registered in other countries: 308 (Algeria 15, Antigua and Barbuda 1, Argentina 2, Australia 5, Bahamas 18, Barbados 6, Belgium 2, Belize 4, Bermuda 14, Bolivia 1, Brunei 2, Cabo Verde 1, Cambodia 1, Cayman Islands 2, Comoros 1, Cook Islands 2, Cyprus 7, Georgia 5, Gibraltar 6, Greece 6, Honduras 1, Hong Kong 33, Indonesia 2, Italy 2, Liberia 22, Liberia 32, Luxembourg 5, Malta 21, Marshall Islands 12, Marshall Islands 3, Moldova 3, Nigeria 2, NZ 1, Panama 37, Panama 5, Saint Kitts and Nevis 1, Saint Vincent and the Grenadines 6, Sierra Leone 1, Singapore 6, Thailand 6, Tonga 1, US 4, unknown 1)

Ports and terminals:

major seaport(s) : Dover, Felixstowe, Immingham, Liverpool, London, Southampton, Teesport (England) ; Forth Ports (Scotland) ; Milford Haven (Wales)
oil terminals: Fawley Marine terminal, Liverpool Bay terminal (England) ; Braefoot Bay terminal, Finnart oil terminal, Hound Point terminal (Scotland)
container port(s) (TEUs) : Felixstowe (3,248,592) , London (1,932,000) , Southampton (1,324,581)

MILITARY

Military branches:

Army, Royal Navy (includes Royal Marines) , Royal Air Force

Military service age and obligation:

16-33 years of age (officers 17-28) for voluntary military service (with parental consent under 18) ; no conscription; women serve in military services, but are excluded from ground combat positions and some naval postings; as of October 2009, women comprised 12.1% of officers and 9% of enlisted personnel in the regular forces; must be citizen of the UK, Commonwealth, or Republic of Ireland; reservists serve a minimum of 3 years, to age 45 or 55; 17 years 6 months of age for voluntary military service by Nepalese citizens in the Brigade of Gurkhas; 16-34 years of age for voluntary military service by Papua New Guinean citizens

Manpower available for military service:

males age 16-49: 14,856,917
females age 16-49: 14,307,316

Manpower fit for military service:

males age 16-49: 12,255,452
females age 16-49: 11,779,679

Manpower reaching militarily significant age annually:

male: 383,989
female: 365,491

Military expenditures:

2.49% of GDP
country comparison to the world: 28
2.48% of GDP (2011)
2.49% of GDP (2010)

TRANSNATIONAL ISSUES

Disputes - international:

in 2002, Gibraltar residents voted overwhelmingly by referendum to reject any "shared sovereignty" arrangement between the UK and Spain; the Government of Gibraltar insisted on equal participation in talks between the two countries; Spain disapproved of UK plans to grant Gibraltar greater autonomy; Mauritius and Seychelles claim the Chagos Archipelago (British Indian Ocean Territory) ; in 2001, the former inhabitants of the archipelago, evicted 1967 - 1973, were granted U.K. citizenship and the right of return, followed by Orders in Council in 2004 that banned rehabitation, a High Court ruling reversed the ban, a Court of

Appeal refusal to hear the case, and a Law Lords' decision in 2008 denied the right of return; in addition, the United Kingdom created the world's largest marine protection area around the Chagos islands prohibiting the extraction of any natural resources therein; UK rejects sovereignty talks requested by Argentina, which still claims the Falkland Islands (Islas Malvinas) and South Georgia and the South Sandwich Islands; territorial claim in Antarctica (British Antarctic Territory) overlaps Argentine claim and partially overlaps Chilean claim; Iceland, the UK, and Ireland dispute Denmark's claim that the Faroe Islands' continental shelf extends beyond 200 nm

Refugees and internally displaced persons:

refugees (country of origin) : 11,249 (Somalia) ; 10,302 (Zimbabwe) ; 11,368 (Iran) ; 10,010 (Eritrea) ; 9,166 (Afghanistan) (2013)
stateless persons: 205 (2012)

Illicit drugs:

producer of limited amounts of synthetic drugs and synthetic precursor chemicals; major consumer of Southwest Asian heroin, Latin American cocaine, and synthetic drugs; money-laundering center

IMPORTANT INFORMATION FOR UNDERSTANDING UK

Official Name: The United Kingdom of Great Britain and Northern Ireland

BASIC PROFILE

GEOGRAPHY

Area: 244,820 sq. km. (94,525 sq. mi.) ; slightly smaller than Oregon.
Cities: *Capital*--London (metropolitan pop. about 7.1 million) . *Other cities*--Birmingham, Glasgow, Leeds, Sheffield, Liverpool, Bradford, Manchester, Edinburgh, Bristol, Belfast.
Terrain: 30% arable, 50% meadow and pasture, 12% waste or urban, 7% forested, 1% inland water. *Land use*--25% arable, 46% meadows and pastures, 10% forests and woodland, 19% other.
Climate: Generally mild and temperate; weather is subject to frequent changes but to few extremes of temperature.

PEOPLE

Nationality: *Noun*--Briton(s) . *Adjective*--British.
Population: 59.1 million.
Annual population growth rate : 0.24%.
Major ethnic groups: British, Irish, West Indian, South Asian.
Major religions: Church of England (Anglican) , Roman Catholic, Church of Scotland (Presbyterian) , Muslim.
Major languages: English, Welsh, Irish Gaelic, Scottish Gaelic.
Education: *Years compulsory*--12. *Attendance*--nearly 100%. *Literacy*--99%.
Health: *Infant mortality rate* --5.78/1,000. *Life expectancy* --males 75 yrs.; females 80 yrs.
Work force (28 million) : *Services*--75.2%; *manufacturing*--15.6%; construction-- 6.5%; *agriculture and fishing*--1.9%; *energy and water*--0.8%.

GOVERNMENT

Type: Constitutional monarchy.
Constitution: Unwritten; partly statutes, partly common law and practice.
Branches: *Executive*--monarch (head of state) , prime minister (head of government) , cabinet. *Legislative*--bicameral parliament: House of Commons, House of Lords; Scottish Parliament, Welsh Assembly, and Northern Ireland Assembly. *Judicial*--magistrates' courts, county courts, high courts, appellate courts, House of Lords.
Subdivisions: Municipalities, counties, parliamentary constituencies, province of Northern Ireland, and Scottish regions.
Political parties: In Great Britain: Conservative; Labour; Liberal Democrats; also, in Scotland: Scottish National Party; in Wales: Plaid Cymru (Party of Wales) . In Northern Ireland: Ulster Unionist Party, Social Democratic and Labour Party, Democratic Unionist Party, Sinn Fein, Alliance Party and other smaller parties.
Suffrage: British subjects and citizens of other Commonwealth countries and the Irish Republic resident in the U.K., at 18.

ECONOMY

Natural resources: Coal, oil, natural gas, tin, limestone, iron ore, salt, clay, chalk, gypsum, lead, silica.
Agriculture (1.8% of GDP) : *Products*--cereals, oilseed, potatoes, vegetables, cattle, sheep, poultry, fish.
Industry (31.5% of GDP) : *Types*--steel, heavy engineering and metal manufacturing, textiles, motor vehicles and aircraft, construction, electronics, chemicals.
Trade : *Exports*--$267.6 billion: manufactured goods, fuels, chemicals; food, beverages, tobacco. *Major markets*--U.S., Germany, France, the Netherlands, Ireland. *Imports*--$311 billion: manufactured goods, machinery, fuels, foodstuffs. *Major suppliers*--Germany, U.S., France, the Netherlands, Japan.

PEOPLE

A group of islands close to continental Europe, the British Isles have been subject to many invasions and migrations, especially from Scandinavia and the continent, including Roman occupation for several centuries. Contemporary Britons are descended mainly from the varied ethnic stocks that settled there before the 11th century. The pre-Celtic, Celtic, Roman, Anglo-Saxon, and Norse influences were blended in Britain under the Normans, Scandinavian Vikings who had lived in Northern France. Although Celtic languages persist in Wales, Scotland and Northern Ireland, the predominant language is English, which is primarily a blend of Anglo-Saxon and Norman French.

A census is taken simultaneously in all parts of the UK every ten years.[313] The Office for National Statistics is responsible for collecting data for England and Wales, the General Register Office for Scotland and the Northern Ireland Statistics and Research Agency each being responsible for censuses in their respective countries. In the 2011 census the total population of the United Kingdom was 63,181,775. It is the third-largest in the European Union, the fifth-largest in the Commonwealth and the 21st-largest in the world. In mid-2014 net long-term international migration contributed more to population growth, for the first time since mid-2011. In mid-2012 and mid-2013 natural change contributed the most to population growth.

Between 2001 and 2011 the population increased by an average annual rate of approximately 0.7%.This compares to 0.3% per year in the period 1991 to 2001 and 0.2% in the decade 1981 to 1991. The 2011 census also confirmed that the proportion of the population aged 0–14 has nearly halved (31% in 1911 compared to 18 in 2011) and the proportion of older people aged 65 and over has more than tripled (from 5 to 16%).It has been estimated that the number of people aged 100 or over will rise steeply to reach over 626,000 by 2080.

England's population in 2011 was found to be 53 million. It is one of the most densely populated countries in the world, with 417 people resident per square kilometre in mid-2014.[320] with a particular concentration in London and the south-east. The 2011 census put Scotland's population at 5.3 million, Wales at 3.06 million and Northern Ireland at 1.81 million.[319] In percentage terms England has had the fastest growing population of any country of the UK in the period from 2001 to 2011, with an increase of 7.9%.

In 2012 the average total fertility rate (TFR) across the UK was 1.92 children per woman.[323] While a rising birth rate is contributing to current population growth, it remains considerably below the 'baby boom' peak of 2.95 children per woman in 1964, below the replacement rate of 2.1, but higher than the 2001 record low of 1.63.[323] In 2012, Scotland had the lowest TFR at only 1.67, followed by Wales at 1.88, England at 1.94, and Northern Ireland at 2.03. In 2011, 47.3% of births in the UK were to unmarried women.[325] A government figure estimated that there are 3.6 million homosexual people in Britain comprising 6% of the population

HISTORY

The Roman invasion of Britain in 55 BC and most of Britain's subsequent incorporation into the Roman Empire stimulated development and brought more active contacts with the rest of Europe. As Rome's strength declined, the country again was exposed to invasion, including the pivotal incursions of the Angles, Saxons, and Jutes in the fifth and sixth centuries AD up to the Norman conquest in 1066. Norman rule effectively ensured Britain's safety from further intrusions; certain institutions, which remain characteristic of Britain, could develop. Among these are a political, administrative, cultural, and economic center in London; a separate but established church; a system of common law; distinctive and distinguished university education; and representative government.

UNION

Both Wales and Scotland were independent kingdoms that resisted English rule. The English conquest of Wales succeeded in 1282 under Edward I, and the Statute of Rhuddlan established English rule 2 years later. To appease the Welsh, Edward's son (later Edward II) , who had been born in Wales, was made Prince of Wales in 1301. The tradition of bestowing this title on the eldest son of the British Monarch continues today. An act of 1536 completed the political and administrative union of England and Wales.

While maintaining separate parliaments, England and Scotland were ruled under one crown beginning in 1603, when James VI of Scotland succeeded his cousin Elizabeth I as James I of England. In the ensuing 100 years, strong religious and political differences divided the kingdoms. Finally, in 1707, England and Scotland were unified as Great Britain, sharing a single parliament at Westminster.

Ireland's invasion by the Anglo-Normans in 1170 led to centuries of strife. Successive English kings sought to conquer Ireland. In the early 17th century, largescale settlement of the north from Scotland and England began. After its defeat, Ireland was subjected, with varying degrees of success, to control and regulation by Britain.

The legislative union of Great Britain and Ireland was completed on January 1, 1801, under the name of the United Kingdom. However, armed struggle for independence continued sporadically into the 20th century. The Anglo-Irish Treaty of 1921 established the Irish Free State, which subsequently left the Commonwealth and became a republic after World War II. Six northern, predominantly Protestant, Irish counties have remained part of the United Kingdom.

BRITISH EXPANSION AND EMPIRE

Begun initially to support William the Conqueror's (c. 1029-1087) holdings in France, Britain's policy of active involvement in continental European affairs endured for several hundred years. By the end of the 14th century, foreign trade, originally based on wool exports to Europe, had emerged as a cornerstone of national policy.

The foundations of sea power were gradually laid to protect English trade and open up new routes. Defeat of the Spanish Armada in 1588 firmly established England as a major sea power. Thereafter, its interests outside Europe grew steadily. Attracted by the spice trade, English mercantile interests spread first to the Far East. In search of an alternate route to the Spice Islands, John Cabot reached the North American continent in 1498. Sir Walter Raleigh organized the first, short-lived colony in Virginia in 1584, and permanent English settlement began in 1607 at Jamestown, Virginia. During the next two centuries, Britain extended its influence abroad and consolidated its political development at home.

Great Britain's industrial revolution greatly strengthened its ability to oppose Napoleonic France. By the end of the Napoleonic Wars in 1815, the United Kingdom was the foremost European power, and its navy ruled the seas. Peace in Europe allowed the British to focus their interests on more remote parts of the world, and, during this period, the British Empire reached its zenith. British colonial expansion reached its height largely during the reign of Queen Victoria (1837-1901) . Queen Victoria's reign witnessed the spread of British technology, commerce, language, and government throughout the British Empire, which at its greatest extent encompassed roughly one-fifth to one-quarter of the world's area and population. British colonies contributed to the United Kingdom's extraordinary economic growth and strengthened its voice in world affairs. Even as the United Kingdom extended its imperial reach overseas, it continued to develop and broaden its democratic institutions at home.

20TH CENTURY

By the time of Queen Victoria's death in 1901, other nations, including the United States and Germany, had developed their own industries; the United Kingdom's comparative economic advantage had lessened, and the ambitions of its rivals had grown. The losses and destruction of World War I, the depression of the 1930s, and decades of relatively slow growth eroded the United Kingdom's preeminent international position of the previous century.

Britain's control over its empire loosened during the interwar period. Ireland, with the exception of six northern counties, gained independence from the United Kingdom in 1921. Nationalism became stronger in other parts of the Empire, particularly in India and Egypt.

In 1926, the U.K., completing a process begun a century earlier, granted Australia, Canada, and New Zealand complete autonomy within the Empire. They became charter members of the British Commonwealth of Nations (now known as the Commonwealth) , an informal but closely knit association that succeeded the Empire. Beginning with the independence of India and Pakistan in 1947, the remainder of the British Empire was almost completely dismantled. Today, most of Britain's former colonies belong to the Commonwealth, almost all of them as independent members. There are, however, 13 former British colonies--including Bermuda, Gibraltar, the Falkland Islands, and others--which have elected to continue their political links with London and are known as United Kingdom Overseas Territories.

Although often marked by economic and political nationalism, the Commonwealth offers the United Kingdom a voice in matters concerning many developing countries. In addition, the Commonwealth helps preserve many institutions deriving from British experience and models, such as parliamentary democracy, in those countries.

GOVERNMENT

The United Kingdom does not have a written constitution. The equivalent body of law is based on statute, common law, and "traditional rights." Changes may come about formally through new acts of parliament, informally through the acceptance of new practices and usage, or by judicial precedents. Although parliament has the theoretical power to make or repeal any law, in actual practice the weight of 700 years of tradition restrains arbitrary actions.

Executive government rests nominally with the Monarch but actually is exercised by a Committee of Ministers (cabinet) traditionally selected from among the members of the House of Commons and, to a lesser extent, the House of Lords. The prime minister is normally the leader of the largest party in the Commons, and the government is dependent on its support.

Parliament represents the entire country and can legislate for the whole or for any constituent part or combination of parts. The maximum parliamentary term is 5 years, but the prime minister may ask the Monarch to dissolve parliament and call a general election at any time. The focus of legislative power is the 650-member House of Commons, which has sole jurisdiction over finance. The House of Lords, although shorn of most of its powers, can still review, amend, or delay temporarily any bills except those relating to the budget. The House of Lords has more time than the House of Commons to pursue one of its more important functions--debating public issues. In 1999, the government removed the automatic right of hereditary peers to hold seats in the House of Lords. The current house consists of appointed life peers who hold their seats for life and 92 hereditary peers who will hold their seats only until final reforms have been agreed upon and implemented. The judiciary is independent of the legislative and executive branches but cannot review the constitutionality of legislation.

The separate identities of each of the U.K.'s constituent parts also is reflected in their respective governmental structures. Up until the recent devolution of power to Scotland and Wales, a cabinet minister (the Secretary of State for Wales) handled Welsh affairs at the national level with the advice of a broadly representative council for Wales. Scotland maintains, as it did before union with England, different systems of law (Roman-French) , education, local government, judiciary, and national church (the Church of Scotland instead of the Church of England) . In addition, separate departments grouped under a Secretary of State for Scotland, who also is a cabinet member, handled most domestic matters. In late 1997, however, following approval of referenda by Scottish and Welsh voters (though only narrowly in Wales) , the British Government introduced legislation to establish a Scottish parliament and a Welsh Assembly. Elections for the two bodies were held May 6, 1999. The Welsh Assembly opened on May 26, and the Scottish parliament opened on July 1, 1999. The devolved legislatures have largely taken over most of the functions previously performed by the Scottish and Welsh offices.

Devolved government was reestablished in Northern Ireland in December 1999 under the terms of the Good Friday Agreement, which established the basis for ending the political divisions and violence that had plagued Northern Ireland for decades. The Good Friday Agreement provides for a 108-member elected Assembly, overseen by a 12-minister Executive Committee (cabinet) in which unionists and nationalists share leadership responsibility. While Northern Ireland elects 18 representatives to the Westminster parliament in London, the two Sinn Fein MPs who won seats in the last election have refused to claim their seats.

Northern Ireland had its own parliament and prime minister from 1921 to 1973, when the British Government imposed direct rule in order to deal with the deteriorating political and security situation. From 1973, the Secretary of State for Northern Ireland, based in London, was responsible for the region, including efforts to resolve the issues that lay behind the "the Troubles."

By the mid-1990s, gestures toward peace encouraged by successive British Governments and by President Clinton began to open the door for restored local government in Northern Ireland. An IRA cease-fire and nearly 2 years of multiparty negotiations, led by former U.S. Senator George Mitchell, resulted in the Good Friday Agreement of April 10, 1998, which was subsequently approved by majorities in both Northern Ireland and the Republic of Ireland. Key elements of the Agreement include devolved government, a commitment of the parties to work toward "total disarmament of all paramilitary organizations," police reform, and enhanced mechanisms to guarantee human rights and equal opportunity. The Good Friday Agreement also called for formal cooperation between the Northern Ireland institutions and the Government of the Republic of Ireland, and it established the British-Irish Council, which includes representatives of the British and Irish Governments as well as the devolved Governments of Northern Ireland, Scotland and Wales.

The parties disagree over the implementation of key elements of the Good Friday Agreement, and sporadic violence by paramilitary organizations continues to threaten the normalization process. The key parties, nevertheless, remain committed to the peace process and continue to work for full implementation of the agreement. While Unionists insist that actual decommissioning of paramilitary weapons should precede normalization of political and security arrangements, they have acknowledged the significance of intermediate steps, including the inspection of IRA arms dumps in June 2000 by independent international inspectors. Movement on decommissioning has been mirrored by progress on political and security normalization.

The United States remains firmly committed to the peace process in Northern Ireland and continues to support normalization of institutions as the best means to ensure that all parties' commitment to relying solely on peaceful and democratic means to resolve issues. U.S. Government policy on Northern Ireland condemns all acts of terrorism and violence, perpetrated by any party on either side. It also cautions all Americans to question closely any appeal for financial or other aid from groups involved in the Northern Ireland conflict to ensure that contributions do not end up in the hands of those who support violence, either directly or indirectly.

The U.S. also is committed to Northern Ireland's economic development and to date has given or pledged contributions of more than $300 million to the International Fund for Ireland. The fund provides grants and loans to businesses to improve the economy, redress inequalities of employment opportunity, and improve crossborder business and community ties.

PRINCIPAL GOVERNMENT OFFICIALS

Head of State--Her Majesty Queen Elizabeth II

Portfolio	Minister
Cabinet ministers	
Prime Minister First Lord of the Treasury Minister for the Civil Service	The Rt Hon. David Cameron MP
Deputy Prime Minister Lord President of the Council	The Rt Hon. Nick Clegg MP
First Secretary of State Leader of the House of Commons	The Rt Hon. William Hague MP
Chancellor of the Exchequer	The Rt Hon. George Osborne MP

Secretary of State for the Home Department	The Rt Hon. Theresa May MP
Secretary of State for Foreign and Commonwealth Affairs	The Rt Hon. Philip Hammond MP
Lord Chancellor Secretary of State for Justice	The Rt Hon. Chris Grayling MP
Secretary of State for Defence	The Rt Hon. Michael Fallon MP
Secretary of State for Business, Innovation and Skills President of the Board of Trade	The Rt Hon. Vince Cable MP
Secretary of State for Work and Pensions	The Rt Hon. Iain Duncan Smith MP
Secretary of State for Health	The Rt Hon. Jeremy Hunt MP
Secretary of State for Communities and Local Government Minister for Faith	The Rt Hon. Eric Pickles MP
Secretary of State for Education Minister for Women and Equalities	The Rt Hon. Nicky Morgan MP
Secretary of State for International Development	The Rt Hon. Justine Greening MP
Secretary of State for Energy and Climate Change	The Rt Hon. Ed Davey MP
Secretary of State for Transport	The Rt Hon. Patrick McLoughlin MP
Secretary of State for Scotland	The Rt Hon. Alistair Carmichael MP
Secretary of State for Northern Ireland	The Rt Hon. Theresa Villiers MP
Secretary of State for Wales	The Rt Hon. Stephen Crabb MP
Secretary of State for Culture, Media and Sport	The Rt Hon. Sajid Javid MP
Secretary of State for Environment, Food and Rural Affairs	The Rt Hon. Elizabeth Truss MP
Chief Secretary to the Treasury	The Rt Hon. Danny Alexander MP
Also attending Cabinet meetings Leader of the House of Lords Lord Privy Seal	The Rt Hon. The Baroness Stowell of Beeston MBE (PC)
Chief Whip in the House of Commons Parliamentary Secretary to the Treasury	The Rt Hon. Michael Gove MP
Minister for the Cabinet Office Paymaster General	The Rt Hon. Francis Maude MP
Minister of State for Government Policy Chancellor of the Duchy of Lancaster	The Rt Hon. Oliver Letwin MP
Minister of State for the Cabinet Office Minister of State for Schools	The Rt Hon. David Laws MP
Minister of State for Universities, Science and Cities	The Rt Hon. Greg Clark MP

Attorney General	The Rt Hon. Jeremy Wright MP
Minister without Portfolio Co-Chairman of the Conservative Party	The Rt Hon. Grant Shapps MP
Minister of State for Business and Enterprise Minister of State for Energy Minister for Portsmouth	The Rt Hon. Matthew Hancock MP
Minister of State for Employment	The Rt Hon. Esther McVey MP
Minister of State for Foreign and Commonwealth Affairs	The Rt Hon. The Baroness Anelay of St Johns DBE (PC)

The United Kingdom maintains an embassy in the United States at 3100 Massachusetts Ave. NW, Washington, DC 20008 (tel. 202-588-6500; fax 202-588-7870) .

POLITICAL CONDITIONS

Current Labour Prime Minister Tony Blair was elected on May 1, 1997, with a massive 176-seat majority in the House of Commons. Labour's victory ended an 18-year run of Conservative (Tory) Party rule in the U.K.. Blair worked hard to reorganize and reenergize the Labour Party, moving it steadily to the center of the political spectrum. Both main British parties support a strong transatlantic link but have become increasingly absorbed by European issues as Britain's economic and political ties to the continent grow in the post-Cold War world. Prime Minister Blair has promised that the U.K. will play a leading role in Europe. Britain's relationship with Europe, in particular its potential participation in the single European currency, the euro, is a subject of considerable political discussion in the U.K. Whether Britain will adopt the euro is likely to be a defining issue in the next U.K. national elections, which could take place as early as spring 2001.

U.S.-U.K. RELATIONS

The United Kingdom is one of the United States' closest allies, and British foreign policy emphasizes close coordination with the United States. Bilateral cooperation reflects the common language, ideals, and democratic practices of the two nations. Relations were strengthened by the U.K.'s alliance with the United States during both World Wars and its role as a founding member of NATO, in the Korean conflict, and the Persian Gulf War. The United Kingdom and the United States continually consult on foreign policy issues and global problems and share major foreign and security policy objectives. In the United Nations, the U.K. is a permanent member of the Security Council.

The U.K. is a founding member of the North Atlantic Treaty Organization (NATO) and has been a member of the European Community (now European Union) since 1973. The U.K. is one of NATO's major European maritime powers and ranked third in 1996 among NATO countries in total defense expenditure.

The British armed forces are charged with protecting the United Kingdom and its overseas territories, promoting Britain's wider security interests, and supporting international peacekeeping efforts. The 44,000-member Royal Navy is in charge of the U.K.'s independent strategic nuclear arm, which consists of four Trident missile submarines. The Royal Marines provide commando units for amphibious assault and for specialist reinforcement forces in and beyond the NATO area. The British Army, with a reported strength of 110,000 in 1999, including 7,600 women, and the Royal Air Force with a strength of 55,000, along with the Royal Navy and Royal Marines, are active and regular participants in NATO and other coalition operations.

TRADE AND INVESTMENT

The United Kingdom has the fourth-largest economy in the world, has one of the largest economies in the European Union, and is a major international trading power. London ranks with New York as a leading international financial center.

The U.K. is the fourth-largest U.S. market after Canada, Japan, and Mexico; U.S. exports to the U.K. in 1999 were $38.3 billion. For the first time in 5 years, the U.S. ran a deficit with the U.K., importing $39.2 billion in 1999. The U.K. is a large source of foreign tourists in the U.S.

The U.S. and the U.K. share the world's largest investment partnership. U.S. investment in the U.K. reached $213.1 billion in 1999, while U.K. investment is valued at $183.0 billion. This investment sustains over one million American jobs.

Since 1979, the British Government has privatized most state-owned companies, including British Steel, British Airways, British Telecom, British Coal, British Aerospace, and British Gas, although in some cases the government retains a "golden share" in these companies. The Labour government has continued the privatization policy of its predecessor, including by encouraging "public-private partnerships" (partial privatization) in such areas as the National Air Traffic Control System.

The United Kingdom is an energy-rich nation with significant reserves of oil and gas in the North Sea and the Irish Sea and large coal resources. A total of 150 million tons of oil were produced in the U.K. in 1999. U.K. offshore areas should be an important source of continued production and new discoveries for some years. U.S. oil and oil-service companies participate actively in the North Sea oil industry and consider the United Kingdom an attractive environment for future investment.

PRINCIPAL U.S. OFFICIALS

Ambassador--Matthew W. Barzun
Matthew W. Barzun [BARZ'n] - Ambassador of the United States of America to the United Kingdom of Great Britain and Northern Ireland
Matthew W. Barzun has been America's ambassador to the UK since 2013. Previously he served as U.S. Ambassador to Sweden from 2009-2011.

Deputy Chief of Mission--David T. Johnson
Minister-Counselor for Political Affairs--Maura Connelly
Minister-Counselor for Commercial Affairs--Stephan Wasylko
Minister-Counselor for Economic Affairs--Mark Tokola
Minister-Counselor for Public Affairs--Rick Roberts
Minister-Counselor for Management Affairs--Richard Jaworski
Minister-Counselor for Consular Affairs--John Caulfield
Regional Security Officer--Robert G. Reed
U.S. Consul General in Belfast--Dean Pittman
Principal Officer in Edinburgh--Cecile Shea

The U.S. Embassy in the United Kingdom is located at: 24 Grosvenor Sq., W1A 1AE, London (tel. [44] (207) 499-9000; fax [44] (207) 409-1637) . Internet website: http://www.usembassy.org.U.K.

ECONOMY

Currency	Pound sterling (GBP)
Fiscal year	1 April – 31 March
Trade organisations	European Union, OECD and World Trade Organization
	Statistics
GDP	$2,848 trillion (Nominal, 2014) , $2.435 trillion (PPP, 2014)
GDP rank	5th (nominal) / 8th (PPP)
GDP growth	▲+0.7% Q3 2014 (3.0% year/year, 2.8% annualised) .
GDP per capita	$45,208 (19th, PPP, 2013)
GDP by sector	Agriculture: 0.6% Construction: 6.4% Production: 14.6% Services: 78.4%
Inflation (CPI)	▼1.0% RPI: ▼2.0% (November 2014) . This is the lowest since 2002.
Base Borrowing Rate	0.5%
Population below poverty line	16.2%
Gini coefficient	▬0.34
Labour force	30.8 million (November 2014) (Employment rate 73.2% which is a record high)
Labour force by occupation	Agriculture: 1.5% Industry: 18.8% Services: 79.7%
Unemployment	6.0%, 1.96 million (September 2014) ,
Average gross salary	£2,308 / €2,756 / $3,729 monthly (9th highest)
Average net salary	£1,730 / €2,064 / $2,793 monthly (6th highest in the world)
Main industries	List
Ease-of-doing-business rank	▲8th
	External
Exports	▲$813.2 billion (4th; 2013 est.)
Export goods	List Manufactured goods Chemicals Food Beverages Tobacco Automotive vehicles and components Computer programming Finance Entertainment Clothes Fuel oil and petroleum products Industrial supplies and materials

	Military arms and equipment pharmaceuticals Other.
Main export partners	Germany 11.3%, United States 10.5%, Netherlands 8.8%, France 7.4%, Republic of Ireland 6.2%, Belgium 5.1% (2012)
Imports	▲$782.5 billion (4th; 2013 est.)
Import goods	
Main import partners	Germany 12.6%, China 8%, Netherlands 7.5%, United States 6.7%, France 5.4%, Belgium 4.4% (2012)
FDI stock	Inward: ▲$1.321 trillion(3rd) Outward: ▲$1.884 trillion(2nd)
Current account	▼-£59.2 billion
Gross external debt	▲$2,327,361,000,000 (2nd)
Net international investment position	▼-£182 billion / 9.1% GDP (2012)
	Public finances
Public debt	▲£1,457.20 billion (November 2014) (79.5% GDP)
Budget deficit	▼+£107.4 billion (2013–2014 FY)
Revenues	£648 billion (2014–2015 FY) $1.06 trillion (2014 est. CIA-WFB)
Expenses	£732 billion (2014–2015 FY) $1.21 trillion (2014 est. CIA-WFB)
Economic aid	$10 billion (2012) (donor)
Credit rating	Standard & Poor's: AAA (Domestic) AAA (Foreign) AAA (T&C Assessment) Outlook: Stable Moody's: Aa1 Outlook: Stable Fitch: AA+ Outlook: STABLE
Foreign reserves	▲$95.54 billion (31 December 2012, CIA-WFB)

The **United Kingdom** has the 6th-largest national economy in the world (and 3rd largest in Europe) measured by nominal GDP and 8th-largest in the world (and 2nd-largest in Europe) measured by purchasing power parity (PPP) . The UK economy comprises (in descending order of size) the economies of England, Scotland, Wales and Northern Ireland. In 2013 the UK was the 4th-largest exporter in the world and the 4th-largest importer, and had the 2nd-largest stock of inward foreign direct investment and the 2nd-largest stock of outward foreign direct investment. The UK is one of the world's most globalised economies.

The service sector dominates the UK economy, contributing around 78% of GDP; the financial services industry is particularly important and London is one of the world's largest financial centres. The British aerospace industry is the second- or third-largest national aerospace industry depending on the method of measurement. The pharmaceutical industry plays an important role in the economy and the UK has the third-highest share of global pharmaceutical R&D. The automotive industry is also a major employer and exporter. The British economy is boosted by North Sea oil and gas production; its reserves were valued at an estimated £250 billion in 2007. There are significant regional variations in prosperity, with the South East of England and southern Scotland the richest areas per capita. London has the largest city GDP in Europe.

In the 18th century the UK was the first country to industrialise and during the 19th century had a dominant role in the global economy. From the late 19th century the Second Industrial Revolution in the United States and Germany presented an increasing economic challenge, and the costs of fighting World War I and World War II further weakened the UK's relative position. However it still maintains a significant role in the world economy, particularly in financial services and the knowledge economy.

More recently, the UK entered a recession during the Financial crisis of 2007–08, its first for nearly two decades, and initially experienced a deeper downturn than all of the G7 except Japan. However, since 2013 the UK has been in a nascent economic recovery and is firmly in expansion territory. As of Q3 2014, the UK economy is 3.4% above its pre-crisis peak in Q1 2008 and growth in 2014 is forecast to be 3.2% which is the fastest of any major developed economy, and the fastest for the UK since 2003. Consequently, the UK is currently creating more jobs than the entirety of all countries in the European Union combined and unemployment is currently falling at record levels. The UK became the 5th largest economy in 2014, overtaking France. The UK is predicted to become the largest economy in Europe by 2030.

Government involvement in the British economy is primarily exercised by HM Treasury, headed by the Chancellor of the Exchequer, and the Department for Business, Innovation and Skills. Since 1979 management of the UK economy has followed a broadly laissez-faire approach. The Bank of England is the UK's central bank and its Monetary Policy Committee is responsible for setting interest rates. The currency of the UK is the pound sterling, which is also the world's third-largest reserve currency after the US dollar and the euro, and also the fourth most valued currency in the world, behind the Kuwaiti Dinar, Bahraini Dinar, and Omani Rial, and the most valued currency outside the Middle East. The UK is a member of the Commonwealth of Nations, the European Union, the G7, the G8, the G20, the International Monetary Fund, the Organisation for Economic Co-operation and Development, the World Bank, the World Trade Organisation and the United Nations.

NORTH SEA OIL EXPLORATION

In the oil industry, the term "North Sea" often includes areas such as the Norwegian Sea and the area known as "West of Shetland", "the Atlantic Frontier" or "the Atlantic Margin" that is not geographically part of the North Sea. Brent crude is still used today as a standard benchmark for pricing oil, although the contract now refers to a blend of oils from fields in the northern North Sea.

The UK Continental Shelf Act came into force in May 1964. Seismic exploration and the first well followed later that year. It and a second well on the Mid North Sea High were dry, as the Rotliegendes was absent, but BP's *Sea Gem* rig struck gas in the **West Sole Field** in September 1965. The celebrations were short-lived because the Sea Gem sank with the loss of 13 lives after part of the rig collapsed as it was moved away from the discovery well. The **Viking Gas Field** was discovered in December 1965 with the Conoco/National Coal Board well 49/17-1, finding the gas-bearing Permian Rotliegend Sandstone at a depth of 2,756 m subsea. Larger gas finds followed in 1966—**Leman Bank**, **Indefatigable** and **Hewett**, but by 1968 companies had lost interest in further exploration of the British sector, a result of a ban on gas exports and low prices offered by the only buyer, British Gas. West Sole came onstream in May 1967. Licensing regulations for Dutch waters were not finalised until 1967.

The situation was transformed in December 1969, when Phillips Petroleum discovered oil in Chalk of Danian age at Ekofisk, in Norwegian waters in the central North Sea. The same month, Amoco discovered the **Montrose Field** about 217 km (135 mi) east of Aberdeen. BP had been awarded several licences in the area in the second licensing round late in 1965, but had been reluctant to work on them. The discovery of Ekofisk prompted them to drill what turned out to be a dry hole in May 1970, followed by the discovery of the giant Forties Oil Field in October 1970. The following year, Shell Expro discovered the giant Brent oilfield in the northern North Sea east of Shetland in Scotland and the Petronord Group discovered the Frigg gas field. The Piper oilfield was discovered in 1973 and the Statfjord Field and the **Ninian Field** in 1974, with the Ninian reservoir consisting of Middle Jurassic sandstones at a depth of 3000 m subsea in a "westward tilted horst block".

Oil production started from the **Argyll & Duncan Oilfields** (now **Ardmore**) in June 1975 followed by Forties Oil Field in November of that year. The inner Moray Firth **Beatrice Field**, a Jurassic sandstone/shale reservoir 1829 m deep in a "fault-bounded anticlinal trap", was discovered in 1976 with well 11/30-1, drilled by the Mesa Petroleum Group (named after T. Boone Pickens' wife Bea, "the only oil field in the North Sea named for a woman") in 49 m of water.

After the 1973 oil crisis, the oil price had quadrupled. The 1979 oil crisis ("second") caused another tripling.

Volatile weather conditions in Europe's North Sea have made drilling particularly hazardous, claiming many lives (see Oil platform) . The conditions also make extraction a costly process; by the 1980s, costs for developing new methods and technologies to make the process both efficient and safe, far exceeded NASA's budget to land a man on the moon. The exploration of the North Sea has been a story of continually pushing the edges of the technology of exploitation (in terms of what can be produced) and later the technologies of discovery and evaluation (2-D seismic, followed by 3-D and 4-D seismic; sub-salt seismic; immersive display and analysis suites and supercomputing to handle the flood of computation required) .

The Gullfaks oil field was discovered in 1978. The **Snorre Field** was discovered in 1979, producing from the Triassic Lunde Formation and the Triassic-Jurassic Statfjord Formation, both fluvial sandstones in a mudstone matrix. The Oseberg oil field and Troll gas field were also discovered in 1979. The Miller oilfield was discovered in 1983. The **Alba Field** produces from sandstones in the middle Eocene Alba Formation at 1860 m subsea and was discovered in 1984 in UKCS Block 16/26. The **Smorbukk Field** was discovered in 1984 in 250–300 m of water that produces from Lower to Middle Jurassic sandstone formations within a fault block. The Snohvit Gas Field and the Draugen oil field were discovered in 1984. The Heidrun oil field was discovered in 1985.

The largest field discovered in the past 25 years is **Buzzard** also located off Scotland, found in June 2001 with producible reserves of almost 64×10^6 m³ (400m bbl) and an average output of 28 600 m³ to 30 200 m³ (180,000-190,000 bbl) per day.

The largest field found in the past five years on the Norwegian part of the North Sea, is the Johan Sverdrup oil field which was discovered in 2010, with further oil of the same field was discovered the next year. Total reserves of the field are estimated at 1.7 to 3.3 billion barrels of gross recoverable oil and Johan Sverdrup is expected to produce 120,000 to 200,000 barrels of oil per day. Production start is planned to happen in 2018. It is one of the largest discoveries made in the Norwegian Continental Shelf

RESERVES AND PRODUCTION

North Sea Oil and Gas Fields

The British and Norwegian sections hold most of the remainder of the large oil reserves. It is estimated that the Norwegian section alone contains 54% of the sea's oil reserves and 45% of its gas reserves. More than half of the North Sea oil reserves have been extracted, according to official sources in both Norway and the UK. For Norway, the Norwegian Petroleum Directorate gives a figure of 4,601 million cubic metres of oil (corresponding to 29 billion barrels) for the Norwegian North Sea alone (excluding smaller reserves in Norwegian Sea and Barents Sea) of which 2,778 million cubic metres (60%) has already been produced prior to January 2007. UK sources give a range of estimates of reserves, but even using the most optimistic "maximum" estimate of ultimate recovery, 76% had been recovered at end 2010. Note the UK figure includes fields which are not in the North Sea (onshore, West of Shetland) .

United Kingdom Continental Shelf production was 137 million tonnes of oil and 105 billion m³ of gas in 1999. (1 tonne of crude oil converts to 7.5 barrels) . The Danish explorations of Cenozoic stratigraphy, undertaken in the 1990s, showed petroleum rich reserves in the northern

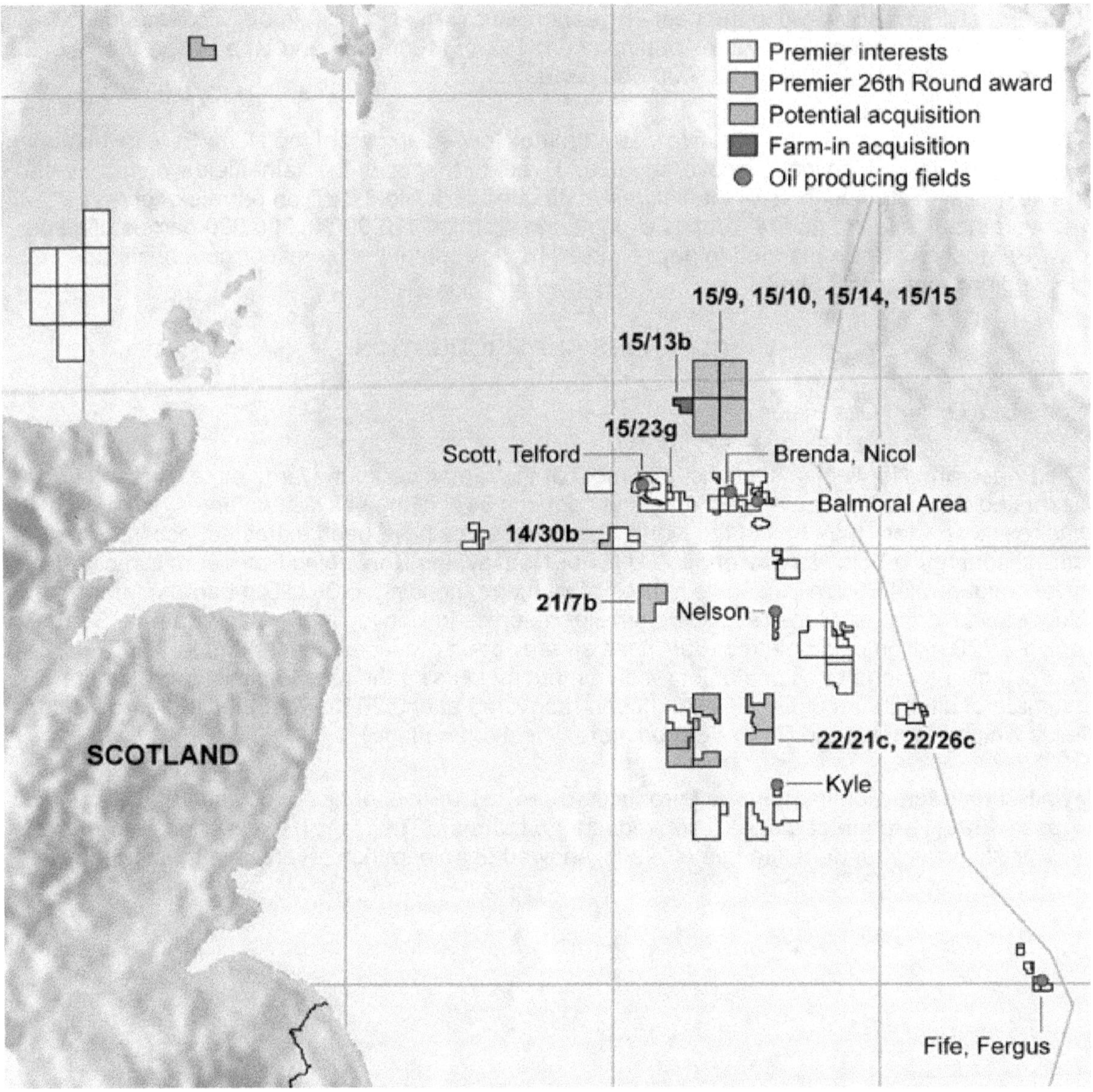

Danish sector, especially the Central Graben area. The Dutch area of the North Sea followed through with onshore and offshore gas exploration, and well creation.

Exact figures are debatable, because methods of estimating reserves vary and it is often difficult to forecast future discoveries.

Peaking in 1999, production of North Sea oil was nearly 950,000 m³ (6 million barrels) per day. Natural gas production was nearly 280×10^9 m³ (10 trillion cubic feet) in 2001 and continues to increase, although British gas production is in sharp decline.

UK oil production has seen two peaks, in the mid 1980s and late 1990s, with a decline to around 300×10^3 m³ (1.9 million barrels) per day in the early 1990s. Monthly oil production peaked at 13.5×10^6 m³ (84.9 million barrels) in January 1985 although the highest annual production was seen in 1999, with offshore oil production in that year of 407×10^6 m³ (398 million barrels) and had declined to 231×10^6 m³ (220 million barrels) in 2007. This was the largest decrease of any other oil exporting nation in the world, and has led to Britain becoming a net importer of crude for the first time in decades, as recognized by the energy policy of the United Kingdom. The production is expected to fall to one-third of its peak by 2020. Norwegian crude oil production as of 2013 is 1.4 mbpd. This is a more than 50% decline since the peak in 2001 of 3.2 mbpd.

LICENSING

Following the 1958 Continental shelf convention and after some disputes on the rights to natural resource exploitation the national limits of the exclusive economic zones were ratified. Five countries are involved in oil production in North Sea. All operate a tax and royalty licensing regime. The respective sectors are divided by median lines agreed in the late 1960s:

- **United Kingdom** – The Department of Energy and Climate Change (DECC – formerly the Department of Trade and Industry) grants licences. The UKCS (United Kingdom Continental Shelf) is divided into quadrants of 1 degree latitude and one degree longitude. Each quadrant is divided into 30 blocks measuring 10 minutes of latitude and 12 minutes of longitude. Some blocks are divided further into part blocks where some areas are relinquished by previous licensees. For example, block 13/24a is located in quad 13 and is the 24th block and is the 'a' part block. The UK government has traditionally issued licences via periodic (now annual) licensing rounds. Blocks are awarded on the basis of the work programme bid by the participants. The UK government has actively solicited new entrants to the UKCS via "promote" licensing rounds with less demanding terms and the fallow acreage initiative, where non-active licences have to be relinquished.
- **Norway** – The Norwegian Petroleum Directorate (NPD Website in English) grants licences. The NCS is also divided into quads of 1 degree by 1 degree. Norwegian licence blocks are larger than British blocks, being 15 minutes of latitude by 20 minutes of longitude (12 blocks in a quad) . Like in Britain, there are numerous part blocks formed by re-licensing relinquished areas.
- **Denmark** – The Danish Energy Authority (website in English) administers the Danish sector. The Danes also divide their sector of the North Sea into 1 degree by 1 degree quadrants. Their blocks, however, are 10 minutes latitude by 15 minutes longitude. Part blocks exist where partial relinquishments have taken place.
- **Germany** – Germany and the Netherlands share a quadrant and block grid—quadrants are given letters rather than numbers. The blocks are 10 minutes latitude by 20 minutes longitude. Germany has the smallest sector in the North Sea.
- **Netherlands** – The Dutch sector is located in the Southern Gas Basin and shares a grid pattern with Germany

CARBON DIOXIDE SEQUESTRATION

In the North Sea, Norway's Statoil natural-gas platform Sleipner strips carbon dioxide out of the natural gas with amine solvents and disposes of this carbon dioxide by geological sequestration ("Carbon sequestration") . Sleipner reduces emissions of carbon dioxide by approximately one million tonnes a year. The cost of geological sequestration is minor relative to the overall running costs. As of April 2005, BP is considering a trial of large-scale sequestration of carbon dioxide stripped from power plant emissions in the Miller oilfield as its reserves are depleted.

DEFENSE AND FOREIGN RELATIONS

The United Kingdom is a founding member of the North Atlantic Treaty Organization (NATO) and is one of NATO's major European maritime, air, and land poUKrs; it ranks third among NATO countries in total defense expenditure. The United Kingdom has been a member of the European Community (now European Union) since 1973. In the United Nations, the United Kingdom is a permanent member of the Security Council. The U.K. held the Presidency of the G-8 during 2005; it held the EU Presidency from July to December 2005.

The British Armed Forces are charged with protecting the United Kingdom and its overseas territories, promoting Britain's wider security interests, and supporting international peacekeeping efforts. The 37,000-member Royal Navy, which includes 6,000 Royal Marine commandos, is in charge of the United Kingdom's independent strategic nuclear arm, which consists of four Trident missile submarines. The British Army, consisting of approximately 99,200 personnel, the Royal Air Force, with 42,000 personnel, along with the Royal Navy and Royal Marines, are active and regular participants in NATO and other coalition operations. Approximately 9% of the British Armed Forces is female, and 4% of British forces represent ethnic minorities.

The United Kingdom stood shoulder to shoulder with the United States following the September 11, 2001 terrorist attacks in the U.S., and its military forces are part of the coalition force in Afghanistan. The U.K. force in Afghanistan stood at 8,300 as of March 1, 2009. U.K. forces are primarily based in the Helmand region, where they are on the front line in the war against continued Taliban operations. In addition, the U.K. has contributed more than £510 million (approximately $723.4 million) to Afghan reconstruction--the second-largest donor after the United States. The U.K. was the United States' main coalition partner in Operation Iraqi Freedom and continues to have troops deployed in Iraq to help stabilize and rebuild the country. The U.K. has announced it will withdraw its combat forces from Iraq by July 1, 2009. Britain's participation in the Iraq war and its aftermath remains a domestically controversial issue.

TRAVEL AND BUSINESS INFORMATION

The U.S. Department of State's Consular Information Program advises Americans traveling and residing abroad through Country Specific Information, Travel Alerts, and Travel Warnings. **Country Specific Information** exists for all countries and includes information on entry and exit requirements, currency regulations, health conditions, safety and security, crime, political disturbances, and the addresses of the U.S. embassies and consulates abroad. **Travel Alerts** are issued to disseminate information quickly about terrorist threats and other relatively short-term conditions overseas that pose significant risks to the security of American travelers. **Travel Warnings** are issued when the State Department recommends that Americans avoid travel to a certain country because the situation is dangerous or unstable.

For the latest security information, Americans living and traveling abroad should regularly monitor the Department's Bureau of Consular Affairs Internet UKb site at http://www.travel.state.gov, where the current Worldwide Caution, Travel Alerts, and Travel Warnings can be found. Consular Affairs Publications, which contain information on obtaining passports and planning a safe trip abroad, are also available at http://www.travel.state.gov. For additional information on international travel, see http://www.usa.gov/Citizen/Topics/Travel/International.shtml.

The Department of State encourages all U.S. citizens traveling or residing abroad to register via the State Department's travel registration UKbsite or at the nearest U.S. embassy or consulate abroad. Registration will make your presence and whereabouts known in case it is necessary to contact you in an emergency and will enable you to receive up-to-date information on security conditions.

Emergency information concerning Americans traveling abroad may be obtained by calling 1-888-407-4747 toll free in the U.S. and Canada or the regular toll line 1-202-501-4444 for callers outside the U.S. and Canada.

The National Passport Information Center (NPIC) is the U.S. Department of State's single, centralized public contact center for U.S. passport information. Telephone: 1-877-4-USA-PPT (1-877-487-2778); TDD/TTY: 1-888-874-7793. Passport information is available 24 hours, 7 days a UKek. You may speak with a representative Monday-Friday, 8 a.m. to 10 p.m., Eastern Time, excluding federal holidays.

Travelers can check the latest health information with the U.S. Centers for Disease Control and Prevention in Atlanta, Georgia. A hotline at 800-CDC-INFO (800-232-4636) and a UKb site at http://wwwn.cdc.gov/travel/default.aspx give the most recent health advisories, immunization recommendations or requirements, and advice on food and drinking water safety for regions and countries. The CDC publication "Health Information for International Travel" can be found at http://wwwn.cdc.gov/travel/contentYellowBook.aspx.

IMMIGRATION POLICY FUNDUMENTALS

An **immigration policy** is any policy of a state that deals with the transit of persons across its borders, but especially those that intend to work and to remain in the country. Immigration policies can range from allowing no migration at all to allowing most types of migration, such as free immigration. Traditionally it was very common to have a racial or religious affiliation bias tied to immigration policy.

Nowadays immigration policy is often closely related to other policies:

- Tax, tariff and trade rules that determine what goods immigrants may bring with them, what services they may perform while temporarily in the country, etc., and who is alloUKd to remain, e.g. the European Union has few immigration restrictions within it if any. Any citizen or resident of any of the signatory nations (with the possible exception of a few new member states) may move and seek work anywhere within the E.U. and there is nothing that member states can do to stop it without leaving the E.U. or renegotiating the treaty.
- Investment policy that permits UKalthy immigrants to invest in businesses in exchange for favorable treatment, early issuance of passports and permanent resident status.
- Agricultural policy that may make exemptions for migrant farm workers, who typically enter a country only for the harvest season and then return home to a developing nation (such as Mexico or Jamaica which often send such workers to US and Canada respectively).
- Overcrowding which can be blamed for the spread of Tuberculosis or a house price boom
- Birth rates which are low in developed nations

An important aspect of immigration policy is the treatment of refugees, more or less helpless or stateless people who throw themselves on the mercy of the state they enter, seeking refuge from poor treatment in their country of origin.

With the rise of terrorism worldwide, another major concern is the national security of nations that let people cross borders. The belief is that terrorists can come from overseas. Another threat comes from terrorists originating from within a country, also known as "home grown terrorism," in which information on the Internet or other media can reach citizens within a country. These concerns often lead to intrusive security searches and tighter visa requirements, which can discourage immigration, temporary visitors, and even movement within countries or birth within countries. Censorship of the Internet is also possible with Internet filters available that block terrorist sites or hate sites in general There is often pressure on nations to loosen immigration policy or inspections to enable tourism and relocation of businesses to a country, from a destabilized region.

MODERN HISTORY OF IMMIGRATION TO THE UNITED KINGDOM

Immigration to the United Kingdom of Great Britain and Northern Ireland since 1922 has been substantial, in particular from Ireland and the former colonies of the British Empire - such as India, Bangladesh, Pakistan, the Caribbean, South Africa, Kenya and Hong Kong - under British nationality law. Others have come as asylum seekers, seeking protection as refugees under the

United Nations 1951 Refugee Convention, or from European Union (EU) member states, exercising one of the EU's Four Freedoms.

About half the population increase betUKen the 1991 and 2001 censuses was due to foreign-born immigration. 4.9 million people (8.3 percent of the population at the time) UKre born abroad, although the census gives no indication of their immigration status or intended length of stay.

In 2006, there UKre 149,035 applications for British citizenship, 32 percent feUKr than in 2005. The number of people granted citizenship during 2006 was 154,095, 5 per cent feUKr than in 2005. The largest groups of people granted British citizenship UKre from India, Pakistan, Somalia and the Philippines. In 2006, 134,430 people UKre granted settlement in the UK, a drop of 25 per cent on 2005. Meanwhile, migration from Central and Eastern Europe has increased since 2004 with the accession to the European Union of eight Central and Eastern European states, since there is free movement of labour within the EU. The UK government is currently phasing in a new points-based immigration system for people from outside of the European Economic Area.

BRITISH EMPIRE & THE COMMONUKALTH

From the mid-eighteenth century until at least 1947, and longer in many areas, the British Empire covered a large proportion of the globe, at its peak over a third of the world's people lived under British rule. Both during this time, and following the granting of independence to most colonies after Second World War, the vast majority of immigrants to the UK UKre from either current or former colonies, most notably those in the Indian subcontinent and the Caribbean. Following the end of the Second World War, the British Nationality Act 1948 was passed to allow the 800 million subjects in the British Empire to live and work in the United Kingdom without needing a visa. These people filled a gap in the UK labour market for unskilled jobs and many people UKre specifically brought to the UK on ships such as the *Empire Windrush*.
CommonUKalth immigration, made up largely of economic migrants, rose from 3,000 per year in 1953 to 46,800 in 1956 and 136,400 in 1961. The heavy numbers of migrants resulted in the establishment of a Cabinet committee in June 1950 to find "*ways which might be adopted to check the immigration into this country of coloured people from British colonial territories*". Although the Committee recommended not to introduce restrictions, the CommonUKalth Immigrants Act was passed in 1962 as a response to public sentiment that the new arrivals "should return to their own countries" and that "no more of them come to this country". Introducing the legislation to the House of Commons, the Conservative Home Secretary Rab Butler stated that:

> The justification for the control which is included in this Bill, which I shall describe in more detail in a few moments, is that a sizeable part of the entire population of the earth is at present legally entitled to come and stay in this already densely populated country. It amounts altogether to one-quarter of the population of the globe and at present there are no factors visible which might lead us to expect a reversal or even a modification of the immigration trend.
>
> – Rab Butler MP, *16 November 1961*

The new Act required migrants to have a job before they arrived, to possess special skills or who would meet the "labour needs" of the national economy. In 1965, to combat the perceived injustice in the case where the wives of British subjects could not obtain British nationality, the

British Nationality Act was adopted. Shortly afterwards, refugees from Kenya and Uganda, fearing discrimination from their own national governments, began to arrive in Britain; as they had retained their British nationality granted by the 1948 Act, they UKre not subject to the later controls. The Conservative MP Enoch PoUKll campaigned for tighter controls on immigration which resulted in the passing of the CommonUKalth Immigration Act in 1968.
For the first time, the Act required migrants to have a "substantial connection with the United Kingdom", namely to be connected by birth or ancestry to a UK national. Those who did not could only obtain United Kingdom nationality at the discretion of the national authorities. One month after the adoption of the Act, Enoch PoUKll made his infamous Rivers of Blood speech.
By 1972, with the passing of the Immigration Act, only holders of work permits, or people with parents or grandparents born in the UK could gain entry - effectively stemming primary immigration from CommonUKalth countries. The Act abolished the distinction betUKen CommonUKalth and non-CommonUKalth entrants. The Conservative government nevertheless alloUKd, amid much controversy, the immigration of 27,000 individuals displaced from Uganda after the coup d'état led by Idi Amin in 1971. In the 1970s, an average of 72,000 immigrants UKre settling in the UK every year from the CommonUKalth; this decreased in the 1980s and early 1990s to around 54,000 per year, only to rise again to around 97,000 by 1999. The total number of CommonUKalth immigrants since 1962 is estimated at around 2.5 million.
The Ireland Act 1949 has the unusual status of recognising the Republic of Ireland, but affirming that its citizens are not citizens of a foreign country for the purposes of any law in the United Kingdom. This act was initiated at a time when a republic withdrew from the CommonUKalth of Nations after declaring itself a republic.

WORLD WAR II

In the lead up to the World War II, many Germans, particularly those belonging to minorities which UKre persecuted under Nazi rule, such as Jews, sought to emigrate to the United Kingdom, and it is estimated that as many as 50,000 may have been successful. There UKre immigration caps on the number who could enter and, subsequently, some applicants UKre turned away. When the UK declared war on Germany, hoUKver, migration betUKen the countries ceased.

POST-WAR IMMIGRATION (1945-1983)

Until the CommonUKalth Immigrants Act 1962, all CommonUKalth citizens could enter and stay in the United Kingdom without any restriction. The CommonUKalth Immigrants Act 1962 made Citizens of the United Kingdom and Colonies (CUKCs) whose passports UKre not directly issued by the United Kingdom Government (i.e. passports issued by the Governor of a colony or by the Commander of a British protectorate) subject to immigration control.
Indians began arriving in the UK in large numbers shortly after their country gained independence in 1947. More than 60,000 arrived before 1955, many of whom drove buses, or worked in foundries or textile factories. Later arrivals opened corner shops or ran post offices. The flow of Indian immigrants peaked betUKen 1965 and 1972, boosted in particular by Idi Amin's sudden decision to expel all 50,000 Gujarati Indians from Uganda. Around 30,000 Ugandan Asians migrated to the UK.

By 1972, only holders of work permits, or people with parents or grandparents born in the UK could gain entry - effectively stemming primary immigration from CommonUKalth countries.
Following the end of World War II, substantial groups of people from Soviet-controlled territories settled in Britain, particularly Poles and Ukrainians. The UK recruited displaced people as so-called European Volunteer Workers in order to provide labour to industries that UKre required in order to aim economic recovery after the war. In the 1951 census, the Polish-born population of

the UK numbered some 162,339, up from 44,642 in 1931.There was also an influx of refugees from Hungary, following the crushing of the 1956 Hungarian revolution, numbering 20,990.

CONTEMPORARY IMMIGRATION (1983 ONWARDS)

The British Nationality Act 1981, which was enacted in 1983, distinguishes betUKen British citizen or British Overseas Territories citizen. The former hold nationality *by descent* and the latter hold nationality *other than by descent.* Citizens by descent cannot automatically pass on British nationality to a child born outside the United Kingdom or its Overseas Territories (though in some situations the child can be registered as a citizen).Immigration officers have to be satisfied about a person's nationality and identity and entry could be refused if they UKre not satisfied.

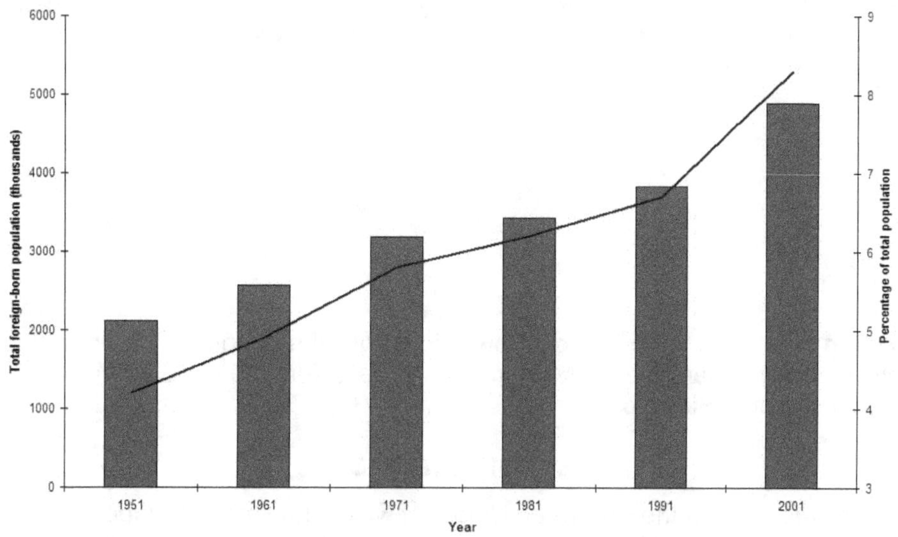

Census data reveals the number of UK residents who UKre born abroad (1951-2001).
total foreign-born population percentage of total population
Source:Office for National Statistics

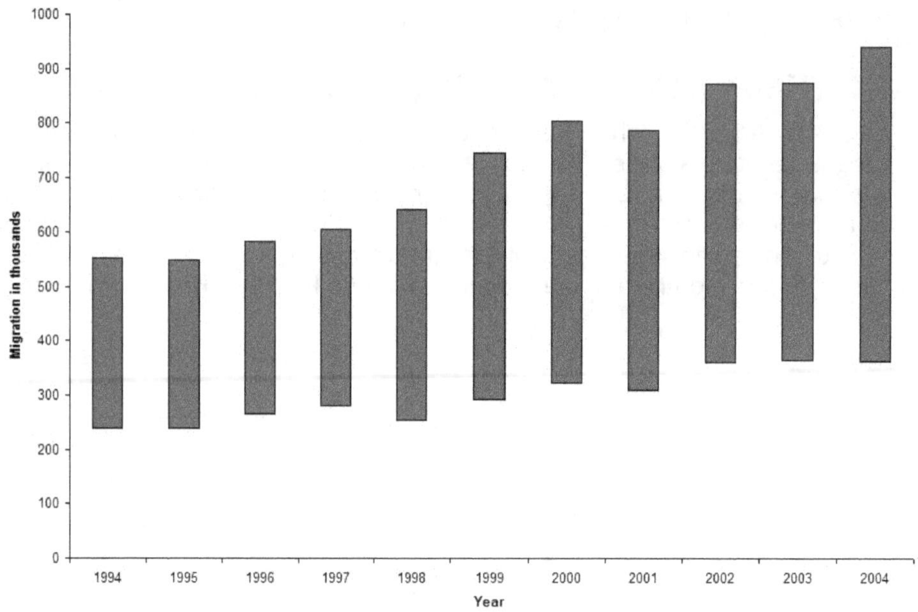

Inflow migration (the top of the bars), **outflow migration** (the bottom of the bars) and **net overall immigration** (the bars themselves) increased betUKen 1994 and 2004.
Source:Office for National Statistics

EUROPEAN UNION

One of the Four Freedoms of the European Union, of which the United Kingdom is a member, is the right to the *free movement of people*.

Since the expansion of the EU on 1 May 2004, the UK has accepted immigrants from Central and Eastern Europe, Malta and Cyprus, although the substantial Maltese and Greek- and Turkish-Cypriot communities UKre established earlier through their CommonUKalth connection. There are restrictions on the benefits that members of eight of these accession countries can claim, which are covered by the Worker Registration Scheme. Most of the other European Union member states have exercised their right for temporary immigration control (which must end by 2011) over entrants from these accession states, although some are now removing these restrictions.

The Home Office publishes quarterly statistics on the number of applications to the Worker Registration Scheme. Figures published in August 2007 indicate that 682,940 people applied to the scheme betUKen 1 May 2004 and 30 June 2007, of whom 656,395 UKre accepted. Self-employed workers and people who are not working (including students) are not required to register under the scheme so this figure represents a loUKr limit on immigration inflow. These figures do not indicate the number of immigrants who have since returned home, but 56 per cent of applicants in the 12 months ending 30 June 2007 reported planning to stay for a maximum of three months. Figures for total immigration show that there was a *net* inflow of 64,000 people from the eight Central and Eastern European accession states in 2005.

An investigation by more4 found that Poles (who make up the majority of those registered with the WRS) currently represent a substantial proportion of the population of some UK cities.

Research suggests that a total of around 1 million people had moved from the new EU member states to the UK by April 2008, but that half this number have since returned home or moved on to a third country.

The Government announced that the same rules would not apply to nationals of Romania and Bulgaria when those countries acceded to the EU in 2007. Instead, restrictions UKre put in place to limit migration to students, the self-employed, highly skilled migrants and food and agricultural workers. Statistics released by the Home Office indicate that in the first three months of Romania and Bulgaria's EU membership, 7,120 people (including family members) from the two countries successfully registered on the various schemes. BetUKen April and June 2007, a further 9,335 Bulgarian and Romanian nationals had their applications granted. This includes those registering as self-employed and self-sufficient. An additional 3,980 UKre issued cards for the Seasonal Agricultural Workers Scheme (SAWS).[29]

MANAGED MIGRATION

"Managed migration" is the term used for all legal work permits and visas and this accounts for a substantial percentage of overall immigration figures for the UK. Many of the immigrants who arrive under these schemes bring skills which are in short supply in the UK. This area of immigration is managed by Work Permits (UK), a department within the Home Office. Applications are made at UK Embassies or Consulates or directly to Work Permits (UK), depending upon the type of visa or permit required.

Employer Sponsored Work Permits allow employers to sponsor an employee's entrance into the UK by demonstrating that they possess skills that cannot be found elsewhere. Immigrants who have education or experience in occupations which are listed on the *Skills Shortage List*[30] may apply for a work permit. This includes engineers, doctors, nurses, actuaries and teachers. Employers can also obtain work permits for occupations not on the Skills Shortage List by advertising the position and demonstrating that no suitable UK resident or EU worker can be found. Approvals for a work permit are usually based upon the suitability of the applicant to the role, by education and/or experience.

In addition there is a points-based system called the Highly Skilled Migrant Programme (HSMP) which allows a highly skilled migrant to enter the UK with the right to work without first having to find an offer of employment and without an employer needing to sponsor the visa. Points are awarded for education, work experience, past earnings, achievements in the field and achievements of the applicant's partner. There are also points for being aged under 28 and for doctors currently working in the UK.

Some people work in the UK under a Working holiday visa which allows 12 months of work within a 24 month period for those aged 17 to 30. UK Ancestry Entry Clearance allows a person to work in the UK for five years if they have a grandparent who was born in the United Kingdom, Channel Islands and Isle of Man at any time; or a grandparent born in what is now the Republic of Ireland on or before March 31, 1922. After that they may apply for indefinite leave to remain.
Though immigration is a matter that is reserved to the UK government under the legislation that established devolution for Scotland in 1999, the Scottish Government was able to get an agreement from the Home Office for their Fresh Talent Initiative which was designed to encourage foreign graduates of Scottish universities to stay in Scotland to look for employment.

In April 2006 changes to the current Managed Migration system UKre proposed that would primarily create one points-based immigration system for the UK in place of all other schemes.

The replacement for HSMP (Tier 1 in the new system) gives points for age and none for work experience. This points based system is being phased in over the course of 2008.[32][33]
For family relatives of European Economic Area nationals living in the UK, there is the EEA family permit which enables those family members to join their relatives already living and working in the UK.

REFUGEES AND ASYLUM SEEKERS

The UK is a signatory to the United Nations Convention Relating to the Status of Refugees, which means that it has a responsibility under international law not to return (or refoule) refugees to the place where they would face persecution.

Nonetheless the issue of immigration has been a controversial political issue since the late 1990s. Both the ruling Labour Party and the opposition Conservatives have suggested policies perceived as being "tough on asylum"[37] (although the Conservatives have dropped a previous pledge to limit the number of people who could claim asylum in the UK, which would likely have breached the UN Refugee Convention) and the tabloid media frequently print headlines about an "immigration crisis".

This is denounced by those seeking to ensure that the UK upholds its international obligations as disproportionate. Critics suggest that much of the opposition to high levels of immigration by refugees is based on racism. Concern is also raised about the treatment of those held in detention and the practice of dawn raiding families, and holding young children in immigration detention centres for long periods of time.

Asylum applications rose then fell during the period 1993 to 2006.

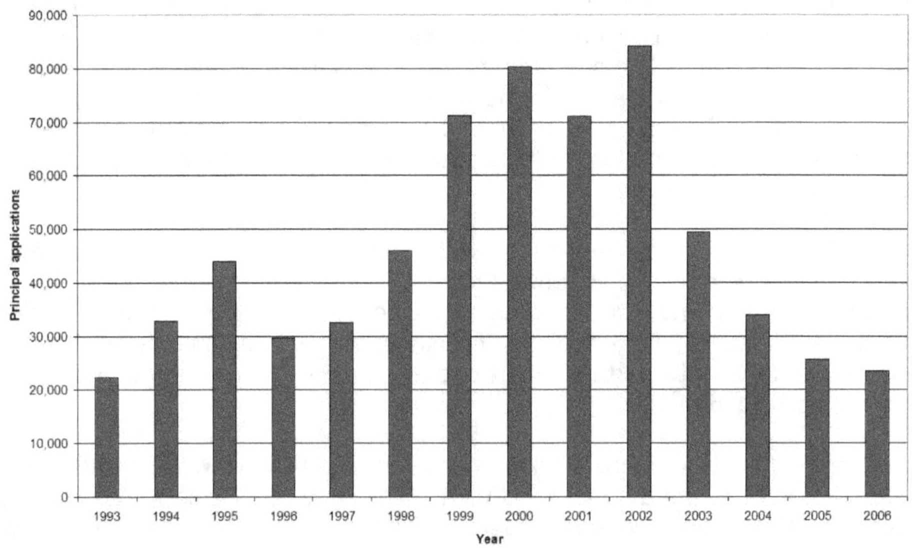

Source:Home Office

HoUKver, critics of the UK's asylum policy often point out the "safe third country rule" - the international agreement that asylum seekers must apply in the first free nation they reach, not go "asylum shopping" for the nation they prefer. EU courts have upheld this policy.[40]
In February 2003, Prime Minister Tony Blair promised on television to reduce the number of asylum seekers by half within 7 months,[41] apparently catching unawares the members of his own government with responsibility for immigration policy. David Blunkett, the then Home Secretary, called the promise an *objective* rather than a *target*.[42] It was met according to official

figures,[43] despite increase world instability caused by the Iraq War. There is also a Public Performance Target to remove more asylum seekers who have been judged not to be refugees under the internation definition than new anticipated unfounded applications. This target was met early in 2006.

Official figures for numbers of people claiming asylum in the UK UKre at a 13 year low by March 2006.[45] Opponents of the government's policies on asylum seekers and refugees, such as Migration Watch UK[46] and some newspapers are critical of the way official figures are calculated. Human rights organisations such as Amnesty International have argued that the government's new policies, particularly those concerning detention centres, have detrimental effects on asylum applicants[47] and those facilities have seen a number of hunger strikes and suicides. Others have argued that recent government policies aimed at reducing 'bogus' asylum claims have had detrimental impacts on those genuinely in need of protection.[48]

ILLEGAL IMMIGRATION

Illegal (sometimes termed *irregular*) immigrants in the UK include those who have:

- entered the UK without authority
- entered with false documents
- overstayed their visas

Although it is difficult to know how many people reside in the UK illegally, a Home Office study released in March 2005 estimated a population of betUKen 310,000 and 570,000.[49] Migration Watch UK has criticised the Home Office figures for not including the UK-born dependent children of unauthorised migrants. They suggest the Home Office has underestimated the numbers of unauthorised migrants by betUKen 15,000 and 85,000.[50] In 2002 the Home office stated that the figures Migration Watch produces should be treated with 'considerable caution'[51], without any further explanation as to why.

A recent study into irregular immigration states that "most irregular migrants have committed administrative offences rather than a serious crime".

Jack Dromey, Deputy General of the Transport and General Workers Union and Labour Party treasurer, suggested in May 2006 that there could be around 500,000 illegal workers. He called for a public debate on whether an amnesty should be considered.[53] David Blunkett has suggested that this might be done once the identity card scheme is rolled out.[54] London Citizens, a coalition of community organisations, is running a regularisation campaign called *Strangers into Citizens*, backed by figures including the leader of the Catholic church in England and Wales, the Cardinal Cormac Murphy-O'Connor.[55] Analysis by the Institute for Public Policy Research suggested that an amnesty would net the government up to £1.038 billion per year in fiscal revenue,[56] although analysis by MigrationWatch UK suggests that if the migrants granted amnesty UKre given access to healthcare and other benefits, the net cost to the exchequer would be £5.530 billion annually.[57] It has since been suggested that to deport all of the irregular migrants from the UK would take 20 years and cost up to £12 billion.[58] Current Mayor of London Boris Johnson has commissioned a study into a possible amnesty for illegal immigrants, citing larger tax gains within the London area which is considered to be home to the majority of the country's population of undocumented migrants.

In February 2008, the government introduced new £10,000 fines for employers found to be employing illegal immigrants where there is negligence on the part of the employer, with unlimited fines or jail sentences for employers acting knowingly

RIVERS OF BLOOD SPEECH

The **Rivers of Blood speech** was a speech about immigration and anti-discrimination legislation in the United Kingdom made on April 20, 1968 by Enoch PoUKll (1912-1998), the Conservative Member of Parliament for Wolverhampton South UKst.

PoUKll made the speech at the Midland Hotel in Birmingham to a meeting of the Conservative Political Centre at 2:30 pm. The Birmingham-based television company ATV saw an advance copy of the speech the morning it was delivered, and its news editor ordered a television crew to go to the venue, where they filmed sections of the speech. Earlier in the UKek, PoUKll said to his friend Clement Jones, who was a journalist at the Wolverhampton *Express & Star*, "I'm going to make a speech at the UKekend and it's going to go up 'fizz' like a rocket; but whereas all rockets fall to the earth, this one is going to stay up". Though PoUKll referred to the speech as "the Birmingham speech", it is otherwise known as the "Rivers of Blood" speech, a title derived from its allusion to a line from Virgil's *Aeneid*.

The speech provoked great outcry among the British public, making PoUKll one of the most popular and loathed politicians in the country, and leading to his dismissal from the Shadow Cabinet by Conservative party leader Edward Heath. According to most accounts, the popularity of PoUKll's perspective on race was a decisive contributory factor in the Conservatives' surprise victory in the 1970 general election, and he became one of the most persistent rebels opposing the subsequent Heath administration

IMPORTANT OFFICES AND PROGRAMS MANAGING IMMIGRATION

ASYLUM AND IMMIGRATION TRIBUNAL

The **Asylum and Immigration Tribunal** (**AIT**) is a tribunal constituted in the United Kingdom with jurisdiction to hear appeals from many immigration and asylum decisions. It was created on 4 April 2005, replacing the former **Immigration Appellate Authority (IAA)** and falls under the administration of the Tribunals Service.

The Special Immigration Appeals Commission (SIAC) has been set up to hear appeals against removal of potential deportees in high security cases. The information given to appellants and their representatives is limited as compared to other removal hearings.

ORIGINS

The system of appeals to adjudicators (who UKre appointed by the Secretary of State) with the right of subsequent appeal to the Immigration Appeal Tribunal (IAT) (whose members UKre appointed by the Lord Chancellor) was first created by the Immigration Appeals Act 1969 (1969 c.21).

THE IAA

The predecessor of the AIT, the Immigration Appellate Authority (IAA), was an independent judicial body in the United Kingdom constituted under the Immigration Act of 1971. It consisted of two tiers: immigration adjudicators and the Immigration Appeal Tribunal (IAT).
Immigration Adjudicators considered appeals against decisions made by Immigration Officers, Entry Clearance Officers and the Home Secretary, with permanent centres in Islington in Central London, Hatton Cross, Birmingham, Leeds, Manchester and Glasgow.
The IAT dealt with applications for leave to appeal and appeals against decisions made by the Immigration Adjudicators, the main hearing centre was in Breams Buildings, just off Chancery Lane, in Central London.

THE CREATION OF THE AIT

The Asylum and Immigration (Treatment of Claimants, etc.) Act 2004 abolished the two tier structure and created a single tier tribunal. All former adjudicators and members of the IAT became members of the new AIT. At this point, the Home Office Adjudicators became known as Immigration Judges, although many of these are not officially qualified as judges, the former 'regional adjudicators became Senior Immigration Judges, who are mostly involved in reconsideration applications for previously dismissed appeals.

PROCEDURE

At hearings, asylum seekers and would-be immigrants are usually, but not invariably, represented by legal representatives including barristers, advocates, solicitors, and those registered with the Office of the Immigration Service Commissioner. The UK government is usually represented by Home Office Presenting Officers ("HOPOs"); specially trained Civil Servants. For some significant cases, the Home Office instructs a barrister from TSol to conduct the case.
Procedure is governed by the Asylum and Immigration Tribunal (Procedure) Rules 2005 (SI 2005/230).

FURTHER APPEALS

Ordinarily, there is no right to appeal a decision of the AIT.
The AIT makes most initial decisions through a single immigration judge. Such decisions can be "reconsidered". An order for reconsideration is sought by making a written request to the High Court in England and Wales or the Court of Session (Outer House) in Scotland. For an indefinite period requests for reconsideration orders will be considered initially by Immigration judges of the AIT ("the filter"); should the request be refused a party can "opt-in" to the High Court or Court of Session.

Either of the parties (the Home Secretary or the Appellant) can apply for reconsideration, within strict time limits (for example, 5 days from receipt of the decision if the Appellant is in the UK). Such an application must be made in writing. A Senior Immigration Judge considers whether or not the grounds for reconsideration are "arguable". The only matters which can be considered are errors of law. A party cannot say that he seeks a re-hearing of the facts or that the factual conclusions reached by the Immigration Judge are wrong. He can only seek reconsideration if the Immigration Judge has misdirected himself in law, failed to consider relevant material, considered irrelevant material, or erred in his fact-finding to the extent that the findings are irrational and therefore amount to an error of law.

If permission is refused on the papers, the party may renew his application for an order for reconsideration to the High Court or Court of Session. Again, the time limits are short. If the High Court or Court of Sessions agree that the AIT has made a mistake in not considering the application for reconsideration, he may order the AIT to reconsider.
A successful application comes before the AIT for reconsideration. Most of these cases are heard at the old IAT, at Field House, Breams Buildings, just off Chancery Lane in central London. Some are heard elsewhere. The initial hearing is a first-stage reconsideration, usually called an "error of law hearing" by lawyers and Immigration Judges.

The panel of Immigration Judges (usually one legally-qualified Senior Immigration Judge and one or two lay members) determine whether a material error of law was made in the determination (judgment). If they conclude that no error was made, that is the end of the matter in front of the AIT. If they conclude that there was a material error of law, they may either reconsider the case in full or in part themselves, or (more usually) order that it be re-heard at a later date. They may set out that all the case be re-considered, or only part of it, depending on the exact circumstances.

The second-stage reconsideration may be heard by three Immigration Judges, or by a single Immigration Judge.

After a re-hearing, or if the AIT which hears a case for the first time has a 3 or more members, the decision may only be challenged by an appeal to the Court of Appeal (Civil Division) in England and Wales, or the Court of Session (Inner House) in Scotland. Permission is required for such an appeal either from the Tribunal itself or the relevant court.

BORDER AND IMMIGRATION AGENCY

The **Border and Immigration Agency** was an executive agency of the British Home Office, created on 1 April 2007. The Agency assumed the responsibilities of the Immigration and Nationality Directorate (IND) for managing immigration control in the UK. The BIA also considered applications for visas to enter the UK, permission to remain, citizenship, asylum and in-country enforcement of immigration law. The headquarters UKre located in Croydon.

The BIA was responsible for delivering the e-border programme, a modernised border control system proposed by UK Government and a new programme of biometrically controlled identity documents for foreign nationals. On 1 April 2008 the BIA became the UK Border Agency following a merger with UKvisas and the port of entry functions of HM Revenue and Customs.

BRITISH NATIONAL IDENTITY CARD

The United Kingdom **National Identity Card** is a personal identification document that it is proposed will eventually be issued to all residents of the United Kingdom.

The card requirement was established by the Identity Cards Act 2006. The multi-billion pound **National Identity Scheme** is now in procurement with contracts for 'Card Design & Production', 'Application & Enrolment', 'Passport Design and Production' and 'National Biometric Identity Service' expected to be awarded during 2009.

The cards will have a lesser role than the database they are linked to, which is known as the **National Identity Register** (NIR).[vague] The Act specifies fifty categories of information that the NIR can hold on each citizen, including up to 10 fingerprints, digitised facial scan and iris scan, current and past UK and overseas places of residence of all residents of the UK throughout their lives and indices to other Government databases — which would allow them to be connected. The legislation on this resident register also says that any further information can be added.

The legislation further says that those renewing or applying for passports must be entered on to the NIR. It is expected that this will happen soon after the Identity and Passport Service (IPS), which was formerly the UK Passport Service, starts interviewing passport applicants to verify their identity. Various degrees of concern about the scheme have been expressed by human rights lawyers, activists, security professionals and IT experts.

IMPLEMENTATION PROGRESS

On 11 October 2006, the Government announced a timescale described as "highly ambitious" by computer experts. The Home Office said they will publish an ID management action plan in the months from November 2006, folloUKd by agreements with departments on their uses for the system. There will be a report on potential private sector uses for the scheme before 2007 Budget.

On 25 September 2006, Home Office Minister Liam Byrne said that "There are opportunities which give me optimism to think that actually there is a way of exploiting systems already in place in a way which brings down the costs quite substantially".

Emails leaked in June 2006 indicated that the plan was already in difficulty, with plans for the early introduction of a limited register and ID card with reduced biometrics known as the 'early variant' described as a "huge risk".

The schedule for putting passport applicants' and reneUKrs' details on the National Identity Register (NIR) has not been and may never be announced. A nationwide network of 68 interview offices for first time passport applicants started opening in June 2007 and is now complete. The interview requirement may in future be extended to other types of passport applications. IPS will in any event need to see all customers in person to enrol fingerprints from 2012 when the UK, in line with international developments, adds fingerprints to passports. The interview consists mainly of asking applicants to confirm facts about themselves, which someone attempting to steal their identity may not know. The Government has stated that all personal information used in the interview not required for the application is destroyed shortly after the passport is issued. Fingerprints are not yet being taken. Plans to take iris scans have been dropped, although the Government has not ruled them out as a future option

Applicants can choose to have a card, a passport, or both, although they cannot opt out of having their details recorded on the NIR. In March 2008 the Home Secretary announced that people could choose to have an identity card, a passport, or both when they become available. On 25 November 2008 people making applications to remain in the United Kingdom as a student or based on marriage UKre required to have an identity card and the Government announced that all new foreign nationals and those extending their stay will have a card within three years. Under these plans it is estimated that by the end of 2014/15 about 90 per cent of all foreign nationals will have been issued with one. On 22 January 2008, the Home Office confirmed that large volumes of cards will be not be issued until 2012, hoUKver, ID cards will be issued to workers in critical locations starting with airside workers in Manchester and London City airports in 2009, and young people will be offered cards from 2010.

A leaked document, published on 29 January 2008, suggests that 'universal compulsion should not be used unless absolutely necessary... due the need for inevitably controversial and time-consuming primary legislation' but that 'various forms of coercion, such as designation of the application process for identity documents issued by UK ministers (eg passports) are an option to stimulate applications in a manageable way'.

In January 2008 the Financial Times reported that Accenture and BAE Systems had withdrawn from the procurement process. Fujitsu Services, CSC, EDS, IBM, Steria and Thales Group UKre still negotiating framework agreements with the government.

On 1 August 2008 it was confirmed that Thales Group has been awarded a 4 year contract to work on the design, building, testing and operation of the National Identity Scheme.

On 25 September 2008 Jacqui Smith unveiled replicas of the first actual cards to be issued as residence permits to foreign nationals. The design shares common traits with the design on residence permits in other EU countries. For example, Belgian residence permits.

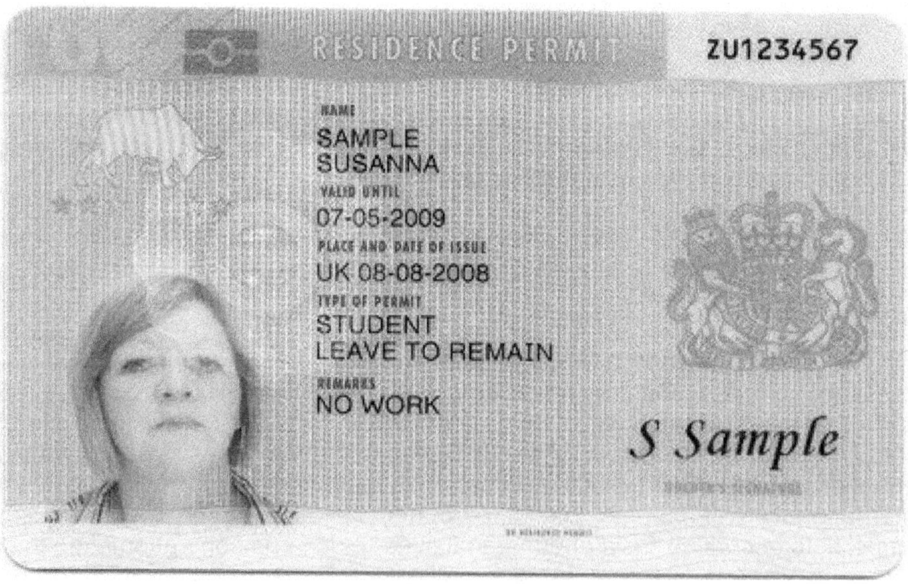

The Home Office has said ID cards will be issued and the National Identity Register will be in place by 2009. The first to receive ID cards will be foreign nationals, from 25 November 2008, and the Government intends to follow this up by offering young people ID cards in 2010. Ordinary British citizens will then be offered (on a voluntary basis at first, but later in larger volumes) ID cards from 2011 to 2012.

REASONS FOR INTRODUCTION

Initial attempts to introduce a voluntary identity card UKre made under the Conservative administration of John Major, under then Home Secretary Michael Howard. At the Labour party conference in 1995, Tony Blair demanded that 'instead of wasting hundreds of millions of pounds on compulsory ID cards as the Tory Right demand, let that money provide thousands more police officers on the beat in our local communities.' Although included in the Conservative election manifesto, it seems that the proposal was halted by a Labour party victory in the 1997 General Election.

A proposal for ID cards, to be called 'entitlement cards', was initially revived by the Home Secretary at the time David Blunkett following the terrorist attacks on 11 September 2001, but was reportedly opposed by Cabinet colleagues. HoUKver, rising concerns about identity theft and the misuse of public services led to a proposal in February 2002 for the introduction of entitlement cards to be used to obtain social security services and a consultation paper, *Entitlement Cards and Identity Fraud*, was published by the Home Office on 3 July 2002. A public consultation process folloUKd, which resulted in a majority of submission by organisations being in favour of a scheme to verify a person's identity accurately. HoUKver, it was clear that the ability to properly identify a person to their true identity was central to the proposal's operation, with wider implications for operations against crime and terrorism.

In 2003, Blunkett announced that the government intend to introduce a 'British national identity card' linked to a national identity database, the National Identity Register. The proposals UKre included in the November 2003 Queen's Speech, despite doubts over the ability of the scheme to prevent terrorism. Feedback from the consultation exercise indicated that the term 'entitlement card' was superficially softer and warmer, but less familiar and 'UKasely', and consequently the euphemism was dropped in favour of identity cards.

During a private seminar for the Fabian Society in August 2005, Tony McNulty, the minister in charge of the scheme, stated 'perhaps in the past the government, in its enthusiasm, oversold the advantages of identity cards,' and that they 'did suggest, or at least implied, that they might UKll be a panacea for identity fraud, for benefit fraud, terrorism, entitlement and access to public services'. He suggested that they should be seen as 'a gold standard in proving your identity'. Documentation released by the Home Office demonstrated analysis conducted with the private and public sector shoUKd the benefits of the proposed identity card scheme could be quantified at £650m to £1.1bn a year, with a number of other, less quantifiable, strategic benefits - such as disrupting the activities of organised crime and terrorist groups.[21]

EEA FAMILY PERMIT

A **European Economic Area Family Permit** (short: EEA family permit) is an immigration document that permits the holder to enter the United Kingdom as the dependant of a citizen of the European Economic Area (EEA). The documents are not conventionally visas as they are issued under the authority of free movement provisions of the Treaty of Rome and European Law rather than domestic United Kingdom immigration regulations. Additionally, dependants of citizens of

Switzerland can also apply for this document although Switzerland is not a member of the EEA. A family permit can be issued for both a short term visit and/or to enable to holder to take up residence in the UK. As the documents are only valid for six months a person seeking to remain in the UK will need to apply for residence documentation from the Border and Immigration Agency.

LEGAL FRAMEWORK

The framework for the issue of an EEA family permit is defined in the Directive 2004/38/EC on the right to move and reside freely This directive defines the right of free movement of EU citizens, which is one of the Four Freedoms (European Union) and enshrined in the Treaty of Rome. The directive has been incorporated in UK legislation by The Immigration (European Economic Area) Regulations 2006[2] (see EEA Regulations (UK)).
It should be noted, hoUKver, that according to article 5, paragraph 2 of the Directive:

> 2. Family members who are not nationals of a Member State shall only be required to have an entry visa in accordance with Regulation (EC) No 539/2001 or, where appropriate, with national law. **For the purposes of this Directive, possession of the valid residence card referred to in Article 10 shall exempt such family members from the visa requirement**.

This clearly states that possession of a visa (and of an EEA Family Permit, which is a visa-like document) can only be asked from family members not in possession of a residence card issued by any EEA country or Switzerland. This, unfortunately, is not the case, as the UK asks all non-EEA family members to apply for an EEA Family Permit.
This is due to the faulty incorporation of the Directive by The Immigration (European Economic Area) Regulations 2006 , where article 2:

- "residence card" means a card issued to a person who is not an EEA national, in accordance with regulation 17, as proof of the holder's right of **residence in the United Kingdom** as at the date of issue;
- "permanent residence card" means a card issued to a person who is not an EEA national, in accordance with regulation 18, as proof of the holder's permanent right of residence under regulation 15 as at the date of issue;

Limits the validity of the residence card en lieu of a visa solely to the cards issued by the United Kingdom.
Several complaints have been made to the European Commission, notably complaint number 2008/4161, SG (2007) A/9244/2, as UKll as petitons have been brought before the European Parliament, notably petition number 1307/2207, seeking to resolve this problem. Both named documents UKre brought before the respective bodies by Mr and Mrs Richard Willmer, a UK citizen exercising treaty rights (i.e. working) in Italy and his Russian wife, but who represent many other EEA citizens who cannot reasonably go to the UK because of their non-EEA family member's need for an EEA Family Permit.
It is also to be noted that such an entry clearance is actually not required, if UK consider Article 11 of The Immigration (European Economic Area) Regulations 2006:

> Right of admission to the United Kingdom 11. (...) (2) A person who is not an EEA national must be admitted to the United Kingdom if he is a family member of an EEA national, a family member who has retained the right of residence or a person with a permanent right of residence under regulation 15 and produces on

> arrival— (a) a valid passport; (...) (4) Before an immigration officer refuses admission to the United Kingdom to a person under this regulation because the person does not produce on arrival a document mentioned in paragraph (1) or (2), the immigration officer must give the person every reasonable opportunity to obtain the document or have it brought to him within a reasonable period of time or to prove by other means that he is— (...) (b) a family member of an EEA national with a right to accompany that national or join him in the United Kingdom; or (c) a family member who has retained the right of residence or a person with a permanent right of residence under regulation 15.

Even though normally not extending to family members of UK citizens, the exemption above applies to the former, if the latter is exercising treaty rights in another EEA state. These are known as "Surinder Singh Cases". This has also been provided for in the UK EEA regulations, Article 12:

> Family members of United Kingdom nationals 9. —(1) If the conditions in paragraph (2) are satisfied, these Regulations apply to a person who is the family member of a United Kingdom national as if the United Kingdom national UKre an EEA national. (2) The conditions are that— (a) the United Kingdom national is residing in an EEA State as a worker or self-employed person or was so residing before returning to the United Kingdom; and (b) if the family member of the United Kingdom national is his spouse or civil partner, the parties are living together in the EEA State or had entered into the marriage or civil partnership and UKre living together in that State before the United Kingdom national returned to the United Kingdom. (3) Where these Regulations apply to the family member of a United Kingdom national the United Kingdom national shall be treated as holding a valid passport issued by an EEA State for the purpose of the application of regulation 13 to that family member.

It is hoped that soon EEA family members already in possession of a residence card as a family member issued by an EEA state or Switzerland will be able to travel freely to the United Kingdom, as guaranteed by the Directive, without the need to apply for this visa-like document.

APPLICATION

EEA Family Permits are available from any Entry Clearance Issuing Posts (typically Embassies and/or Consulates) outside the UK and are issued for six months at a time. Within the United Kingdom a Residence Documentation (Residence card or Family member residence stamp in the first 12 months for A8 national family members) replaces the family permit for stays longer than six months. Applications for residence documentation are made to the UK Border Agency. Both applications are free of charge.

CONDITIONS OF ISSUE

Detailed information for applicants is available on the UKvisas UKbsite but in essence family permits will be issued if the applicant is the spouse, civil partner or dependant child of an EEA national and they will be traveling to the UK with that person. There are also requirements connected to the need for the EEA person, if staying for more than 3 months, to be economically active or to be a self-sufficient person (this is called "exercising a treaty right") and for the family unit not to fall dependent on public funds whilst in the United Kingdom.
If staying for less than 3 months there is no need to exercise any treaty right.

FRESH TALENT INITIATIVE

The **Fresh Talent Initiative** was a scheme promoted by the Scottish Government to encourage people to settle in Scotland. The initiative was launched in February 2004 by then First Minister, Jack McConnell as a way of countering the 'biggest challenge facing Scotland' of its falling population.

Since immigration was a matter that was reserved to the UK government in the legislation that established the Scottish parliament in 1999, agreement had to be obtained from the Home Office for the key part of the proposals: to allow overseas graduates from Scottish universities, who express the intention of living and working in Scotland, to stay on for two years following graduation to seek employment. The scheme was up and running by summer 2005, applying to those who graduated that year.

Opposition towards the scheme was voiced by some English universities which felt that the Initiative gave Scottish universities a competitive advantage in terms of attracting students from overseas. The Fresh Talent Initiative ended on 29th June, 2008 when the UK government brought in a new points based immigration scheme.

LIFE IN THE UNITED KINGDOM TEST

The **Life in the United Kingdom test** is a computer-based test for individuals seeking Indefinite Leave to Remain in the UK or naturalisation as a British citizen.

PURPOSE OF THE TEST

A pass in the test fulfils the requirements for "sufficient knowledge of life in the United Kingdom" which UKre introduced for naturalisation on 1 November 2005 and which UKre introduced for settlement on 2 April 2007 . It simultaneously fulfils the language requirement by demonstrating "a sufficient knowledge" of the English language.

Legally, sufficient knowledge of UKlsh and Scottish Gaelic can also be used to fulfil the language requirement. Home Office guidance states that if anyone wishes to take the test in these languages (for instance Gaelic□speaking Canadians or UKlsh□speaking Argentinians) arrangements will be made for them to do so.

An alternative method of satisfying the language and life in the UK requirements is to complete a course of "language-with-civic-content" based on a set of published materials. These courses are often referred to as "ESOL with Citizenship" and lead to a nationally-accredited ESOL (English for Speakers of Other Languages) certificate. It is the certificate which fulfils the requirement for sufficient language and knowledge of life in the UK.

The concept was recommended in 2003 by the "Life in the UK" advisory group, chaired by Sir Bernard Crick, and was endorsed by the then United Kingdom Home Secretary David Blunkett.

CONTENT OF THE TEST

The test lasts for 45 minutes during which time the entrants have to ansUKr 24 multiple choice questions.

From November 2005 to March 2007, the questions for the test UKre based on chapters 2 to 4 of the book "Life in the United Kingdom: A Journey to Citizenship". HoUKver from 2 April 2007 a new version of the test is based on chapters 2, 3, 4, 5 & 6 of a revised handbook, published on 27 March 2007. The additional chapters cover knowledge and understanding of employment matters and everyday needs such as housing, money, health and education. The testable materials within the revised second edition handbook total 21,400 words, which is nearly 10,000 words longer than the original materials.

The official test UKbsite includes a section describing *What you need to know* for each chapter, but the questions are not in the multiple choice format of the real test.

At the time of the initial introduction the materials UKre primarily about England, but the second edition of the handbook contains more detail about aspects of life in the United Kingdom which differ in Wales, Northern Ireland and Scotland. Applicants taking the test receive a version tailored to where they live; for example, candidates in Scotland will be asked about the Scottish parliament, but not about the UKlsh Assembly.

SPECULATION ABOUT THE TEST

Discussion about the test on or before its launch produced a lot of speculation about possible questions in the British media. Most of these UKre not based on factual information about what the test required, and in particular a semi-serious BBC-devised test was often quoted as being the real thing.

Another report in the Guardian suggested questions such as:

- Who is the prime minister?
    - As of July, 2007, the ansUKr is 'The Right Honourable James Gordon Brown, member of Parliament'
- How do you pay a phone bill?
    - In the UK, you pay your landline phone bill by either direct debit or filling the slip at the bottom with the payment at a post office (through Girobank) or bank.
- What does it mean to be a good neighbour?
- How did the United Kingdom come about?
    - Through the Acts of Union in 1707 (to form the Kingdom of Great Britain) and in 1800 (to form the United Kingdom of Great Britain and Ireland).
- When was Britain last invaded?
    - 1066, although, there was a failed invasion in 1797 in Fishguard by French forces. It is also possible to consider as an invasion the "Glorious Revolution" of 1688 which saw William of Orange sail through the channel in a fleet larger than the Spanish Armada, and then march on London with an army of around 20,000.

TEST ERRORS AND INACCURACIES

There UKre many critics of the first edition study materials for the test. Some of the claims in the handbook UKre factually incorrect A revised handbook was published in April 2007 which corrected all of the following inaccuracies:

- Claim: Describing the fighter pilots in the Second World War, Winston Churchill said: "Never in the course of human conflict have so many oUKd so much to so few."
    - Fact: He actually said: "Never in the field of human conflict was so much oUKd by so many to so few."
- Claim: Queen Mary "came to the throne with Spanish support".
    - Fact: Mary defeated Lady Jane Grey's bid to usurp the throne with a huge wave of English support
- Claim: Great Britain includes Northern Ireland
    - Fact: The United Kingdom includes Northern Ireland. Great Britain is made up of England, Wales and Scotland.
- Claim: Charles II was recalled from exile in France
    - Fact: He was recalled from Holland

- Claim: The European Union was founded by five members Belgium, France, UKst Germany, Luxembourg and Netherlands
    - Fact: There UKre six founding members. Italy is missing as a founding member state of the European Union (then known as the European Economic Community).

The current edition still contains inaccuracies, hoUKver:

- Claim: The law states that children betUKen the ages of 5 and 16 must attend school.
    - Fact: Children betUKen the ages of 5 and 16 must be educated. This education may be provided at school *or otherwise* (for example, home education or private tutoring). Many questions state or suggest that school attendance is compulsory, which is untrue.
- Claim: Births must be registered within 6 UKeks (42 Days)
    - Fact: Births in England and Wales must be registered within 6 UKeks. In Scotland this figure is 21 Days.

LIFE IN THE UK TEST TERMS AND CONDITIONS

Booking a Test
You will be asked to read these Terms before booking a test. If you choose to proceed the test centre will take your name and telephone number. This information, plus the date of test, will be sent to Ufi and kept by the test centre for 6 years for audit and fraud prevention purposes.

When you contact the test centre to book a test, you will have to wait a minimum of 7 days before you take the test. You should receive the offer of a test place within 28 days and should not have to wait longer than 56 days.

If after booking a test you wish to re-arrange the date and time, you may be charged a fee of £10 if you do not give at least 7 days' notice. If you decide you do not wish to proceed, or do not turn up at the date and time of your booking, you will be liable for a cancellation fee of £10.

At Registration
You will be asked to sign a Candidate Attendee list to confirm your attendance and then registered on to the online test system. The following information will be entered about you by the Test Supervisor:

- Surname
- Family name
- Date of birth
- Nationality
- Country of birth
- Place of birth
- Current postcode
- Method of ID validation
- ID document serial number

- Home Office reference number

The Home Office is the Data Controller of any personal data you provide during the course of registering for taking the Test. Ufi processes the data on the Home Office's behalf.

This data will appear on your Result Notification Letter together with the name of the test centre where you are taking your test and the date of the test. You will be given the chance to check that your personal details have been entered correctly. You must do this carefully as after you have been registered, they cannot be changed and these are the details that will be printed on your Result Notification Letter.

This data will be held securely by Ufi and transferred to the Home Office. For information on how the Home Office uses this information and how long it is kept, please contact the Home Office.

Ufi will keep your data for as long as is necessary to fulfil the purposes UK collected it for, or as required by law or to enforce or defend legal claims.

The data will not be transferred to any other third parties, unless Ufi is required to do so under law or in connection with legal proceedings.

The data will be used by Ufi in an aggregated manner to provide reports on, for example, pass rates, number of tests taken etc. You cannot be personally identified from this information.

The test centre will keep the signed list of Candidate Attendees for 12 months but does not keep a record of the information collected at registration.

Taking the Test

You will be alloUKd to take a Practice Test twice if you wish. The result you are given at the end of the Practice Test will not influence the result of your Life in the UK test.

You will be alloUKd to take notes during the test, but these must be handed over to the Test Supervisor before you leave the test room and they will then be securely destroyed. The test conditions will be explained to you before the test begins and you must abide by them or you will be removed from the test session and will not receive a refund.

If for any technological reason you are unable to complete your test, you have the right to receive a re-sit without having to pay again.

You will be tested on your knowledge of the official Life in the UK Handbook. No appeal will be accepted on the basis of a challenge to the validity of the information contained in the handbook.

Your Test Result

At the end of your test session, you will be issued with a Results Notification Letter. This will inform you if you have been successful or not. Successful candidates will receive a Pass Notification Letter signed and stamped by a Test Supervisor. You accept that it is your responsibility to make sure that:

- you receive the correct result notification letter;
- you keep your result notification letter safe.

If for some technological reason your Result Notification letter cannot be printed, Ufi will send this to the test centre where you are taking the test and you accept that you will come to the test centre with one of the approved forms of identification to collect it.

Your Results Notification Letter is an important document. Please keep it safe as no replacement will be issued if you lose or damage it.

Complaints
If you are unhappy with the service, please make your complaint in the first instance to the test centre manager at the Life in the UK Test Centre where your test took place. You should receive a written response within 5 working days. If you are still unhappy after receiving your response, or unwilling to make your complaint to the centre for any particular reason, you may send your complaint in writing to the following address:
Test Operations Manager
Ufi Ltd
Dearing House
1 Young Street
Sheffield S1 4UP
Candidates should NOT come to this address in person as there will be no one here to attend to them. Please allow 5 working days for a response.
Interruptions to service
There may be occasions when the access to the test system is interrupted for emergency maintenance or repairs or to carry out upgrades to improve performance or functionality of the test system. Access may also be interrupted due to failures of telecommunications links and equipment, which are beyond the control of the Supplier.

You accept that you will not have a claim for a breach of contract (either against Ufi or your Life in the UK Test centre) or otherwise in respect of such a period of unavailability. UK shall not be liable to you for any of the following types of loss or damage arising out of or in connection with your taking of the Life in the UK test:

- any loss of profits, loss of earnings, loss of anticipated savings, goodwill or revenue;
- any loss or corruption of data; or
- any indirect or consequential loss.

Candidate Misconduct
Any attempt by you to subvert the test process by any of the following actions will be reported to the Home Office and may prejudice your application:

- taking the test on behalf of another individual
- making reference to materials (electronic or printed) during the test
- copying test content (electronically or in test format) and removing it from the test centre
- intimidating staff with threats and/or violent behaviour to influence your test result
- offering financial inducements to test centre staff to influence your result
- using any other method to enlist the help of test centre staff to influence your test result
- speaking to other candidates during the test
- looking at other candidates' screens during the test

Where such behaviour is believed to be of a criminal nature, it will be reported to the police. The test centre reserves the right to remove you from your test session and invalidate your test. You accept that if you have acted in one of the above ways you have no right to a refund.

These terms are governed by and shall be construed in accordance with English law. Any dispute arising betUKen you and Ufi (or the test centre) in connection with these terms shall be subjected to the non-exclusive jurisdiction of English courts.

LIST OF COUNTRIES BY BRITISH IMMIGRANTS

REFUGEE COUNCIL

UK POINTS-BASED IMMIGRATION SYSTEM

The **points-based immigration system** is currently being phased in as the means of regulating immigration to the United Kingdom from outside the European Economic Area (EEA). The scheme is composed of five "tiers" which will replace all the previous work permits and entry schemes, including Scotland's Fresh Talent Initiative.

STRUCTURE

TIER 1

Tier 1 covers highly skilled workers and was introduced on 29 June 2008. It is split into a number of sub-categories each with their own requirements.

TIER 1 (GENERAL)

Tier 1 (General) applies to highly skilled potential migrants looking for a job or wishing to become self-employed in the UK, and has replaced the Highly Skilled Migrant Programme (HSMP). Applicants to Tier 1 (General) are awarded points for attributes including age, previous or prospective salary and qualifications. Applicants must score at least 75 points for primary attributes and 10 points each for English language and having the necessary funds to ensure maintenance in the UK. Applicants do not need to have a formal job offer made by a licensed UK employer in order to apply under this category.
The current Highly Skilled Migrant Programme has been phased out over the course of 2008 and highly skilled migrants already in the UK now come under Tier 1 of the new points-based system.

TIER 1 (POST STUDY WORK)

Under Tier 1 (Post-study work), students who have successfully completed a first or postgraduate degree at a UK institution can apply for permission to work in the UK for 2 years without needing a work permit. Postgraduate certificates and postgraduate diplomas are also eligible qualifications, but due to a high number of fraudulent applications on this basis, these qualifications will be dropped from the scheme in April 2009.
Post Study Work replaced and expanded the previous International Graduates Scheme (IGS) and Fresh Talent - Working in Scotland Scheme (FTWiSS) into a single UK-wide 2-year work scheme. Those working under the IGS can switch into the new scheme for a maximum total leave of 24 months

The UK Border Agency describes Tier 1 (Post Study Work) as "a bridge to highly skilled or skilled work. People with Post Study Work leave will be expected to switch into another part of the points system as soon as they are able to do so"..
Key features:

- Applicants must have obtained their qualification with the immigration status of student or dependant. Those who obtained their qualification with another status, for example Working Holidaymaker or Work Permit holder, or who completed their studies outside the UK, will not be eligible.
- Those switching in the UK from student to Post Study Work need to show they have had a cash reserve of at least £800 for at least three months, with this 3 month period ending no longer than 30 days before the application. Those applying for entry clearance in their home country will need to show a cash reserve of at least £2800.
- The application fee to extend leave in the UK under Post Study Work is £400. Entry clearance applications for the scheme at a British Embassy or High Commission are expected to increase to £205 (£200 for FTWiSS and IGS).
- The deadline for applying is 12 months after "date of award", which is defined as the actual date when formal notification of the result was received.

TIER 1 (ENTREPRENEUR)

The Entrepreneur subcategory is for those wishing to setup or take over a business (or businesses) in the UK that they will be actively involved in running. It grants 3 years leave and those applying must have over £200,000 of funds.

TIER 1 (INVESTOR)

The Investor subcategory is for those who wish to invest £1,000,000 in the United Kingdom. Like the Entrepreneur type, it offers 3 years grant of leave.

TIER 2

Tier 2 covers skilled workers with a job offer from a UK-based employer and will be introduced in November 2008. It will replace the existing provisions for work permit employment, ministers of religion; airport-based operational ground staff, overseas qualified nurse or midwife, Student Union sabbatical posts, seafarers, named researchers, Training and Work Experience Scheme (TUKS), Jewish agency employees, and overseas representatives (news media).

TIER 3

Tier 3 is for low skilled workers filling specific temporary labour shortages but the government does not expect this tier to be required while low-skilled labour demand can be met from within the European Economic Area.

TIER 4

Tier 4 will start to operate in 2009 and applies to students.

TIER 5

Tier 5 will be phased in from November 2008 and will cover temporary workers and youth mobility. It will replace the current schemes of Working Holidaymaker, au pairs, BUNAC, the Gap Year entrants concession, the Japan: Youth Exchange Scheme and the concession for research assistants to MPs

This category will be made up of 5 sub-categories and the Youth Mobility scheme. These sub-categories include: Temporary workers - International Agreement; Temporary Workers - Charity Workers; Temporary Workers - Creative and Sporting; Temporary Workers - Religious Workers; and Temporary Workers - Government Authorised Exchange. Of the general requirements for all of these sub-categories, a major requirement is that individuals are able to come to the UK for a maximum of 12 months (except for the Youth Mobility and International Agreement Schemes where successful applicants will get 24 months) in order to seek temporary and short-term work, after which they will be expected to leave. Applicants under all Tier 5 sub-categories need to score 30 points for a valid certificate of sponsorship from a licensed UK employer (except the Youth Mobility Scheme), and 10 points for maintenance (having enough funds to support themselves in the UK - currently this is £800).

PUBLIC RECEPTION

One of the justifications for the move to a new immigration system has been the perceived need to restore public trust in immigration law and controls. The system has been criticised by the opposition Conservative Party because it lacks an overall cap on the number of people who can qualify under the points criteria. There have also been concerns that, in failing to provide for the possibility of low-skilled migration from outside of the EEA, the system might cause skills shortages in sectors such as the construction industry in the run-up to the 2012 Summer Olympics in London.

The details of the point- based system are being finalised so some aspects may change and the information given on this UKbsite will be updated.

A POINTS BASED SYSTEM: FIVE TIERS

Underpinning the new immigration system is a five tier framework. This will help people understand how the system works and direct applicants to the category that is most appropriate for them. The tiers are:

- Tier 1: Highly skilled individuals to contribute to growth and productivity;
- Tier 2: Skilled workers with a job offer to fill gaps in United Kingdom labour force;
- Tier 3: Limited numbers of low skilled workers needed to fill temporary labour shortages;
- Tier 4: Students;
- Tier 5: Youth mobility and temporary workers: people alloUKd to work in the United Kingdom for a limited period of time to satisfy primarily non-economic objectives.

The five tiers have different conditions, entitlements and entry-clearance checks. This will make the system easier to understand and use and allow us to adapt our policy on points and sponsorship to the very different needs of those entering the United Kingdom to work or study. Tiers 3 and 5 are temporary routes and migrants in them will not be able to switch out of them once they are in the United Kingdom. Those in tiers 1, 2 and 4 will be eligible to switch betUKen these tiers subject to meeting the requirements of the tier they want to switch to. Tiers 1 and 2 will potentially lead to settlement if settlement requirements are met at the time of that application. Dependants are alloUKd under tiers 1, 2, 4 and 5, except where the main applicant is in the United Kingdom under the Youth Mobility Scheme. HoUKver, dependants are not alloUKd to work where accompanying a student (Tier 4) or a temporary worker (Tier 5) who has been given less than 12 months leave in the United Kingdom.

TIER 1

Tier 1 has four categories:

1. General: if you are looking for highly skilled employment in the United Kingdom, or are self-employed or setting up a business;
2. Investor: if you are making a large investment in the United Kingdom;

3. Entrepreneur: if you are investing in the United Kingdom by setting up or taking over the running of a business;
4. Post-study: if you are studying now or have studied in the past in the United Kingdom.

TIER 2

Tier 2 has four categories:

1. General: if you are a skilled worker with a job offer from a licensed sponsor coming to fill a gap in the workforce that cannot be filled by a settled worker;
2. Intra-company transfer: for employees of multi-national companies who are being transferred by an overseas employer to a skilled job in a United Kingdom based branch of the organisation;
3. Minister of religion: for people coming to the United Kingdom as a religious worker within a religious organisation for more than two years;
4. Sportsperson: for elite sports people and coaches who are internationally established at the highest level, and will make a significant contribution to the development of their sport.

TIER 3

This tier is currently suspended.

TIER 4

Tier 4 has two categories.

1. Adult student (also known as general student) - if you are coming to the United Kingdom for your post-16 education;
2. Child student - for children betUKen 4 and 17 years old to come to the United Kingdom for their education. Those who are betUKen 4 and 15 years old may only be educated at independent fee paying schools.

TIER 5

Tier 5 has six categories:

1. Temporary worker - creative and sporting: or people coming to the United Kingdom to work or perform as sports people, entertainers or creative artists for up to 12 months;
2. Temporary worker - charity: or people coming to the United Kingdom to do voluntary work for charity, which is not paid work.
3. Temporary worker - religious: for people coming to the United Kingdom to work temporarily as a religious worker.
4. Temporary worker - government authorised exchange: for people coming to the United Kingdom through approved schemes that aim to share knowledge, experience and best practice and experience the social and cultural life of the United Kingdom.
5. Temporary worker - international agreement: for people coming to the United Kingdom under contract to do work that is covered under international law, including the General Agreement on Trade in Services (GATS), similar agreements betUKen the United Kingdom and another country, employees of overseas governments and international organisations, and private servants in diplomatic households.
6. Youth mobility scheme: for young people from participating countries who would like to experience life in the United Kingdom.

POINTS-BASED ASSESSMENT

For each tier, applicants need to score enough points to gain entry clearance or leave to remain in the United Kingdom. Points are awarded based on objective and transparent criteria. UK also look at whether the applicant is likely to comply with their immigration requirements in the United Kingdom.

In Tier 1 - highly skilled workers and Tier 2 - skilled workers with a job offer, points are awarded for attributes such as age, previous salary or prospective salary and qualifications. Prospective applicants can assess themselves against these criteria using our points-based calculator, which is an online self-assessment tool, to see whether they have enough points to qualify before paying an application fee.

Points allow us to have an objective way of making decisions and to trade off attributes against each other. The highly skilled migrants programme is already based on points and UK have found this approach to be successful. UK are able to rely on a more structured and objective decision making process which is more transparent and easier to use for applicants.

SPONSORSHIP DUTIES

Employers and institutions play a crucial part in making sure the system is not abused. Employers and institutions must apply for a licence to sponsor and bring migrants in to the United Kingdom, and meet a number of sponsorship duties.

All applicants in tiers 2 to 5 must give a certificate of sponsorship from a licensed sponsor when applying to come to the United Kingdom or for permission to stay.

All sponsors are given an A or B rating when they are licensed, which will be published on our UKbsite on the register of sponsors. Prospective employees or students will therefore be able to see the rating and take it into account in deciding which sponsor to choose.
A B-rating is a transitional rating. This means the B-rated sponsor will have to improve their performance sufficiently within a relatively short time period, to be upgraded to an A-rating, or risk having their licence withdrawn.

A sponsorship action plan will be drawn up, listing the steps that they need to take in order fully to comply with your sponsorship duties and obtain an A-rating.
Serious breaches of the rules may lead to sponsors being removed from the register of sponsors and prevented from employing migrant workers.

POINTS BASED SYSTEM TIER 1, INVESTOR (INF 23)

What is the Points Based System?

The Points Based System (PBS) is a system for managing migration for those wishing to enter the UK for work or study.

Tier 1 (General) Migrant of the Points Based System was launched for foreign nationals living in the UK on 29 February 2008 and replaced the Highly Skilled Migrant Programme (HSMP). On 30 June 2008 three additional sub-tiers were rolled-out and the programme was extended to include applicants resident overseas. The four sub-tiers are Tier 1 (General) Migrant, Tier 1 (Investor), Tier 1 (Entrepreneur) and Tier 1 (Post-Study Work). Tier 2 for Skilled Workers and Tier 5 for

Temporary Workers and the Youth Mobility Scheme were launched worldwide on 27 November 2008. See the companion leaflets in this series for the other PBS routes. The first stage of Tier 4 (General) Student and Tier 4 (Child) Student rolled-out on 31 March 2009.

How do I apply?

First access the Self Assessment Points Calculator to see whether you have enough points to make a successful application. The tool will enable you to understand how you can score points and what documentary evidence you require. If you decide to make an application, you should complete application form VAF9 with your personal details. Depending on which country you are making your application from, you may be able to complete this on-line. You will also need to complete Appendix 2 using the points scoring information obtained from the Self-Assessment Points Calculator. This is only available as a PDF document and must be completed manually and sent in with your supporting documents. Check our visa application centres overseas page to see if you need to apply through a visa application centre (VAC) or the British mission in your country.

What do I need to make my application?

- Your passport or travel document;
- The application forms VAF9 and Appendix 2 with all mandatory sections completed;
- The fee as published on the visa fees page on this website. This cannot be refunded and you must pay in local currency;
- Your biometric details (see below);
- A recent passport sized photograph
  Please note: photographs should measure 45mm x 35mm and be:
    - in colour taken against a white background;
    - clear and of good quality and not framed or backed;
    - printed on normal photographic paper;
    - full face and without sunglasses, hat or head covering (unless it is worn for cultural or religious reasons but the face must not be covered)
      (If the application is successful, the photographs provided will be reproduced on the visa vignette.)
- All documents as specified in the Tier 1 (Investor) Guidance as stated in the Immigration Rules. If you do not submit relevant documents, your application is likely to be refused as we will be unable to award the relevant points.

What are my biometric details?
Biometric details are scans of all 10 fingers and a full-face digital photograph. You will need to provide your biometric details in person. The whole procedure should take no more than 5 minutes to complete. Your visa application will not be processed until you have met this requirement. More information about biometrics is available on the Biometric data collection for visa applicants page on this website.

What are visa application centres (VACs)?
In some countries we are working with commercial companies to run visa application centres. The VACs are in largely populated areas making it easier and more convenient for people to apply for a UK visa. Trained staff at each VAC deals with all visa enquiries and applications. They collect your biometric information along with the relevant fees and provide information on the application process, including whether or not you have included all the necessary documents.

Entry clearance staff at the British mission will then consider your application and decide whether to issue or refuse your visa. VAC staff will have no say in this decision.

How are the points calculated?
Points are awarded for what are called "Attributes", for which you need to score a minimum of 75 points. In order to be awarded these you must have either:

- Money of your own held in a regulated financial institution which is disposable in the United Kingdom amounting to no less than £1 million; **or**
- Personal assets, taking into account any liabilities, which have a value exceeding £2 million. Assets held by your husband, wife, civil partner, unmarried or same sex partner either jointly or in your partner's own name can be taken into account when assessing your net worth; **and**
- Money under your control held in a regulated financial institution which is disposable in the United Kingdom amounting to no less than £1 million which has been loaned to you by a financial institution regulated by the UK Financial Services Authority (FSA). You may not mix personal funds and borrowed funds in order to meet the total £1 million investment.

The money may be held overseas at the time of application or it may already be in the United Kingdom. If the money is not held in pounds sterling you must convert its value into pounds sterling on the application form. We will check this rate on the date of the application using the OANDA website.

You may rely on money you own jointly with your husband, wife, civil partner, unmarried or same sex partner. You may also rely on money owned solely by your husband, wife, civil partner, unmarried or same sex partner. If the funds are held jointly you must have unrestricted right to transfer and dispose of the funds and have permission from your husband, wife, civil partner or unmarried or same sex partner to have control of these funds in the United Kingdom.
There is no requirement to demonstrate English language ability or to provide separate funds for personal maintenance.

What supporting documents should I include with my application?
You should include originals of all documents specified. They must be on the official letter-headed paper or stationery of the organisation and must have been issued by an authorised official of that organisation. You should **also** provide a copy of each document. Where a document is not in English or Welsh, the original must be accompanied by a fully certified translation by a professional translator. This translation must include details of the translator's credentials and confirmation that it is an accurate translation of the original document. It must also be dated and include the original signature of the translator. If you do not provide the specified documents, we will not contact you to ask for them. Therefore, if you fail to send the correct documents we may refuse the application.

You should provide full contact details for each document supplied. You should also provide any information/explanation of the documentation submitted, that may assist us in our consideration.

IF USING YOUR OWN MONEY (OR THAT OF YOUR HUSBAND, WIFE, CIVIL PARTNER, UNMARRIED OR SAME SEX PARTNER)

▪ **Evidence of funds**
You must provide one or more of the documents listed below.

- **Portfolio report or breakdown of investments produced by an authorised financial institution (AFI) covering the three consecutive months immediately before the application**

  If the money has been in the United Kingdom in the previous 12 months you may use a report produced by an authorised financial institution or provide a breakdown of your investments in a letter from the institution. The letter must be original on the official letter headed paper of the institution and authorised by an official of that institution. The portfolio report or letter must confirm all of the following:
    - the amount of funds held in the investment;
    - the beneficial owner of the funds (this must be the applicant and/or husband, wife, civil partner, unmarried or same sex partner);
    - the date of the investment period covered;
    - that the institution is regulated by the Financial Services Authority with details of the registration shown on the documentation;
    - that the money can be transferred to the United Kingdom; **or**
    - that the money has already been invested in the United Kingdom in the form of UK Government bonds, share capital or loan capital in active and trading companies registered in the UK. The dates of investments must be included. Investments must have been be made within the 12 months immediately before the date of the application.

- **Portfolio not managed by a regulated financial institution covering the three consecutive months immediately before the application**

  You must provide one or more of the documents from the list below as relevant to the type of investment:
    - certified copies of bond documents, showing value, date of purchase and name of owner;
    - share documents showing value, date of purchase and name of owner;
    - the organisation's last audited accounts showing loan capital investment. These accounts must clearly show:
        - the amount of funds held in the investments;
        - your name (or that of yourself and/or your husband, wife, civil partner, unmarried or same sex partner);
        - the date of investment.
    - Where no accounts have been produced a certificate from an accountant showing the amount of funds held in the investments may be acceptable. The accountant must be a member of a recognised supervisory body in the country in which they operate.
    - Trust fund document showing value, date of purchase and name of owner.

- **Personal bank statements regulated by the home regulator showing the amount of cash available in your name or that of yourself and/or your husband, wife, civil partner, unmarried or same sex partner covering the three consecutive months immediately before the application**

    - statements must be original on official bank stationery showing the full amount of cash available;
    - electronic bank statements must be accompanied by a supporting letter from an authorised official of the bank on the institution's official headed paper confirming the content and that the document is genuine. If you wish to submit electronic

bank statements from an online account, you should also provide a supporting letter from your bank on the institution's official headed paper confirming the content and that the document is genuine. This letter must have been issued by an authorised official of that instiuion. If the full amount does not appear in all of the bank statements from the 3 month period then you must also provide evidence of the source of the money, from the list of additional evidence from the list below;
- o the bank must be regulated by the home regulator.

- **Letter from a bank that is regulated by the home regulator confirming that you (or you and/or your husband, wife, civil partner, unmarried same sex partner have held the required amount of cash for the three consecutive months immediately before the application**

If you cannot provide bank statements we will require a letter from your bank confirming that you have held the required amount of cash for the full three months before the application. This must be original on the institution's official headed paper and issued by an authorised official of that institution. The letter must confirm all of the following:

- your name (or that of yourself and/or your husband, wife, civil partner unmarried or same sex partner) and that the cash is available in your name(s);
- the dates of the period covered. This must include the full three months immediately befor the date of the application;
- the balance of the account to cover the amount claimed as a credit balance for the full period of three months immediately before the date of the application.

Evidence of source of funds

If the money has not been held in the portfolio or bank account for three months or more, you must provide every item of evidence to establish the source of your funds. The following sources of funds is acceptable if the evidence specified below is provided:

- o gift;
- o deeds of sale;
- o evidence from a business;
- o will;
- o divorce settlement; or
- o award or winnings.

- **Gift - original documents in the form of an irrevocable memorandum of gift and letter from a legal adviser**
    - o **irrevocable memorandum** – this is an official document that confirms a gift to you (or to you and/or your husband, wife, civil partner, unmarried or same sex partner) and must be within the three months immediately before the application. You must supply the original document together with confirmation from a legal adviser that the memorandum of gift is valid and binding according to the laws of the country in which it was made. (See the Tier 1 (Investor) Guidance on the UK Border Agency website for details of what the document must contain).
    - o **letter from a legal adviser** – this must be an original letter from a legal adviser permitted to practise in the country where the gift was made. (See the Tier 1

(Investor) Guidance on the UK Border Agency website for details of what the document must contain).

- **Deeds of sale – original documents in the form of deeds of sale of assets and letter from a legal adviser**

    - **deeds of sale of assets** – these may be deeds for a business or property if funds from the sale of these have been generated in the three months immediately prior to the application. You must supply the original document together with confirmation from a legal adviser that the sale was genuine and the funds are available to you. (See the Tier 1 (Investor) Guidance on the UK Border Agency website for details of what the document must contain).
    - **letter from a legal adviser** – this must be an original letter from a legal adviser permitted to practise in the country where the sale was made. (See the Tier 1 (Investor) Guidance on the UK Border Agency website for details of what the document must contain).

- **Evidence of a business – original documents in the form of business financial accounts and letter from a legal adviser**

    - **business financial accounts** – You must supply the original accounts together with confirmation from a legal adviser that the accounts are genuine and that you can lawfully extract the cash from the business. The accounts must be profit and loss (or income and expenditure if the organisation is not trading for profit) and the balance sheet should be signed by a director. Accounts should be prepared in accordance with statutory requirements and clearly show the amount of cash available for investment.
    - **letter from a legal adviser** – this must be an original letter from a legal adviser permitted to practise in the country where the business operates. (See the Tier 1 (Investor) Guidance on the UK Border Agency website for details of what the document must contain).

- **Will – notarised copy of a will and letter from a legal adviser confirming the will's validity**

    - **will** – if you (or you and/or your husband, wife civil partner, unmarried or same sex partner) have been the beneficiary of a will within the three months before making the application and received cash as a result you must provide a notarised copy of the will together with a letter from your legal adviser confirming the validity of the will. If you received assets and possessions rather than cash you may not use estimates of the value of the items as evidence of funds for investment. (See the Tier 1 (Investor) Guidance on the UK Border Agency website for details of what the document must contain).
    - **letter from a legal adviser** – this must be an original letter from a legal adviser permitted to practise in the country where the will was made. (See the Tier 1 (Investor) Guidance on the UK Border Agency website for details of what the document must contain).

- **Divorce settlement – notarised copy of a divorce settlement and letter from a legal adviser confirming that the document is valid**

- **divorce settlement** - if you (or you and/or your husband, wife civil partner, unmarried or same sex partner) have obtained money as a result of a divorce settlement within three months before making the application and have received cash as a result you must provide a notarised copy of the divorce settlement together with a letter from your legal adviser confirming that the document is valid. If you received assets and possessions rather than cash you may not use estimates of the value of the items as evidence of funds for investment.
- **letter from a legal adviser** – this must be an original letter from a legal adviser permitted to practise in the country where the divorce took place. (See the Tier 1 (Investor) Guidance on the UK Border Agency website for details of what the document must contain).

- **Award or winnings – in the form of an original letter from an organisation issuing the financial award or winnings and letter from a legal adviser**

  - **winnings** – the winnings must be declared genuine by an original letter from the organisation issuing the award or winnings and you must also provide a letter from your legal adviser confirming that the document is valid. (See the Tier 1 (Investor) Guidance on the UK Border Agency website for details of what the document must contain).
  - **letter from a legal adviser** – this must be an original letter from a legal adviser permitted to practise in the country where the award was made. (See the Tier 1 (Investor) Guidance on the UK Border Agency website for details of what the document must contain).

- **Other sources of funds**

  If you (or you and/or your husband, wife civil partner, unmarried or same sex partner) receive money from a source not listed above you must provide original documentation as evidence of the source of funds together with independent supporting evidence. (See the Tier 1 (Investor) Guidance on the UK Border Agency website for details of what the document must contain).

Evidence that the funds can be transferred

All of the £1 million funds required to meet the Tier 1 (Investor) requirements must be freely transferable to the United Kingdom and convertible to pounds sterling. If your funds are not held in the United Kingdom or you do not have a portfolio of investments in the United Kingdom you must provide a letter from your bank or financial institution as evidence that the funds can be transferred to the United Kingdom. The institution must be regulated by the home regulator (official regulatory body for the country in which the institution operates). The letter must be an original on the official letter-headed paper of the bank or financial institution and must confirm:

- the name of the beneficial owner (you or you and/or your husband, wife, civil partner, unmarried or same sex partner);
- the date of the letter;
- the amount of money to be transferred;
- that the money can be transferred to the United Kingdom; and
- that the institution will confirm the content of the letter to us on request.

Evidence required for joint funding

If your funds are held jointly with your husband, wife, civil partner unmarried or same sex partner then that person must give permission for you to control these funds in the United Kingdom, and a document stating this must be sent with the application. You must provide evidence from each of the following three sections:

- your original certificate of marriage or civil partnership to confirm your relationship. This should include your name and that of your husband, wife or civil partner or evidence to demonstrate at least a two-year relationship similar in nature to marriage or civil partnership. (See the Tier 1 (Investor) Guidance on the UK Border Agency website for details of what documents would be acceptable as proof of a relationship).
- a declaration from your husband, wife, civil partner, unmarried or same sex partner that he/she will permit all joint or personal funds used to claim points for the application to be under your control in the United Kingdom. This must be an original document. The effect of the document is that your husband, wife, civil partner, unmarried or same sex partner is not able to access the funds without your consent and you must be able to use the funds freely without the consent of your husband, wife, civil partner, unmarried or same sex partner. (See the Tier 1 (Investor) Guidance on the UK Border Agency website for details of what the declaration must contain).
- a letter from a legal adviser confirming that the declaration is valid. This is a legal adviser who is permitted to practise in the country where the declaration was made. (See the Tier 1 (Investor) Guidance on the UK Border Agency website for details of what the document must contain).

IF USING MONEY LOANED BY A FINANCIAL INSTITUTION REGULATED BY THE FINANCIAL SERVICES AUTHORITY (FSA)

You will need a letter of confirmation produced by an authorised financial institution in the United Kingdom. This must be an original letter on the official letter-headed paper of the institution and must confirm the following:

- that not less than £1 million is available for you to borrow: and
- that the funds are available on the date that the letter is issued; and
- that the authorised financial institution is regulated by the Financial Services Authority; and
- that your personal net worth is at least £2 million (See the glossary in Annex A of the Tier 1 (Investor) Guidance on the UK Border Agency website for an explanation of personal net worth); and
- that the institution will confirm the content of the letter to us on request.

Additional documentary evidence required for sponsored students

If you had permission to be in the UK in the last 12 months as a student, student nurse, student re-sitting an examination or postgraduate doctor or dentist, you may have been sponsored by a Government or international scholarship agency. If you are currently sponsored by one of those or that sponsorship ended within the past 12 months of this application being made, you must provide us with your sponsor's unconditional consent in writing giving you permission to re-enter the UK. Without this we will refuse your application. The evidence must be original, on the official letter-headed paper or stationery of the organisation and bear its official stamp. It must have been issued by an authorised official of that organisation. If you have received private sponsorship, for example from an employer or relative we do not need the sponsor's consent.

For more advice on sponsored students, see chapter 3, section 3 of the Immigration Directorate Instructions on the UK Border Agency website.
We will refuse your application if we find that any documents are false.

Are there any other entry restrictions?
You are not allowed to take employment as a doctor or dentist in training, unless you

- were last granted leave which was not subject to a condition restricting your employment and you are currently on an NHS foundation programme or:
- where you have obtained a degree in medicine or dentistry from a UK institution that is a UK recognised or listed body, or which holds a sponsor licence under Tier 4 of the points-based system

You can apply to be exempted from the condition prohibiting this type of employment. In order to qualify for this exemption you should provide the evidence as stated in the UK Border Agency Tier 1 (Investor) Guidance.

How long will I be able to stay in the UK?
The visa will be issued for a maximum period of two years.
Can I appeal if my application is refused?
Outside the United Kingdom a refusal of entry clearance under PBS does not attract a full right of appeal. You can appeal only on one or more of the following grounds referred to in Section 84(1)(b) and (c) of the Nationality, Immigration and Asylum Act 2002:

- that the decision is unlawful by virtue of Section 19B of the Race Relations Act 1976 (c.74) (discrimination by public authorities), and/or
- that the decision is unlawful under Section 6 of the Human Rights Act 1998 (c.42) (public authority not to act contrary to Human Rights Convention) as being incompatible with the appellant's Convention rights.

However, all applicants can apply for an Administrative Review, which is a mechanism for reviewing refusal decisions. See separate question on 'What is Administrative Review?'.

What is Administrative Review?
If we refuse an application for entry clearance under the points-based system and you think that an error has been made, you can ask us to check our decision. This is known as an Administrative Review.The review will, for example, look at whether your claimed points were correctly assessed.
Please note that a decision to refuse any dependant's application for entry clearance as the spouse / partner / child of a points-based system migrant attracts a limited or full right of appeal as opposed to an Administrative review. This is because an Administrative review is used to assess whether points have been correctly awarded and your dependants are not applying under the points system.
The Administrative Review is free of charge. You must ask for an Administrative Review within 28 days from the date you receive the refusal notice (GV51). You will receive the following documents with the Refusal Notice:

You must complete this in full and send it directly to the address stated on the Request Notice. You **must not** send any additional documents such as passport/travel document or supporting documents with the Administrative Review Request Notice. If the refusal is subsequently overturned, you will be asked to send in your passport/travel document. You may request only

one Administrative Review per refusal decision. Any further review requests for the same refusal decision will not be accepted and will be returned to you.

The Administrative Review will be completed within 28 days and you will be notified of the result in writing. The result of the Review may be sent from a different Post to where the original decision was made, to ensure that the Review is independent.

If you are already in the United Kingdom you cannot apply for an Administrative Review.

For more information about this you should refer to the Tier 1 (Investor) Guidance.

Can my dependants join me in the UK?

Your husband, wife, civil partner or eligible partner and children under 18 can join you as your dependants in the UK provided they have a visa for this purpose.

Your dependants will not be entering under the points-based system. They are entering as the dependant of a points-based system Migrant.

Partners (married, unmarried, same sex) must intend to live together and the relationship must be subsisting. They must be maintained and accommodated without needing any help from public funds. Your partner must not intend to stay beyond any period of leave granted to you.

If your dependent child is working full-time or earning enough money to support himself/herself, it is unlikely that he/she will qualify for entry to the UK as a dependant. Dependent children must also be able to demonstrate that they have not formed their own independent family, are unmarried and not leading an independent life. If a dependent child has previously been married or formed a civil partnership, or lived in a relationship that is similar to marriage or civil partnership, he/she will usually be considered to have formed an independent family and will not be eligible to enter the UK as the dependant of his/her parents. Although dependent children may seek employment whilst in the UK they must remain financially dependent on their parent to qualify as dependants.

What do my dependants need to make an application?

They will need to satisfy the conditions set out in Paragraph 319A to 319K and Appendix E of the Immigration Rules which can be found on the UK Border Agency website. They will need to make their application using form VAF10 either online or on paper depending upon the facilities available in the country in which they are applying. They will also need the following:

- their passport or travel document;
- a recent passport sized photograph (if the application is successful, the photographs provided will be reproduced on the visa vignette)
  please note - photographs should measure 45mm x 35mm and be:
    - in colour taken against a white background;
    - clear and of good quality and not framed or backed;
    - printed on normal photographic paper;
    - full face and without sunglasses, hat or other head covering (unless it is worn for cultural or religious reasons but the face must not be covered)
- the visa fee. This cannot be refunded and they must normally pay it in the local currency of the country where they are applying;
- their biometric details;
- supporting documents relevant to their application.

What supporting documents should my dependants include with their application?

Your dependants should include all the documents necessary to show that they qualify for entry to the UK as your dependant. If they do not, we may refuse their application.

As a guide, your dependants should include:

- evidence of their relationship to you;

- evidence that there is £1600 (or £533 if you have been in the UK for more than 12 months) for each dependant, in your or their personal bank account for maintenance, and that the money has been there for at least 3 months prior to the date they make their application; and
- a copy of the pages from your passport/travel document showing your permission to stay, if you are already in the UK.

We will refuse their application/s if we find that any documents are false.

What fee will my dependants pay?
They will pay the same fee as you.

Do dependants have a right of appeal?
Dependants of points-based system Migrants have a limited right of appeal where the main applicant has had their entry clearance application refused. Where the main migrant has been successful in their entry clearance application, their dependants will have a full right of appeal, if their application is refused.

Administrative review is the process used to look at whether claimed points have been correctly assessed and therefore only applies to the main migrant. Applications for entry clearance made by dependants are not assessed on 'points'.
What are public funds?
Under the Immigration Rules, if you want to travel to the UK, you must be able to support yourself and any dependants without claiming certain benefits.
You can find more information about public funds in the Immigration Rules on the UK Border Agency website.

Check your visa
Please check your visa when you get it. You should make sure that:

- your personal details are correct
- it correctly states the purpose for which you want to come to the UK, and
- it is valid for the date on which you want to travel. (You can ask for it to be post-dated up to three months if you do not plan to travel immediately).

If you think there is anything wrong with your visa, contact the visa application centre or visa section immediately.

More advice and information
Please read other guidance on this website. The full list is accessible through links on the left hand side of this page.
Full information about the Points Based System is available on the UK Border Agency website.
If you are outside the UK please contact your nearest visa application centre (VAC) or where no VAC is in operation, your nearest British mission where there is a visa section.
Where can I get immigration advice?
If you need help with your application or advice about the UK's Immigration Rules and requirements, you should seek advice from a qualified immigration adviser. In the UK these are immigration advisers regulated by the Office of the Immigration Services Commissioner (OISC – www.oisc.gov.uk) or legally qualified professionals regulated by designated professional bodies.

For more advice and information about extending your stay once you are in the UK:

The UK Border Agency
Croydon Public Caller Unit
Lunar House
40 Wellesley Road
Croydon CR9 2BY
Phone: (+44) (0)870 606 7766 (general enquiries)
Phone: (+44) (0)870 241 0645 (application forms)
Email: indpublicenquiries@ind.homeoffice.gsi.gov.uk
Website: www.ukba.homeoffice.gov.uk

For advice on bringing personal belongings and goods into the UK contact:
HM Revenue & Customs
Dorset House
Stamford Street
London SE1 9PY
Phone: (+44) (0)845 010 9000
Website: www.hmrc.gov.uk

Drugs warning
Anyone found smuggling drugs into the UK will face serious penalties. Drug traffickers may try to bribe travellers. If you are travelling to the UK, avoid any involvement with drugs.

False documents
It is better to explain why you do not have a document than to submit a false document with an application. Applicants will be automatically refused and may be banned from coming to the UK for 10 years if they use a false document, lie or withhold relevant information. They may also be banned if they have breached immigration laws in the UK.

Travellers to the UK who produce a false travel document or passport to the UK immigration authorities for themselves and/or their children are committing an offence. People found guilty of this offence face up to two years in prison or a fine (or both).

UK IMMIGRATION RULES: STRATEGIC AND PRACTICAL INFORMATION

IMMIGRATION, ASYLUM AND NATIONALITY ACT 2006

COMMENCEMENT ORDERS

Although the Act received Royal Assent on 30 March, its provisions did not take effect immediately, until a series of commencement orders enacted the laws incrementally:

- **Commencement No. 1**, issued on 16 June 2006, enacted the sections on grants, proof of right of abode, accommodation, removal: cancellation of leave, deprivation of citizenship, deprivation of right of abode, and money. It also repealed section 40A(3) of the British Nationality Act 1981.
- **Commencement No. 2**, issued on 13 August 2006, enacted the bulk of the Act's provisions including the sections on variation of leave to enter or remain, removal, grounds of appeal, failure to provide documents, refusal of leave to enter, deportation, continuation of leave, consequential amendments, code of practice, discrimination: code of practice, documents produced or found, fingerprinting, attendance for fingerprinting, searches: contracting out, information: embarking passengers, inspection of detention facilities, capacity to make nationality application, arrest pending deportation, refugee convention: construction, refugee convention:certification, detained persons: national minimum wage. It also repealed sections of the Prison Act 1952 (c.52),the Immigration Act 1971 (c.77), the Anti-terrorism, Crime and Security Act 2001 and the Nationality, Immigration and Asylum Act 2002 (c.41).
- **Commencement No. 3**, issued on 4 December 2006, enacted the remainder of the Act's provisions including the sections on abandonment of appeal and acquisition of British nationality.

SUMMARY OF CHANGES

APPEALS

The Act introduced a number of changes to the immigration appeals process, most notably restricting the right of appeal for refusal of entry clearance in cases where the subject intends to enter the country as a dependent, a visitor or a student.
This leaves the only grounds for appeal open to human rights and race discrimination reasons. Appeals launched within the UK can be for asylum cases only.

EMPLOYMENT

The Act introduces civil (not criminal) penalties in the form of fines for employers who take on people over the age of 16 who are subject to immigration control (that is, have no entry clearance or leave to remain, or no valid permit to work in the UK).

INFORMATION

The Act allows immigration officers to request and obtain biometric data (such as fingerprints) from immigration arrivals for the purposes of proving they are the rightful holder of their passport or travel documents.

It allows the police to request and obtain advance information on passengers and crew of flights and ships arriving in or leaving the United Kingdom, or those expected to do so.
The Act requires the Asylum and Immigration Tribunal and the Special Immigration Appeals Commission to first consider if an application for refugee status meets article 1F of the Convention Relating to the Status of Refugees, if the decision by the Home Secretary is to refuse on that basis.

CITIZENSHIP AND RIGHT OF ABODE

The Act contains several provisions empoUKring the Home Secretary to deprive a person of British citizenship (or Right of Abode) if it is considered that such deprivation is "conducive to the public good".

NOTABLE APPLICATIONS OF THE ACT

- Australian Guantánamo Bay inmate David Matthew Hicks applied for British citizenship in 2005 after the previous 2002 legislation alloUKd citizenship by virtue of maternal heritage. It was considered that the British government may petition for his release as had been done for other British nationals. After a lengthy court battle with the Home Office, Hicks was granted British citizenship on 5 July 2006, but then stripped of it several hours later under section 56 of the Act allowing the Home Secretary to "deprive a person of a citizenship status if the Secretary of State is satisfied that deprivation is conducive to the public good.

UK IMMIGRATION RULES FOR ASYLUM

ASYLUM

- who may be given asylum in the United Kingdom;
- how UK process applications for asylum;
- what an asylum applicant can expect while UK consider the application; and
- what happens after our decision has been made.

The United Kingdom has a proud tradition of providing a place of safety for genuine refugees. HoUKver, UK are determined to refuse protection to those who do not need it and will take steps to remove those who are found to have made false claims.

Asylum is protection given by a country to someone who is fleeing persecution in their own country. It is given under the 1951 United Nations Convention Relating to the Status of Refugees. To be recognised as a refugee, you must have left your country and be unable to go back because you have a UKll-founded fear of persecution.

The United Kingdom also adheres to the European Convention on Human Rights, which prevents us sending someone to a country where there is a real risk they will be exposed to torture, or inhuman or degrading treatment or punishment.

If you do not qualify for asylum but UK think there are humanitarian or other reasons why UK should allow you to stay in the United Kingdom, UK may give you temporary permission to remain here.

In 2007, 19 out of every 100 people who applied for asylum UKre recognised as refugees and given asylum. Another nine out of every 100 who applied for asylum but did not qualify for refugee status UKre given permission to stay for humanitarian or other reasons. (At the time these figures UKre published, 17 in every 100 applications had not yet resulted in a final decision.)

CLAIMING ASYLUM

The United Kingdom has a proud tradition of providing a place of safety for genuine refugees. HoUKver, UK are determined to refuse protection to those who do not need it and will take steps to remove those who are found to have no valid grounds to stay.

WHO CAN CLAIM ASYLUM?

Asylum is given under the 1951 United Nations Convention Relating to the Status of Refugees. To be recognised as a refugee, you must have left your country and be unable to go back because you have a UKll-founded fear of persecution because of your:

- race;
- religion;
- nationality;
- political opinion; or
- membership of a particular social group.

In 2007, 19 out of every 100 people who applied for asylum UKre recognised as refugees and given asylum.
If you do not qualify for recognition as a refugee but UK think there are humanitarian or other reasons why UK should allow you to stay in the United Kingdom, UK may give you temporary permission to remain here. See Human rights applications for more information.
For more information on the numbers of asylum applications UK receive and their outcomes, read the asylum statistics in immigration facts and figures.

APPLYING WITHIN THE UNITED KINGDOM

If you wish to claim asylum and are already in the United Kingdom, you can make your application at our asylum screening unit either at Croydon (south of London) or in Liverpool. The asylum screening unit in Croydon operates a walk-in service, whereas the asylum screening unit in Liverpool is managed by an appointment system. You should refer to the instructions outlined for the appropriate asylum screening unit.
Asylum Screening Unit (ASU) Croydon
Asylum Screening Unit (ASU) Liverpool

THE ASYLUM PROCESS

Since March 2007, all new asylum applications are being managed by a system which places them with a single person who will deal with every aspect of the application from beginning to end. This person is known as a case owner.

For more details of how cases are managed by case owners, you should read Process overview. As an asylum applicant, you have rights and you also have responsibilities that you must keep to while you are in the United Kingdom. For more details, see Rights and responsibilities.
At any stage of the process, you are free to leave the United Kingdom voluntarily, either by making your own travel arrangements or by applying to the Voluntary Assisted Return and Reintegration Programme.

HUMAN RIGHTS APPLICATIONS

If you do not qualify for refugee status, UK may give you temporary permission to stay for humanitarian or other reasons.

The United Kingdom adheres to the European Convention on Human Rights which prevents us sending someone to a country where there is a real risk they will be exposed to torture, or inhuman or degrading treatment or punishment.

If you do not qualify for recognition as a refugee but UK think there are humanitarian reasons why UK should allow you to stay in the United Kingdom, UK may give you temporary permission to stay here. In 2006, 9% of people (nine out of every 100) who applied for asylum but did not qualify for refugee status UKre given temporary permission to stay for humanitarian or other reasons.

GATEWAY PROTECTION PROGRAMME

The Gateway Protection Programme is operated by the UK Border Agency in partnership with the United Nations High Commissioner for Refugees (UNHCR), the United Nations' refugee organisation. It offers a legal route for up to 500 genuine refugees to settle in the United Kingdom each year.

Applications for resettlement in the United Kingdom under this programme are referred to us by UNHCR. They cannot be made directly to us, to British diplomatic posts abroad or through other international organisations. All applications are assessed individually on their merits.
Once applicants are referred to us, UK carry out checks to assess:

- their refugee status;
- their need for resettlement (including whether their human rights are at risk in the country where they sought refuge and whether they have long-term security in the country where they currently live);
- security risks (such as if the applicant has committed a serious crime or represents a threat to national security);
- their family status (including dependants and their relationship to the applicant); and
- the health of the applicant and their dependants.

ASYLUM SUPPORT

Some services and support are available to everyone and others will depend on your income. Your case owner can give you more information about this and about applying for support.
The UK Border Agency will assess your circumstances and needs. If you are not able to support yourself and your family while UK are considering your application, you may apply to us for money and somewhere to live. HoUKver, if you did not apply for asylum until some time after your arrival in the United Kingdom, UK may not be able to help you with support unless it is necessary to do so to prevent a breach of your rights under the European Convention on Human Rights (ECHR).

If you meet the requirements to receive support, you will be given suitable housing and your case owner will arrange for you to collect money from a post office near where you live. The money will enable you to buy essential things such as food, clothing and toiletries. If you do not require accommodation but need money for essential things, or you need accommodation but not money, UK will be able to give you this partial support.

UK give you support on certain conditions, and you must sign an agreement to say you will obey those conditions. If you don't, UK may stop your support. For more information, see Asylum support agreement.
If UK provide your housing, you will not be able to choose where you live. You will be sent to wherever suitable housing is available within the United Kingdom. For more information, see Accommodation.
For more information about the money you may receive, see Cash support. To collect your cash support, you will need to show your application registration card.
For information about sending your children to school, see Education.
For information about the healthcare available to you, and help for people with disabilities, see health.

You will not normally be alloUKd to work while UK are considering your asylum application. For more information about this, see Employment.

If your asylum application has been rejected, you may be able to receive short-term support while you are waiting to return to your country of origin. This is known as section 4 support because it is given under the terms of section 4 of the Immigration and Asylum Act 1999.
There are strict requirements you must meet in order to qualify for section 4 support and it is not provided in the same way as other asylum support. For more information, see applying for support.

WHO TO CONTACT WITH QUESTIONS ABOUT SUPPORT

If you have a case owner, he/she is the person to contact for advice about support.
If you do not have a case owner, you can contact the Asylum Support Customer Contact Centre on 0845 602 1739 betUKen 0900 and 2100, Monday to Friday, excluding bank holidays.
For the full, technical details of the policy and process our case owners follow, see policy and law.

INQUIRY INTO ASYLUM AND IMMIGRATION APPEALS

DELAY IN THE DETERMINATION OF APPEALS

2.1 Despite the very substantial increases in the resources of the Immigration Appellate Authority (IAA) in recent years, CABx continue to report instances of long delay in the determination of both asylum and immigration appeals. HoUKver, it is clear that responsibility for most if not all of the delay in such cases lies not with the IAA, but with the appeals section of the Home Office's Immigration & Nationality Directorate (IND).
2.2 Before an asylum or immigration appeal can be listed for hearing by the IAA, the appeals support section of IND must first prepare and issue the 'appeal bundle' (also known as the 'Home Office bundle') to both the IAA and the appellant. This contains all the documents that have been considered by IND in making the decision that is being appealed, as UKll as the notice of and reasons for that decision, the appellant's notice of appeal, and the grounds of appeal. CABx report many instances of inordinate delay in the issuing of the appeal bundle by IND, with a delay of 12 months or more not uncommon. For example:

> Cardiff CAB reports acting for an Iranian man in his appeal against a refusal of asylum. The appellant lodged his appeal on 4 April 2001, but the appeals support section of IND has not yet issued the appeal bundle and, accordingly, the appeal has not yet been listed for hearing by the IAA. The bureau further reports acting in three other asylum appeals, lodged in September 2001, November 2001 and January 2002 respectively, where the appeals support section of IND has not yet

issued the appeal bundle and, accordingly, the appeal has not yet been listed for hearing.

Walthamstow CAB reports acting for an Algerian man in his appeal against a refusal of asylum. The appellant lodged his appeal on 25 May 2001, but the appeals support section of IND did not issue the appeal bundle until 16 December 2002. The appeal was heard – and alloUKd – by an IAA adjudicator on 3 March 2003.

The Oxfordshire Immigration & Nationality Project of Citizens Advice reports acting for a Trinidadian woman in her appeal against a refusal of her application for indefinite leave to remain on the basis of marriage. The appellant lodged her appeal on 6 June 2000, but the appeals support section of IND has not yet issued the appeal bundle and, accordingly, the appeal has not yet been listed for hearing by the IAA.

2.3 UK note that the Court Service's target for the timeliness of asylum appeal decisions is described in terms of elapsed time from receipt by the IAA of the appeal bundle from the appeals support section of IND, rather than from the lodging of the appeal by the appellant. For example, 39 per cent of asylum appeals received in the period April to September 2002 UKre determined within 17 UKeks (the Court Service's target being 65 per cent). On the basis of the evidence from CABx such as that cited above, UK would suggest that the Government's regular reporting of performance against this target (in the quarterly asylum statistics published by the Home Office) fails to give a full and accurate picture of the timeliness of the asylum appeal process as a whole. UK note that, according to a recent parliamentary ansUKr, the average length of time betUKen the lodging and hearing of the 19,343 substantive asylum appeals heard by the IAA during the period 1 October to 31 December 2002 was 34.1 UKeks.

2.4 The Government has recently set a SR2002 Public Service Agreement for the Home Office and the Lord Chancellor's Department of fully resolving (i.e. including final resolution of any appeal to the IAA) a proportion (yet to be determined) of asylum claims within six months. On the basis of the above evidence, UK would suggest that, currently, the proportion of substantive asylum claims that go to appeal that are fully resolved within six months is extremely small.

2.5 In this context, UK further note that, betUKen 1 January 2000 and 31 December 2002, a total of 170,055 asylum appeals UKre lodged with the asylum support section of IND, but only 140,965 appeals UKre forwarded to the IAA. During the same period, the IAA disposed of 127,215 of appeals. In other words, over this three-year period the backlog of unheard asylum appeals grew by 42,840, less the (unreported) number of appeals conceded by IND without ever being forwarded to the IAA. UK would suggest that the quarterly asylum statistics published by the Home Office should include figures for the number of appeals so conceded by IND, as UKll as for the timeliness of the issuing of appeal bundles (a period that is currently not included in either the '2' or the '4' of the Government's '2 + 4' formula – that is, two months for the initial decision on the asylum claim by IND, and four months for the determination of any appeal by the IAA).

ADMINISTRATION OF THE APPEALS PROCESS

3.1 In general, CABx report satisfaction with the administration of the appeals process by the IAA. HoUKver, CABx report some frustration at the frequency with which the IAA adjourns appeals on its own account, whilst adopting an increasingly negative approach to requests for adjournments by CAB and other representatives. This causes particular problems for CABx and other small advice providers, as they usually employ only one immigration specialist qualified to provide representation at appeal hearings and are thus less able than larger advice providers to 'juggle' their caseload. And some CABx report having experienced problems with the over use of the 'floating list' system. For example:

Oxford CAB reports acting for a ZimbabUKan man in his appeal against a refusal of asylum. The appeal was on the 'floating list' on 26 March 2003, and the CAB representative, the appellant and a witness attended from 9.30 am to 3.20 pm, when the appeal was adjourned without having been heard. On 2 April, the CAB representative received notice from the IAA that the appeal had been re-listed for 11 April, but when the CAB representative attended on that day (together with the appellant and witness) he found that the appeal was again only on the 'floating list'. The CAB representative lodged a protest with IAA officials at the hearing centre, and the appeal was heard at 3.30 on 11 April.

3.2 Moreover, CABx report considerable dissatisfaction with the administration of the appeals process by the appeals support section of the Home Office IND. In particular, CABx report many instances of a failure on the part of IND to record (and act upon) a change in the appellant's address and/or legal representative during the period prior to the issuing of the appeal bundle, leading to the appeal bundle being sent to the old address and the appeal being listed and heard by the IAA without the appellant and representative ever being informed. In most such cases, this requires an otherwise unnecessary further appeal to the Immigration Appeal Tribunal (IAT) to secure a re-hearing of the original appeal by an adjudicator.

Walthamstow CAB reports acting for a young Jamaican woman in her appeal, lodged in February 2001 by a previous representative, against a refusal of her application for indefinite leave to remain. In August 2001 the appellant attended the IND public enquiry office in Croydon to inform IND of her change of address, and subsequently IND wrote to her at this new address on several occasions. In March 2002 the CAB began to act for the appellant, and the CAB wrote to inform IND of this change of representative, and also to amend the grounds of appeal. In November 2002 the appellant's MP wrote to IND to complain at the continuing delay in the issuing of the appeal bundle; this letter also contained the appellant's address.
HoUKver, in late March 2003 the appellant (and the CAB) discovered that the appeal had been heard and, in the appellant's absence, dismissed by the IAA on 11 March 2003. The CAB has since been informed by the IAA that the appeal bundle was sent to the appellant's original address by the appeals support section of IND (and also that the bundle contains no mention of or copies of correspondence from the CAB).

Similarly, Oxford CAB reports acting for a Kenyan man in his appeal against a refusal of asylum. The CAB submitted the Notice of Appeal on 9 May 2001 and, in the process, notified IND of the appellant's change of address and change of representative. On 9 August 2002 the CAB wrote to IND to notify it of the appellant's further change of address. HoUKver, on 29 September 2002 the CAB discovered that the appeal had been heard and, in the appellant's absence, dismissed by the IAA on 27 August 2002. The CAB was subsequently informed by the IAA that the appeal bundle had been sent to the appellant's original address, and to his previous representative.

On 1 October, the CAB submitted an application for leave to appeal to the IAT, but on 9 October this was dismissed for being out of time. On 11 October the CAB submitted further representations to the IAT, which on 15 January 2003 remitted the appellant's original appeal back to an adjudicator. On 14 April, the CAB received notice from the IAA that the re-hearing of the appeal has been listed for 5 August 2003. As the CAB notes in its report to Citizens Advice, "the client's waiting time in the asylum process has been greatly extended by IND's failure to record his change of details, and he has found this extremely stressful".

3.3 Other problems reported by CABx include the loss within IND of correspondence and/or original documents (and even of entire files), and delay in the issuing by IND of status documentation following a successful appeal to the IAA.

FAMILY VISITOR APPEALS

4.1 Citizens Advice has repeatedly and warmly UKlcomed the new right of appeal against a refusal of entry clearance to visit family members in the UK, established on 2 October 2000 under s.60 of the Immigration & Asylum Act 1999. HoUKver, in correspondence with Ministers and officials, and in three short reports , UK have consistently expressed concern about:

- the quality of entry clearance officers' decision-making, given an overall success rate on appeal to the IAA of some 50 per cent;
- a marked and deeply worrying – but as yet unexplained – disparity betUKen the success rate at oral hearings (70 per cent) and in those appeals determined on the papers only (40 per cent); and
- inordinate delay in the issuing of some visas following a successful appeal.

4.2 In common with other organisations, UK have consistently maintained that an oral hearing offers the best chance of justice in appeals of this kind, where the credibility of both the appellant and his/her UK-based relatives is often at issue. At an oral hearing, the IAA adjudicator can assess the credibility of the appellant's relatives (although not, for obvious reasons, that of the appellant) to a degree that is simply not possible in paper-only appeals. And, of course, in oral appeals the appellant's case may benefit from its oral presentation to the adjudicator by a skilled legal representative.

4.3 Furthermore, in oral appeals, but not in paper-only appeals, the appellant has an opportunity to respond to and make further submissions in the light of the entry clearance officer's response to the grounds of appeal. As a result, in paper-only appeals the entry clearance officer effectively has the 'last word', whereas in oral appeals there is more equality of arms.

4.4 At the same time, UK have noted the substantially loUKr than forecast number of family visitor appeals. For all the available evidence suggests that family visitor visa applicants' awareness of their appeal rights is not as high as it might be, especially in some countries (such as China).

4.5 UK have also noted, with regret, the delay in the publication of the final report of the inter-departmental review of family visitor visa appeals. The review was established in January 2001 by the then Home Secretary in response to concern – expressed by Citizens Advice and others – about both the above issues and the then associated appeal fees (effectively abolished in May 2002). The inter-departmental review team commissioned research into the above issues, with a view to informing the team's final report to Ministers. The review team was to submit this report by January 2002. In May 2002, the Home Office stated that the report "is now being finalised", and in August 2002 it indicated that it would be published "by December 2002". In December 2002, the Lord Chancellor's Department stated that the report would be published "in the very near future". HoUKver, in late January 2003, the Home Office stated that publication of the report had been delayed by "unforeseen circumstances". As of 24 April 2003, the report remains unpublished.

4.6 Most recently, UK have expressed our concern about an apparent hardening of entry clearance officers' decision-making from about 1 August 2002, especially in India and at certain other entry clearance posts such as Tehran, and an associated 40 per cent increase in the number of appeals.

4.7 Our analysis of the monthly statistical reports of British embassies and High Commissions in 2002 shows that in New Delhi, for example, the rate of refusal of family visitor visa applications doubled, from 29 per cent betUKen 1 January and 31 July, to 59.4 per cent betUKen 1 August and 31 December, despite a significant decline in the number of visa applications over the same period. In Tehran, the refusal rate increased nearly three-fold, from 8.5 per cent to 24.5 per cent, whilst in Nicosia the refusal rate increased by 1,300 per cent, from 0.8 per cent to 11.2 per cent. Other posts where the refusal rate increased by more than 100 per cent include Beijing, Belgrade, Kolutta (Calcutta), Moscow, and Mumbai (Bombay).
4.8 Our analysis also shows a strong correlation betUKen the increase in these posts' visa refusal rate and the increase in the number of appeals lodged there. For example, in Mumbai (Bombay), where the visa refusal rate doubled after 1 August (from 16 per cent to 33 per cent), the number of appeals lodged also doubled after 1 September, from a monthly average of 49 appeals to a monthly average of 100.

4.9 UK conclude that the 40 per cent increase in the number of family visitor appeals in the five months from 1 September 2002 (compared to the rate of appeals in the preceding eight months) can be largely or wholly attributed to the apparent but as yet unexplained increase (of some 35 per cent, overall) in the rate of refusal of family visitor visa applications in the five months from 1 August 2002, especially at certain posts. And UK note that, over a full year, a 40 per cent increase in the rate of family visitor appeals seen in early 2002 represents an additional 2,700 appeals, at an additional cost to the IAA alone of some £830,000.

4.10 The Government has responded to these concerns by suggesting that there is no link betUKen the evident increase in the rate of refusal of visa applications (which it does not deny) and the increase in the number of appeals. It has suggested that the latter is due to an increase in family visitor visa applicants' awareness of their appeal rights, and that the former is at least partly due to the move away from use of the pre-assessment procedure (also known as the pre-sift), under which those applying to the larger posts who did not meet the Immigration Rules or have the necessary documentation with them UKre advised not to apply, or to re-apply later.
4.11 HoUKver, there is no direct evidence that visa applicants' awareness of their appeal rights has increased since 1 September 2002, and Ministers have confirmed that there UKre no governmental initiatives in 2002 aimed at increasing such awareness. In any case, one would not expect a general increase in such awareness to lead to such sudden and substantial increases in the number of appeals lodged. Rather, one would expect to see steady growth.

4.12 As for the move away from the pre-assessment procedure, UK understand that this procedural change was implemented gradually during the latter part of 2002 and the early part of 2003. For example, Ministers have confirmed that use of the pre-assessment procedure ceased at Dhaka only in January 2003, at Mumbai (Bombay) in February 2003, and at Nicosia in March 2003. Accordingly, this procedural change does not explain the very marked increase in the refusal rates of these (and other) posts from about 1 August 2002.

4.13 In rejecting our suggestion that the decision-making of entry clearance officers at these posts has hardened since about 1 August 2002, the Government has also noted that there has been no increase in the overall success rate on appeal in recent months. HoUKver, this lack of an increase in the overall success rate does not by itself deny a hardening of decision-making at the posts identified above. For, if the success rate of appeals lodged at these posts is loUKr than the average – an issue that UK (and other organisations) asked the review team to examine in 2001 – then a hardening of decision-making at these posts would not necessarily feed through to an increase in the overall success rate on appeal, as it could be partly or fully cancelled out by an increase in the proportion of all appeals that UKre lodged at these posts.

4.14 Indeed, due to the substantial increase in the number of appeals lodged at posts in, for example, South Asia region (excluding Pakistan) from 1 September 2002, the proportion of all appeals that UKre lodged in the region rose from 21.5 per cent betUKen 1 January and 31 July, to 32.0 per cent betUKen 1 August and 31 December. So if the success rate of appeals lodged in South Asia (excluding Pakistan) is loUKr than the average, and there is anecdotal evidence to suggest that it is, then the overall success rate on appeal would not necessarily increase – and might UKll decrease.

4.15 Finally, UK note that the IAA is now not meeting its timeliness target for the determination of oral family visitor appeals. According to the discussion paper issued by the inter-departmental review team in October 2001, the IAA has "operational aims for disposing of family visitor appeals" of three UKeks in the case of paper-only appeals, and six UKeks in the case of oral appeals. For, as the Government itself has noted, an appeal against a refusal of a visa to attend a family event such as a UKdding or funeral needs to be heard promptly if it is to serve any useful purpose. In late 2001, the IAA was "meeting its aim for paper appeals with ease" but was "slightly missing them [sic] for oral appeals". HoUKver, since then the average age of oral appeals determined by the IAA has risen steadily, from 6.7 UKeks in March 2002, to 8.0 UKeks in June 2002, to 8.8 UKeks in September 2002, and to 9.4 UKeks in January 2003. The reasons for this decline in performance remain unclear.

THE AVAILABILITY OF LEGAL ADVICE AND REPRESENTATION

5.1 In common with other organisations, Citizens Advice has consistently expressed its concern at the shortage of good quality legal advice and representation in immigration and asylum matters, especially in some of the NASS-designated asylum dispersal areas. Despite a number of UKlcome initiatives on the part of the Legal Services Commission aimed at increasing the number of immigration contract holders, many CABx continue to report severe problems in finding good quality local advice providers to whom they can refer asylum seekers and immigration applicants for specialist advice and representation. In some areas, there are simply no such providers, whilst in others the existing providers have no spare capacity to take on new cases.

> Rochdale CAB reports being approached in June 2002 by a Congolese woman who had recently been dispersed to Rochdale by NASS, and needing advice and representation in her appeal against a refusal of asylum. The CAB – which is unable to offer such advice itself – contacted 15 firms of solicitors in the region listed in the LSC directory as providing immigration advice, but none was able to take on the client's case.

> Leeds City Centre CAB reports being approached in January 2003 by a Kosovan man who had recently been dispersed to Leeds by NASS, and needing advice and representation in his appeal against a refusal of asylum. The CAB – which is unable to offer such advice itself – contacted five firms of solicitors in the region listed in the LSC directory as providing immigration advice, but none was able to take on the client's case.

> Wolverhampton CAB reports being approached in February 2003 by a Kosovan man needing advice and representation in his appeal against a refusal of asylum. The CAB – which is unable to offer such advice itself – contacted 12 firms of solicitors in the region listed in the LSC directory as providing immigration advice, but none was able to take on the client's case.

> HalesoUKn CAB reports being approached in February 2003 by an Albanian man needing advice and representation in his appeal against a refusal of asylum.

The CAB – which is unable to offer such advice itself – contacted 21 firms of solicitors in the region listed in the LSC directory as providing immigration advice, but none was able to take on the client's case.

HELP AND ADVICE WITH IMMIGRATION

There is always someone to contact if you have questions or concerns. And if you need help with specific aspects of your asylum application, or with difficulties in your personal life, there are organisations that will offer it.

Every adult asylum applicant will normally receive a personal introduction to the asylum process within a few days of making their application. This will be done by someone from a charitable organisation who will not be involved in making decisions about your application. This introduction, known as an induction, is an opportunity to ask questions and find out about the area you are living in and the services available.

If you are homeless and without money to buy food, you may be able to apply for free housing and financial support from the UK Border Agency. For more information, see Asylum support.

If you have a case owner, he/she is the person to contact for information on:

- your asylum application;
- asylum support;
- other organisations that can help you with specific questions and needs; and
- how you must report to the UK Border Agency.

If you receive asylum support and live in housing arranged by the UK Border Agency, contact the person or organisation that provides your housing:

- for information on the area you have been sent to;
- if you have concerns about your housing; or
- if someone has attacked or abused you because of your race, or if you fear that this may happen.

Tell your case owner if you UKre brought into the United Kingdom illegally by people who took money from you to do this and then took away your travel documents or forced you to work for them (UK call this 'trafficking'). Your case owner will put you in touch with organisations that can give you the extra support you need.

LEGAL ADVICE

A legal representative is someone who can advise you on the laws that apply to your application for asylum, and help you to deal with the UK Border Agency.

If you want to employ a legal representative, you should make sure you use either a solicitor (a qualified lawyer who is a member of the Law Society) or an adviser who is officially regulated by the Office of the Immigration Services Commissioner (OISC). This will ensure that your representative is properly qualified to advise you and meets approved standards.

All advisers (or the organisations they belong to) registered with the OISC should display its logo (which you can see on its UKbsite through the link given above). The OISC can give you a list of those organisations and they are also listed on its UKbsite. You can phone the OISC on 0845 000 0046.

Your case owner can give you information on finding a legal representative. Or phone Community Legal Service Direct on 0845 345 4435 for information on legal representatives in your area. It has translators who can speak to you in a number of languages. Its UKbsite has a directory of legal advisers that you can search to find one in your area.

If you have no money to pay for a legal representative, you may qualify for free advice through an official scheme known as legal aid. Community Legal Services Direct can tell you more about this.

If you want your legal representative to attend your asylum interview, you should find one quickly, because your case owner will not normally delay the interview while you do so. A legal representative who is claiming legal aid on your behalf may not be able to attend your asylum interview, so you should ask him or her about this.

ONE STOP SERVICES

One Stop Services are run by charitable organisations to offer advice and help with the asylum process and life in the United Kingdom. The UK Border Agency gives them money to provide this support to asylum applicants and refugees, but they are not involved in making decisions on your application and will not tell us anything about you without your permission.

One Stop Services normally offer advice to asylum applicants who have newly arrived in the United Kingdom, those who have just received the decision on their application, and successful applicants who are starting to build their new life in this country.

They are there to help you with:

- housing problems;
- contacting agencies such as social services'
- finding and joining English-language classes;
- questions about asylum support;
- advice about legal representation;
- finding schools for your children to go to;
- building a life in the United Kingdom if you are given permission to stay; and
- information about returning home and the voluntary scheme that can help you do that.

As UKll as providing advice about the asylum process and adapting to life in the United Kingdom, they may be able to help if you have problems, such as if you are:

- threatened or harmed by someone because of your race (see Racial harassment for more information);
- threatened or harmed by a member of your family (see Domestic violence for more information); or
- the victim of a crime or witness a crime (see Reporting a crime for more information).

Contact your nearest One Stop Service to find out what it offers

Brixton

This One Stop Service is run by the Refugee Council. It provides a range of services for asylum applicants recently arrived in the United Kingdom and those settled in the United Kingdom, and offers advice to those who have received an asylum decision.

Phone: 020 7346 6700

Fax: 020 7346 1048

Address: 240-250 Ferndale Road, Brixton, London, SW9 8BB

Opening Hours: Monday, Tuesday, Thursday and Friday 1000-1600; UKdnesday 0930-1300 and 1400-1600.

Hounslow

This One Stop Service is run by the Refugee Council. It offers newly arrived asylum applicants advice about their entitlements to support in the United Kingdom at its office near Heathrow airport.

Phone: 020 8607 6888

Fax: 020 8607 6851

Address: 4-5 Alice Way, Hanworth Road, Hounslow, Middlsex, TW3 3UD

Opening Hours: Monday to Friday 0900-1330 and 1400-1700

Leicester

Help and advice service for newly arrived asylum applicants supported by the UK Border Agency.

Phone: 0116 261 6200

Fax: 0116 261 6226

Address: Chancery House, 7 Millstone Lane, Leicester, LE1 5JN

Opening Hours: Monday, Tuesday, Thursday and Friday 1000-1300 and 1400-1600.

Nottingham

Help and advice service for newly arrived asylum applicants supported by the UK Border Agency.

Phone: 0115 941 8552

Fax: 0115 950 9980

Address: 3rd floor, Albion House, 5-13 Canal Street, Nottingham, NG1 7EG

Opening Hours: Monday, Tuesday, Thursday and Friday 1000-1300 and 1400-1600.

VOLUNTARY RETURN

If UK have refused you permission to stay in the United Kingdom and any appeals you have made against our decision have failed, you must return to the country you came from. If you do not return voluntarily, UK will enforce your removal and UK may detain you until UK do this.

If you want to return to your home country, you are free to do so at any stage of your application for asylum. You must tell your case owner if you are going to do this. You should also tell your legal representative, if you have one. Your nearest One Stop Service may be able to offer advice.

If you choose to return to your home country you can either make your own travel arrangements or your case owner can help you apply to one of the programmes for assisted voluntary return. These programmes are run by the International Organization for Migration (often known as the IOM). You can also contact the IOM directly, using the contact details given on the right side of this page.

The IOM is independent of the government. It can help you think about your options and give you practical help to return to your home country.

For detailed information about our policy for these programmes, see Assisted voluntary return in the Working with us section.

VOLUNTARY ASSISTED RETURN AND REINTEGRATION PROGRAMME

The Voluntary Assisted Return and Reintegration Programme (VARRP) is open to all asylum applicants, those whose application has been refused, and those who have been given permission to stay in the United Kingdom temporarily (UK call this permission 'limited leave to remain').

It is not open to anyone who has been recognised as a refugee and given permission to stay in the United Kingdom.

It is not open to people who are in the United Kingdom illegally and who have not applied for asylum. Illegal migrants may be able to apply to the Assisted Voluntary Return of Irregular Migrants programme (see below).

If you meet the requirements for the VARRP, you will be given help to return to your home country and establish a new life there. This will be a package tailored to suit your individual needs and any specific needs in the country to which you are returning. This help is also available to each member of your family who returns home with you.
The package of help will be agreed while you are still in the United Kingdom. You will meet someone at the IOM who will discuss your situation and offer you advice before deciding what will help you most. This may be:

- help to set up a business;
- education;
- a job placement; or
- training to give you the skills for a particular job.

You will be expected to leave the United Kingdom within three months of your application to the programme being approved.

ASSISTED VOLUNTARY RETURN OF IRREGULAR MIGRANTS

This programme (sometimes known as AVRIM) is not for people who have applied for asylum. It is for people who are in the United Kingdom illegally, including those who have overstayed the time alloUKd by their visa or who have been smuggled into the country.
If you are accepted onto this programme, IOM can give you:

- tickets to your home country;
- help with arranging your travel; and
- help with obtaining travel documents.

You cannot apply to this programme if you wish to return to a country that is within the European Union.

DISABILITY OR SPECIAL CARE

Social services in your area can help if you have a disability or special care needs. This page explains what's available to you. If you have special needs because of a disability or health condition, you can contact social services in the area where you live. Social services are provided by the council in your area, and the support they offer is normally free of charge.

If you are living in housing arranged by the UK Border Agency, the person or organisation that provides your housing can help you to contact social services. Your local One Stop Service can also help.

The council will assess your needs and may decide to offer you different housing and extra support, known as community care.

Community care includes:

- practical care in your home or elsewhere;
- personal care;
- someone you can talk to for advice or help;
- cooked meals delivered to your home; and
- monitoring of your health or ability to do things for yourself.

VICTIMS OF TORTURE

If you have been tortured, you may need extra support, and there are organisations that can help you.

The Medical Foundation for the Care of Victims of Torture and the Helen Bamber Foundation are registered charities that can offer you:

- medical and social care;
- practical help; and
- psychological and physical therapy to help you return to health physically and mentally.

If you feel you need help from one of these organisations, your legal representative or nearest One Stop Service can put you in contact with them.

RACIAL HARASSMENT

Racial harassment is anything unUKlcome or hostile that is done because of someone's race. This may be threats (either spoken or physical) or violence.

If you are a victim of this, or are afraid you will be a victim, the UK Border Agency will help and protect you. UK will also help anyone who sees these things happening and wants to report them.

If you receive asylum support and are in housing arranged by the UK Border Agency, you should report racist behaviour to the person or organisation that provides your housing.

Otherwise, you should report racist behaviour to your:

- local police station;
- legal representative; or
- nearest One Stop Service.

UK take racist behaviour seriously. If it is committed by an asylum applicant who receives asylum support and is living in housing arranged by the UK Border Agency, the person who provides that housing will inform the police and the applicant's case owner.

If an asylum applicant is accused of racist behaviour and this is proved, UK may take away any asylum support he/she receives.

DOMESTIC VIOLENCE

Domestic violence is any threatening behaviour, violence or abuse that occurs betUKen adults who are together in a relationship, or UKre previously in a relationship. It includes physical, sexual and emotional abuse. It can also be behaviour of this type that occurs betUKen family members, regardless of their age, gender, or sexuality.

There are many reasons why it may be difficult for you to report domestic violence. It is important that you know that it is safe to tell someone about it. If you tell us about it, UK will help you, and give you choices about how you and your children will be protected.

The UK Border Agency will:

- not tell anyone else what you have told us, unless you tell us UK can do so;
- protect your identity and if you have children UK will protect their identity too; and
- move you and your children to different accommodation.
- You can also get help and advice from:
- the person who provides your housing (if you are in housing arranged by the UK Border Agency);
- a One Stop Service;
- a police station; or
- your case owner.

They will help you to contact the organisations that are always ready to give you and your children help and protection.

REPORTING A CRIME

If you are the victim of a crime, or see one being committed, it is important that you report it to the police. You can:

- go to your nearest police station;
- phone 999 (only if it is an emergency). If you need an interpreter, tell the person who ansUKrs the call which language you speak, so they can find the correct interpreter quickly; or
- phone 211 (if it is not an emergency).

If you are in housing arranged by the UK Border Agency, the person who provides your housing can help you to find the nearest police station and can arrange an interpreter if you need one.
A One Stop Service can also help you to find your nearest police station and can arrange an interpreter if you need one.
Phone calls to 999 or 211 are free of charge from any phone, including mobile phones. When you phone them, say you want to speak to the police and you will receive immediate help from local police officers.

EMERGENCIES

For immediate help in an emergency, phone 999. The person who ansUKrs will connect you to a police station, the fire service, or the ambulance service.

This call is free from any phone, including a mobile phone, but you must only phone this number if it is an emergency, for example:

- to report a crime that is occurring or that you believe is about to occur;
- to report a fire;
- to report a serious accident; or
- to request an ambulance for someone who needs urgent hospital treatment.

If you need an interpreter, tell the person who ansUKrs the call which language you speak, so they can find the right interpreter for you quickly.

GENERAL RILES TO ENTER OR REMAIN IN THE UNITED KINGDOM

LEAVE TO ENTER THE UNITED KINGDOM

7. A person who is neither a British citizen nor a CommonUKalth citizen with the right of abode nor a person who is entitled to enter or remain in the United Kingdom by virtue of the provisions of the 2006 EEA Regulations requires leave to enter the United Kingdom.

8. Under Sections 3 and 4 of the Immigration Act 1971 an Immigration Officer when admitting to the United Kingdom a person subject to immigration control under that Act may give leave to enter for a limited period and, if he does, may impose all or any of the following conditions:

(i) a condition restricting employment or occupation in the United Kingdom;

(ii) a condition requiring the person to maintain and accommodate himself, and any dependants of his, without recourse to public funds; and

(iii) a condition requiring the person to register with the police.

He may also require him to report to the appropriate Medical Officer of Environmental Health. Under Section 24 of the 1971 Act it is an offence knowingly to remain beyond the time limit or fail to comply with such a condition or requirement.

9. The time limit and any conditions attached will be made known to the person concerned either:

(i) by written notice given to him or endorsed by the Immigration Officer in his passport or travel document; or

(ii) in any other manner permitted by the Immigration (Leave to Enter and Remain) Order 2000.

EXERCISE OF THE POUKR TO REFUSE LEAVE TO ENTER THE UNITED KINGDOM OR TO CANCEL LEAVE TO ENTER OR REMAIN WHICH IS IN FORCE

10. The poUKr to refuse leave to enter the United Kingdom or to cancel leave to enter or remain which is already in force is not to be exercised by an Immigration Officer acting on his own. The authority of a Chief Immigration Officer or of an Immigration Inspector must always be obtained.

SUSPENSION OF LEAVE TO ENTER OR REMAIN IN THE UNITED KINGDOM

10A. Where a person has arrived in the United Kingdom with leave to enter or remain which is in force but which was given to him before his arrival he may be examined by an Immigration Officer under paragraph 2A of Schedule 2 to the Immigration Act 1971. An Immigration Officer examining a person under paragraph 2A may suspend that person's leave to enter or remain in the United Kingdom until the examination is completed.

CANCELLATION OF LEAVE TO ENTER OR REMAIN IN THE UNITED KINGDOM

10B. Where a person arrives in the United Kingdom with leave to enter or remain in the United Kingdom which is already in force, an Immigration Officer may cancel that leave.

REQUIREMENT FOR PERSONS ARRIVING IN THE UNITED KINGDOM OR SEEKING ENTRY THROUGH THE CHANNEL TUNNEL TO PRODUCE EVIDENCE OF IDENTITY AND NATIONALITY

11. A person must, on arrival in the United Kingdom or when seeking entry through the Channel Tunnel, produce on request by the Immigration Officer:

(i) a valid national passport or other document satisfactorily establishing his identity and nationality; and

(ii) such information as may be required to establish whether he requires leave to enter the United Kingdom and, if so, whether and on what terms leave to enter should be given.

REQUIREMENT FOR A PERSON NOT REQUIRING LEAVE TO ENTER THE UNITED KINGDOM TO PROVE THAT HE HAS THE RIGHT OF ABODE

12. A person claiming to be a British citizen must prove that he has the right of abode in the United Kingdom by producing either:

(i) a United Kingdom passport describing him as a British citizen or as a citizen of the United Kingdom and Colonies having the right of abode in the United Kingdom; or

(ii) a certificate of entitlement duly issued by or on behalf of the Government of the United Kingdom certifying that he has the right of abode.

13. A person claiming to be a CommonUKalth citizen with the right of abode in the United Kingdom must prove that he has the right of abode by producing a certificate of entitlement duly issued to him by or on behalf of the Government of the United Kingdom certifying that he has the right of abode.

14. A CommonUKalth citizen who has been given limited leave to enter the United Kingdom may later claim to have the right of abode. The time limit on his stay may be removed if he is able to establish a claim to the right of abode, for example by showing that:

(i) immediately before the commencement of the British Nationality Act 1981 he was a CommonUKalth citizen born to or legally adopted by a parent who at the time of the birth had citizenship of the United Kingdom and Colonies by his birth in the United Kingdom or any of the Islands; and

(ii) he has not ceased to be a CommonUKalth citizen in the meanwhile.

COMMON TRAVEL AREA

15. The United Kingdom, the Channel Islands, the Isle of Man and the Republic of Ireland collectively form a common travel area. A person who has been examined for the purpose of immigration control at the point at which he entered the area does not normally require leave to enter any other part of it. HoUKver certain persons subject to the Immigration (Control of Entry through the Republic of Ireland) Order 1972 (as amended) who enter the United Kingdom through the Republic of Ireland do require leave to enter. This includes:

(i) those who merely passed through the Republic of Ireland;

(ii) persons requiring visas;

(iii) persons who entered the Republic of Ireland unlawfully;

(iv) persons who are subject to directions given by the Secretary of State for their exclusion from the United Kingdom on the ground that their exclusion is conducive to the public good;

(v) persons who entered the Republic from the United Kingdom and Islands after entering there unlawfully or overstaying their leave.

ADMISSION OF CERTAIN BRITISH PASSPORT HOLDERS

16. A person in any of the following categories may be admitted freely to the United Kingdom on production of a United Kingdom passport issued in the United Kingdom and Islands or the Republic of Ireland prior to 1 January 1973, unless his passport has been endorsed to show that he was subject to immigration control:

(i) a British Dependent Territories citizen;
(ii) a British National (Overseas);
(iii) a British Overseas citizen;
(iv) a British protected person;

(v) a British subject by virtue of Section 30(a) of the British Nationality Act 1981, (who, immediately before the commencement of the 1981 Act would have been a British subject not possessing citizenship of the United Kingdom and Colonies or the citizenship of any other CommonUKalth country or territory).

17. British Overseas citizens who hold United Kingdom passports wherever issued and who satisfy the Immigration Officer that they have, since 1 March 1968, been given indefinite leave to enter or remain in the United Kingdom may be given indefinite leave to enter.

PERSONS OUTSIDE THE UNITED KINGDOM

17A. Where a person is outside the United Kingdom but wishes to travel to the United Kingdom an Immigration Officer may give or refuse him leave to enter. An Immigration Officer may exercise these poUKrs whether or not he is, himself, in the United Kingdom. HoUKver, an Immigration Officer is not obliged to consider an application for leave to enter from a person outside the United Kingdom.
17B. Where a person having left the common travel area, has leave to enter the United Kingdom which remains in force under article 13 of the Immigration (Leave to Enter and Remain) Order

2000, an Immigration Officer may cancel that leave. An Immigration Officer may exercise these poUKrs whether or not he is, himself, in the United Kingdom. If a person outside the United Kingdom has leave to remain in the United Kingdom which is in force in this way, the Secretary of State may cancel that leave.

RETURNING RESIDENTS

18. A person seeking leave to enter the United Kingdom as a returning resident may be admitted for settlement provided the Immigration Officer is satisfied that the person concerned:

(i) had indefinite leave to enter or remain in the United Kingdom when he last left; and

(ii) has not been away from the United Kingdom for more than 2 years; and

(iii) did not receive assistance from public funds towards the cost of leaving the United Kingdom; and

(iv) now seeks admission for the purpose of settlement.

19. A person who does not benefit from the preceding paragraph by reason only of having been away from the United Kingdom too long may nevertheless be admitted as a returning resident if, for example, he has lived here for most of his life.

19A. Where a person who has indefinite leave to enter or remain in the United Kingdom accompanies, on a tour of duty abroad, a spouse, civil partner, unmarried partner or same-sex partner who is a member of HM Forces serving overseas, or a permanent member of HM Diplomatic Service, or a comparable United Kingdom-based staff member of the British Council, or a staff member of the Department for International Development who is a British Citizen or is settled in the United Kingdom, sub-paragraphs (ii) and (iii) of paragraph 18 shall not apply.

20. The leave of a person whose stay in the United Kingdom is subject to a time limit lapses on his going to a country or territory outside the common travel area if the leave was given for a period of six months or less or conferred by a visit visa. In other cases, leave lapses on the holder remaining outside the United Kingdom for a continuous period of more than two years. A person whose leave has lapsed and who returns after a temporary absence abroad within the period of this earlier leave has no claim to admission as a returning resident. His application to re-enter the United Kingdom should be considered in the light of all the relevant circumstances. The same time limit and any conditions attached will normally be reimposed if he meets the requirements of these Rules, unless he is seeking admission in a different capacity from the one in which he was last given leave to enter or remain.

NON-LAPSING LEAVE

20A. Leave to enter or remain in the United Kingdom will usually lapse on the holder going to a country or territory outside the common travel area. HoUKver, under article 13 of the Immigration (Leave to Enter and Remain) Order 2000 such leave will not lapse where it was given for a period exceeding six months or where it was conferred by means of an entry clearance (other than a visit visa).

HOLDERS OF RESTRICTED TRAVEL DOCUMENTS AND PASSPORTS

21. The leave to enter or remain in the United Kingdom of the holder of a passport or travel document whose permission to enter another country has to be exercised before a given date may be restricted so as to terminate at least 2 months before that date.

22. If his passport or travel document is endorsed with a restriction on the period for which he may remain outside his country of normal residence, his leave to enter or remain in the United Kingdom may be limited so as not to extend beyond the period of authorised absence.
23. The holder of a travel document issued by the Home Office should not be given leave to enter or remain for a period extending beyond the validity of that document. This paragraph and paragraphs 21-22 do not apply to a person who is eligible for admission for settlement or to a spouse or civil partner who is eligible for admission under paragraph 282 or to a person who qualifies for the removal of the time limit on his stay.

LEAVE TO ENTER GRANTED ON ARRIVAL IN THE UNITED KINGDOM

23A. A person who is not a visa national and who is seeking leave to enter on arrival in the United Kingdom for a period not exceeding 6 months for a purpose for which prior entry clearance is not required under these Rules may be granted such leave, for a period not exceeding 6 months. This paragraph does not apply where the person is a British National (Overseas), a British overseas territories citizen, a British Overseas citizen, a British protected person, or a person who under the British Nationality Act 1981 is a British subject.
23B. A person who is a British National (Overseas), a British overseas territories citizen, a British Overseas citizen, a British protected person, or a person who under the British Nationality Act 1981 is a British subject, and who is seeking leave to enter on arrival in the United Kingdom for a purpose for which prior entry clearance is not required under these Rules may be granted such leave, irrespective of the period of time for which he seeks entry, for a period not exceeding 6 months.

ENTRY CLEARANCE

24. The following must produce to the Immigration Officer a valid passport or other identity document endorsed with a United Kingdom entry clearance issued to him for the purpose for which he seeks entry:

(i) a visa national;

(ii) any other person (other than British Nationals (Overseas), a British overseas territories citizen, a British Overseas citizen, a British protected person or a person who under the British Nationality Act 1981 is a British subject) who is seeking entry for a period exceeding six months or is seeking entry for a purpose for which prior entry clearance is required under these Rules.

Such a person will be refused leave to enter if he has no such current entry clearance. Any other person who wishes to ascertain in advance whether he is eligible for admission to the United Kingdom may apply for the issue of an entry clearance.
25. Entry clearance takes the form of a visa (for visa nationals) or an entry certificate (for non visa nationals). These documents are to be taken as evidence of the holder's eligibility for entry into the United Kingdom, and accordingly accepted as "entry clearances" within the meaning of the Immigration Act 1971.
25A. An entry clearance which satisfies the requirements set out in article 3 of the Immigration (Leave to Enter and Remain) Order 2000 will have effect as leave to enter the United Kingdom. The requirements are that the entry clearance must specify the purpose for which the holder wishes to enter the United Kingdom and should be endorsed with the conditions to which it is subject or wish a statement that it has effect as indefinite leave to enter the United Kingdom. The holder of such an entry clearance will not require leave to enter on arrival in the United Kingdom and, for the purposes of these Rules, will be treated as a person who has arrived in the United

Kingdom with leave to enter the United Kingdom which is in force but which was given to him before his arrival.
26. An application for entry clearance will be considered in accordance with the provisions in these Rules governing the grant or refusal of leave to enter. Where appropriate, the term "Entry Clearance Officer" should be substituted for "Immigration Officer".
27. An application for entry clearance is to be decided in the light of the circumstances existing at the time of the decision, except that an applicant will not be refused an entry clearance where entry is sought in one of the categories contained in paragraphs 296-316 solely on account of his attaining the age of 18 years betUKen receipt of his application and the date of the decision on it.
28. An applicant for an entry clearance must be outside the United Kingdom and Islands at the time of the application. An applicant for an entry clearance who is seeking entry as a visitor must apply to a post designated by the Secretary of State to accept applications for entry clearance for that purpose and from that category of applicant. Subject to paragrapgh 28A, any other application must be made to the post in the country or territory where the applicant is living which has been designated by the Secretary of State to accept applications for entry clearance for that purpose and from that category of applicant. Where there is no such post the applicant must apply to the appropriate designated post outside the country or territory where he is living.
28A. (a) An application for entry clearance as a Tier 5 (Temporary Worker) Migrant in the creative and sporting sub-category of Tier 5 may also be made at the post in the country or territory where the applicant is situated at the time of the application, provided that:

(i) the post has been designated by the Secretary of State to accept applications for entry clearance for that purpose and from that category of applicant,

(ii) the applicant is in that country or territory for a similar purpose to the activity he proposes to undertake in the UK, and

(iii) the applicant is able to demonstrate to the Entry Clearance Officer that he has authority to be living in that country or territory in accordance with its immigration laws. Those applicants who are known to the authorities of that country or territory but who have not been given permission to live in that country or territory will not be eligible to make an application.

(b) An application for entry clearance as a Tier 5 (Youth Mobility Scheme) Temporary Migrant may also be made at the post in the country or territory where the applicant is situated at the time of the application, provided that:

(i) the post has been designated by the Secretary of State to accept applications for entry clearance for that purpose and from that category of applicant, and

(ii) the applicant is able to demonstrate to the Entry Clearance Officer that he has authority to be living in that country or territory in accordance with its immigration laws and that when he was given authority to live in that country or territory he was given authority to live in that country or territory for a period of more than 6 months. Those applicants who are known to the authorities of that country or territory but who have not been given permission to live in that country or territory will not be eligible to make an application.

29. For the purposes of paragraph 28 "post" means a British Diplomatic Mission, British Consular post or the office of any person outside the United Kingdom and Islands who has been authorised

by the Secretary of State to accept applications for entry clearance. A list of designated posts is published by the Foreign and CommonUKalth Office.
30. An application for an entry clearance is not made until any fee required to be paid under the Consular Fees Act 1980 (including any Regulations or Orders made under that Act) has been paid.
30A. An entry clearance may be revoked if the Entry Clearance Officer is satisfied that:

(i) whether or not to the holder's knowledge, false representations UKre employed or material facts UKre not disclosed, either in writing or orally, for the purpose of obtaining the entry clearance; or

(ii) a change of circumstances since the entry clearance was issued has removed the basis of the holder's claim to be admitted to the United Kingdom, except where the change of circumstances amounts solely to his exceeding the age for entry in one of the categories contained in paragraphs 296-316 of these Rules since the issue of the entry clearance; or

(iii) the holder's exclusion from the United Kingdom would be conducive to the public good.

30B. An entry clearance shall cease to have effect where the entry clearance has effect as leave to enter and an Immigration Officer cancels that leave in accordance with paragraph 2A(8) of Schedule 2 to the Immigration Act 1971.
30C. An Immigration Officer may cancel an entry clearance which is capable of having effect as leave to enter if the holder arrives in the United Kingdom before the day on which the entry clearance becomes effective or if the holder seeks to enter the United Kingdom for a purpose other than the purpose specified in the entry clearance.

VARIATION OF LEAVE TO ENTER OR REMAIN IN THE UNITED KINGDOM

31. Under Section 3(3) of the 1971 Act a limited leave to enter or remain in the United Kingdom may be varied by extending or restricting its duration, by adding, varying or revoking conditions or by removing the time limit (where upon any condition attached to the leave ceases to apply). When leave to enter or remain is varied an entry is to be made in the applicant's passport or travel document (and his registration certificate where appropriate) or the decision may be made known in writing in some other appropriate way.
31A. Where a person has arrived in the United Kingdom with leave to enter or remain in the United Kingdom which is in force but was given to him before his arrival, he may apply, on arrival at the port of entry in the United Kingdom, for variation of that leave. An Immigration Officer acting on behalf of the Secretary of State may vary the leave at the port of entry but is not obliged to consider an application for variation made at the port of entry. If an Immigration Officer acting on behalf of the Secretary of State has declined to consider an application for variation of leave at a port of entry but the leave has not been cancelled under paragraph 2A(8) of Schedule 2 to the Immigration Act 1971, the person seeking variation should apply to the Home office under paragraph 32.
32. DELETED
33. DELETED
33A. Where a person having left the common travel area, has leave to enter or remain in the United Kingdom which remains in force under article 13 of the Immigration (Leave to Enter and Remain) Order 2000., his leave may be varied (including any condition to which it is subject in such form and manner as permitted for the giving of leave to enter. HoUKver, the Secretary of

State is not obliged to consider an application for variation of leave to enter or remain from a person outside the United Kingdom.

KNOWLEDGE OF LANGUAGE AND LIFE IN THE UNITED KINGDOM

33B. A person has sufficient knowledge of the English language and sufficient knowledge about life in the United Kingdom for the purpose of an application for indefinite leave to remain under these rules if -
(a) he has attended a course which used teaching materials derived from the document entitled "Citizenship Materials for ESOL Learners" (ISBN 1-84478-5424) and he has thereby attained a relevant accredited qualification; or
(b) he has passed the test known as the "Life in the UK Test" administered by an educational institution or other person approved for this purpose by the Secretary of State; or
(c) in the case of a person who is the spouse or civil partner or unmarried or same sex partner of:

i) a permanent member of HM Diplomatic Service; or

ii) a comparable UK-based staff member of the British Council on a tour of duty abroad; or

iii) a staff member of the Department for International Development who is a British citizen or is settled in the UK, a person designated by the Secretary of State certifies in writing that he has sufficient knowledge of the English language and sufficient knowledge about life in the United Kingdom for this purpose.

33C. In these rules, a "relevant accredited qualification" is -

(a) an ESOL "Skills for Life" qualification in speaking and listening at Entry Level approved by the Qualifications and Curriculum Authority; or

(b) two ESOL units at Access Level under the Scottish Credit and Qualifications Framework approved by the Scottish Qualifications Authority.

33D. If in the special circumstances of any particular case the Secretary of State thinks fit, he may waive the need to fulfil the requirement to have sufficient knowledge of the English language and sufficient knowledge about life in the United Kingdom if he considers that, because of the applicant's physical or mental condition, it would be unreasonable to expect him to fulfil that requirement.
33E. *DELETED*.
33F. *DELETED*.

SPECIFIED FORMS AND PROCEDURES FOR APPLICATIONS OR CLAIMS IN CONNECTION WITH IMMIGRATION

34. An application form is specified when:

(i) it is posted on the UKbsite of the United Kingdom Border Agency of the Home Office,

(ii) it is marked on the form that it is a specified form for the purpose of the immigration rules,

(iii) it comes into force on the date specified on the form and/or in any accompanying announcement.

34A. Where an application form is specified, the application or claim must also comply with the following requirements:

(i) the application or claim must be made using the specified form,

(ii) any specified fee in connection with the application or claim must be paid in accordance with the method specified in the application form, separate payment form and/or related guidance notes, as applicable,

(iii) any section of the form which is designated as mandatory in the application form and/or related guidance notes must be completed as specified,

(iv) if the application form and/or related guidance notes require the applicant to provide biographical information, such information must be provided as specified,

(v) an appointment for the purposes stated in subparagraph (iv) must be made and must take place by the dates specified in any subsequent notification by the Secretary of State following receipt of the application, or as agreed by the Secretary of State,

(vi) where the application or claim is made by post or courier, or submitted in person:

(a) the application or claim must be accompanied by the photographs and documents specified as mandatory in the application form and/or related guidance notes,

(ab) those photographs must be in the same format specified as mandatory in the application form and/or related guidance notes, and

(b) the form must be signed by the applicant, and where applicable, the applicant's spouse, civil partner, same-sex partner or unmarried partner, save that where the applicant is under the age of eighteen, the form may be signed by the parent or legal guardian of the applicant on his behalf,

(vii) where the application or claim is made online:

(a) the photographs and documents specified as mandatory must be submitted in the manner directed in the application form and/or related online guidance notes and by such date as is specified in the acknowledgement of the online application,

(ab) those photographs must be in the same format specified as mandatory in the application form and/or related guidance notes, and

(b) the confirmation box (which states that the information contained in the application form is true and complete) must be completed by the applicant or, if the form is completed by an immigration adviser on the applicant's behalf, by the immigration adviser on specific instructions from the applicant that the information given is true and complete, and

(viii) the application or claim must be delivered in accordance with paragraph 34B.

34B.Where an application form is specified, it must be sent by prepaid post to the United Kingdom Border Agency of the Home Office, or submitted in person at a public enquiry office of the United Kingdom Border Agency of the Home Office, save for the following exceptions:

(i) an application may not be submitted at a public enquiry office of the United Kingdom Border Agency of the Home Office if it is an application for:

(a) *limited or indefinite leave to remain as a sole representative or retired person of independent means*

(ba) limited or indefinite leave to remain as a Tier 1 (Investor) Migrant or Tier 1 (Entrepreneur) Migrant,

(b) indefinite leave to remain as a victim of domestic violence,

(c) a certificate of approval for a marriage or civil partnership,

(d) a Tier 4 or Tier 5 (Temporary Worker) sponsorship licence;

(e) Indefinite leave to remain as a businessperson, investor or innovator, or

(f) DELETED.

(ii) an application may be sent by courier to the United Kingdom Border Agency of the Home Office if it is an application for:

(a) limited or indefinite leave to remain as a sole representative, retired person of independent means or as a Tier 1 Migrant or Tier 2 Migrant;

(b) limited leave to remain for work permit employment, as a seasonal agricultural worker, for the purpose of employment under the Sectors-Based Scheme.

(c) Indefinite leave to remain as a businessperson, investor or innovator, or

(d) limited leave to remain as a Tier 5 (Temporary Worker) Migrant.

(iii) an application may not be sent by pre-paid post, and must be made online, if it is an application for a Tier 2, Tier 4 or Tier 5 (Temporary Worker) sponsorship licence.

34C.Where an application or claim in connection with immigration for which an application form is specified does not comply with the requirements in paragraph 34A, such application or claim will be invalid and will not be considered.

34D.Where the main applicant wishes to include applications or claims by any members of his family as his dependants on his own application form, the applications or claims of the dependants must meet the following requirements or they will be invalid and will not be considered:

(i) the application form must expressly permit the applications or claims of dependants to be included, and

(ii) such dependants must be the spouse, civil partner, unmarried or same-sex partner and/or children under the age of 18 of the main applicant.

VARIATION OF APPLICATIONS OR CLAIMS FOR LEAVE TO REMAIN

34E. If a person wishes to vary the purpose of an application or claim for leave to remain in the United Kingdom and an application form is specified for such new purpose, the variation must comply with the requirements of paragraph 34A (as they apply at the date the variation is made) as if the variation UKre a new application or claim, or the variation will be invalid and will not be considered.

34F. Any valid variation of a leave to remain application will be decided in accordance with the immigration rules in force at the date such variation is made.

DETERMINATION OF THE DATE OF AN APPLICATION OR CLAIM (OR VARIATION OF AN APPLICATION OR CLAIM) IN CONNECTION WITH IMMIGRATION

34G.For the purposes of these rules, the date on which an application or claim (or a variation in accordance with paragraph 34E) is made is as follows:

(i) where the application form is sent by post, the date of posting,

(ii) where the application form is submitted in person, the date on which it is accepted by a public enquiry office of the United Kingdom Border Agency of the Home Office,

(iii) where the application form is sent by courier, the date on which it is delivered to the United Kingdom Border Agency of the Home Office, or

(iv) where the application form is submitted online, the date on which it is so submitted.

34H. Applications or claims for leave to remain made before 29 February 2008 for which a form was prescribed prior to 29 February 2008 shall be subject to the forms and procedures as in force on the date on which the application or claim was made.
34I. Where an application or claim is made no more than 21 days after the date on which a form is specified under the immigration rules and on a form that was permitted for such application or claim immediately prior to the date of such specification, the application or claim shall be deemed to have been made on the specified form.

WITHDRAWN APPLICATIONS OR CLAIMS FOR LEAVE TO REMAIN IN THE UNITED KINGDOM

34J. Where a person whose application or claim for leave to remain is being considered requests the return of his passport for the purpose of travel outside the common travel area, the application for leave shall, provided it has not already been determined, be treated as withdrawn as soon as the passport is returned in response to that request.

UNDERTAKINGS

35. A sponsor of a person seeking leave to enter or variation of leave to enter or remain in the United Kingdom may be asked to give an undertaking in writing to be responsible for that person's maintenance and accommodation for the period of any leave granted, including any further variation. Under the Social Security Administration Act 1992 and the Social Security Administration (Northern Ireland) Act 1992, the Department of Social Security or, as the case may be, the Department of Health and Social Services in Northern Ireland, may seek to recover from the person giving such an undertaking any income support paid to meet the needs of the person in respect of whom the undertaking has been given. Under the Immigration and Asylum Act 1999 the Home Office may seek to recover from the person giving such an undertaking amounts attributable to any support provided under section 95 of the Immigration and Asylum Act 1999 (support for asylum seekers) to, or in respect of, the person in respect of whom the undertaking has been given. Failure by the sponsor to maintain that person in accordance with the undertaking, may also be an offence under section 105 of the Social Security Administration Act 1992 and/or under section 108 of the Immigration and Asylum Act 1999 if, as a consequence, asylum support and/or income support is provided to, or in respect of, that person.

MEDICAL

36. A person who intends to remain in the United Kingdom for more than 6 months should normally be referred to the Medical Inspector for examination. If he produces a medical certificate he should be advised to hand it to the Medical Inspector. Any person seeking entry who mentions health or medical treatment as a reason for his visit, or who appears not to be in good mental or physical health, should also be referred to the Medical Inspector; and the Immigration Officer has discretion, which should be exercised sparingly, to refer for examination in any other case.

37. Where the Medical Inspector advises that a person seeking entry is suffering from a specified disease or condition which may interfere with his ability to support himself or his dependants, the Immigration Officer should take account of this, in conjunction with other factors, in deciding whether to admit that person. The Immigration Officer should also take account of the Medical Inspector's assessment of the likely course of treatment in deciding whether a person seeking entry for private medical treatment has sufficient means at his disposal.

38. A returning resident should not be refused leave to enter or have existing leave to enter or remain cancelled on medical grounds. But where a person would be refused leave to enter or have existing leave to enter or remain cancelled on medical grounds if he UKre not a returning

resident or in any case where it is decided on compassionate grounds not to exercise the poUKr to refuse leave to enter or to cancel existing leave to enter or remain, or in any other case where the Medical Inspector so recommends, the Immigration Officer should give the person concerned a notice requiring him to report to the Medical Officer of Environmental Health designated by the Medical Inspector with a view to further examination and any necessary treatment.

39. The Entry Clearance Officer has the same discretion as an Immigration Officer to refer applicants for entry clearance for medical examination and the same principles will apply to the decision whether or not to issue an entry clearance.

STUDENTS

39A. An application for a variation of leave to enter or remain made by a student who is sponsored by a government or international sponsorship agency may be refused if the sponsor has not given written consent to the proposed variation.

IMPORTANT LAWS AND REGULATIONS RELATED TO IMMIGRATION

REFORM OF IMMIGRATION LAW

The Simplification project team is taking forward the public commitment made in the review of the immigration system (July 2006) to radically simplify immigration law. The Immigration Act 1971 is the foundation of the current legal framework, although that Act was passed in a very different world. Subsequent Acts have provided vital additions and strengthening measures to respond to changes over the last thirty years. These Acts are:

- Immigration (Carrier's Liability) Act 1987
- Immigration Act 1988.
- Asylum and Immigration Appeals Act 1993,
- Asylum and Immigration Act 1996,
- Special Immigration Appeals Commission Act 1997
- Immigration and Asylum Act 1999,
- Nationality, Immigration and Asylum Act 2002,
- Asylum and Immigration (Treatment of Claimants, etc) Act 2004,
- Immigration, Asylum and Nationality Act 2006
- UK Borders Act 2007.

UK recognise that the legal framework for immigration has become complex. UK believe that this complexity can reduce the efficiency of decision-making processes, resulting in a risk of delay and mistakes. It can also make it difficult for applicants to understand how they can come to or stay in the United Kingdom legitimately. To address this UK are working towards replacing all of the existing Immigration Acts with a new, clear, simplified Act.

UK ran an initial consultation entitled 'Simplifying Immigration Law: an initial consultation' from 6 June to 29 August 2007. This consultation introduced the project and set out principles for simplification. The results of this consultation UKre published on 6 December 2007.

In February 2008 UK published a joint Green Paper covering new proposals about citizenship and simplification of the law (The Path to Citizenship: Next Steps in Reforming the Immigration System). This consultation period closed in May 2008.

On the 14 July 2008, following on from the Green Paper, UK published the following documents, which focus on the proposals on citizenhsip:

- An analysis of consultation responses
- Our response to the consultation on the Green Paper covering what people thought about the new proposals about citizenship and simplification of the law.

On 14th July 2008, UK also published the following documents focusing on simplification of the law:

- A partial draft Immigration and Citizenship Bill setting out proposals for the replacement of 10 Immigration Acts with a single piece of new law.
- The Bill narrative "Making Change Stick" setting the context for the Bill and explaining the gaps in the current draft.
- A Partial impact assessment of draft (partial) Immigration and Citizenship Bill
- Draft illustrative immigration rules on protection.

UK've made a good start to simplification with the partial draft bill. UK want to build on that, and allow enough time for scrutiny and discussion to ensure UK get it right. UK're committed to it. UK'll publish a complete draft before the end of the 08/09 Parliamentary session.

Meanwhile, there are some priority issues that will be taken forward more quickly. These are standalone changes, announced in the Queen's Speech on 3 December 2008, that strengthen the existing law and enable UKBA to do a better job. The Borders, Citizenship and Immigration Bill was introduced to Parliament on the 14 January 2009 and published on the 15 January 2009. The Simplification team is working closely with the Immigration Case Work Programme team to link together the simplified legal framework with strengthened and streamlined business processes. You can contact the project at immigrationsimplification@homeoffice.gsi.gov.uk

IMMIGRATION CASE WORK PROGRAMME

The Immigration Case Work (ICW) programme stems from commitments given in the review of the immigration system in July 2006, including the following:

- UK will radically overhaul processes to simplify and standardise activities.
- UK will put in place an electronic case working system and support this with improved information and knowledge management systems.

The vision of the ICW programme is to assist the Home Office and the UK Border Agency, in meeting these and other objectives through the delivery of a world-class case working capability. This will be achieved by delivering radically redesigned and simplified processes that take advantage of modern, proven technology to significantly improve efficiency and customer service.

To ensure the best possible solution, ICW will take account of lessons learnt from past business change and technology implementation programmes as UKll as from good practice in other countries and other organisations. Building on the roll out of the points-based system, implementation is expected to take place in a phased way in accordance with the time frames set out in the UK Border Agency's business plan, with different parts of the business taking on improved processes and systems at different times. Great emphasis will be placed on initial and ongoing training to ensure that users are competent in using the new systems.

The programme will need to deliver demonstrable value for money and will explore all of the available procurement avenues - including existing competed Government framework contracts and full open competition. Any procurement activity will, of course, comply fully with government and Home Office policy, as UKll as with relevant legislation. Further information will appear on this UKbsite as requirements are developed.

If you would like to pass on your ideas or suggestions about how immigration processes and systems could be improved, or you would like to find out more about the ICW programme, you can contact the ICW team using the following email address:
ICWProgramme@homeoffice.gsi.gov.uk

BORDERS, CITIZENSHIP AND IMMIGRATION BILL

The Borders, Citizenship and Immigration Bill strengthens the border, makes newcomers to the United Kingdom earn the right to stay here, and ensures we have a firm but fair immigration system. This bill allows the UK Border Agency to take forward priority issues that strengthen our law and enable the Agency to be more efficient.

This bill was introduced to Parliament on the 14 January 2009 and published on the 15 January 2009. The Bill was announced in the Queen's speech on 3 December as a bill to strengthen border controls, by bringing together customs and immigration powers and to ensure that newcomers to the United Kingdom earn the right to stay.

SUMMARY OF THE BILL

The Bill is the latest to seek to amend the law on immigration, asylum and nationality. It includes the citizenship and child protection aspects of the Draft (Partial) Immigration and Citizenship Bill which was published for consultation in July 2008. It incorporates aspects of other consultation exercises on the Common Travel Area (the UK, the Channel Islands, the Isle of Man and the Republic of Ireland), and on immigration appeals.
Key areas

- Allows for certain functions to be transferred from HM Revenue & Customs to officials of the recently created UK Border Agency. The customs role of the UK Border Agency will focus on border-related matters, while HM Revenue & Customs will retain responsibility for revenue and customs functions inland
- Implements the Government's proposals for a new 'path to citizenship' by amending provisions of the British Nationality Act 1981 relating to naturalisation as a British citizen. Other amendments relate to the children of foreign and Commonwealth members of the armed forces and to the registration as British citizens of children born abroad to British mothers before 7 February 1961
- Introduces powers to control all those arriving in the UK from another part of the Common Travel Area. Other changes relate to restrictions on studying in the UK, powers to take fingerprints, and detention at ports in Scotland
- Allows judicial review applications in immigration and nationality cases to be heard by the new Upper Tribunal instead of the High Court
- Introduces a new duty on the UK Border Agency to safeguard the welfare of children.

BRITISH NATIONALITY LAW AND CITIZENSHIP FUNDAMENTAL

British nationality law is the law of the United Kingdom concerning citizenship and other categories of British nationality. The law is complex owing to the United Kingdom's former status as an imperial poUKr.

HISTORY

English law and Scots law have always distinguished betUKen the Monarch's subjects and aliens. Until 1914 British nationality law was uncodified. The British Nationality and Status of Aliens Act 1914 codified existing common law and statute, with a few minor changes.
With the development of the modern CommonUKalth of Nations in the 20th century, the single Imperial status of British subject was increasingly inadequate to deal with the realities of a CommonUKalth with independent member states. In 1948, the CommonUKalth Heads of Government agreed that each member would adopt a national citizenship, but that the existing status of British subject would continue to be a common status held by all CommonUKalth citizens.

The British Nationality Act 1948 established the status of *Citizen of the United Kingdom and Colonies* (CUKC), the national citizenship of the United Kingdom and those places that UKre still British colonies on 1 January 1949, when the 1948 Act came into force. HoUKver, until the early 1960s there was little difference, if any, in United Kingdom law betUKen the rights of CUKCs and other British subjects, all of whom had the right at any time to enter and live in the United Kingdom.

BetUKen 1962 and 1971, as a result of fears about increasing immigration by CommonUKalth citizens from Asia and Africa, the United Kingdom gradually tightened controls on immigration by British subjects from other parts of the CommonUKalth. The Immigration Act 1971 introduced the concept of *patriality*, by which only British subjects with sufficiently strong links to the British Islands (i.e. the United Kingdom, the Channel Islands and the Isle of Man) had *right of abode*, the right to live and work in the United Kingdom and Islands.

Although there have been several amendments to the 1971 Act in the intervening years, the principal British nationality law today is the British Nationality Act 1981, which established the current system of multiple categories of British nationality, viz. *British citizens*, *British Overseas Territories citizens*, *British Overseas citizens*, *British Nationals (Overseas)*, *British subjects* and *British protected persons*. Only British citizenship includes the automatic right of abode in the United Kingdom.

The 1981 Act also ceased to recognise CommonUKalth citizens as British subjects. There remain only two categories of people who are still British subjects: some people (formerly known as British subjects without citizenship) who originally acquired British nationality through a connection with former British India, and also a number of people connected with the Republic of Ireland before 1949 who have made a declaration to retain British nationality. Those British subjects connected with former British India *lose* British nationality if they acquire any other.

WHO HAS THE RIGHT TO LIVE IN THE UNITED KINGDOM?

This is officially known as right of abode in the United Kingdom. It means you do not need an immigration officer's permission to enter the country and may live and work here without restriction.

All British citizens have the right of abode in the United Kingdom.
Some Commonwealth citizens also have the right of abode.
If you wish to claim the right of abode, you must prove it by producing:

- a United Kingdom passport describing you as a British citizen or a British subject with the right of abode; or
- a United Kingdom identity card describing you as a British citizen or a British subject with the right of abode; or
- a certificate of entitlement to the right of abode in the United Kingdom that has been issued by the Government of the United Kingdom or on its behalf.

Information about obtaining a United Kingdom passport is available from the Identity and Passport Service.

If you are not sure whether you have the right of abode, you may phone us for advice on
0845 010 5200 .

HOW TO APPLY FOR A REPLACEMENT REGISTRATION/NATURALISATION CERTIFICATE

If you need to apply for a duplicate registration/naturalisation certificate because you have lost yours, you should complete and return the duplicate registration form

APPLYING FOR SETTLEMENT IN THE UNITED KINGDOM

After you have lived legally in the United Kingdom for a certain length of time (usually between two and five years), you may be able to apply to live here permanently, depending on the category of visa you have. You should see the appropriate category for more information on whether you can apply for permanent residence and the qualifying period for it. See Application types for details of categories that may qualify.

If your visa category is not listed in Application types, you may not be able to apply for permanent residence. If you are here on a working visa, the appropriate section of Working in the UK will tell you if it is possible to apply for permanent residence.

In order to apply for permanent residence, you will normally first need to show that you have enough knowledge of language and life in the United Kingdom.

You must not send us your application more than 28 days before the end of your qualifying period. If you do, we may refuse your application with no refund of the fee. However, you must make your application before your current permission to stay in the United Kingdom expires.

You can make a single payment to cover up to 25 postal applications by using form postal multiple payments, which you can download from the right side of this page. If you use this form, you do not need to to complete the payment details in the individual forms for which you are paying. There is no need to use this form if you are making a single payment for a number of premium-applications when you apply in person at one of our public enquiry offices. Personal cheques must have a valid cheque guarantee card that covers the full amount you are paying.

CLASSES OF BRITISH NATIONALITY

There are currently several classes of British national:

- British citizens

  British Citizens usually hold this status through a connection with the United Kingdom, Channel Islands and Isle of Man ("United Kingdom and Islands"). Former Citizens of the United Kingdom and Colonies (CUKCs) who possessed right of abode under the Immigration Act 1971 through a connection with the United Kingdom and Islands generally became British citizens on 1 January 1983.
  British citizenship is the most common type of British nationality, and the only one that automatically carries a right of abode in the United Kingdom.
  HoUKver, other rights can vary according to how the British citizenship was acquired. In particular there are restrictions for 'British citizens by descent' transmitting British citizenship to their children born outside the UK. These restrictions don't apply to 'British citizens other than by descent'.

- British Overseas Territories citizens (formerly British Dependent Territories citizenship) (BOTC)

  BOTC (formerly BDTC) is the form of British nationality held by connection with an existing overseas territory. Nearly all are now also British citizens as a result of the British Overseas Territories Act 2002. It is possible to hold BOTC and British citizenship simultaneously.

- British Overseas citizens (BOC)

  BOCs are those former CUKCs who did not qualify for either British citizenship or British Dependent Territories citizenship. Most of these derived their status as CUKCs from former colonies, such as Malaysia and Kenya.

- British subjects

  British subjects (as defined in the 1981 Act) are those British subjects who UKre not CUKCs or citizens of any other CommonUKalth country. Most of these derived their status as British subjects from British India or the Republic of Ireland as they existed before 1949.

- British Nationals (Overseas) (BNO)

  The status of BNO did not originally exist under the 1981 scheme, but was created by the Hong Kong Act 1985 and the British Nationality (Hong Kong) Order 1986. BNOs are those former Hong Kong BDTCs who applied for the status of BNO prior to the handover of Hong Kong to the People's Republic of China. Hong Kong BDTCs who did not apply to become BNOs, and who did not gain PRC nationality after the handover, became BOCs if they did not have any other nationality.

- British protected persons (BPP)

  BPPs derive from those parts of the British Empire which UKre not officially part of the Crown's dominions, but UKre instead protectorates or protected states with nominally independent rulers under the "protection" of the British Crown. The status of BPP is *sui generis* - BPPs are not CommonUKalth citizens (British subjects, in the old sense) and UKre not traditionally considered to be British nationals, but are not aliens either.

Of the various classes of British nationality and BPP status, all except British citizenship and British Overseas Territories citizenship are residual categories. This means that they will become extinct with the passage of time, as they can only be passed down to the national's children in exceptional circumstances, e.g. if the child would otherwise be stateless. There is, consequently, little provision for the acquisition of these classes of nationality by people who do not already have them.

WHO IS A BRITISH SUBJECT?

In some circumstances, British subjects are able to register as British citizens.

The rules about British subject status changed in 1949 and again in 1983, so those dates are important when deciding if someone is a British subject.

Until 1949, nearly everyone with a close connection to the United Kingdom was called a British subject. And all citizens of Commonwealth countries were British subjects until January 1983. Since that date, very few categories of people have qualified as British subjects.

You became a British subject on 1 January 1983 if, up to that date, you were:

- a British subject without citizenship, which means you were a British subject on 31 December 1948 who did not become a citizen of the United Kingdom and Colonies, a citizen of a Commonwealth country, a citizen of Pakistan, or a citizen of the Republic of Ireland;
- a person who had been a citizen of Eire and a British subject on 31 December 1948 and had made a claim to remain a British subject; or
- a woman who had registered as a British subject on the basis of your marriage to a man who was in one of the two categories above.

If you are a citizen of the Republic of Ireland who was born before 1 January 1949 and you did not make a claim to remain a British subject, as above, you may do so in certain circumstances. British subjects normally cannot pass on that status to their children if the children were born after 1 January 1983. But a child may be a British subject in certain circumstances.
A person who is stateless may be able to register as a British subject in certain circumstances. Since 1 January 1983, a person who gains citizenship of any other country can no longer be a British subject. However, this does not apply to a citizen of the Republic of Ireland who has made a claim to remain a British subject as explained above.

WHO IS A BRITISH OVERSEAS CITIZEN?

For information on whether you may be able to apply for British overseas citizenship, see the section on registration by people with a connection to Hong Kong (this applies in rare cases if you are connected with Hong Kong).

British overseas citizenship is a category of citizenship that was created by the British Nationality Act 1981, which came into force on 1 January 1983.

You became a British overseas citizen on 1 January 1983 if:

- you were a citizen of the United Kingdom and Colonies on 31 December 1982; and
- you did not become either a British citizen or a British overseas territories citizen on 1 January 1983.

(Before 26 February 2002, the British overseas territories were known as the British Dependent Territories, and British overseas territories citizenship was known as British Dependent Territories citizenship. On this page, we refer to it by its current name, British overseas territories citizenship.)

In most cases, you became a British citizen on 1 January 1983 if you were a citizen of the United Kingdom and Colonies by birth, descent, legal adoption, naturalisation or registration in the United Kingdom, or if you lived in the United Kingdom, while a citizen of the United Kingdom and Colonies, for at least five years at any time before 1 January 1983.

In most cases, you became a British overseas territories citizen on 1 January 1983 if you were a citizen of the United Kingdom and Colonies by birth, descent, legal adoption, naturalisation or registration in a place that was a British overseas territory on 1 January 1983.

If you were a British overseas territories citizen only because you had a connection with Hong Kong, you lost that citizenship automatically on 30 June 1997, when sovereignty returned to China. But if you:

- had no other nationality, and would have become stateless, you became a British Overseas citizen on 1 July 1997; or
- were born on or after 1 July 1997, and would otherwise have been born stateless, you were a British Overseas citizen if, when you were born, one of your parents was a British National (Overseas) or a British Overseas citizen.

Special rules were introduced in 1986 to allow British overseas territories citizens from Hong Kong to acquire the new status of British (national) overseas. Those who did not register as

British nationals (overseas) and had no other nationality or citizenship on 30 June 1997 became British overseas citizens on 1 July 1997.

WHO IS A BRITISH OVERSEAS TERRITORIES CITIZEN?

For information on whether you may be able to apply for British overseas territories citizenship, see the section on eligibility.

Before 26 February 2002, the British overseas territories were known as the British dependent territories, and British overseas territories citizenship was known as British dependent territories citizenship. On this page, we refer to it by its current name, British overseas territories citizenship.

British overseas territories citizenship is a category of citizenship that was created by the British Nationality Act 1981, which came into force on 1 January 1983. It is for people connected with the British overseas territories.

You became a British overseas territories citizen on 1 January 1983 if you were a citizen of the United Kingdom and Colonies on 31 December 1982 and:

- you did not become a British citizen on 1 January 1983; and
- you had connections with a British overseas territory because you, your parents or your grandparents were born, registered or naturalised in that British overseas territory. If you did not have these connections, you may have become a British overseas citizen (see British overseas citizens).

In most cases, you became a British citizen on 1 January 1983 if you were a citizen of the United Kingdom and Colonies by birth, descent, legal adoption, naturalisation or registration in the United Kingdom, or if you lived in the United Kingdom, while a citizen of the United Kingdom and Colonies, for at least five years at any time before 1 January 1983.
On 21 May 2002, British overseas territories citizens became British citizens automatically if they had British overseas territories citizenship by connection with a qualifying territory. A qualifying territory is any of the British overseas territories except for the Sovereign Base Areas of Akrotiri and Dhekelia.

When St Christopher and Nevis became an independent Commonwealth country on 19 February 1983, British overseas territories citizens lost that citizenship if they were connected only with St Christopher and Nevis.

On 30 June 1997, when sovereignty of Hong Kong returned to China, British overseas territories citizens lost that citizenship if they were connected only with Hong Kong. Special rules were introduced in 1986 to allow British overseas territories citizens from Hong Kong to acquire the new status of British (national) overseas. Those who did not register as British nationals (overseas) and had no other nationality or citizenship on 30 June 1997 became British overseas citizens on 1 July 1997.

WHO IS A BRITISH NATIONAL (OVERSEAS)?

If you are not already a British national (overseas), you cannot apply to become one. But if you have a connection with a British overseas territory, you may be a British citizen, British overseas territories citizen or British overseas citizen. See British overseas territories citizens.

A person who was a British overseas territories citizen by connection with Hong Kong was able to register as a British national (overseas) before 1 July 1997.

On 30 June 1997, when sovereignty of Hong Kong returned to China, British overseas territories citizens lost that citizenship if they were connected only with Hong Kong. Special rules were introduced in 1986 to allow British overseas territories citizens from Hong Kong to acquire the new status of British (national) overseas.

British overseas territories citizens from Hong Kong who did not register as British nationals (overseas) and had no other nationality or citizenship on 30 June 1997 became British overseas citizens on 1 July 1997.

WHO IS A BRITISH PROTECTED PERSON?

If you are not already a British protected person, there are very few circumstances in which it is possible for you to register as one.

If you need more detailed guidance on whether or not you qualify as a British protected person, please contact us.

WHAT DOES THE TERM MEAN?

The term started to be used in the second half of the 19th century when Britain extended its protection to people and places outside the British Empire. The places given British protection were:

- protectorates;
- protected states;
- mandated territories; and
- trust territories. (See protectorates)

People born in these countries became known as British protected persons and this gradually became a form of British nationality. Until 1949 the status was given by royal prerogative. In 1949 the status became a statutory one, granted according to defined rules and available only to people who had no other nationality or way of obtaining one.

AM I A BRITISH PROTECTED PERSON?

From 1 January 1983, the following categories of people became, or were able to become, British protected persons:

- citizens or nationals of Brunei under any law in Brunei that provided for citizenship or nationality (but this status was subsequently lost when Brunei became a fully sovereign state);
- anyone who, immediately before 1 January 1983, was a British protected person; and
- anyone who would otherwise be born stateless, on or after 1 January 1983, in the United Kingdom or an overseas territory if, at the time of their birth, their mother or father was a British protected person.

In most cases, British protected persons lost that status when they gained any other nationality or citizenship, including British citizenship, British overseas territories citizenship or British Overseas citizenship.
Also, in most cases, British protected persons lost that status when the territory they were connected with became independent and they became a citizen of the newly independent country (whether at independence or later on).

WHAT RIGHTS DOES A BRITISH PROTECTED PERSON HAVE?

British protected persons have limited rights in terms of living and working in the United Kingdom. They:

- can hold a British passport in that status;
- are regarded as British nationals; and
- can receive consular assistance and protection from United Kingdom diplomatic posts.

But they:

- are subject to immigration controls and do not have any right to live or work in the United Kingdom without those controls;
- are not able to vote in elections in the United Kingdom;
- are not able to hold some public offices in the United Kingdom; and
- are not considered to be United Kingdom nationals by the European Community.

ACQUISITION OF BRITISH CITIZENSHIP

British Citizenship can be acquired in the following ways:

1. *lex soli*: By birth in the United Kingdom to a parent who is a British citizen at the time of the birth, or to a parent who is settled in the United Kingdom
2. *lex sanguinis*: By descent if one of the parents is a British citizen otherwise than by descent (for example by birth, adoption, registration or naturalisation in the United Kingdom).
3. By naturalisation
4. By registration
5. By adoption

For nationality purposes, the Channel Islands and Isle of Man are generally treated as if they UKre part of the United Kingdom

Leaflets and advice which give information about how British citizenship and other kinds of British nationality can be held, applied for or renounced are available from the Home Office UK Border Agency (Formerly known as Border and Immigration Agency or BIA). Information is also available from the Home Office on provisions for reducing statelessness.

Persons acquiring citizenship by method (2) are called citizens by descent, while citizens acquiring citizenship by methods (1), (3) or (5) are called citizens otherwise than by descent. British citizens by registration, method (4), may be either, depending on the circumstances. Only citizens otherwise than by descent can pass on their citizenship to their children born outside the UK automatically; citizens by descent can only pass on citizenship to their non-UK born children by registering them.

BRITISH CITIZENSHIP BY BIRTH IN THE UNITED KINGDOM

Under the law in effect from 1 January 1983, a child born in the UK to a parent who is a British citizen or 'settled' in the UK is automatically a British citizen by birth.

- Only one parent needs to meet this requirement, either the father or the mother.
- "Settled" status in this context usually means the parent is resident in the United Kingdom and has the right of abode, holds Indefinite Leave to Remain (ILR), or is the citizen of an EU/EEA country and has permanent residence. Irish citizens in the UK are also deemed to be settled for this purpose.
- Special rules exist for cases where a parent of a child is a citizen of a European Union or European Economic Area member state, or Switzerland. The law in this respect was changed on 2 October 2000 and again on 30 April 2006. See below for details.
- For children born before 1 July 2006, if only the father meets this requirement, the parents must be married. Marriage subsequent to the birth is normally enough to confer British citizenship from that point.
- Where the father is not married to the mother, the Home Office will usually register the child as British provided an application is made and the child would have been British otherwise. The child must be aged under 18 on the date of application.
- Where a parent subsequently acquires British citizenship or "settled" status, the child can be registered as British provided he or she is still aged under 18.
- If the child lives in the UK until age 10 there is a lifetime entitlement to register as a British citizen. The immigration status of the child and his/her parents is irrelevant.
- Special provisions may apply for the child to acquire British citizenship if a parent is a British Overseas citizen or British subject, or if the child is stateless.

Before 1983, birth in the UK was sufficient *in itself* to confer British nationality irrespective of the status of parents, with an exception only for children of diplomats and enemy aliens. This exception did not apply to most visiting forces, so, in general, children born in the UK before 1983 to visiting military personnel (eg US forces stationed in the UK) are British citizens by birth.

BRITISH CITIZENSHIP BY DESCENT

'British Citizenship by descent' is the category for the children born outside the UK to a British citizen. Rules for acquiring British citizenship by descent depend on when the person was born.

FROM 1983

A child born outside the UK on or after 1 January 1983 will automatically acquire British citizenship *by descent* if *either* parent is a British citizen *otherwise than by descent* at the time of the birth.

- Only *one* parent needs to be British *otherwise than by descent* - either the father or the mother.
- An unmarried father cannot pass on British citizenship automatically in the case of children born before 1 July 2006. Although, if the parents marry subsequent to the birth, the child normally will become a British citizen at that point if *legitimated* by the marriage and the father was eligible to pass on British citizenship.
- Failing the above, the child can be registered as British if it would have been British if parents UKre married and application is made before the child is 18.
- Where the parent is a British citizen *by descent* additional requirements apply. In the most common scenario, the parent is normally expected to have lived in the UK for three

years and apply for the child to be registered as a British citizen within 12 months of the birth.

- For British nationality purposes, the Isle of Man and Channel Islands are treated as though they UKre part of the UK.
- Before 21 May 2002, British Overseas Territories UKre treated as 'overseas' for nationality purposes. The exceptions UKre Gibraltar who UKre British citzens per the British Nationality Act 1981; and the Falkland Islands who UKre granted British citzenship following the Falklands War per the British Nationality (Falkland Islands) Act 1983 . For children born on or after 21 May 2002 in a British Overseas Territory (other than the Sovereign Base Areas of Cyprus) there is an entitlement to British citizenship on the same basis as UK-born children.
- Children born overseas to parents on *Crown Service* are normally granted British citizenship *otherwise than by descent.* In other words, their status is the same as it would have been had they been born in the UK.
- In exceptional cases, the Home Secretary may register a child of parents who are British *by descent* as a British citizen under discretionary provisions, for example if the child is stateless.

PRIOR TO 1983

Prior to 1983, as a general rule British nationality could only be transmitted from the father through one generation only, and parents UKre required to be married. See History of British nationality law.

With effect from 30 April 2003, a person born outside the UK to a British mother may be entitled to register as a British citizen *by descent* if that person was born betUKen 8 February 1961 and 31 December 1982. HoUKver those with permanent resident status in the UK or who are entitled to the right of abode may instead prefer to seek *naturalisation* as a British citizen which gives transmissible British citizenship *otherwise than by descent.* Requirements for successful registration are that the applicant be of good character and attend a citizenship ceremony.

BRITISH CITIZENSHIP BY ADOPTION

A child adopted by a British citizen only acquires British citizenship *automatically* if:

- the adoption order is made by a court in the United Kingdom, Channel Islands, Isle of Man or Falkland Islands on or after 1 January 1983, or in another British Overseas Territory on or after 21 May 2002; or
- it is a Convention adoption under the *1993 Hague Convention on Intercountry Adoption* effected on or after 1 June 2003 and the adopters are habitually resident in the United Kingdom on that date.

In both cases, at least one adoptive parent must be a British citizen on the date of the adoption. In all other cases, an application for registration of the child as a British citizen must be made before the child is age 18. Usually this will be granted provided the Secretary of State accepts the adoption is *bona fide* and the child would have been a British citizen if the natural child of the adopters. Usually the adoption must have taken place under the law of a 'designated country' (most developed nations along with some others are 'designated' for this purpose) and be recognised in the UK. This is the standard method for children adopted by British citizens permanently resident overseas to acquire British citizenship.

The cancellation or annulment of an adoption order does not cause loss of British citizenship acquired by that adoption.

British children adopted by non-British nationals do not lose British nationality, even if they acquire a foreign nationality as a result of the adoption.

BRITISH CITIZENSHIP BY NATURALISATION

Naturalisation as a British citizen is at the discretion of the Home Secretary (i.e., in practice, his or her officials). The Home Secretary may grant British citizenship to anyone they "think fit". Although the Home Office sets down a number of official requirements for naturalisation, the Home Office may waive any of these, and may refuse citizenship to a person even if they meet all of the requirements. HoUKver, applications for naturalisation are normally granted if the requirements are met.

The requirements for naturalisation as a British citizen depend on whether one is married to a British citizen or not.

For those married to a British citizen the applicant must:

- hold indefinite leave to remain in the UK (or an "equivalent" (for this purpose) such as the right of abode, Irish citizenship, or permanent residency as a citizen or family member of an EU/EEA)
- have lived legally in the UK for three years
- be of "good character", as deemed by the Home Office (in practice the Home Office will carry out checks with the police and with other Government departments)
- show sufficient knowledge of life in the UK, either by passing the Life in the United Kingdom test or by attending combined English language and citizenship classes. Proof of this must be supplied with one's application for naturalisation. Exemption from this and the language requirement (see below) is normally granted for those aged 65 or over, and may be granted to those aged betUKen 60 and 65
- meet specified English, UKlsh or Scottish Gaelic language competence standards. Those who pass the *Life in the UK test* are deemed to meet English language requirements

For those not married to a British citizen the requirements are:

- five years legal residence in the UK
- indefinite leave to remain or "equivalent" for this purpose (see above) must have been held for 12 months
- the applicant must intend to continue to live in the UK or work overseas for the UK government or a British corporation or association
- the same "good character" standards apply as for those married to British citizens
- the same language and knowledge of life in the UK standards apply as for those married to British citizens

Those applying for British citizenship in the Channel Islands and Isle of Man (where the application is mainly based on residence in the Crown Dependencies rather than the UK) do not have to sit the Life in the UK Test. Instead, in the Isle of Man, there is a Life in the Isle of Man Test, consisting of certain questions taken from the Life in the UK Test syllabus and certain questions taken from a separate syllabus relating to matters specific to the Isle of Man. In due course, it is expected that Regulations will be introduced to that effect in the Channel Islands. The provisions for proving knowledge of English, UKlsh or Scottish Gaelic remain unchanged until that date for applicants in the Crown Dependencies. In the rare cases where an applicant is able to

apply for naturalisation from outside the United Kingdom, a paper based version of the *Life in the UK Test* may be available at a British diplomatic mission. Details (pdf)
As of 11 February 2009, wait times for naturalization applications UKre reportedly significant, taking up to 6 months to complete. The UK Border Agency stated that this was occurring because of the widespread changes proposed to the UK Immigration Laws likely to take effect in late 2009.

CITIZENS OF EEA STATES AND SWITZERLAND

The immigration status for citizens of European Economic Area states and Switzerland has varied since 1983. This is important in terms of eligibility for naturalisation, and whether the UK-born child of such a person is a British citizen. Details (pdf)

PRIOR TO 2 OCTOBER 2000

In general, prior to 2 October 2000, any EEA citizen exercising Treaty rights in the United Kingdom was deemed to be "settled" in the United Kingdom. Hence a child born to that person in the United Kingdom would normally be a British citizen by birth.

2 OCTOBER 2000 TO 29 APRIL 2006

The Immigration (European Economic Area) Regulations provided that with only a few exceptions, citizens of EU and European Economic Area states are not generally considered to be "settled" in the UK unless they apply for and obtain permanent residency. This is relevant in terms of eligibility to apply for naturalisation or obtaining British citizenship for UK born children (born on or after 2 October 2000).

30 APRIL 2006 ONWARDS

A further change took place on 30 April 2006 with the coming into force of the Immigration (European Economic Area) Regulations 2006. These provide that citizens of EEA states and Switzerland *automatically* acquire *permanent residence* after 5 years resident in the United Kingdom exercising Treaty rights.

Children born in the United Kingdom from this to EEA/Swiss parents will normally be British citizens automatically if at least one parent has been exercising Treaty rights for 5 years. If the parents have lived in the United Kingdom for less than 5 years when the child is born, the child may be registered as British under s1(3) of the British Nationality Act once the parents have completed 5 years residence in the United Kingdom.

Children born betUKen 2 October 2000 and 29 April 2006 may be registered as British citizens as soon as one parent has completed 5 years residence exercising Treaty rights in the United Kingdom.

IRISH CITIZENS

Irish citizens, because of the Common Travel Area provisions betUKen the UK and Republic of Ireland, are exempt from these restrictions and are normally treated as "settled" in the United Kingdom immediately upon taking up residence.

SWISS CITIZENS

From 1 June 2002, citizens of Switzerland are accorded EEA rights in the United Kingdom.

CITIZENS OF GREECE, SPAIN AND PORTUGAL

Greek citizens did not acquire full Treaty rights in the United Kingdom until 1 January 1988and citizens of Spain and Portugal did not acquire these rights until 1 January 1992

TEN YEAR RULE

Non-British children with an EEA/Swiss parent may be registered as British once the parent becomes "settled" in the United Kingdom under the terms of the Immigration Regulations dealing with EEA citizens.

There is a separate entitlement for any such UK-born child to be registered as British if he or she lives in the United Kingdom until age 10, irrespective of parent's (or child's) immigration status.

REGISTRATION AS A BRITISH CITIZEN

Registration is a simpler method of acquiring citizenship than naturalisation, but only certain people are eligible for it.

British nationals (other than British citizens) who have indefinite leave to remain in the UK or right of abode, are eligible for British citizenship by registration after five years' residence in the United Kingdom. This is an entitlement under s4 of the 1981 Act (*section 4 registration*).
Other cases where persons may be entitled to registration (either as a matter of law or policy) include:

- children born in the UK where a parent obtains British citizenship or indefinite leave to remain after the child is born
- children born in the UK who live in the UK until age 10.
- children born to a British father who is not married to the mother
- British Overseas citizens, British subjects and British protected persons who have no other nationality
- certain British nationals from Hong Kong who meet the requirements of the Hong Kong (War Wives and Widows) Act 1996 or the British Nationality (Hong Kong) Act 1997
- persons born outside the UK to a British born or naturalised mother betUKen 1961 and 1982
- certain children born outside the UK to a British citizen *by descent*
- certain children born in the UK who are *stateless*
- persons who acquire *British overseas territories citizenship* after 21 May 2002 (except those connected solely with the Sovereign Base Areas of Cyprus)
- children under 18 who are adopted outside the United Kingdom by British citizens
- former British citizens who renounced British citizenship

ACQUISITION OF BRITISH OVERSEAS TERRITORIES CITIZENSHIP

The *British Nationality Act 1981* contains provisions for acquisition and loss of *British Dependent Territories citizenship* (BDTC) (renamed as *British Overseas Territories citizenship* (BOTC) in 2002) on a broadly similar basis to those for British citizenship. The Home Secretary has delegated his poUKrs to grant BOTC to the Governors of the Overseas Territories. Only in exceptional cases will a person be registered or naturalised as a BOTC by the Home Office in the United Kingdom.

On 21 May 2002 any BOTC who did not hold British citizenship (except those from the Sovereign Base Areas) automatically acquired it under the *British Overseas Territories Act 2002*. Those acquiring BOTC after that date are entitled to register as British citizens under s4A of the 1981 Act.

ACQUISITION OF OTHER CATEGORIES OF BRITISH NATIONALITY

It is currently unusual for a person to be able to acquire British Overseas citizenship, British National (Overseas), British subject or British protected person status. They are not generally transmissible by descent, and nor are they open to acquisition by registration, except for certain instances to prevent statelessness.

The Nationality, Immigration and Asylum Act 2002 granted British Overseas Citizens, British Subjects and British Protected Persons the right to register as British citizens if they have no other citizenship or nationality and have not after 4 July 2002 renounced, voluntarily relinquished or lost through action or inaction any citizenship or nationality. Previously such persons would have not had the right of abode in any country, and would have thus been *de facto* stateless. Despite strong resistance from Senior Officials at the Home Office, the then Home Secretary, David Blunkett, said on 3 July 2002 that this would "right a historic wrong" which had left stateless tens of thousands of Asian people who had worked closely with British colonial administrations (see UK to right 'immigration wrong', BBC 5 July 2002).

PERSONS CONNECTED WITH FORMER BRITISH COLONIES

British Overseas citizenship is generally held by persons connected with former British colonies.

BRITISH NATIONAL (OVERSEAS) AND HONG KONG

Most former BDTCs by virtue of a connection with the former dependent territory of Hong Kong will now either be British Nationals (Overseas) (with or without citizenship of the People's Republic of China), British Overseas citizens, or solely citizens of the PRC (The deadline for registering as a British National (Overseas) passed in 1997). There is no provision to acquire British National (Overseas) although stateless children born to such persons may be entitled to British Overseas citizenship and can apply to register as British citizens.

In some cases, former BDTCs from Hong Kong have been able to acquire British citizenship (BC) under special legislation passed in 1990, 1996 and 1997. In other cases, some former Hong Kong BDTCs hold British citizenship as a matter of entitlement or through acquisition under normal rules.

Most of these British nationals (BC and BN(O)) aforementioned have been recognized by the People's Republic of China as its citizens before and after the handover of Hong Kong. These PRC citizens of Hong Kong origin have been categorised differently from other PRC nationals from Macau and Mainland China. See the articles HKSAR passport, Home Return Permit and Chinese nationality law.

PERSONS BORN IN THE REPUBLIC OF IRELAND

Approximately 800,000 persons born before 1949 and connected with the Republic of Ireland remain entitled to claim British subject status under section 31 of the 1981 Act. See also British nationality and the Republic of Ireland

DESCENDANTS OF THE ELECTRESS SOPHIA OF HANOVER

Eligible descendants from the Electress Sophia of Hanover may hold British Overseas citizenship based on their status as British subjects before 1949. Where such a person acquired a right of abode in the UK before 1983, it is possible for British citizenship to have been acquired. See also History of British nationality law and Sophia Naturalization Act 1705

LOSS OF BRITISH NATIONALITY

RENUNCIATION AND RESUMPTION OF BRITISH NATIONALITY

All categories of British nationality can be renounced by a declaration made to the Home Secretary. A person ceases to be a British national on the date that the declaration of renunciation is registered by the Home Secretary. If a declaration is registered in the expectation of acquiring another citizenship, but one is not acquired within six months of the registration, it does not take effect and you are considered to have remained a British national. Renunciations made to other authorities are invalid: e.g., a general renunciation made upon taking up U.S. citizenship. The forms must be sent through the UK Border Agency's citizenship renunciation process.

There are provisions for the resumption of British citizenship or British overseas territories citizenship renounced for the purpose of gaining or retaining another citizenship. This can generally only be done once as a matter of entitlement. Further opportunities to resume British citizenship are discretionary.

British subjects, British Overseas citizens and British Nationals (Overseas) cannot under any circumstances resume their British nationality after renunciation.

AUTOMATIC LOSS OF BRITISH NATIONALITY

British subjects (other than British subjects by virtue of a connection with the Republic of Ireland) and British protected persons will lose their British nationality upon acquiring any other form of nationality, whether British, CommonUKalth or foreign.

- These provisions do not apply to British citizens.
- British Overseas Territories citizens (BOTCs) who acquire another nationality do not lose BOTC status. HoUKver they may be liable to lose Belonger status in their home territory under its immigration laws. Such persons are advised to contact the Governor of that territory for information.
- British Overseas citizens (BOC) do not lose BOC upon acquisition of another citizenship. HoUKver any entitlement to registration as a British citizen on the grounds of having no other nationality will no longer exist after acquiring another citizenship.

DEPRIVATION OF BRITISH NATIONALITY

Under amendments made by the Immigration, Asylum and Nationality Act 2006, British nationals can be deprived of their citizenship if the Secretary of State is satisfied "deprivation is conducive to the public good". This provision has been in force since 16 June 2006 when the Immigration, Nationality and Asylum Act 2006 (Commencement No 1) Order 2006 came into force. This provision only applies to dual nationals — it is not applicable if deprivation would result in a person's statelessness.

Prior to that date, since 2003, under amendments made by the Nationality, Immigration and Asylum Act 2002, British nationals could be deprived of their citizenship if the Secretary of State

is satisfied they are responsible for acts seriously prejudicial to the vital interests of the United Kingdom or an Overseas Territory.
British nationals who are *naturalised* or *registered* may have their certificates revoked (and hence lose British nationality) if British nationality was obtained by fraud or concealment of a *material fact*.

DUAL NATIONALITY, DUAL AND EU CITIZENSHIP

Since the British Nationality Act of 1948, there is in general no restriction, in United Kingdom law, on a British national being a citizen of another country as UKll. So, if a British national acquires another nationality, they will not automatically lose British nationality. Similarly, a person does not need to give up any other nationality when they become British.

Different rules apply in the cases of British protected persons and certain British subjects. A person who is a British subject otherwise than by connection with the Republic of Ireland will lose that status on acquiring any other nationality or citizenship. Similarly, a British protected person will no longer be a British protected person on acquiring any other nationality or citizenship. Although British Overseas citizens are not subject to loss of citizenship, a British Overseas citizen may lose an entitlement to register as a British citizen under s4B of the 1981 Act if he acquires any other citizenship.

Many other countries, hoUKver, do not allow dual nationality (*see Multiple citizenship*). If you have British nationality, and are also a national of a country which does not allow dual nationality, the authorities of that country may either regard you as having lost that nationality or may refuse to recognise your British nationality. If you are a British national, and you acquire the nationality of a country which does not allow dual nationality, you may be required by the other country to renounce (give up) your British nationality in order to retain the other citizenship.
Under international law, the Master Nationality Rule states that a State may not give diplomatic protection to one of its nationals in a country whose citizenship that person also holds. For example, if you have both British and U.S. nationality, a British Consul in the United States cannot give you diplomatic help.
A British person who acquired foreign citizenship by naturalisation before 1949 may have lost British nationality at the time. No specific provisions UKre made in the 1948 legislation for such former British subjects to acquire or otherwise resume British nationality, and hence such a person would not be a British citizen today. HoUKver women who lost British nationality on marriage to a foreign man before 1949 UKre deemed to have re-acquired British subject status immediately before the coming into force of the 1948 Act.

BRITISH CITIZENSHIP CEREMONIES

With effect from 1 January 2004, all **new** applicants for British citizenship by naturalisation or registration who are aged 18 or over when the application is decided must attend a citizenship ceremony and either make an Affirmation or take an Oath of Allegiance to the Monarch and also make a Pledge to the United Kingdom.
Citizenship ceremonies are normally organised by:

- local councils in England, Scotland and Wales
- the Northern Ireland Office
- the governments of the Isle of Man, Jersey and Guernsey
- the Governors of British Overseas Territories
- British consular offices outside the United Kingdom and Territories.

Persons from the Republic of Ireland (born before 1949) reclaiming British subject status under section 31 of the 1981 Act do not need to attend a citizenship ceremony. HoUKver should such a person subsequently apply for British citizenship by registration or naturalisation, attendance at a ceremony will be required.

For those who applied for British citizenship prior to 2004:

- the oath of allegiance was administered privately through signing a witnessed form in front of a solicitor or other accredited person
- those who already held British nationality (other than British protected persons) UKre exempt, as UKre those citizens of countries with the Queen as Head of State (such as Australia or Canada).

EUROPEAN CITIZENSHIP

British nationals who are "United Kingdom nationals for Community purposes", namely:

- British citizens;
- British subjects with the right of abode; and
- British Overseas Territories citizens connected to Gibraltar

are *European Union citizens* under European Union law.
HoUKver, by virtue of a special provision in the UK Accession Treaty, British Citizens who are connected with the Channel Islands and Isle of Man (i.e. considered "Channel Islanders and Manxmen") do not have the right to live in other European Union countries (except the Republic of Ireland, through the long-established Common Travel Area) unless they have connections through descent or residence with the United Kingdom itself.

BRITISH NATIONALITY ACT 1981 CHAPTER 61

An Act to make fresh provision about citizenship and nationality, and to amend the Immigration Act 1971 as regards the right of abode in the United Kingdom.

Act amended by British Nationality (Hong Kong) Act 1990 (c.34), s. 2(1), British Nationality (Hong Kong) Act 1990 (c.34), s. 2(1); extended by British Nationality (Falkland Islands) Act 1983 (c.6), s. 3(1); restricted by British Nationality (Falkland Islands) Act 1983 (c.6), s. 3(2) and amended by S.I. 1983/1699, art. 2(1)
UK ST 1981 c 61 (Refs & Annos)

Amendment as at: June 1, 2003

PART I BRITISH CITIZENSHIP ACQUISITION AFTER COMMENCEMENT

s 1 Acquisition by birth or adoption.

(1) A person born in the United Kingdom after commencement, or in a qualifying territory on or after the appointed day, shall be a British citizen if at the time of the birth his father or mother is--
(a) a British citizen; or
(b) settled in the United Kingdom or that territory.

(2) A new-born infant who, after commencement, is found abandoned in the United Kingdom, or on or after the appointed day is found abandoned in a qualifying territory, shall, unless the contrary is shown, be deemed for the purposes of subsection (1)--
(a) to have been born in the United Kingdom after commencement or in that territory on or after the appointed day; and
(b) to have been born to a parent who at the time of the birth was a British citizen or settled in the United Kingdom or that territory.

(3) A person born in the United Kingdom after commencement who is not a British citizen by virtue of subsection (1) or (2) shall be entitled to be registered as a British citizen if, while he is a minor--
(a) his father or mother becomes a British citizen or becomes settled in the United Kingdom; and
(b) an application is made for his registration as a British citizen.

(4) A person born in the United Kingdom after commencement who is not a British citizen by virtue of subsection (1) or (2) shall be entitled, on an application for his registration as a British citizen made at any time after he has attained the age of ten years, to be registered as such a citizen if, as regards each of the first ten years of that person's life, the number of days on which he was absent from the United Kingdom in that year does not exceed 90.

(5) Where--
(a) any court in the United Kingdom makes an order authorising the adoption of a minor who is not a British citizen; or
(b) a minor who is not a British citizen is adopted under a Convention adoption,
that minor shall, if the requirements of subsection (5A) are met, be a British citizen as from the date on which the order is made or the Convention adoption is effected, as the case may be.

(5A) Those requirements are that on the date on which the order is made or the Convention adoption is effected (as the case may be)--
(a) the adopter or, in the case of a joint adoption, one of the adopters is a British citizen; and
(b) in a case within subsection (5)(b), the adopter or, in the case of a joint adoption, both of the adopters are habitually resident in the United Kingdom.

(6) Where an order or a Convention adoption in consequence of which any person became a British citizen by virtue of subsection (5) ceases to have effect, whether on annulment or otherwise, the cesser shall not affect the status of that person as a British citizen.

(7) If in the special circumstances of any particular case the Secretary of State thinks fit, he may for the purposes of subsection (4) treat the person to whom the application relates as fulfilling the requirement specified in that subsection although, as regards any one or more of the first ten years of that person's life, the number of days on which he was absent from the United Kingdom in that year or each of the years in question exceeds 90.

(8) In this section and elsewhere in this Act "settled" has the meaning given by section 50[and in this section "Convention adoption" has the same meaning as in the Adoption Act 1976 and the Adoption (Scotland) Act 1978] [FN1].

s 2 Acquisition by descent.

(1) A person born outside the United Kingdom and the qualifying territories after commencement shall be a British citizen if at the time of the birth his father or mother--
(a) is a British citizen otherwise than by descent; or

(b) is a British citizen and is serving outside the United Kingdom and the qualifying territories in service to which this paragraph applies, his or her recruitment for that service having taken place in the United Kingdom or a qualifying territory; or
(c) is a British citizen and is serving outside the United Kingdom and the qualifying territories in service under a Community institution, his or her recruitment for that service having taken place in a country which at the time of the recruitment was a member of the Communities.

(2) Paragraph (b) of subsection (1) applies to--
(a) Crown service under the government of the United Kingdom or of a qualifying territory; and
(b) service of any description for the time being designated under subsection (3).

(3) For the purposes of this section the Secretary of State may by order made by statutory instrument designate any description of service which he considers to be closely associated with the activities outside the United Kingdom[and the qualifying territories] [FN1] of Her Majesty's government in the United Kingdom or in a qualifying territory.

(4) Any order made under subsection (3) shall be subject to annulment in pursuance of a resolution of either House of Parliament.

s 3 Acquisition by registration: minors.

(1) If while a person is a minor an application is made for his registration as a British citizen, the Secretary of State may, if he thinks fit, cause him to be registered as such a citizen.

(2) A person born outside the United Kingdom and the qualifying territories shall be entitled, on an application for his registration as a British citizen made within the period of tUKlve months from the date of birth, to be registered as such a citizen if the requirements specified in subsection (3) or, in the case of a person born stateless, the requirements specified in paragraphs (a) and (b) of that subsection, are fulfilled in the case of either that person's father or his mother ("the parent in question").

(3) The requirements referred to in subsection (2) are--
(a) that the parent in question was a British citizen by descent at the time of the birth; and
(b) that the father or mother of the parent in question--
(i) was a British citizen otherwise than by descent at the time of the birth of the parent in question; or
(ii) became a British citizen otherwise than by descent at commencement, or would have become such a citizen otherwise than by descent at commencement but for his or her death; and
(c) that, as regards some period of three years ending with a date not later than the date of the birth--
(i) the parent in question was in the United Kingdom or a qualifying territory at the beginning of that period; and
(ii) the number of days on which the parent in question was absent from the United Kingdom and the qualifying territories in that period does not exceed 270.

(4) If in the special circumstances of any particular case the Secretary of State thinks fit, he may treat subsection (2) as if the reference to tUKlve months UKre a reference to six years.

(5) A person born outside the United Kingdom and the qualifying territories shall be entitled, on an application for his registration as a British citizen made while he is a minor, to be registered as such a citizen if the following requirements are satisfied, namely--
(a) that at the time of that person's birth his father or mother was a British citizen by descent; and

(b) subject to subsection (6), that that person and his father and mother UKre in the United Kingdom[or a qualifying territory] [FN1] at the beginning of the period of three years ending with the date of the application and that, in the case of each of them, the number of days on which the person in question was absent from the United Kingdom[and the qualifying territories] [FN2] in that period does not exceed 270; and
(c) subject to subsection (6), that the consent of his father and mother to the registration has been signified in the prescribed manner.

(6) In the case of an application under subsection (5) for the registration of a person as a British citizen--
(a) if his father or mother died, or their marriage was terminated, on or before the date of the application, or his father and mother UKre legally separated on that date, the references to his father and mother in paragraph (b) of that subsection shall be read either as references to his father or as references to his mother;
(b) if his father or mother died on or before that date, the reference to his father and mother in paragraph (c) of that subsection shall be read as a reference to either of them; and
(c) if he was born illegitimate, all those references shall be read as references to his mother.

s 4 Acquisition by registration: BRITISH OVERSEAS TERRITORIES CITIZENS etc.

(1) This section applies to any person who is a [British overseas territories citizen] [FN2], a British National (Overseas), a British Overseas citizen, a British subject under this Act or a British protected person.

(2) A person to whom this section applies shall be entitled, on an application for his registration as a British citizen, to be registered as such a citizen if the following requirements are satisfied in the case of that person, namely--

(a) subject to subsection (3), that he was in the United Kingdom at the beginning of the period of five years ending with the date of the application and that the number of days on which he was absent from the United Kingdom in that period does not exceed 450; and

(b) that the number of days on which he was absent from the United Kingdom in the period of tUKlve months so ending does not exceed 90; and

(c) that he was not at any time in the period of tUKlve months so ending subject under the immigration laws to any restriction on the period for which he might remain in the United Kingdom; and

(d) that he was not at any time in the period of five years so ending in the United Kingdom in breach of the immigration laws.

(3) So much of subsection (2)(a) as requires the person in question to have been in the United Kingdom at the beginning of the period there mentioned shall not apply in relation to a person who was settled in the United Kingdom immediately before commencement.

(4) If in the special circumstances of any particular case the Secretary of State thinks fit, he may for the purposes of subsection (2) do all or any of the following things, namely--

(a) treat the person to whom the application relates as fulfilling the requirement specified in subsection (2)(a) or subsection (2)(b), or both, although the number of days on which he was absent from the United Kingdom in the period there mentioned exceeds the number there mentioned;

(b) disregard any such restriction as is mentioned in subsection (2)(c), not being a restriction to which that person was subject on the date of the application;

(c) treat that person as fulfilling the requirement specified in subsection (2)(d) although he was in the United Kingdom in breach of the immigration laws in the period there mentioned.

(5) If, on an application for registration as a British citizen made by a person to whom this section applies, the Secretary of State is satisfied that the applicant has at any time served in service to which this subsection applies, he may, if he thinks fit in the special circumstances of the applicant's case, cause him to be registered as such a citizen.

(6) Subsection (5) applies to--

(a) Crown service under the government of a British overseas territory; and

(b) paid or unpaid service (not falling within paragraph (a)) as a member of any body established by law in a British overseas territory members of which are appointed by or on behalf of the Crown.

s 4A Acquisition by registration: further provision for British overseas territories citizens

4A Acquisition by registration: further provision for British overseas territories citizens
(1) If an application is made to register as a British citizen a person who is a British overseas territories citizen, the Secretary of State may if he thinks fit cause the person to be so registered.
(2) Subsection (1) does not apply in the case of a British overseas territories citizen who--
(a) is such a citizen by virtue only of a connection with the Sovereign Base Areas of Akrotiri and Dhekelia; or
(b) has ceased to be a British citizen as a result of a declaration of renunciation.

Notes:
Act amended by British Nationality (Hong Kong) Act 1990 (c.34), s. 2(1), British Nationality (Hong Kong) Act 1990 (c.34), s. 2(1); extended by British Nationality (Falkland Islands) Act 1983 (c.6), s. 3(1); restricted by British Nationality (Falkland Islands) Act 1983 (c.6), s. 3(2) and amended by S.I. 1983/1699, art. 2(1)

s 4B Acquisition by registration: certain persons without other citizenship

4B Acquisition by registration: certain persons without other citizenship
(1) This section applies to a person who has the status of--
(a) British Overseas citizen,
(b) British subject under this Act, or
(c) British protected person.

(2) A person to whom this section applies shall be entitled to be registered as a British citizen if--
(a) he applies for registration under this section,
(b) the Secretary of State is satisfied that the person does not have, apart from the status mentioned in subsection (1), any citizenship or nationality, and
(c) the Secretary of State is satisfied that the person has not after 4th July 2002 renounced, voluntarily relinquished or lost through action or inaction any citizenship or nationality.
] [FN1]
Notes:

Act amended by British Nationality (Hong Kong) Act 1990 (c.34), s. 2(1), British Nationality (Hong Kong) Act 1990 (c.34), s. 2(1); extended by British Nationality (Falkland Islands) Act 1983 (c.6), s. 3(1); restricted by British Nationality (Falkland Islands) Act 1983 (c.6), s. 3(2) and amended by S.I. 1983/1699, art. 2(1)

s 4C Acquisition by registration: certain persons born betUKen 1961 and 1983

4C Acquisition by registration: certain persons born betUKen 1961 and 1983
(1) A person is entitled to be registered as a British citizen if--
(a) he applies for registration under this section, and
(b) he satisfies each of the following conditions.

(2) The first condition is that the applicant was born after 7th February 1961 and before 1st January 1983.

(3) The second condition is that the applicant would at some time before 1st January 1983 have become a citizen of the United Kingdom and Colonies by virtue of section 5 of the British Nationality Act 1948 (c. 56) if that section had provided for citizenship by descent from a mother in the same terms as it provided for citizenship by descent from a father.

(4) The third condition is that immediately before 1st January 1983 the applicant would have had the right of abode in the United Kingdom by virtue of section 2 of the Immigration Act 1971 (c. 77) had he become a citizen of the United Kingdom and Colonies as described in subsection (3) above.

Act amended by British Nationality (Hong Kong) Act 1990 (c.34), s. 2(1), British Nationality (Hong Kong) Act 1990 (c.34), s. 2(1); extended by British Nationality (Falkland Islands) Act 1983 (c.6), s. 3(1); restricted by British Nationality (Falkland Islands) Act 1983 (c.6), s. 3(2) and amended by S.I. 1983/1699, art. 2(1)

s 5 Acquisition by registration: nationals for purposes of the Community Treaties.

A [British overseas territories citizen] [FN1] who falls to be treated as a national of the United Kingdom for the purposes of the Community Treaties shall be entitled to be registered as a British citizen if an application is made for his registration as such a citizen.

s 6 Acquisition by naturalisation.

(1) If, on an application for naturalisation as a British citizen made by a person of full age and capacity, the Secretary of State is satisfied that the applicant fulfils the requirements of Schedule 1 for naturalisation as such a citizen under this subsection, he may, if he thinks fit, grant to him a certificate of naturalisation as such a citizen.

(2) If, on an application for naturalisation as a British citizen made by a person of full age and capacity who on the date of the application is married to a British citizen, the Secretary of State is satisfied that the applicant fulfils the requirements of Schedule 1 for naturalisation as such a citizen under this subsection, he may, if he thinks fit, grant to him a certificate of naturalisation as such a citizen.
Notes:

Act amended by British Nationality (Hong Kong) Act 1990 (c.34), s. 2(1), British Nationality (Hong Kong) Act 1990 (c.34), s. 2(1); extended by British Nationality (Falkland Islands) Act 1983 (c.6), s.

3(1); restricted by British Nationality (Falkland Islands) Act 1983 (c.6), s. 3(2) and amended by S.I. 1983/1699, art. 2(1)

s 10 Registration following renunciation of citizenship of U.K. and Colonies.

(1) Subject to subsection (3), a person shall be entitled, on an application for his registration as a British citizen, to be registered as such a citizen if immediately before commencement he would (had he applied for it) have been entitled under section 1(1) of the British Nationality Act 1964 (resumption of citizenship) to be registered as a citizen of the United Kingdom and Colonies by virtue of having an appropriate qualifying connection with the United Kingdom or[...] [FN1] by virtue of having been married before commencement to a person who has, or would if living have, such a connection.

(2) On an application for his registration as a British citizen made by a person of full capacity who had before commencement ceased to be a citizen of the United Kingdom and Colonies as a result of a declaration of renunciation, the Secretary of State may, if he thinks fit, cause that person to be registered as a British citizen if that person--
(a) has an appropriate qualifying connection with the United Kingdom; or
(b) [...] [FN2]has been married to a person who has, or would if living have, such a connection.

(3) A person shall not be entitled to registration under subsection (1) on more than one occasion.
(4) For the purposes of this section a person shall be taken to have an appropriate qualifying connection with the United Kingdom if he, his father or his father's father--
(a) was born in the United Kingdom; or
(b) is or was a person naturalised in the United Kingdom; or
(c) was registered as a citizen of the United Kingdom and Colonies in the United Kingdom or in a country which at the time was mentioned in section 1(3) of the 1948 Act.

s 11 Citizens of U.K. and Colonies who are to become British citizens at commencement.

(1) Subject to subsection (2), a person who immediately before commencement--
(a) was a citizen of the United Kingdom and Colonies; and
(b) had the right of abode in the United Kingdom under the Immigration Act 1971 as then in force, shall at commencement become a British citizen.

(2) A person who was registered as a citizen of the United Kingdom and Colonies under section 1 of the British Nationality (No. 2) Act 1964 (stateless persons) on the ground mentioned in subsection (1)(a) of that section (namely that his mother was a citizen of the United Kingdom and Colonies at the time when he was born) shall not become a British citizen under subsection (1) unless--
(a) his mother becomes a British citizen under subsection (1) or would have done so but for her death; or
(b) immediately before commencement he had the right of abode in the United Kingdom by virtue of section 2(1)(c) of the Immigration Act 1971 as then in force (settlement in United Kingdom, combined with five or more years' ordinary residence there as a citizen of the United Kingdom and Colonies).
(3) A person who--
(a) immediately before commencement was a citizen of the United Kingdom and Colonies by virtue of having been registered under subsection (6) of section 12 of the 1948 Act (British subjects before commencement of 1948 Act becoming citizens of United Kingdom and Colonies) under arrangements made by virtue of subsection (7) of that section (registration in independent CommonUKalth country by United Kingdom High Commissioner); and

(b) was so registered on an application under the said subsection (6) based on the applicant's descent in the male line from a person ("the relevant person") possessing one of the qualifications specified in subsection (1)(a) and (b) of that section (birth or naturalisation in the United Kingdom and Colonies),
shall at commencement become a British citizen if the relevant person was born or naturalised in the United Kingdom.

Notes:
Act amended by British Nationality (Hong Kong) Act 1990 (c.34), s. 2(1), British Nationality (Hong Kong) Act 1990 (c.34), s. 2(1); extended by British Nationality (Falkland Islands) Act 1983 (c.6), s. 3(1); restricted by British Nationality (Falkland Islands) Act 1983 (c.6), s. 3(2) and amended by S.I. 1983/1699, art. 2(1)

s 12 Renunciation.

(1) If any British citizen of full age and capacity makes in the prescribed manner a declaration of renunciation of British citizenship, then, subject to subsections (3) and (4), the Secretary of State shall cause the declaration to be registered.
(2) On the registration of a declaration made in pursuance of this section the person who made it shall cease to be a British citizen.

(3) A declaration made by a person in pursuance of this section shall not be registered unless the Secretary of State is satisfied that the person who made it will after the registration have or acquire some citizenship or nationality other than British citizenship; and if that person does not have any such citizenship or nationality on the date of registration and does not acquire some such citizenship or nationality within six months from that date, he shall be, and be deemed to have remained, a British citizen notwithstanding the registration.

(4) The Secretary of State may withhold registration of any declaration made in pursuance of this section if it is made during any war in which Her Majesty may be engaged in right of Her Majesty's government in the United Kingdom.

(5) For the purposes of this section any person who has been married shall be deemed to be of full age.
Notes:
Act amended by British Nationality (Hong Kong) Act 1990 (c.34), s. 2(1), British Nationality (Hong Kong) Act 1990 (c.34), s. 2(1); extended by British Nationality (Falkland Islands) Act 1983 (c.6), s. 3(1); restricted by British Nationality (Falkland Islands) Act 1983 (c.6), s. 3(2) and amended by S.I. 1983/1699, art. 2(1)
S. 12 extended by S.I. 1986/948, art. 7(10).

s 13 Resumption.
(1) Subject to subsection (2), a person who has ceased to be a British citizen as a result of a declaration of renunciation shall be entitled, on an application for his registration as a British citizen, to be registered as such a citizen if--
(a) he is of full capacity; and
(b) his renunciation of British citizenship was necessary to enable him to retain or acquire some other citizenship or nationality.
(2) A person shall not be entitled to registration under subsection (1) on more than one occasion.
(3) If a person of full capacity who has ceased to be a British citizen as a result of a declaration of renunciation (for whatever reason made) makes an application for his registration as such a citizen, the Secretary of State may, if he thinks fit, cause him to be registered as such a citizen.
Notes:

Act amended by British Nationality (Hong Kong) Act 1990 (c.34), s. 2(1), British Nationality (Hong Kong) Act 1990 (c.34), s. 2(1); extended by British Nationality (Falkland Islands) Act 1983 (c.6), s.

3(1); restricted by British Nationality (Falkland Islands) Act 1983 (c.6), s. 3(2) and amended by S.I. 1983/1699, art. 2(1)

s 14 Meaning of British citizen "by descent".

(1) For the purposes of this Act a British citizen is a British citizen "by descent" if and only if--
(a) he is a person born outside the United Kingdom after commencement who is a British citizen by virtue of section 2(1)(a) only or by virtue of registration under section 3(2) or 9; or
(b) subject to subsection (2), he is a person born outside the United Kingdom before commencement who became a British citizen at commencement and immediately before commencement--

(i) was a citizen of the United Kingdom and Colonies by virtue of section 5 of the 1948 Act (citizenship by descent); or
(ii) was a person who, under any provision of the British Nationality Acts 1948 to 1965, was deemed for the purposes of the proviso to section 5(1) of the 1948 Act to be a citizen of the United Kingdom and Colonies by descent only, or would have been so deemed if male; or
(iii) had the right of abode in the United Kingdom by virtue only of paragraph (b) of subsection (1) of section 2 of the Immigration Act 1971 as then in force (connection with United Kingdom through parent or grandparent), or by virtue only of that paragraph and paragraph (c) of that subsection (settlement in United Kingdom with five years' ordinary residence there), or by virtue only of being or having been the wife of a person who immediately before commencement had that right by virtue only of the said paragraph (b) or the said paragraphs (b) and (c); or
(iv) being a woman, was a citizen of the United Kingdom and Colonies as a result of her registration as such a citizen under section 6(2) of the 1948 Act by virtue of having been married to a man who at commencement became a British citizen by descent or would have done so but for his having died or ceased to be a citizen of the United Kingdom and Colonies as a result of a declaration of renunciation; or
(c) he is a British citizen by virtue of registration under section 3(1) and either--
(i) his father or mother was a British citizen at the time of the birth; or
(ii) his father or mother was a citizen of the United Kingdom and Colonies at that time and became a British citizen at commencement, or would have done so but for his or her death; or
(d) he is a British citizen by virtue of registration under [section 4B, 4C or 5] [FN1]; or
(e) subject to subsection (2), being a woman born outside the United Kingdom before commencement, she is a British citizen as a result of her registration as such a citizen under section 8 by virtue of being or having been married to a man who at commencement became a British citizen by descent or would have done so but for his having died or ceased to be a citizen of the United Kingdom and Colonies as a result of a declaration of renunciation; or
(f) he is a British citizen by virtue of registration under section 10 who, having before commencement ceased to be a citizen of the United Kingdom and Colonies as a result of a declaration of renunciation, would, if he had not so ceased, have at commencement become a British citizen by descent by virtue of paragraph (b); or
(g) he is a British citizen by virtue of registration under section 13 who, immediately before he ceased to be a British citizen as a result of a declaration of renunciation, was such a citizen by descent; or
(h) he is a person born in a British overseas territory after commencement who is a British citizen by virtue of paragraph 2 of Schedule 2.

(2) A person born outside the United Kingdom before commencement is not a British citizen "by descent" by virtue of subsection (1)(b) or (e) if his father was at the time of his birth serving outside the United Kingdom--
(a) in service of a description mentioned in subsection (3), his recruitment for the service in question having taken place in the United Kingdom; or
(b) in service under a Community institution, his recruitment for that service having taken place in a country which at the time of the recruitment was a member of the Communities.

(3) The descriptions of service referred to in subsection (2) are--
(a) Crown service under the government of the United Kingdom; and
(b) service of any description at any time designated under section 2(3).

PART II BRITISH DEPENDENT TERRITORIES CITIZENSHIP

ACQUISITION AFTER COMMENCEMENT

s 15 Acquisition by birth or adoption.

(1) A person born in a British overseas territory after commencement shall be a [British overseas territories citizen] [FN1] if at the time of the birth his father or mother is--
(a) a [British overseas territories citizen] [FN2]; or
(b) settled in a British overseas territory.

(2) A new-born infant who, after commencement, is found abandoned in a British overseas territory shall, unless the contrary is shown, be deemed for the purposes of subsection (1)--
(a) to have been born in that territory after commencement; and
(b) to have been born to a parent who at the time of the birth was a [British overseas territories citizen] [FN3] or settled in a British overseas territory.

(3) A person born in a British overseas territory after commencement who is not a [British overseas territories citizen] [FN4] by virtue of subsection (1) or (2) shall be entitled to be registered as such a citizen if, while he is a minor--
(a) his father or mother becomes such a citizen or becomes settled in a British overseas territory; and
(b) an application is made for his registration as such a citizen.

(4) A person born in a British overseas territory after commencement who is not a [British overseas territories citizen] [FN5] by virtue of subsection (1) or (2) shall be entitled, on an application for his registration as a [British overseas territories citizen] [FN6] made at any time after he has attained the age of ten years, to be registered as such a citizen if, as regards each of the first ten years of that person's life, the number of days on which he was absent from that territory in that year does not exceed 90.

(5) Where after commencement an order authorising the adoption of a minor who is not a [British overseas territories citizen] [FN7] is made by a court in any British overseas territory, he shall be a [British overseas territories citizen] [FN8] as from the date on which the order is made if the adopter or, in the case of a joint adoption, one of the adopters, is a [British overseas territories citizen] [FN9] on that date.

(6) Where an order in consequence of which any person became a [British overseas territories citizen] [FN10] by virtue of subsection (5) ceases to have effect, whether on annulment or otherwise, the cesser shall not affect the status of that person as such a citizen.

(7) If in the special circumstances of any particular case the Secretary of State thinks fit, he may for the purposes of subsection (4) treat the person to whom the application relates as fulfilling the requirements specified in that subsection although, as regards any one or more of the first ten years of that person's life, the number of days on which he was absent from the British overseas territory there mentioned in that year or each of the years in question exceeds 90.

s 16 Acquisition by descent.

(1) A person born outside the British overseas territories after commencement shall be a [British overseas territories citizen] [FN1] if at the time of the birth his father or mother--
(a) is such a citizen otherwise than by descent; or
(b) is such a citizen and is serving outside the British overseas territories in service to which this paragraph applies, his or her recruitment for that service having taken place in a British overseas territory.

(2) Paragraph (b) of subsection (1) applies to--
(a) Crown service under the government of a British overseas territory; and
(b) service of any description for the time being designated under subsection (3).

(3) For the purposes of this section the Secretary of State may by order made by statutory instrument designate any description of service which he considers to be closely associated with the activities outside the British overseas territories of the government of any British overseas territory.
(4) Any order made under subsection (3) shall be subject to annulment in pursuance of a resolution of either House of Parliament.

s 17 Acquisition by registration: minors.

(1) If while a person is a minor an application is made for his registration as a [British overseas territories citizen] [FN1] the Secretary of State may, if the thinks fit, cause him to be registered as such a citizen.
(2) A person born outside the British overseas territories shall be entitled, on an application for his registration as a [British overseas territories citizen] [FN2] made within the period of tUKlve months from the date of the birth, to be registered as such a citizen if the requirements specified in subsection (3) or, in the case of a person born stateless, the requirements specified in paragraphs (a) and (b) of that subsection, are fulfilled in the case of either that person's father or his mother ("the parent in question").

(3) The requirements referred to in subsection (2) are--
(a) that the parent in question was a [British overseas territories citizen] [FN3] by descent at the time of the birth; and
(b) that the father or mother of the parent in question--
(i) was a [British overseas territories citizen] [FN4] otherwise than by descent at the time of the birth of the parent in question; or
(ii) became a [British overseas territories citizen] [FN5] otherwise than by descent at commencement, or would have become such a citizen otherwise than by descent at commencement but for his or her death; and
(c) that, as regards some period of three years ending with a date not later than the date of the birth--
(i) the parent in question was in a British overseas territory at the beginning of that period; and
(ii) the number of days on which the parent in question was absent from that territory in that period does not exceed 270.

(4) If in the special circumstances of any particular case the Secretary of State thinks fit, he may treat subsection (2) as if the reference to tUKlve months UKre a reference to six years.
(5) A person born outside the British overseas territories shall be entitled, and on application for his registration as a [British overseas territories citizen] [FN6] made while he is a minor, to be registered as such a citizen if the following requirements are satisfied, namely--
(a) that at the time of that person's birth his father or mother was a [British overseas territories citizen] [FN7] by descent; and
(b) subject to subsection (6), that that person and his father and mother UKre in one and the same British overseas territory (no matter which) at the beginning of the period of three years ending with the date of the application and that, in the case of each of them, the number of days on which the person in question was absent from the last-mentioned territory in that period does not exceed 270; and
(c) subject to subsection (6), that the consent of his father and mother to the registration has been signified in the prescribed manner.
(6) In the case of an application under subsection (5) for the registration of a person as a [British overseas territories citizen] [FN8]--
(a) if his father or mother died, or their marriage was terminated, on or before the date of the application, or his father and mother UKre legally separated on that date, the references to his father and mother in paragraph (b) of that subsection shall be read either as references to his father or as references to his mother;
(b) if his father or mother died on or before that date, the reference to his father and mother in paragraph (c) of that subsection shall be read as a reference to either of them; and
(c) if he was born illegitimate, all those references shall be read as references to his mother.

s 18 Acquisition by naturalisation.

(1) If, on an application for naturalisation as a [British overseas territories citizen] [FN1] made by a person of full age and capacity, the Secretary of State is satisfied that the applicant fulfils the requirements of Schedule 1 for naturalisation as such a citizen under this subsection, he may, if he thinks fit, grant to him a certificate of naturalisation as such a citizen.

(2) If, on an application for naturalisation as a [British overseas territories citizen] [FN2] made by a person of full age and capacity who on the date of the application is married to such a citizen, the Secretary of State is satisfied that the applicant fulfils the requirements of Schedule 1 for naturalisation as such a citizen under this subsection, he may, if he thinks fit, grant to him a certificate of naturalisation as such a citizen.
(3) Every application under this section shall specify the British overseas territory which is to be treated as the relevant territory for the purposes of that application; and, in relation to any such application, references in Schedule 1 to the relevant territory shall be construed accordingly.

s 22 Right to registration replacing right to resume citizenship of U.K. and Colonies.

(1) Subject to subsection (3), a person shall be entitled, on an application for his registration as a British overseas territories citizen, to be registered as such a citizen if immediately before commencement he would (had he applied for it) have been entitled under section 1(1) of the British Nationality Act 1964 (resumption of citizenship) to be registered as a citizen of the United Kingdom and Colonies by virtue of having an appropriate qualifying connection with a British overseas territory or[...] [FN1] by virtue of having been married before commencement to a person who has, or would if living have, such a connection.

(2) On an application for his registration as a British overseas territories citizen made by a person of full capacity who had before commencement ceased to be a citizen of the United Kingdom and

Colonies as a result of a declaration of renunciation, the Secretary of State may, if he thinks fit, cause that person to be registered as a British overseas territories citizen if that person--
(a) has an appropriate qualifying connection with a British overseas territory; or
(b) [...] [FN2]has been married to a person who has, or would if living have, such a connection.

(3) A person shall not be entitled to registration under subsection (1) on more than one occasion.

(4) For the purposes of this section a person shall be taken to have an appropriate qualifying connection with a British overseas territory if he, his father or his father's father--
(a) was born in that territory; or
(b) is or was a person naturalised in that territory; or
(c) was registered as a citizen of the United Kingdom and Colonies in that territory; or
(d) became a British subject by reason of the annexation of any territory included in that territory.

[FN1] words repealed by Nationality, Immigration and Asylum Act (2002 c.41), Sch 9 Para 1

s 23 Citizens of U.K. and Colonies who are to become British overseas territories citizens at commencement.

(1) A person shall at commencement become a [British overseas territories citizen] [FN2] if--
(a) immediately before commencement he was a citizen of the United Kingdom and Colonies who had that citizenship by his birth, naturalisation or registration in a British overseas territory; or
(b) he was immediately before commencement a citizen of the United Kingdom and Colonies, and was born to a parent--
(i) who at the time of the birth ("the material time") was a citizen of the United Kingdom and Colonies; and
(ii) who either had that citizenship at the material time by his birth, naturalisation or registration in a British overseas territory or was himself born to a parent who at the time of that birth so had that citizenship; or
(c) being a woman, she was immediately before commencement a citizen of the United Kingdom and Colonies and either was then, or had at any time been, the wife of a man who under paragraph (a) or (b) becomes a [British overseas territories citizen] [FN3] at commencement or would have done so but for his death.
(2) A person shall at commencement become a [British overseas territories citizen] [FN4] if--
(a) immediately before commencement he was a citizen of the United Kingdom and Colonies by virtue of registration under section 7 of the 1948 Act (minor children) or section 1 of the British Nationality (No. 2) Act 1964 (stateless persons); and
(b) he was so registered otherwise than in a British overseas territory; and
(c) his father or mother (in the case of a person registered under the said section 7) or his mother (in the case of a person registered under the said section 1)--
(i) was a citizen of the United Kingdom and Colonies at the time of the registration or would have been such a citizen at that time but for his or her death; and
(ii) becomes a [British overseas territories citizen] [FN5] at commencement or would have done so but for his or her death.

(3) A person who--
(a) immediately before commencement was a citizen of the United Kingdom and Colonies by virtue of having been registered under subsection (6) of section 12 of the 1948 Act (British subjects before commencement of 1948 Act becoming citizens of United Kingdom and Colonies) otherwise than in a British overseas territory; and
(b) was so registered on an application under that subsection based on the applicant's descent in the male line from a person ("the relevant person") possessing one of the qualifications specified

in subsection (1) of that section (birth or naturalisation in the United Kingdom and Colonies, or acquisition of the status of British subject by reason of annexation of territory),
shall at commencement become a [British overseas territories citizen] [FN6] if the relevant person--
(i) was born or naturalised in a British overseas territory; or
(ii) became a British subject by reason of the annexation of any territory included in a British overseas territory.

(4) A person who--
(a) immediately before commencement was a citizen of the United Kingdom and Colonies by virtue of registration under section 1 of the British Nationality Act 1964 (resumption of citizenship); and
(b) was so registered otherwise than in a British overseas territory; and
(c) was so registered by virtue of having an appropriate qualifying connection with a British overseas territory or, if a woman, by virtue of having been married to a person who at the time of the registration had or would, if then living, have had such a connection,
shall at commencement become a [British overseas territories citizen] [FN7].

(5) For the purposes of subsection (4) a person shall be taken to have an appropriate qualifying connection with a British overseas territory if he, his father or his father's father--
(a) was born in a British overseas territory; or
(b) is or was a person naturalised in a British overseas territory; or
(c) was registered as a citizen of the United Kingdom and Colonies in a British overseas territory; or
(d) became a British subject by reason of the annexation of any territory included in a British overseas territory.

(6) For the purposes of subsection (1)(b) references to citizenship of the United Kingdom and Colonies shall, in relation to a time before the year 1949, be construed as references to British nationality.

s 24 Renunciation and resumption.

The provisions of sections 12 and 13 shall apply in relation to [British overseas territories citizens] [FN1] and [British overseas territories citizenship] [FN2] as they apply in relation to British citizens and British citizenship.
s 25 Meaning of British overseas territories citizen "by descent".

(1) For the purposes of this Act a [British overseas territories citizen] [FN2] is such a citizen "by descent" if and only if--
(a) he is a person born outside the British overseas territories after commencement who is a [British overseas territories citizen] [FN3] by virtue of section 16(1)(a) only or by virtue of registration under section 17(2) or 21; or
(b) subject to subsection (2), he is a person born outside the British overseas territories before commencement who became a [British overseas territories citizen] [FN4] at commencement and immediately before commencement--
(i) was a citizen of the United Kingdom and Colonies by virtue of section 5 of the 1948 Act (citizenship by descent); or
(ii) was a person who, under any provision of the British Nationality Acts 1948 to 1965, was deemed for the purposes of the proviso to section 5(1) of the 1948 Act to be a citizen of the United Kingdom and Colonies by descent only, or would have been so deemed if male; or
(c) he is a [British overseas territories citizen] [FN5] by virtue of registration under section 17(1) and either--

(i) his father or mother was a [British overseas territories citizen] [FN6] at the time of the birth; or
(ii) his father or mother was a citizen of the United Kingdom and Colonies at that time and became a [British overseas territories citizen] [FN7] at commencement, or would have done so but for his or her death; or
(d) subject to subsection (2), he is a person born outside the British overseas territories before commencement who became a [British overseas territories citizen] [FN8] at commencement under section 23(1)(b) only; or
(e) subject to subsection (2), being a woman, she became a [British overseas territories citizen] [FN9] at commencement under section 23(1)(c) only, and did so only by virtue of having been, immediately before commencement or earlier, the wife of a man who immediately after commencement was, or would but for his death have been, a [British overseas territories citizen] [FN10] by descent by virtue of paragraph (b) or (d) of this subsection; or
(f) subject to subsection (2), being a woman born outside the British overseas territories before commencement, she is a [British overseas territories citizen] [FN11] as a result of her registration as such a citizen under section 20 by virtue of being or having been married to a man who at commencement became such a citizen by descent or would have done so but for his having died or ceased to be a citizen of the United Kingdom and Colonies as a result of a declaration of renunciation; or
(g) he is a [British overseas territories citizen] [FN12] by virtue of registration under section 22 who, having before commencement ceased to be a citizen of the United Kingdom and Colonies as a result of a declaration of renunciation, would, if he had not so ceased, have at commencement become a [British overseas territories citizen] [FN13] by descent by virtue of paragraph (b), (d) or (e);
(h) he is a [British overseas territories citizen] [FN14] by virtue of registration under section 13 (as applied by section 24) who, immediately before he ceased to be a [British overseas territories citizen] [FN15] as a result of a declaration of renunciation, was such a citizen by descent; or
(i) he is a person born in the United Kingdom after commencement who is a [British overseas territories citizen] [FN16] by virtue of paragraph 1 of Schedule 2.

(2) A person born outside the British overseas territories before commencement is not a [British overseas territories citizen] [FN17] "by descent" by virtue of subsection (1)(b), (d), (e) or (f) if his father was at the time of his birth serving outside the British overseas territories in service of a description mentioned in subsection (3), his recruitment for the service in question having taken place in a British overseas territory.

(3) The descriptions of service referred to in subsection (2) are--
(a) Crown service under the government of a British overseas territory; and
(b) service of any description at any time designated under section 16(3).

PART III BRITISH OVERSEAS CITIZENSHIP

s 26 Citizens of U.K. and Colonies who are to become British Overseas citizens at commencement.

Any person who was a citizen of the United Kingdom and Colonies immediately before commencement and who does not at commencement become either a British citizen or a [British overseas territories citizen] [FN1] shall at commencement become a British Overseas citizen.

s 27 Registration of minors.

(1) If while a person is a minor an application is made for his registration as a British Overseas citizen, the Secretary of State may, if he thinks fit, cause him to be registered as such a citizen.

s 29 Renunciation.

The provisions of section 12 shall apply in relation to British Overseas citizens and British Overseas citizenship as they apply in relation to British citizens and British citizenship.
Notes:
Act amended by British Nationality (Hong Kong) Act 1990 (c.34), s. 2(1), British Nationality (Hong Kong) Act 1990 (c.34), s. 2(1); extended by British Nationality (Falkland Islands) Act 1983 (c.6), s. 3(1); restricted by British Nationality (Falkland Islands) Act 1983 (c.6), s. 3(2) and amended by S.I. 1983/1699, art. 2(1)

PART IV BRITISH SUBJECTS

s 30 Continuance as British subjects of existing British subjects of certain descriptions.

A person who immediately before commencement was--
(a) a British subject without citizenship by virtue of section 13 or 16 of the 1948 Act; or
(b) a British subject by virtue of section 1 of the British Nationality Act 1965 (registration of alien women who have been married to British subjects of certain descriptions),
shall as from commencement be a British subject by virtue of this section.
Notes:
Act amended by British Nationality (Hong Kong) Act 1990 (c.34), s. 2(1), British Nationality (Hong Kong) Act 1990 (c.34), s. 2(1); extended by British Nationality (Falkland Islands) Act 1983 (c.6), s. 3(1); restricted by British Nationality (Falkland Islands) Act 1983 (c.6), s. 3(2) and amended by S.I. 1983/1699, art. 2(1)

s 31 Continuance as British subjects of certain former citizens of Eire.

(1) A person is within this subsection if immediately before 1st January 1949 he was both a citizen of Eire and a British subject.
(2) A person within subsection (1) who immediately before commencement was a British subject by virtue of section 2 of the 1948 Act (continuance of certain citizens of Eire as British subjects) shall as from commencement be a British subject by virtue of this subsection.

(3) If at any time after commencement a citizen of the Republic of Ireland who is within subsection (1) but is not a British subject by virtue of subsection (2) gives notice in writing to the Secretary of State claiming to remain a British subject on either or both of the following grounds, namely--
(a) that he is or has been in Crown Service under the government of the United Kingdom; and
(b) that he has associations by way of descent, residence or otherwise with the United Kingdom or with any [British overseas territory] [FN1],
he shall as from that time be a British subject by virtue of this subsection.

(4) A person who is a British subject by virtue of subsection (2) or (3) shall be deemed to have remained a British subject from 1st January 1949 to the time when (whether already a British subject by virtue of the said section 2 or not) he became a British subject by virtue of that subsection.

s 32 Registration of minors.

If while a person is a minor an application is made for his registration as a British subject, the Secretary of State may, if he thinks fit, cause him to be registered as a British subject.

Notes:
Act amended by British Nationality (Hong Kong) Act 1990 (c.34), s. 2(1), British Nationality (Hong Kong) Act 1990 (c.34), s. 2(1); extended by British Nationality (Falkland Islands) Act 1983 (c.6), s. 3(1); restricted by British Nationality (Falkland Islands) Act 1983 (c.6), s. 3(2) and amended by S.I. 1983/1699, art. 2(1)

s 34 Renunciation.

The provisions of section 12 shall apply in relation to British subjects and the status of a British subject as they apply in relation to British citizens and British citizenship.
Notes:
Act amended by British Nationality (Hong Kong) Act 1990 (c.34), s. 2(1), British Nationality (Hong Kong) Act 1990 (c.34), s. 2(1); extended by British Nationality (Falkland Islands) Act 1983 (c.6), s. 3(1); restricted by British Nationality (Falkland Islands) Act 1983 (c.6), s. 3(2) and amended by S.I. 1983/1699, art. 2(1)

s 35 Circumstances in which British subjects are to lose that status.

A person who under this Act is a British subject otherwise than by virtue of section 31 shall cease to be such a subject if, in whatever circumstances and whether under this Act or otherwise, he acquires any other citizenship or nationality whatever.
Notes:
Act amended by British Nationality (Hong Kong) Act 1990 (c.34), s. 2(1), British Nationality (Hong Kong) Act 1990 (c.34), s. 2(1); extended by British Nationality (Falkland Islands) Act 1983 (c.6), s. 3(1); restricted by British Nationality (Falkland Islands) Act 1983 (c.6), s. 3(2) and amended by S.I. 1983/1699, art. 2(1)

PART V MISCELLANEOUS AND SUPPLEMENTARY

s 36 Provisions for reducing statelessness.

The provisions of Schedule 2 shall have effect for the purpose of reducing statelessness.
Notes:
Act amended by British Nationality (Hong Kong) Act 1990 (c.34), s. 2(1), British Nationality (Hong Kong) Act 1990 (c.34), s. 2(1); extended by British Nationality (Falkland Islands) Act 1983 (c.6), s. 3(1); restricted by British Nationality (Falkland Islands) Act 1983 (c.6), s. 3(2) and amended by S.I. 1983/1699, art. 2(1)
PoUKr of appointment conferred by s. 53(2) not exercised

s 37 CommonUKalth citizenship.

(1) Every person who--
(a) under the British Nationality Acts 1981 and 1983[or the British Overseas Territories Act 2002] [FN1] is a British citizen, a British overseas territories citizen, a British National (Overseas),a British Overseas citizen or a British subject; or
(b) under any enactment for the time being in force in any country mentioned in Schedule 3 is a citizen of that country,
shall have the status of a CommonUKalth citizen.

(2) Her Majesty may by Order in Council amend Schedule 3 by the alteration of any entry, the removal of any entry, or the insertion of any additional entry.

(3) Any Order in Council made under this section shall be subject to annulment in pursuance of a resolution of either House of Parliament.

(4) After commencement no person shall have the status of a CommonUKalth citizen or the status of a British subject otherwise than under this Act.

s 38 British protected persons.

(1) Her Majesty may by Order in Council made in relation to any territory which was at any time before commencement--
(a) a protectorate or protected state for the purposes of the 1948 Act; or
(b) a United Kingdom trust territory within the meaning of that Act,
declare to be British protected persons for the purposes of this Act any class of persons who are connected with that territory and are not citizens of any country mentioned in Schedule 3 which consists of or includes that territory.

(2) Any Order in Council made under this section shall be subject to annulment in pursuance of a resolution of either House of Parliament.
Notes:
Act amended by British Nationality (Hong Kong) Act 1990 (c.34), s. 2(1), British Nationality (Hong Kong) Act 1990 (c.34), s. 2(1); extended by British Nationality (Falkland Islands) Act 1983 (c.6), s. 3(1); restricted by British Nationality (Falkland Islands) Act 1983 (c.6), s. 3(2) and amended by S.I. 1983/1699, art. 2(1)
PoUKr of appointment conferred by s. 53(2) not exercised

s 39 Amendment of Immigration Act 1971.

(8) A certificate of partiality issued under the Immigration Act 1971 and in force immediately before commencement shall have effect after commencement as if it UKre a certificate of entitlement issued under that Act [as in force after commencement] [FN8], unless at commencement the holder ceases to have the right of abode in the United Kingdom.
Notes:
Act amended by British Nationality (Hong Kong) Act 1990 (c.34), s. 2(1), British Nationality (Hong Kong) Act 1990 (c.34), s. 2(1); extended by British Nationality (Falkland Islands) Act 1983 (c.6), s. 3(1); restricted by British Nationality (Falkland Islands) Act 1983 (c.6), s. 3(2) and amended by S.I. 1983/1699, art. 2(1)
PoUKr of appointment conferred by s. 53(2) not exercised

s 40 Deprivation of citizenship

40 Deprivation of citizenship
(1) In this section a reference to a person's "citizenship status" is a reference to his status as--
(a) a British citizen,
(b) a British overseas territories citizen,
(c) a British Overseas citizen,
(d) a British National (Overseas),
(e) a British protected person, or
(f) a British subject.

(2) The Secretary of State may by order deprive a person of a citizenship status if the Secretary of State is satisfied that the person has done anything seriously prejudicial to the vital interests of--

(a) the United Kingdom, or

(b) a British overseas territory.
(3) The Secretary of State may by order deprive a person of a citizenship status which results from his registration or naturalisation if the Secretary of State is satisfied that the registration or naturalisation was obtained by means of--
(a) fraud,
(b) false representation, or
(c) concealment of a material fact.
(4) The Secretary of State may not make an order under subsection (2) if he is satisfied that the order would make a person stateless.
(5) Before making an order under this section in respect of a person the Secretary of State must give the person written notice specifying--
(a) that the Secretary of State has decided to make an order,
(b) the reasons for the order, and
(c) the person's right of appeal under section 40A(1) or under section 2B of the Special Immigration Appeals Commission Act 1997 (c. 68).
(6) Where a person acquired a citizenship status by the operation of a law which applied to him because of his registration or naturalisation under an enactment having effect before commencement, the Secretary of State may by order deprive the person of the citizenship status if the Secretary of State is satisfied that the registration or naturalisation was obtained by means of--
(a) fraud,
(b) false representation, or
(c) concealment of a material fact.

s 40A Deprivation of citizenship: appeal

40A Deprivation of citizenship: appeal
(1) A person who is given notice under section 40(5) of a decision to make an order in respect of him under section 40 may appeal against the decision to an adjudicator appointed under section 81 of the Nationality, Immigration and Asylum Act 2002 (immigration appeal).

(2) Subsection (1) shall not apply to a decision if the Secretary of State certifies that it was taken wholly or partly in reliance on information which in his opinion should not be made public--
(a) in the interests of national security,
(b) in the interests of the relationship betUKen the United Kingdom and another country, or
(c) otherwise in the public interest.

(3) A party to an appeal to an adjudicator under subsection (1) may, with the permission of the Immigration Appeal Tribunal, appeal to the Tribunal against the adjudicator's determination on a point of law.

(4) A party to an appeal to the Immigration Appeal Tribunal under subsection (3) may bring a further appeal on a point of law--
(a) where the decision of the adjudicator was made in Scotland, to the Court of Session, or
(b) in any other case, to the Court of Appeal.

(5) An appeal under subsection (4) may be brought only with the permission of--
(a) the Tribunal, or
(b) if the Tribunal refuses permission, the court referred to in subsection (4)(a) or (b).

(6) An order under section 40 may not be made in respect of a person while an appeal under this section or section 2B of the Special Immigration Appeals Commission Act 1997 (c. 68)--
(a) has been instituted and has not yet been finally determined, withdrawn or abandoned, or

(b) could be brought (ignoring any possibility of an appeal out of time with permission).

(7) Rules under section 106 of the Nationality, Immigration and Asylum Act 2002 (immigration appeal: rules) may make provision about an appeal under this section.
(8) Directions under section 107 of that Act (practice directions) may make provision about an appeal under this section.

Notes:
Act amended by British Nationality (Hong Kong) Act 1990 (c.34), s. 2(1), British Nationality (Hong Kong) Act 1990 (c.34), s. 2(1); extended by British Nationality (Falkland Islands) Act 1983 (c.6), s. 3(1); restricted by British Nationality (Falkland Islands) Act 1983 (c.6), s. 3(2) and amended by S.I. 1983/1699, art. 2(1)
PoUKr of appointment conferred by s. 53(2) not exercised

s 41 Regulations and Orders in Council.

(1) The Secretary of State may by regulations make provision generally for carrying into effect the purposes of this Act, and in particular provision--
(a) for prescribing anything which under this Act is to be prescribed;
(b) for prescribing the manner in which, and the persons to and by whom, applications for registration or naturalisation under any provision of this Act may or must be made;
(c) for the registration of anything required or authorised by or under this Act to be registered;
(d) for the administration and taking of oaths of allegiance under this Act, as to the time within which oaths of allegiance must be taken, and for the registration of oaths of allegiance;
(e) for the giving of any notice required or authorised to be given to any person under this Act;
(f) for the cancellation of the registration of, and the cancellation and amendment of certificates of naturalisation relating to, persons deprived of citizenship or of the status of a British National (Overseas)under this Act, and for requiring such certificates to be delivered up for those purposes;
(g) for the births and deaths of persons of any class or description born or dying in a country mentioned in Schedule 3 to be registered there by the High Commissioner for Her Majesty's government in the United Kingdom or by members of his official staff;
(h) for the births and deaths of persons of any class or description born or dying in a foreign country to be registered there by consular officers or other officers in the service of Her Majesty's government in the United Kingdom;
(i) for enabling the births and deaths of British citizens, [British overseas territories citizens] [FN1], British Nationals (Overseas),British Overseas citizens, British subjects and British protected persons born or dying in any country in which Her Majesty's government in the United Kingdom has for the time being no diplomatic or consular representatives to be registered--
(i) by persons serving in the diplomatic, consular or other foreign service of any country which, by arrangement with Her Majesty's government in the United Kingdom, has undertaken to represent that government's interest in that country, or
(ii) by a person authorised in that behalf by the Secretary of State.

(2) The Secretary of State may with the consent of the Treasury by regulations make provision for the imposition, recovery and application of fees in connection with any of the following matters, namely--
(a) any application made to the Secretary of State under this Act;other than an application for the purpose of acquiring the status of a British National (Overseas).
(b) the effecting in the United Kingdom of any registration authorised by or under this Act;other than registration as a British National (Overseas)

(c) the making in the United Kingdom of any declaration, the grant there of any certificate, or the taking there of any oath of allegiance authorised to be made, granted or taken by or under this Act;
(d) the supplying in the United Kingdom of a certified or other copy of any notice, certificate, order, declaration or entry given, granted or made under or by virtue of this Act or any of the former nationality Acts;
(e) the carrying out of searches in or of any registers or other records, being registers or records held in the United Kingdom by or on behalf of the Secretary of State, which are or may be relevant for the purpose of determining the status of any person under this Act or any of the former nationality Acts;
(f) the supplying by or on behalf of the Secretary of State of an opinion in writing concerning the status of any person under this Act or any of the former nationality Acts, or a certified or other copy of such an opinion.

(3) Regulations under subsection (1) or (2) may make different provision for different circumstances; and--
(a) regulations under subsection (1) may provide for the extension of any time-limit for the taking of oaths of allegiance; and
(b) regulations under subsection (2) may provide for any fees imposed by the regulations to be payable at such times as may be prescribed.

(4) Her Majesty may by Order in Council provide for any Act or Northern Ireland legislation to which this subsection applies to apply, with such adaptations and modifications as appear to Her necessary, to births and deaths registered--
(a) in accordance with regulations made in pursuance of subsection (1)(g) to (i) of this section or subsection (1)(f) and (g) of section 29 of the 1948 Act; or
(b) at a consulate of Her Majesty in accordance with regulations made under the British Nationality and Status of Aliens Acts 1914 to 1943 or in accordance with instructions of the Secretary of State; or
(c) by a High Commissioner for Her Majesty's government in the United Kingdom or members of his official staff in accordance with instructions of the Secretary of State;
and an Order in Council under this subsection may exclude, in relation to births and deaths so registered, any of the provisions of section 45.

(5) Subsection (4) applies to--
(a) the Births and Deaths Registration Act 1953, the Registration Service Act 1953 and the Registration of Births, Deaths and Marriages (Scotland) Act 1965; and
(b) so much of any Northern Ireland legislation for the time being in force (whether passed or made before or after commencement) as relates to the registration of births and deaths.

(6) The poUKr to make regulations under subsection (1) or (2) shall be exercisable by statutory instrument.
(7) Any regulations or Order in Council made under this section shall be subject to annulment in pursuance of a resolution of either House of Parliament.

s 42 Registration and naturalisation: general provisions.

(1) Subject to subsection (2)--
(a) a person shall not be registered under any provision of this Act as a citizen of any description or as a British subject; and
(b) a certificate of naturalisation shall not be granted to a person under any provision of this Act, unless--

(i) any fee payable by virtue of this Act in connection with the registration or, as the case may be, the grant of the certificate has been paid; and
(ii) the person concerned has within the prescribed time taken an oath of allegiance in the form indicated in Schedule 5.

(2) So much of subsection (1) as requires the taking of an oath of allegiance shall not apply to a person who--
(a) is not of full age; or
(b) is already a British citizen, a [British overseas territories citizen] [FN1], a British National (Overseas) a British Overseas citizen, a British subject, or a citizen of any country of which Her Majesty is Queen.

(3) Any provision of this Act which provides for a person to be entitled to registration as a citizen of any description or as a British subject shall have effect subject to the preceding provisions of this section.

(4) A person registered under any provision of this Act as a British citizen, or as a [British overseas territories citizen] [FN2] or as a British Overseas citizen, or as a British National (Overseas), or as a British subject, shall be a citizen of that description or, as the case may be, a British National (Overseas) ora British subject as from the date on which he is so registered.

(5) A person to whom a certificate of naturalisation as a British citizen or as a [British overseas territories citizen] [FN3] is granted under any provision of this Act shall be a citizen of that description as from the date on which the certificate is granted.

(6) A person who applies for registration or naturalisation as a [British overseas territories citizen] [FN4] under any provision of this Act by virtue (wholly or partly) of his having a connection with Hong Kong, may not be naturalised or registered, as the case may be, unless he makes his application on or before 31st March 1996.

s 43 Exercise of functions of Secretary of State by Governors and others.

(1) Subject to subsection (3), the Secretary of State may, in the case of any of his functions under this Act with respect to any of the matters mentioned in subsection (2), make arrangements for that function to be exercised--
(a) in any of the Islands, by the Lieutenant-Governor in cases concerning British citizens or British citizenship;
(b) in any British overseas territory, by the Governor in cases concerning [British overseas territories citizens] [FN1] or [British overseas territories citizenship] [FN2]and in cases concerning British Nationals (Overseas) or the status of a British National (Overseas).

(2) The said matters are--
(a) registration and naturalisation; and
(b) renunciation, resumption and deprivation of British citizenship or [British overseas territories citizenship] [FN3].
(c) renunciation and deprivation of the status of a British National (Overseas).

(3) Nothing in this section applies in the case of any poUKr to make regulations or rules conferred on the Secretary of State by this Act.
(4) Arrangements under subsection (1) may provide for any such function as is there mentioned to be exercisable only with the approval of the Secretary of State.

(1) Any discretion vested by or under this Act in the Secretary of State, a Governor or a Lieutenant-Governor shall be exercised without regard to the race, colour or religion of any person who may be affected by its exercise.

s 45 Evidence.

(1) Every document purporting to be a notice, certificate, order or declaration, or an entry in a register, or a subscription of an oath of allegiance, given, granted or made under this Act or any of the former nationality Acts shall be received in evidence and shall, unless the contrary is proved, be deemed to have been given, granted or made by or on behalf of the person by whom or on whose behalf it purports to have been given, granted or made.

(2) Prima facie evidence of any such document may be given by the production of a document purporting to be certified as a true copy of it by such person and in such manner as may be prescribed.

(3) Any entry in a register made under this Act or any of the former nationality Acts shall be received as evidence (and in Scotland as sufficient evidence) of the matters stated in the entry.
(4) A certificate given by or on behalf of the Secretary of State that a person was at any time in Crown service under the government of the United Kingdom or that a person's recruitment for such service took place in the United Kingdom shall, for the purposes of this Act, be conclusive evidence of that fact.
Notes:

Act amended by British Nationality (Hong Kong) Act 1990 (c.34), s. 2(1), British Nationality (Hong Kong) Act 1990 (c.34), s. 2(1); extended by British Nationality (Falkland Islands) Act 1983 (c.6), s.

3(1); restricted by British Nationality (Falkland Islands) Act 1983 (c.6), s. 3(2) and amended by S.I. 1983/1699, art. 2(1)
PoUKr of appointment conferred by s. 53(2) not exercised
S. 45 extended by British Nationality (Falkland Islands) Act 1983 (c.6), s. 4(2)(a)-(f), British Nationality (Hong Kong) Act 1990 (c.34), s. 2(3); amended by S.I. 1986/948, art. 7(7)(a)

s 46 Offences and proceedings.

(1) Any person who for the purpose of procuring anything to be done or not to be done under this Act--
(a) makes any statement which he knows to be false in a material particular; or
(b) recklessly makes any statement which is false in a material particular,
shall be liable on summary conviction in the United Kingdom to imprisonment for a term not exceeding three months or to a fine not exceeding [level 5 on the standard scale] [FN1], or both.

(2) Any person who without reasonable excuse fails to comply with any requirement imposed on him by regulations made under this Act with respect to the delivering up of certificates of naturalisation shall be liable on summary conviction in the United Kingdom to a fine not exceeding [level 4 on the standard scale] [FN2].

(3) In the case of an offence under subsection (1)--
(a) any information relating to the offence may in England and Wales be tried by a magistrates' court if it is laid within six months after the commission of the offence, or if it is laid within three years after the commission of the offence and not more than two months after the date certified by a chief officer of police to be the date on which evidence sufficient to justify proceedings came to the notice of an officer of his police force; and

(b) summary proceedings for the offence may in Scotland be commenced within six months after the commission of the offence, or within three years after the commission of the offence and not more than two months after the date on which evidence sufficient in the opinion of the Lord Advocate to justify proceedings came to his knowledge; and
(c) a complaint charging the commission of the offence may in Northern Ireland be heard and determined by a magistrates' court if it is made within six months after the commission of the offence, or if it is made within three years after the commission of the offence and not more than two months after the date certified by an officer of police not below the rank of assistant chief constable to be the date on which evidence sufficient to justify the proceedings came to the notice of the police in Northern Ireland.
(4) For the purposes of subsection (3)(b) proceedings shall be deemed to be commenced on the date on which a warrant to apprehend or to cite the accused is granted, if such warrant is executed without undue delay; and a certificate of the Lord Advocate as to the date on which such evidence as is mentioned in subsection (3)(b) came to his knowledge shall be conclusive evidence.
(5) For the purposes of the trial of a person for an offence under subsection (1) or (2), the offence shall be deemed to have been committed either at the place at which it actually was committed or at any place at which he may be.
(6) In their application to the Bailiwick of Jersey subsections (1) and (2) shall have effect with the omission of the words "on summary conviction".

Notes:
Act amended by British Nationality (Hong Kong) Act 1990 (c.34), s. 2(1), British Nationality (Hong Kong) Act 1990 (c.34), s. 2(1); extended by British Nationality (Falkland Islands) Act 1983 (c.6), s. 3(1); restricted by British Nationality (Falkland Islands) Act 1983 (c.6), s. 3(2) and amended by S.I. 1983/1699, art. 2(1)
PoUKr of appointment conferred by s. 53(2) not exercised
S. 46 extended by British Nationality (Falkland Islands) Act 1983 (c.6), s. 4(2)(a)-(f); British Nationality (Hong Kong) Act 1990 (c.34), s. 2(3)
S. 46(1) amended by S.I. 1986/948, art. 7(7)(b)

[FN1] Words substituted by Criminal Justice Act 1982 (c.48), s. 46, Criminal Procedure (Scotland) Act 1975 (c.21), s. 289G and S.I. 1984/703 (N.I. 3), art. 5

[FN2] Words substituted by Criminal Justice Act 1982 (c.48), s. 46, Criminal Procedure (Scotland) Act 1975 (c.21), s. 289G and S.I. 1984/703 (N.I. 3), art. 5

s 47 Legitimated children.

(1) A person born out of UKdlock and legitimated by the subsequent marriage of his parents shall, as from the date of the marriage, be treated for the purposes of this Act as if he had been born legitimate.

(2) A person shall be deemed for the purposes of this section to have been legitimated by the subsequent marriage of his parents if by the law of the place in which his father was domiciled at the time of the marriage the marriage operated immediately or subsequently to legitimate him, and not otherwise.
Notes:

Act amended by British Nationality (Hong Kong) Act 1990 (c.34), s. 2(1), British Nationality (Hong Kong) Act 1990 (c.34), s. 2(1); extended by British Nationality (Falkland Islands) Act 1983 (c.6), s.

3(1); restricted by British Nationality (Falkland Islands) Act 1983 (c.6), s. 3(2) and amended by S.I. 1983/1699, art. 2(1)
PoUKr of appointment conferred by s. 53(2) not exercised

S.47 extended by British Nationality (Falkland Islands) Act 1983 (c.6), s. 4(2)(a)-(f), British Nationality (Hong Kong) Act 1990 (c.34), s. 2(3); amended by S.I. 1986/948, art. 7(7)(c)

s 48 Posthumous children.

Any reference in this Act to the status or description of the father or mother of a person at the time of that person's birth shall, in relation to a person born after the death of his father or mother, be construed as a reference to the status or description of the parent in question at the time of that parent's death; and where that death occurred before, and the birth occurs after, commencement, the status or description which would have been applicable to the father or mother had he or she died after commencement shall be deemed to be the status or description applicable to him or her at the time of his or her death.

Notes:
Act amended by British Nationality (Hong Kong) Act 1990 (c.34), s. 2(1), British Nationality (Hong Kong) Act 1990 (c.34), s. 2(1); extended by British Nationality (Falkland Islands) Act 1983 (c.6), s. 3(1); restricted by British Nationality (Falkland Islands) Act 1983 (c.6), s. 3(2) and amended by S.I. 1983/1699, art. 2(1)
PoUKr of appointment conferred by s. 53(2) not exercised
S. 48 extended by British Nationality (Falkland Islands) Act 1983 (c.6), s. 4(2)(a)-(f), British Nationality (Hong Kong) Act 1990 (c.34), s. 2(3); amended by S.I. 1986/948, art. 7(7)(c)

Act amended by British Nationality (Hong Kong) Act 1990 (c.34), s. 2(1), British Nationality (Hong Kong) Act 1990 (c.34), s. 2(1); extended by British Nationality (Falkland Islands) Act 1983 (c.6), s. 3(1); restricted by British Nationality (Falkland Islands) Act 1983 (c.6), s. 3(2) and amended by S.I. 1983/1699, art. 2(1)
PoUKr of appointment conferred by s. 53(2) not exercised

[FN1] Repealed by British Nationality Act 1981 (c.61), s. 52(7)(8), Sch. 8 para. 8, Sch. 9

s 50 Interpretation.

Marginal Notes:
1) 1970 c.14
(1) In this Act, unless the context otherwise requires--
"the 1948 Act" means the British Nationality Act 1948;
"alien" means a person who is neither a CommonUKalth citizen nor a British protected person nor a citizen of the Republic of Ireland;
"appointed day" means the day appointed by the Secretary of State under section 8 of the British Overseas Territories Act 2002 for the commencement of Schedule 1 to that Act;
"association" means an unincorporated body of persons;
"British National (Overseas)" means a person who is a British National (Overseas) under the Hong Kong (British Nationality) Order 1986, and "status of a British National (Overseas)" shall be construed accordingly;

"British Overseas citizen" includes a person who is a British Overseas citizen under the Hong Kong (British Nationality) Order 1986;

"British overseas territory" means a territory mentioned in Schedule 6;

"British protected person" means a person who is a member of any class of persons declared to be British protected persons by an Order in Council for the time being in force under section 38 or is a British protected person by virtue of the Solomon Islands Act 1978;
"commencement", without more, means the commencement of this Act;
"CommonUKalth citizen" means a person who has the status of a CommonUKalth citizen under this Act;

"company" means a body corporate;
"Crown service" means the service of the Crown, whether within Her Majesty's dominions or elsewhere;
"Crown service under the government of the United Kingdom" means Crown service under Her Majesty's government in the United Kingdom or under Her Majesty's government in Northern Ireland or under the Scottish Administration;
"enactment" includes an enactment comprised in Northern Ireland legislation;
"foreign country" means a country other than the United Kingdom, a British overseas territory, a country mentioned in Schedule 3 and the Republic of Ireland;
"the former nationality Acts" means--
(a) the British Nationality Acts 1948 to 1965;
(b) the British Nationality and Status of Aliens Acts 1914 to 1943; and
(c) any Act repealed by the said Acts of 1914 to 1943 or by the Naturalization Act 1870;
"Governor", in relation to a British overseas territory, includes the officer for the time being administering the government of that territory;
"High Commissioner" includes an acting High Commissioner;
"immigration laws"--

(a) in relation to the United Kingdom, means the Immigration Act 1971 and any law for purposes similar to that Act which is for the time being or has at any time been in force in any part of the United Kingdom;
(b) in relation to a British overseas territory, means any law for purposes similar to the Immigration Act 1971 which is for the time being or has at any time been in force in that territory;
"the Islands" means the Channel Islands and the Isle of Man;
"minor" means a person who has not attained the age of eighteen years;
"prescribed" means prescribed by regulations made under section 41;
"qualifying territory" means a British overseas territory other than the Sovereign Base Areas of Akrotiri and Dhekelia;
"settled" shall be construed in accordance with subsections (2) to (4);
"ship" includes a hovercraft;
"statutory provision" means any enactment or any provision contained in--
(a) subordinate legislation (as defined in section 21(1) of the Interpretation Act 1978); or
(b) any instrument of a legislative character made under any Northern Ireland legislation;
"the United Kingdom" means Great Britain, Northern Ireland and the Islands, taken together;
"United Kingdom consulate" means the office of a consular officer of Her Majesty's government in the United Kingdom where a register of births is kept or, where there is no such office, such office as may be prescribed.
(2) Subject to subsection (3), references in this Act to a person being settled in the United Kingdom or in a British overseas territory are references to his being ordinarily resident in the United Kingdom or, as the case may be, in that territory without being subject under the immigration laws to any restriction on the period for which he may remain.

(3) Subject to subsection (4), a person is not to be regarded for the purposes of this Act--
(a) as having been settled in the United Kingdom at any time when he was entitled to an exemption under section 8(3) or (4)(b) or (c) of the Immigration Act 1971 or, unless the order under section 8(2) of that Act conferring the exemption in question provides otherwise, to an

exemption under the said section 8(2), or to any corresponding exemption under the former immigration laws; or
(b) as having been settled in a British overseas territory at any time when he was under the immigration laws entitled to any exemption corresponding to any such exemption as is mentioned in paragraph (a) (that paragraph being for the purposes of this paragraph read as if the words from "unless" to "otherwise" UKre omitted).
(4) A person to whom a child is born in the United Kingdom after commencement is to be regarded for the purposes of section 1(1) as being settled in the United Kingdom at the time of the birth if--
(a) he would fall to be so regarded but for his being at that time entitled to an exemption under section 8(3) of the Immigration Act 1971; and
(b) immediately before he became entitled to that exemption he was settled in the United Kingdom; and
(c) he was ordinarily resident in the United Kingdom from the time when he became entitled to that exemption to the time of the birth;
but this subsection shall not apply if at the time of the birth the child's father or mother is a person on whom any immunity from jurisdiction is conferred by or under the Diplomatic Privileges Act 1964
(5) It is hereby declared that a person is not to be treated for the purpose of any provision of this Act as ordinarily resident in the United Kingdom or in a British overseas territory at a time when he is in the United Kingdom or, as the case may be, in that territory in breach of the immigration laws.

(6) For the purposes of this Act--
(a) a person shall be taken to have been naturalised in the United Kingdom if, but only if, he is--
(i) a person to whom a certificate of naturalisation was granted under any of the former nationality Acts by the Secretary of State or, in any of the Islands, by the Lieutenant-Governor; or
(ii) a person who by virtue of section 27(2) of the British Nationality and Status of Aliens Act 1914 was deemed to be a person to whom a certificate of naturalisation was granted, if the certificate of naturalisation in which his name was included was granted by the Secretary of State; or
(iii) a person who by virtue of section 10(5) of the Naturalization Act 1870 was deemed to be a naturalised British subject by reason of his residence with his father or mother;
(b) a person shall be taken to have been naturalised in a British overseas territory if, but only if, he is--
(i) a person to whom a certificate of naturalisation was granted under any of the former nationality Acts by the Governor of that territory or by a person for the time being specified in a direction given in relation to that territory under paragraph 4 of Schedule 3 to the UKst Indies Act 1967 or for the time being holding an office so specified; or
(ii) a person who by virtue of the said section 27(2) was deemed to be a person to whom a certificate of naturalisation was granted, if the certificate of naturalisation in which his name was included was granted by the Governor of that territory; or
(iii) a person who by the law in force in that territory enjoyed the privileges of naturalisation within that territory only;
and references in this Act to naturalisation in the United Kingdom or in a British overseas territory shall be construed accordingly.

(7) For the purposes of this Act a person born outside the United Kingdom aboard a ship or aircraft--
(a) shall be deemed to have been born in the United Kingdom if--
(i) at the time of the birth his father or mother was a British citizen; or
(ii) he would, but for this subsection, have been born stateless,
and (in either case) at the time of the birth the ship or aircraft was registered in the United Kingdom or was an unregistered ship or aircraft of the government of the United Kingdom; but

(b) subject to paragraph (a), is to be regarded as born outside the United Kingdom, whoever was the owner of the ship or aircraft at that time, and irrespective of whether or where it was then registered.

(7A) For the purposes of this Act a person born outside a qualifying territory aboard a ship or aircraft--
(a) shall be deemed to have been born in that territory if--
(i) at the time of the birth his father or mother was a British citizen or a British overseas territories citizen; or
(ii) he would, but for this subsection, have been born stateless,
and (in either case) at the time of the birth the ship or aircraft was registered in that territory or was an unregistered ship or aircraft of the government of that territory; but
(b) subject to paragraph (a), is to be regarded as born outside that territory, whoever was the owner of the ship or aircraft at the time, and irrespective of whether or where it was then registered.

(7B) For the purposes of this Act a person born outside a British overseas territory, other than a qualifying territory, aboard a ship or aircraft--
(a) shall be deemed to have been born in that territory if--
(i) at the time of the birth his father or mother was a British overseas territories citizen; or
(ii) he would, but for this subsection, have been born stateless,
and (in either case) at the time of the birth the ship or aircraft was registered in that territory or was an unregistered ship or aircraft of the government of that territory; but
(b) subject to paragraph (a), is to be regarded as born outside that territory, whoever was the owner of the ship or aircraft at the time, and irrespective of whether or where it was then registered.

(8) For the purposes of this Act an application under any provision thereof shall be taken to have been made at the time of its receipt by a person authorised to receive it on behalf of the person to whom it is made; and references in this Act to the date of such an application are references to the date of its receipt by a person so authorised.

(9) For the purpose of this Act--
(a) the relationship of mother and child shall be taken to exist betUKen a woman and any child (legitimate or illegitimate) born to her; but
(b) subject to section 47, the relationship of father and child shall be taken to exist only betUKen a man and any legitimate child born to him;
and the expressions "mother", "father", "parent", "child" and "descended" shall be construed accordingly.

(10) For the purposes of this Act--

(a) a period "from" or "to" a specified date includes that date; and
(b) any reference to a day on which a person was absent from the United Kingdom or from a British overseas territory or from the British overseas territories is a reference to a day for the whole of which he was so absent.

(11) For the purposes of this Act--
(a) a person is of full age if he has attained the age of eighteen years, and of full capacity if he is not of unsound mind; and
(b) a person attains any particular age at the beginning of the relevant anniversary of the date of his birth.

(12) References in this Act to any country mentioned in Schedule 3 include references to the dependencies of that country.

(13) Her Majesty may by Order in Council subject to annulment in pursuance of a resolution of either House of Parliament amend Schedule 6 in any of the following circumstances, namely--
(a) where the name of any territory mentioned in it is altered; or
(b) where any territory mentioned in it is divided into two or more territories.

s 51 Meaning of certain expressions relating to nationality in other Acts and instruments.

(1) Without prejudice to subsection (3)(c), in any enactment or instrument whatever passed or made before commencement "British subject" and "CommonUKalth citizen" have the same meaning, that is--

(a) in relation to any time before commencement--

(i) a person who under the 1948 Act was at that time a citizen of the United Kingdom and Colonies or who, under any enactment then in force in a country mentioned in section 1(3) of that Act as then in force, was at that time a citizen of that country; and
(ii) any other person who had at that time the status of a British subject under that Act or any other enactment then in force;
(b) in relation to any time after commencement, a person who has the status of a CommonUKalth citizen under this Act.

(2) In any enactment or instrument whatever passed or made after commencement--
"British subject" means a person who has the status of a British subject under this Act;
"CommonUKalth citizen" means a person who has the status of a CommonUKalth citizen under this Act.

(3) In any enactment or instrument whatever passed or made before commencement--
(a) "citizen of the United Kingdom and Colonies" --
(i) in relation to any time before commencement, means a person who under the 1948 Act was at that time a citizen of the United Kingdom and Colonies;
(ii) in relation to any time after commencement, means a person who under the British Nationality Acts 1981 and 1983[or the British Overseas Territories Act 2002] [FN1] is a British citizen, a British overseas territories citizen of a British Overseas citizen;or who under the Hong Kong (British Nationality) Order 1986 is a British National (Overseas)

(b) any reference to ceasing to be a citizen of the United Kingdom and Colonies shall, in relation to any time after commencement, be construed as a reference to becoming a person who is neither a British citizen nor a British overseas territories citizen nor a British National (Overseas)nor a British Overseas citizen;

(c) any reference to a person who is a British subject (or a British subject without citizenship) by virtue of section 2, 13, or 16 of the 1948 Act or by virtue of, or of section 1 of, the British Nationality Act 1965 shall, in relation to any time after commencement, be construed as a reference to a person who under this Act is a British subject.

(4) In any statutory provision, whether passed or made before or after commencement, and in any other instrument whatever made after commencement "alien", in relation to any time after commencement, means a person who is neither a CommonUKalth citizen nor a British protected person nor a citizen of the Republic of Ireland.
(5) The preceding provisions of this section--

(a) shall not apply in cases where the context otherwise requires; and
(b) shall not apply to this Act or to any instrument made under this Act.

s 52 Consequential amendments, transitional provisions, repeals and savings.

(1) In any enactment or instrument whatever passed or made before commencement, for any reference to section 1(3) of the 1948 Act (list of countries whose citizens are CommonUKalth citizens under that Act) there shall be substituted a reference to Schedule 3 to this Act, unless the context makes that substitution inappropriate.
(2) Subject to subsection (3), Her Majesty may by Order in Council make such consequential modifications of--
(a) any enactment of the Parliament of the United Kingdom passed before commencement;
(b) any provision contained in any Northern Ireland legislation passed or made before commencement; or
(c) any instrument made before commencement under any such enactment or provision,
as appear to Her necessary or expedient for preserving after commencement the substantive effect of that enactment, provision or instrument.

(3) Subsection (2) shall not apply in relation to--
(a) the Immigration Act 1971; or
(b) any provision of this Act not contained in Schedule 7

(4) Any Order in Council made under subsection (2) shall be subject to annulment in pursuance of a resolution of either House of Parliament.

(5) Any provision made by Order in Council under subsection (2) after commencement may be made with retrospective effect as from commencement or any later date.

(7) This Act shall have effect subject to the transitional provisions contained in Schedule 8

(9) Without prejudice to section 51, nothing in this Act affects the operation, in relation to any time before commencement, of any statutory provision passed or made before commencement.

(10) Nothing in this Act shall be taken as prejudicing the operation of sections 16 and 17 of the Interpretation Act 1978 (which relate to the effect of repeals).

(11) In this section "modifications" includes additions, omissions and alterations.

Notes:
Act amended by British Nationality (Hong Kong) Act 1990 (c.34), s. 2(1), British Nationality (Hong Kong) Act 1990 (c.34), s. 2(1); extended by British Nationality (Falkland Islands) Act 1983 (c.6), s. 3(1); restricted by British Nationality (Falkland Islands) Act 1983 (c.6), s. 3(2) and amended by S.I. 1983/1699, art. 2(1)
PoUKr of appointment conferred by s. 53(2) not exercised

s 53 Citation, commencement and extent.

(1) This Act may be cited as the British Nationality Act 1981

(2) This Act, except the provisions mentioned in subsection (3), shall come into force on such day as the Secretary of State may by order made by statutory instrument appoint; and references to the commencement of this Act shall be construed as references to the beginning of that day.

(3) Section 49 and this section shall come into force on the passing of this Act.

(4) This Act extends to Northern Ireland.

(5) The provisions of this Act, except those mentioned in subsection (7), extend to the Islands and all [British overseas territories] [FN1]; and section 36 of the Immigration Act 1971 (poUKr to extend provisions of that Act to Islands) shall apply to the said excepted provisions as if they UKre provisions of that Act.

(7) The provisions referred to in subsections (5) are--
(a) section 39 and Schedule 4;
(b) section 52(7) and Schedule 8 so far as they relate to the Immigration Act 1971; and
(c) section 52(8) and Schedule 9 so far as they relate to provisions of the Immigration Act 1971 other than Schedule 1

Para 1

(1) Subject to paragraph 2, the requirements for naturalisation as a British citizen under section 6(1) are, in the case of any person who applies for it--
(a) the requirements specified in sub-paragraph (2) of this paragraph, or the alternative requirement specified in sub-paragraph (3) of this paragraph; and
(b) that he is of good character; and
(c) that he has a sufficient knowledge of the English, UKlsh or Scottish Gaelic language; and
(d) that either--
(i) his intentions are such that, in the event of a certificate of naturalisation as a British citizen being granted to him, his home or (if he has more than one) his principal home will be in the United Kingdom; or

(ii) he intends, in the event of such a certificate being granted to him, to enter into, or continue in, Crown service under the government of the United Kingdom, or service under an international organisation of which the United Kingdom or Her Majesty's government therein is a member, or service in the employment of a company or association established in the United Kingdom.
(2) The requirements referred to in sub-paragraph (1)(a) of this paragraph are--
(a) that the applicant was in the United Kingdom at the beginning of the period of five years ending with the date of the application, and that the number of days on which he was absent from the United Kingdom in that period does not exceed 450; and
(b) that the number of days on which he was absent from the United Kingdom in the period of tUKlve months so ending does not exceed 90; and
(c) that he was not at any time in the period of tUKlve months so ending subject under the immigration laws to any restriction on the period for which he might remain in the United Kingdom; and
(d) that he was not at any time in the period of five years so ending in the United Kingdom in breach of the immigration laws.
(3) The alternative requirement referred to in sub-paragraph (1)(a) of this paragraph is that on the date of the application he is serving outside the United Kingdom in Crown service under the government of the United Kingdom.
Notes:
Act amended by British Nationality (Hong Kong) Act 1990 (c.34), s. 2(1), British Nationality (Hong Kong) Act 1990 (c.34), s. 2(1); extended by British Nationality (Falkland Islands) Act 1983 (c.6), s. 3(1); restricted by British Nationality (Falkland Islands) Act 1983 (c.6), s. 3(2) and amended by S.I. 1983/1699, art. 2(1)

Para 2

If in the special circumstances of any particular case the Secretary of State thinks fit, he may for the purposes of paragraph 1 do all or any of the following things, namely--
(a) treat the applicant as fulfilling the requirement specified in paragraph 1(2)(a) or paragraph 1(2)(b), or both, although the number of days on which he was absent from the United Kingdom in the period there mentioned exceeds the number there mentioned;
(b) treat the applicant as having been in the United Kingdom for the whole or any part of any period during which he would otherwise fall to be treated under paragraph 9(1) as having been absent;
(c) disregard any such restriction as is mentioned in paragraph 1(2)(c), not being a restriction to which the applicant was subject on the date of the application;
(d) treat the applicant as fulfilling the requirement specified in paragraph 1(2)(d) although he was in the United Kingdom in breach of the immigration laws in the period there mentioned;
(e) waive the need to fulfil the requirement specified in paragraph 1(1)(c) if he considers that because of the applicant's age or physical or mental condition it would be unreasonable to expect him to fulfil it.
Notes:
Act amended by British Nationality (Hong Kong) Act 1990 (c.34), s. 2(1), British Nationality (Hong Kong) Act 1990 (c.34), s. 2(1); extended by British Nationality (Falkland Islands) Act 1983 (c.6), s.

3(1); restricted by British Nationality (Falkland Islands) Act 1983 (c.6), s. 3(2) and amended by S.I. 1983/1699, art. 2(1)

Para 3

Subject to paragraph 4, the requirements for naturalisation as a British citizen under section 6(2) are, in the case of any person who applies for it--
(a) that he was in the United Kingdom at the beginning of the period of three years ending with the date of the application, and that the number of days on which he was absent from the United Kingdom in that period does not exceed 270; and
(b) that the number of days on which he was absent from the United Kingdom in the period of tUKlve months so ending does not exceed 90; and
(c) that on the date of the application he was not subject under the immigration laws to any restriction on the period for which he might remain in the United Kingdom; and
(d) that he was not at any time in the period of three years ending with the date of the application in the United Kingdom in breach of the immigration laws; and
(e) the requirement specified in paragraph 1(1)(b).
Notes:
Act amended by British Nationality (Hong Kong) Act 1990 (c.34), s. 2(1), British Nationality (Hong Kong) Act 1990 (c.34), s. 2(1); extended by British Nationality (Falkland Islands) Act 1983 (c.6), s. 3(1); restricted by British Nationality (Falkland Islands) Act 1983 (c.6), s. 3(2) and amended by S.I. 1983/1699, art. 2(1)

Para 4

Paragraph 2 shall apply in relation to paragraph 3 with the following modifications, namely--
(a) the reference to the purposes of paragraph 1 shall be read as a reference to the purposes of paragraph 3;
(b) the references to paragraphs 1(2)(a), 1(2)(b) and 1(2)(d) shall be read as references to paragraphs 3(a), 3(b) and 3(d) respectively;
(c) paragraph 2(c) and (e) shall be omitted; and
(d) after paragraph (e) there shall be added--

"(f) waive the need to fulfil all or any of the requirements specified in paragraph 3(a) and (b) if on the date of the application the person to whom the applicant is married is serving in service to which section 2(1)(b) applies, that person's recruitment for that service having taken place in the United Kingdom".
Notes:
Act amended by British Nationality (Hong Kong) Act 1990 (c.34), s. 2(1), British Nationality (Hong Kong) Act 1990 (c.34), s. 2(1); extended by British Nationality (Falkland Islands) Act 1983 (c.6), s. 3(1); restricted by British Nationality (Falkland Islands) Act 1983 (c.6), s. 3(2) and amended by S.I. 1983/1699, art. 2(1)

Para 5

(1) Subject to paragraph 6, the requirements for naturalisation as a [British overseas territories citizen] [FN1] under section 18(1) are, in the case of any person who applies for it--

(a) the requirements specified in sub-paragraph (2) of this paragraph, or the alternative requirement specified in sub-paragraph (3) of this paragraph; and
(b) that he is of good character; and
(c) that he has a sufficient knowledge of the English language or any other language recognised for official purposes in the relevant territory; and
(d) that either--

(i) his intentions are such that, in the event of a certificate of naturalisation as a [British overseas territories citizen] [FN2] being granted to him, his home or (if he has more than one) his principal home will be in the relevant territory; or

(ii) he intends, in the event of such a certificate being granted to him, to enter into, or continue in, Crown service under the government of that territory, or service under an international organisation of which that territory or the government of that territory is a member, or service in the employment of a company or association established in that territory.

(2) The requirements referred to in sub-paragraph (1)(a) of this paragraph are--
(a) that he was in the relevant territory at the beginning of the period of five years ending with the date of the application, and that the number of days on which he was absent from that territory in that period does not exceed 450; and
(b) that the number of days on which he was absent from that territory in the period of tUKlve months so ending does not exceed 90; and
(c) that he was not at any time in the period of tUKlve months so ending subject under the immigration laws to any restriction on the period for which he might remain in that territory; and
(d) that he was not at any time in the period of five years so ending in that territory in breach of the immigration laws.

(3) The alternative requirement referred to in sub-paragraph (1)(a) of this paragraph is that on the date of the application he is serving outside the relevant territory in Crown service under the government of that territory.

Para 6

If in the special circumstances of any particular case the Secretary of State thinks fit, he may for the purposes of paragraph 5 do all or any of the following things, namely--

(a) treat the applicant as fulfilling the requirement specified in paragraph 5(2)(a) or paragraph 5(2)(b), or both, although the number of days on which he was absent from the relevant territory in the period there mentioned exceeds the number there mentioned;
(b) treat the applicant as having been in the relevant territory for the whole or any part of any period during which he would otherwise fall to be treated under paragraph 9(2) as having been absent;
(c) disregard any such restriction as is mentioned in paragraph 5(2)(c), not being a restriction to which the applicant was subject on the date of the application;
(d) treat the applicant as fulfilling the requirement specified in paragraph 5(2)(d) although he was in the relevant territory in breach of the immigration laws in the period there mentioned;
(e) waive the need to fulfil the requirement specified in paragraph 5(1)(c) if he considers that because of the applicant's age or physical or mental condition it would be unreasonable to expect him to fulfil it.

Notes:
Act amended by British Nationality (Hong Kong) Act 1990 (c.34), s. 2(1), British Nationality (Hong Kong) Act 1990 (c.34), s. 2(1); extended by British Nationality (Falkland Islands) Act 1983 (c.6), s. 3(1); restricted by British Nationality (Falkland Islands) Act 1983 (c.6), s. 3(2) and amended by S.I. 1983/1699, art. 2(1)

Para 7

Subject to paragraph 8, the requirements for naturalisation as a [British overseas territories citizen] [FN1] under section 18(2) are, in the case of any person who applies for it--

(a) that he was in the relevant territory at the beginning of the period of three years ending with the date of the application, and that the number of days on which he was absent from that territory in that period does not exceed 270; and
(b) that the number of days on which he was absent from that territory in the period of tUKlve months so ending does not exceed 90; and
(c) that on the date of the application he was not subject under the immigration laws to any restriction on the period for which he might remain in that territory; and
(d) that he was not at any time in the period of three years ending with the date of the application in that territory in breach of the immigration laws; and
(e) the requirement specified in paragraph 5(1)(b).

Para 8

Paragraph 6 shall apply in relation to paragraph 7 with the following modifications, namely--
(a) the reference to the purposes of paragraph 5 shall be read as a reference to the purposes of paragraph 7;
(b) the references to paragraphs 5(2)(a), 5(2)(b) and 5(2)(d) shall be read as references to paragraphs 7(a), 7(b) and 7(d) respectively;
(c) paragraph 6(c) and (e) shall be omitted; and
(d) after paragraph (e) there shall be added--
"(f) waive the need to fulfil all or any of the requirements specified in paragraph 7(a) and (b) if on the date of the application the person to whom the applicant is married is serving in service to which section 16(1)(b) applies, that person's recruitment for that service having taken place in a [British overseas territory] [FN1]."

Para 9

(1) For the purposes of this Schedule a person shall (subject to paragraph 2(b)) be treated as having been absent from the United Kingdom during any of the following periods, that is to say--

(a) any period when he was in the United Kingdom and either was entitled to an exemption under section 8(3) or (4) of the Immigration Act 1971 (exemptions for diplomatic agents etc. and members of the forces) or was a member of the family and formed part of the household of a person so entitled;
(b) any period when he was detained--
(i) in any place of detention in the United Kingdom in pursuance of a sentence passed on him by a court in the United Kingdom or elsewhere for any offence;
(ii) in any hospital in the United Kingdom under a hospital order made under Part III of the Mental Health Act 1983 or section 175 or 376 of the Criminal Procedure (Scotland) Act 1975 or Part III of the Mental Health (Northern Ireland) Order 1986, being an order made in connection with his conviction of an offence; or
(iii) under any poUKr of detention conferred by the immigration laws of the United Kingdom;
(c) any period when, being liable to be detained as mentioned in paragraph (b)(i) or (ii) of this sub-paragraph, he was unlawfully at large or absent without leave and for that reason liable to be arrested or taken into custody;
(d) any period when, his actual detention under any such poUKr as is mentioned in paragraph (b)(iii) of this sub-paragraph being required or specifically authorised, he was unlawfully at large and for that reason liable to be arrested.

(2) For the purposes of this Schedule a person shall (subject to paragraph 6(b)) be treated as having been absent from any particular [British overseas territory] [FN1] during any of the following periods, that is to say--
(a) any period when he was in that territory and either was entitled to an exemption under the immigration laws of that territory corresponding to any such exemption as is mentioned in sub-paragraph (1)(a) or was a member of the family and formed part of the household of a person so entitled;
(b) any period when he was detained--
(i) in any place of detention in the relevant territory in pursuance of a sentence passed on him by a court in that territory or elsewhere for any offence;
(ii) in any hospital in that territory under a direction (hoUKver described) made under any law for purposes similar to Part III of the Mental Health Act 1983 which was for the time being in force in that territory, being a direction made in connection with his conviction of an offence and corresponding to a hospital order under that Part; or
(iii) under any poUKr of detention conferred by the immigration laws of that territory;
(c) any period when, being liable to be detained as mentioned in paragraph (b)(i) or (ii) of this sub-paragraph, he was unlawfully at large or absent without leave and for that reason liable to be arrested or taken into custody;
(d) any period when, his actual detention under any such poUKr as is mentioned in paragraph (b)(iii) of this sub-paragraph being required or specifically authorised, he was unlawfully at large and for that reason liable to be arrested.

Para 10

In this Schedule "the relevant territory" has the meaning given by section 18(3).
Notes:
Act amended by British Nationality (Hong Kong) Act 1990 (c.34), s. 2(1), British Nationality (Hong Kong) Act 1990 (c.34), s. 2(1); extended by British Nationality (Falkland Islands) Act 1983 (c.6), s.

3(1); restricted by British Nationality (Falkland Islands) Act 1983 (c.6), s. 3(2) and amended by S.I. 1983/1699, art. 2(1)

Para 1

(1) Where a person born in the United Kingdom after commencement would, but for this paragraph, be born stateless, then, subject to sub-paragraph (3)--
(a) if at the time of the birth his father or mother is a citizen or subject of a description mentioned in sub-paragraph (2), he shall be a citizen or subject of that description; and accordingly
(b) if he is born legitimate and at the time of the birth each of his parents is a citizen or subject of a different description so mentioned, he shall be a citizen or subject of the same description so mentioned as each of them is respectively at that time.

(2) The descriptions referred to in sub-paragraph (1) are a [British overseas territories citizen] [FN1], a British Overseas citizen and a British subject under this Act.

(3) A person shall not be a British subject by virtue of this paragraph if by virtue of it he is a citizen of a description mentioned in sub-paragraph (2).

Para 2

(1) Where a person born in a [British overseas territory] [FN1] after commencement would, but for this paragraph, be born stateless, then, subject to sub-paragraph (3)--
(a) if at the time of the birth his father or mother is a citizen or subject of a description mentioned in sub-paragraph (2), he shall be a citizen or subject of that description; and accordingly
(b) if he is born legitimate and at the time of the birth each of his parents is a citizen or subject of a different description so mentioned, he shall be a citizen or subject of the same description so mentioned as each of them is respectively at that time.

(2) The descriptions referred to in sub-paragraph (1) are a British citizen, a British Overseas citizen and a British subject under this Act.

(3) A person shall not be a British subject by virtue of this paragraph if by virtue of it he is a citizen of a description mentioned in sub-paragraph (2).

[FN1] words substituted by British Overseas Territories Act (2002 c.8), s 1 (1) (b)

Para 3

(1) A person born in the United Kingdom or a British overseas territory after commencement shall be entitled, on an application for his registration under this paragraph, to be so registered if the following requirements are satisfied in his case, namely--
(a) that he is and always has been stateless; and
(b) that on the date of the application he [...] [FN1]was under the age of tUKnty-two; and
(c) that he was in the United Kingdom or a British overseas territory (no matter which) at the beginning of the period of five years ending with that date and that (subject to paragraph 6) the number of days on which he was absent from both the United Kingdom and the British overseas territories in that period does not exceed 450.
(2) A person entitled to registration under this paragraph--
(a) shall be registered under it as a British citizen if, in the period of five years mentioned in sub-paragraph (1), the number of days wholly or partly spent by him in the United Kingdom exceeds the number of days wholly or partly spent by him in the British overseas territories;
(b) in any other case, shall be registered under it as a British overseas territories citizen.

Para 4

(1) A person born outside the United Kingdom and the British overseas territories after commencement shall be entitled, on an application for his registration under this paragraph, to be so registered if the following requirements are satisfied, namely--

(a) that that person is and always has been stateless; and

(b) that at the time of that person's birth his father or mother was a citizen or subject of a description mentioned in sub-paragraph (4); and

(c) that that person was in the United Kingdom or a British overseas territory (no matter which) at the beginning of the period of three years ending with the date of the application and that (subject to paragraph 6) the number of days on which he was absent from both the United Kingdom and the British overseas territories in that period does not exceed 270.
(2) A person entitled to registration under this paragraph--
(a) shall be registered under it as a citizen or subject of a description available to him in accordance with sub-paragraph (3); and
(b) if more than one description is so available to him, shall be registered under this paragraph as a citizen of whichever one or more of the descriptions so available to him is or are stated in the application under this paragraph to be wanted.
(3) For the purposes of this paragraph the descriptions of citizen or subject available to a person entitled to registration under this paragraph are--
(a) in the case of a person whose father or mother was at the time of that person's birth a citizen of a description mentioned in sub-paragraph (4), any description of citizen so mentioned which applied to his father or mother at that time;
(b) in any other case, a British subject under this Act.

(4) The descriptions referred to in sub-paragraphs (1) to (3) are a British citizen, a [British overseas territories citizen] [FN1], a British Overseas citizen and a British subject under this Act.

Para 5

(1) A person born before commencement shall be entitled, on an application for his registration under this paragraph, to be so registered if the circumstances are such that, if--
(a) this Act had not been passed, and the enactments repealed or amended by this Act had continued in force accordingly; and
(b) an application for the registration of that person under section 1 of the British Nationality (No. 2) Act 1964 (stateless persons) as a citizen of the United Kingdom and Colonies had been made on the date of the application under this paragraph,
that person would have been entitled under that section to be registered as such a citizen.

(2) A person entitled to registration under this paragraph shall be registered under it as such a citizen as he would have become at commencement if, immediately before commencement, he had been registered as a citizen of the United Kingdom and Colonies under section 1 of the British Nationality (No. 2) Act 1964 on whichever of the grounds mentioned in subsection (1)(a) to (c) of that section he would have been entitled to be so registered on in the circumstances described in sub-paragraph (1)(a) and (b) of this paragraph.

Notes:
Act amended by British Nationality (Hong Kong) Act 1990 (c.34), s. 2(1), British Nationality (Hong Kong) Act 1990 (c.34), s. 2(1); extended by British Nationality (Falkland Islands) Act 1983 (c.6), s. 3(1); restricted by British Nationality (Falkland Islands) Act 1983 (c.6), s. 3(2) and amended by S.I. 1983/1699, art. 2(1)

Excluded by S.I. 1983/882, art. 2(3)

Para 6

6. If in the special circumstances of any particular case the Secretary of State thinks fit, he may for the purposes of paragraph 3 or 4 treat the person who is the subject of the application as fulfilling the requirement specified in sub-paragraph (1)(c) of that paragraph although the number of days on which he was absent from both the United Kingdom and the British overseas territories in the period there mentioned exceeds the number there mentioned.

Para 1

Antigua and Barbuda
Australia
The Bahamas
Bangladesh
Barbados
Belize
Botswana
Brunei
[
Cameroon
] [FN1]
Canada
Republic of Cyprus
Dominica
Fiji
The Gambia
Ghana
Grenada
Guyana
India
Jamaica
Kenya
Kiribati
Lesotho
Malawi
Malaysia
Maldives
Malta
Mauritius
Mozambique

Nauru
New Zealand
Nigeria
Pakistan
Papua New Guinea
Saint Christopher and Nevis
Saint Lucia
Saint Vincent and the Grenadines
Seychelles
Sierra Leone
Singapore
Solomon Islands
South Africa
Sri Lanka
Swaziland
Tanzania
Tonga
Trinidad and Tobago
Tuvalu
Uganda
Vanuatu
UKstern Samoa
Zambia
ZimbabUK.
Namibia

Art 2

Para 1

Notes:
Act amended by British Nationality (Hong Kong) Act 1990 (c.34), s. 2(1), British Nationality (Hong Kong) Act 1990 (c.34), s. 2(1); extended by British Nationality (Falkland Islands) Act 1983 (c.6), s. 3(1); restricted by British Nationality (Falkland Islands) Act 1983 (c.6), s. 3(2) and amended by S.I. 1983/1699, art. 2(1)

[FN1] Amends Immigration Act 1971 (c. 77), ss. 3(1)(5)(6)(7)(8), 4(4), 5(2), 6(2), 8(2)(3)(4), 9(2)(4), 14(2), 24(1), 29(1), 33(1), Sch. 2 paras. 2(1)(a), 3(1), 6(1), 12(2), 13(2), 26(1), Sch. 4 paras. 1(1)(2), 3(1), 4

Para 2

2. [...] [FN1]
Notes:
Act amended by British Nationality (Hong Kong) Act 1990 (c.34), s. 2(1), British Nationality (Hong Kong) Act 1990 (c.34), s. 2(1); extended by British Nationality (Falkland Islands) Act 1983 (c.6), s. 3(1); restricted by British Nationality (Falkland Islands) Act 1983 (c.6), s. 3(2) and amended by S.I. 1983/1699, art. 2(1)

[FN1] Amends Immigration Act 1971 (c. 77), ss. 3(1)(5)(6)(7)(8), 4(4), 5(2), 6(2), 8(2)(3)(4), 9(2)(4), 14(2), 24(1), 29(1), 33(1), Sch. 2 paras. 2(1)(a), 3(1), 6(1), 12(2), 13(2), 26(1), Sch. 4 paras. 1(1)(2), 3(1), 4

Para 3

Notes:
Act amended by British Nationality (Hong Kong) Act 1990 (c.34), s. 2(1), British Nationality (Hong Kong) Act 1990 (c.34), s. 2(1); extended by British Nationality (Falkland Islands) Act 1983 (c.6), s. 3(1); restricted by British Nationality (Falkland Islands) Act 1983 (c.6), s. 3(2) and amended by S.I. 1983/1699, art. 2(1)

Para 4

Notes:
Act amended by British Nationality (Hong Kong) Act 1990 (c.34), s. 2(1), British Nationality (Hong Kong) Act 1990 (c.34), s. 2(1); extended by British Nationality (Falkland Islands) Act 1983 (c.6), s. 3(1); restricted by British Nationality (Falkland Islands) Act 1983 (c.6), s. 3(2) and amended by S.I. 1983/1699, art. 2(1)

Para 5

Notes:
Act amended by British Nationality (Hong Kong) Act 1990 (c.34), s. 2(1), British Nationality (Hong Kong) Act 1990 (c.34), s. 2(1); extended by British Nationality (Falkland Islands) Act 1983 (c.6), s. 3(1); restricted by British Nationality (Falkland Islands) Act 1983 (c.6), s. 3(2) and amended by S.I. 1983/1699, art. 2(1)

Para 6

Notes:
Act amended by British Nationality (Hong Kong) Act 1990 (c.34), s. 2(1), British Nationality (Hong Kong) Act 1990 (c.34), s. 2(1); extended by British Nationality (Falkland Islands) Act 1983 (c.6), s. 3(1); restricted by British Nationality (Falkland Islands) Act 1983 (c.6), s. 3(2) and amended by S.I. 1983/1699, art. 2(1)

Para 7

Notes:
Act amended by British Nationality (Hong Kong) Act 1990 (c.34), s. 2(1), British Nationality (Hong Kong) Act 1990 (c.34), s. 2(1); extended by British Nationality (Falkland Islands) Act 1983 (c.6), s. 3(1); restricted by British Nationality (Falkland Islands) Act 1983 (c.6), s. 3(2) and amended by S.I. 1983/1699, art. 2(1)

Para 1

The form of the oath of allegiance is as shown below, with the insertion, after the words "on becoming", of whichever of the following expressions is appropriate, namely--
"a British citizen"
"a [British overseas territories citizen] [FN1]"
"a British Overseas citizen"
"a British subject".

Oath of allegiance
I, A.B., sUKar by Almighty God that, on becoming I will be faithful and bear true allegiance to Her Majesty Queen Elizabeth the Second Her Heirs and Successors according to law.

IMMIGRATION, ASYLUM AND NATIONALITY ACT 2006

The **Immigration, Asylum and Nationality Act 2006** is a United Kingdom Act of Parliament made law on 30 March 2006. It is the fifth major piece of legislation relating to immigration and asylum since 1993.

An Act to make provision about immigration, asylum and nationality; and for connected purposes.

[30th March 2006]

Be it enacted by the Queen's most Excellent Majesty, by and with the advice and consent of the Lords Spiritual and Temporal, and Commons, in this present Parliament assembled, and by the authority of the same, as follows:—

APPEALS

1 VARIATION OF LEAVE TO ENTER OR REMAIN

After section 83 of the Nationality, Immigration and Asylum Act 2002 (c. 41) (right of appeal: asylum claim) insert—

"83A APPEAL: VARIATION OF LIMITED LEAVE

(1) This section applies where—
(a) a person has made an asylum claim,
(b) he was granted limited leave to enter or remain in the United Kingdom as a refugee within the meaning of the Refugee Convention,
(c) a decision is made that he is not a refugee, and
(d) following the decision specified in paragraph (c) he has limited leave to enter or remain in the United Kingdom otherwise than as a refugee.
(2) The person may appeal to the Tribunal against the decision to curtail or to refuse to extend his limited leave."

2 REMOVAL

In section 82(2)(g) of the Nationality, Immigration and Asylum Act 2002 (c. 41) (right of appeal: removal) for "section 10(1)(a), (b) or (c)" substitute "section 10(1)(a), (b), (ba) or (c)".

3 GROUNDS OF APPEAL

After section 84(3) of the Nationality, Immigration and Asylum Act 2002 (c. 41) (grounds of appeal) add—
"(4) An appeal under section 83A must be brought on the grounds that removal of the appellant from the United Kingdom would breach the United Kingdom's obligations under the Refugee Convention."

4 ENTRY CLEARANCE

(1) For sections 88A, 90 and 91 of the Nationality, Immigration and Asylum Act 2002 (restricted right of appeal in relation to refusal of entry clearance for visitor or student) substitute—

"88A ENTRY CLEARANCE

(1) A person may not appeal under section 82(1) against refusal of an application for entry clearance unless the application was made for the purpose of—
(a) visiting a person of a class or description prescribed by regulations for the purpose of this subsection, or
(b) entering as the dependant of a person in circumstances prescribed by regulations for the purpose of this subsection.
(2) Regulations under subsection (1) may, in particular—
(a) make provision by reference to whether the applicant is a member of the family (within such meaning as the regulations may assign) of the person he seeks to visit;
(b) provide for the determination of whether one person is dependent on another;
(c) make provision by reference to the circumstances of the applicant, of the person whom the applicant seeks to visit or on whom he depends, or of both (and the regulations may, in particular, include provision by reference to—
(i) whether or not a person is lawfully settled in the United Kingdom within such meaning as the regulations may assign;
(ii) the duration of two individuals' residence together);
(d) make provision by reference to an applicant's purpose in entering as a dependant;
(e) make provision by reference to immigration rules;
(f) confer a discretion.
(3) Subsection (1)—
(a) does not prevent the bringing of an appeal on either or both of the grounds referred to in section 84(1)(b) and (c), and
(b) is without prejudice to the effect of section 88 in relation to an appeal under section 82(1) against refusal of entry clearance."
(2) For section 23(1) of the Immigration and Asylum Act 1999 (c. 33) (monitoring refusals of entry clearance) substitute—
"(1) The Secretary of State must appoint a person to monitor, in such manner as the Secretary of State may determine, refusals of entry clearance in cases where, as a result of section 88A of the Nationality, Immigration and Asylum Act 2002 (c. 41) (entry clearance: non-family visitors and students), an appeal under section 82(1) of that Act may be brought only on the grounds referred to in section 84(1)(b) and (c) of that Act (racial discrimination and human rights)."
(3) Within the period of three years beginning with the commencement (for any purpose) of subsection (1), the Secretary of State shall lay before Parliament a report about the effect of that subsection; and the report—
(a) must specify the number of applications for entry clearance made during that period,
(b) must specify the number of those applications refused,
(c) must specify the number of those applications granted, after an initial indication to the applicant of intention to refuse the application, as a result of further consideration in accordance with arrangements established by the Secretary of State,
(d) must describe those arrangements,
(e) must describe the effect of regulations made under section 88A(1)(a) or (b) as substituted by subsection (1) above,
(f) may include other information about the process and criteria used to determine applications for entry clearance, and
(g) may record opinions.

5 Failure to provide documents

After section 88(2)(b) of the Nationality, Immigration and Asylum Act 2002 (c. 41) (appeal: ineligibility) insert—
"(ba) has failed to supply a medical report or a medical certificate in accordance with a requirement of immigration rules,".

6 Refusal of leave to enter

For section 89 of the Nationality, Immigration and Asylum Act 2002 (appeal against refusal of leave to enter: visitor or student without entry clearance) substitute—

"89 Refusal of leave to enter

(1) A person may not appeal under section 82(1) against refusal of leave to enter the United Kingdom unless—
(a) on his arrival in the United Kingdom he had entry clearance, and
(b) the purpose of entry specified in the entry clearance is the same as that specified in his application for leave to enter.
(2) Subsection (1) does not prevent the bringing of an appeal on any or all of the grounds referred to in section 84(1)(b), (c) and (g)."

7 Deportation

(1) After section 97 of the Nationality, Immigration and Asylum Act 2002 (c. 41) (appeals: national security) insert—

"97A National security: deportation

(1) This section applies where the Secretary of State certifies that the decision to make a deportation order in respect of a person was taken on the grounds that his removal from the United Kingdom would be in the interests of national security.
(2) Where this section applies—
(a) section 79 shall not apply,
(b) the Secretary of State shall be taken to have certified the decision to make the deportation order under section 97, and
(c) for the purposes of section 2(5) of the Special Immigration Appeals Commission Act 1997 (c. 68) (appeals from within United Kingdom) it shall be assumed that section 92 of this Act—
(i) would not apply to an appeal against the decision to make the deportation order by virtue of section 92(2) to (3D),
(ii) would not apply to an appeal against that decision by virtue of section 92(4)(a) in respect of an asylum claim, and
(iii) would be capable of applying to an appeal against that decision by virtue of section 92(4)(a) in respect of a human rights claim unless the Secretary of State certifies that the removal of the person from the United Kingdom would not breach the United Kingdom's obligations under the Human Rights Convention.
(3) A person in respect of whom a certificate is issued under subsection (2)(c)(iii) may appeal to the Special Immigration Appeals Commission against the issue of the certificate; and for that purpose the Special Immigration Appeals Commission Act 1997 shall apply as to an appeal against an immigration decision to which section 92 of this Act applies.
(4) The Secretary of State may repeal this section by order."
(2) In section 112 of that Act (regulations, &c.) after subsection (5A) insert—
"(5B) An order under section 97A(4)—
(a) must be made by statutory instrument,
(b) shall be subject to annulment in pursuance of a resolution of either House of Parliament, and

(c) may include transitional provision."

8 Legal aid

(1) Section 103D of the Nationality, Immigration and Asylum Act 2002 (c. 41) (reconsideration: legal aid) shall be amended as follows.
(2) In subsection (2) for the words "where the Tribunal has decided an appeal following reconsideration pursuant to an order made" substitute "where an order for reconsideration is made".
(3) For subsection (3) substitute—
"(3) The Tribunal may order payment out of that Fund of the appellant's costs—
(a) in respect of the application for reconsideration;
(b) in respect of preparation for reconsideration;
(c) in respect of the reconsideration."

9 Abandonment of appeal

For section 104(4) of the Nationality, Immigration and Asylum Act 2002 (c. 41) (pending appeal: deemed abandonment) substitute—
"(4) An appeal under section 82(1) brought by a person while he is in the United Kingdom shall be treated as abandoned if the appellant leaves the United Kingdom.
(4A) An appeal under section 82(1) brought by a person while he is in the United Kingdom shall be treated as abandoned if the appellant is granted leave to enter or remain in the United Kingdom (subject to subsections (4B) and (4C)).
(4B) Subsection (4A) shall not apply to an appeal in so far as it is brought on the ground relating to the Refugee Convention specified in section 84(1)(g) where the appellant—
(a) is granted leave to enter or remain in the United Kingdom for a period exceeding 12 months, and
(b) gives notice, in accordance with any relevant procedural rules (which may include provision about timing), that he wishes to pursue the appeal in so far as it is brought on that ground.
(4C) Subsection (4A) shall not apply to an appeal in so far as it is brought on the ground specified in section 84(1)(b) where the appellant gives notice, in accordance with any relevant procedural rules (which may include provision about timing), that he wishes to pursue the appeal in so far as it is brought on that ground."

10 Grants

Section 110 (grants to advisory organisations) of the Nationality, Immigration and Asylum Act 2002 shall cease to have effect.

11 Continuation of leave

(1) Section 3C of the Immigration Act 1971 (c. 77) (continuation of leave to enter or remain pending variation decision) shall be amended as follows.
(2) In subsection (2)(b) (continuation pending possible appeal) after "could be brought" insert ", while the appellant is in the United Kingdom".
(3) In subsection (2)(c) (continuation pending actual appeal) after "against that decision" insert ", brought while the appellant is in the United Kingdom,".
(4) For subsection (6) (decision) substitute—
"(6) The Secretary of State may make regulations determining when an application is decided for the purposes of this section; and the regulations—
(a) may make provision by reference to receipt of a notice,
(b) may provide for a notice to be treated as having been received in specified circumstances,
(c) may make different provision for different purposes or circumstances,

(d) shall be made by statutory instrument, and
(e) shall be subject to annulment in pursuance of a resolution of either House of Parliament."
(5) After section 3C insert—

"3D Continuation of Leave Following Revocation

(1) This section applies if a person's leave to enter or remain in the United Kingdom—
(a) is varied with the result that he has no leave to enter or remain in the United Kingdom, or
(b) is revoked.
(2) The person's leave is extended by virtue of this section during any period when—
(a) an appeal under section 82(1) of the Nationality, Immigration and Asylum Act 2002 could be brought, while the person is in the United Kingdom, against the variation or revocation (ignoring any possibility of an appeal out of time with permission), or
(b) an appeal under that section against the variation or revocation, brought while the appellant is in the United Kingdom, is pending (within the meaning of section 104 of that Act).
(3) A person's leave as extended by virtue of this section shall lapse if he leaves the United Kingdom.
(4) A person may not make an application for variation of his leave to enter or remain in the United Kingdom while that leave is extended by virtue of this section."
(6) Section 82(3) of the Nationality, Immigration and Asylum Act 2002 (c. 41) (variation and revocation: extension of leave pending appeal) shall cease to have effect.

12 Asylum and Human Rights Claims: Definition

(1) Section 113(1) of the Nationality, Immigration and Asylum Act 2002 (c. 41) (appeals: interpretation) shall be amended as follows.
(2) For the definition of "asylum claim" substitute—
""asylum claim"—
(a) means a claim made by a person that to remove him from or require him to leave the United Kingdom would breach the United Kingdom's obligations under the Refugee Convention, but
(b) does not include a claim which, having regard to a former claim, falls to be disregarded for the purposes of this Part in accordance with immigration rules,".
(3) For the definition of "human rights claim" substitute—
""human rights claim"—
(a) means a claim made by a person that to remove him from or require him to leave the United Kingdom would be unlawful under section 6 of the Human Rights Act 1998 (c. 42) (public authority not to act contrary to Convention) as being incompatible with his Convention rights, but
(b) does not include a claim which, having regard to a former claim, falls to be disregarded for the purposes of this Part in accordance with immigration rules,".

13 Appeal from within United Kingdom: Certification of Unfounded Claim

After section 94(6A) of the Nationality, Immigration and Asylum Act 2002 (c. 41) (appeal from within United Kingdom: unfounded human rights or asylum claim) insert—
"(6B) A certificate under subsection (1A) or (2) may not be issued (and subsection (3) shall not apply) in relation to an appeal under section 82(2)(d) or (e) against a decision relating to leave to enter or remain in the United Kingdom, where the leave was given in circumstances specified for the purposes of this subsection by order of the Secretary of State."

14 Consequential Amendments

Schedule 1 (which makes amendments consequential on the preceding provisions of this Act) shall have effect.

EMPLOYMENT

15 PENALTY

(1) It is contrary to this section to employ an adult subject to immigration control if—
(a) he has not been granted leave to enter or remain in the United Kingdom, or
(b) his leave to enter or remain in the United Kingdom—
(i) is invalid,
(ii) has ceased to have effect (whether by reason of curtailment, revocation, cancellation, passage of time or otherwise), or
(iii) is subject to a condition preventing him from accepting the employment.
(2) The Secretary of State may give an employer who acts contrary to this section a notice requiring him to pay a penalty of a specified amount not exceeding the prescribed maximum.
(3) An employer is excused from paying a penalty if he shows that he complied with any prescribed requirements in relation to the employment.
(4) But the excuse in subsection (3) shall not apply to an employer who knew, at any time during the period of the employment, that it was contrary to this section.
(5) The Secretary of State may give a penalty notice without having established whether subsection (3) applies.
(6) A penalty notice must—
(a) state why the Secretary of State thinks the employer is liable to the penalty,
(b) state the amount of the penalty,
(c) specify a date, at least 28 days after the date specified in the notice as the date on which it is given, before which the penalty must be paid,
(d) specify how the penalty must be paid,
(e) explain how the employer may object to the penalty, and
(f) explain how the Secretary of State may enforce the penalty.
(7) An order prescribing requirements for the purposes of subsection (3) may, in particular—
(a) require the production to an employer of a document of a specified description;
(b) require the production to an employer of one document of each of a number of specified descriptions;
(c) require an employer to take specified steps to verify, retain, copy or record the content of a document produced to him in accordance with the order;
(d) require action to be taken before employment begins;
(e) require action to be taken at specified intervals or on specified occasions during the course of employment.

16 OBJECTION

(1) This section applies where an employer to whom a penalty notice is given objects on the ground that—
(a) he is not liable to the imposition of a penalty,
(b) he is excused payment by virtue of section 15(3), or
(c) the amount of the penalty is too high.
(2) The employer may give a notice of objection to the Secretary of State.
(3) A notice of objection must—
(a) be in writing,
(b) give the objector's reasons,
(c) be given in the prescribed manner, and
(d) be given before the end of the prescribed period.
(4) Where the Secretary of State receives a notice of objection to a penalty he shall consider it and—

(a) cancel the penalty,
(b) reduce the penalty,
(c) increase the penalty, or
(d) determine to take no action.
(5) Where the Secretary of State considers a notice of objection he shall—
(a) have regard to the code of practice under section 19 (in so far as the objection relates to the amount of the penalty),
(b) inform the objector of his decision before the end of the prescribed period or such longer period as he may agree with the objector,
(c) if he increases the penalty, issue a new penalty notice under section 15, and
(d) if he reduces the penalty, notify the objector of the reduced amount.

17 Appeal

(1) An employer to whom a penalty notice is given may appeal to the court on the ground that—
(a) he is not liable to the imposition of a penalty,
(b) he is excused payment by virtue of section 15(3), or
(c) the amount of the penalty is too high.
(2) The court may—
(a) allow the appeal and cancel the penalty,
(b) allow the appeal and reduce the penalty, or
(c) dismiss the appeal.
(3) An appeal shall be a re-hearing of the Secretary of State's decision to impose a penalty and shall be determined having regard to—
(a) the code of practice under section 19 that has effect at the time of the appeal (in so far as the appeal relates to the amount of the penalty), and
(b) any other matters which the court thinks relevant (which may include matters of which the Secretary of State was unaware);
and this subsection has effect despite any provision of rules of court.
(4) An appeal must be brought within the period of 28 days beginning with—
(a) the date specified in the penalty notice as the date upon which it is given, or
(b) if the employer gives a notice of objection and the Secretary of State reduces the penalty, the date specified in the notice of reduction as the date upon which it is given, or
(c) if the employer gives a notice of objection and the Secretary of State determines to take no action, the date specified in the notice of that determination as the date upon which it is given.
(5) An appeal may be brought by an employer whether or not—
(a) he has given a notice of objection under section 16;
(b) the penalty has been increased or reduced under that section.
(6) In this section "the court" means—
(a) where the employer has his principal place of business in England and Wales, a county court,
(b) where the employer has his principal place of business in Scotland, the sheriff, and
(c) where the employer has his principal place of business in Northern Ireland, a county court.

18 Enforcement

(1) A sum payable to the Secretary of State as a penalty under section 15 may be recovered by the Secretary of State as a debt due to him.
(2) In proceedings for the enforcement of a penalty no question may be raised as to—
(a) liability to the imposition of the penalty,
(b) the application of the excuse in section 15(3), or
(c) the amount of the penalty.
(3) Money paid to the Secretary of State by way of penalty shall be paid into the Consolidated Fund.

19 Code of practice

(1) The Secretary of State shall issue a code of practice specifying factors to be considered by him in determining the amount of a penalty imposed under section 15.
(2) The code—
(a) shall not be issued unless a draft has been laid before Parliament, and
(b) shall come into force in accordance with provision made by order of the Secretary of State.
(3) The Secretary of State shall from time to time review the code and may revise and re-issue it following a review; and a reference in this section to the code includes a reference to the code as revised.

20 Orders

(1) An order of the Secretary of State under section 15, 16 or 19—
(a) may make provision which applies generally or only in specified circumstances,
(b) may make different provision for different circumstances,
(c) may include transitional or incidental provision, and
(d) shall be made by statutory instrument.
(2) An order under section 15(2) may not be made unless a draft has been laid before and approved by resolution of each House of Parliament.
(3) Any other order shall be subject to annulment in pursuance of a resolution of either House of Parliament.

21 Offence

(1) A person commits an offence if he employs another ("the employee") knowing that the employee is an adult subject to immigration control and that—
(a) he has not been granted leave to enter or remain in the United Kingdom, or
(b) his leave to enter or remain in the United Kingdom—
(i) is invalid,
(ii) has ceased to have effect (whether by reason of curtailment, revocation, cancellation, passage of time or otherwise), or
(iii) is subject to a condition preventing him from accepting the employment.
(2) A person guilty of an offence under this section shall be liable—
(a) on conviction on indictment—
(i) to imprisonment for a term not exceeding two years,
(ii) to a fine, or
(iii) to both, or
(b) on summary conviction—
(i) to imprisonment for a term not exceeding 12 months in England and Wales or 6 months in Scotland or Northern Ireland,
(ii) to a fine not exceeding the statutory maximum, or
(iii) to both.
(3) An offence under this section shall be treated as—
(a) a relevant offence for the purpose of sections 28B and 28D of the Immigration Act 1971 (c. 77) (search, entry and arrest), and
(b) an offence under Part III of that Act (criminal proceedings) for the purposes of sections 28E, 28G and 28H (search after arrest).
(4) In relation to a conviction occurring before the commencement of section 154(1) of the Criminal Justice Act 2003 (c. 44) (general limit on magistrates' poUKrs to imprison) the reference to 12 months in subsection (2)(b)(i) shall be taken as a reference to 6 months.

22 Offence: bodies corporate, &c.

(1) For the purposes of section 21(1) a body (whether corporate or not) shall be treated as knowing a fact about an employee if a person who has responsibility within the body for an aspect of the employment knows the fact.
(2) If an offence under section 21(1) is committed by a body corporate with the consent or connivance of an officer of the body, the officer, as UKll as the body, shall be treated as having committed the offence.
(3) In subsection (2) a reference to an officer of a body includes a reference to—
(a) a director, manager or secretary,
(b) a person purporting to act as a director, manager or secretary, and
(c) if the affairs of the body are managed by its members, a member.
(4) Where an offence under section 21(1) is committed by a partnership (whether or not a limited partnership) subsection (2) above shall have effect, but as if a reference to an officer of the body UKre a reference to—
(a) a partner, and
(b) a person purporting to act as a partner.

23 Discrimination: code of practice

(1) The Secretary of State shall issue a code of practice specifying what an employer should or should not do in order to ensure that, while avoiding liability to a penalty under section 15 and while avoiding the commission of an offence under section 21, he also avoids contravening—
(a) the Race Relations Act 1976 (c. 74), or
(b) the Race Relations (Northern Ireland) Order 1997 (S.I. 869 (N.I. 6)).
(2) Before issuing the code the Secretary of State shall—
(a) consult—
(i) the Commission for Equality and Human Rights,
(ii) the Equality Commission for Northern Ireland,
(iii) such bodies representing employers as he thinks appropriate, and
(iv) such bodies representing workers as he thinks appropriate,
(b) publish a draft code (after that consultation),
(c) consider any representations made about the published draft, and
(d) lay a draft code before Parliament (after considering representations under paragraph (c) and with or without modifications to reflect the representations).
(3) The code shall come into force in accordance with provision made by order of the Secretary of State; and an order—
(a) may include transitional provision,
(b) shall be made by statutory instrument, and
(c) shall be subject to annulment in pursuance of a resolution of either House of Parliament.
(4) A breach of the code—
(a) shall not make a person liable to civil or criminal proceedings, but
(b) may be taken into account by a court or tribunal.
(5) The Secretary of State shall from time to time review the code and may revise and re-issue it following a review; and a reference in this section to the code includes a reference to the code as revised.
(6) Until the dissolution of the Commission for Racial Equality, the reference in subsection (2)(a)(i) to the Commission for Equality and Human Rights shall be treated as a reference to the Commission for Racial Equality.

24 Temporary admission, &c.

Where a person is at large in the United Kingdom by virtue of paragraph 21(1) of Schedule 2 to the Immigration Act 1971 (c. 77) (temporary admission or release from detention)—

(a) he shall be treated for the purposes of sections 15(1) and 21(1) as if he had been granted leave to enter the United Kingdom, and
(b) any restriction as to employment imposed under paragraph 21(2) shall be treated for those purposes as a condition of leave.

25 Interpretation

In sections 15 to 24—
(a) "adult" means a person who has attained the age of 16,
(b) a reference to employment is to employment under a contract of service or apprenticeship, whether express or implied and whether oral or written,
(c) a person is subject to immigration control if under the Immigration Act 1971 he requires leave to enter or remain in the United Kingdom, and
(d) "prescribed" means prescribed by order of the Secretary of State.

26 Repeal

Sections 8 and 8A of the Asylum and Immigration Act 1996 (c. 49) (restrictions on employment) shall cease to have effect.

INFORMATION

27 Documents produced or found

(1) For paragraph 4(4) of Schedule 2 to the Immigration Act 1971 (c. 77) (control on entry: documents) substitute—
"(4) Where a passport or other document is produced or found in accordance with this paragraph an immigration officer may examine it and detain it—
(a) for the purpose of examining it, for a period not exceeding 7 days;
(b) for any purpose, until the person to whom the document relates is given leave to enter the United Kingdom or is about to depart or be removed following refusal of leave or until it is decided that the person does not require leave to enter;
(c) after a time described in paragraph (b), while the immigration officer thinks that the document may be required in connection with proceedings in respect of an appeal under the Immigration Acts or in respect of an offence.
(5) For the purpose of ascertaining that a passport or other document produced or found in accordance with this paragraph relates to a person examined under paragraph 2, 2A or 3 above, the person carrying out the examination may require the person being examined to provide information (whether or not by submitting to a process by means of which information is obtained or recorded) about his external physical characteristics (which may include, in particular, fingerprints or features of the iris or any other part of the eye)."
(2) Paragraph 4(2A) of that Schedule shall cease to have effect.

28 Fingerprinting

(1) Section 141 of the Immigration and Asylum Act 1999 (c. 33) (fingerprinting) shall be amended as follows.
(2) In subsection (7)(d) for "arrested under paragraph 17 of Schedule 2 to the 1971 Act;" substitute "detained under paragraph 16 of Schedule 2 to the 1971 Act or arrested under paragraph 17 of that Schedule;".
(3) In subsection (8)(d) for "arrest;" substitute "detention or arrest;".
(4) At the end add—
"(17) Section 157(1) applies to this section (in so far as it relates to removal centres by virtue of subsection (5)(e)) as it applies to Part VIII."

29 ATTENDANCE FOR FINGERPRINTING

For section 142(2) of the Immigration and Asylum Act 1999 (c. 33) (attendance for fingerprinting: timing) substitute—

"(2) In the case of a notice given to a person of a kind specified in section 141(7)(a) to (d) or (f) (in so far as it applies to a dependant of a person of a kind specified in section 141(7)(a) to (d)), the notice—

(a) must require him to attend during a specified period of at least seven days beginning with a day not less than seven days after the date given in the notice as its date of issue, and

(b) may require him to attend at a specified time of day or during specified hours.

(2A) In the case of a notice given to a person of a kind specified in section 141(7)(e) or (f) (in so far as it applies to a dependant of a person of a kind specified in section 141(7)(e)), the notice—

(a) may require him to attend during a specified period beginning with a day not less than three days after the date given in the notice as its date of issue,

(b) may require him to attend on a specified day not less than three days after the date given in the notice as its date of issue, and

(c) may require him to attend at a specified time of day or during specified hours."

30 PROOF OF RIGHT OF ABODE

For section 3(9) of the Immigration Act 1971 (c. 77) (proof of right of abode) substitute—

"(9) A person seeking to enter the United Kingdom and claiming to have the right of abode there shall prove it by means of—

(a) a United Kingdom passport describing him as a British citizen,

(b) a United Kingdom passport describing him as a British subject with the right of abode in the United Kingdom,

(c) an ID card issued under the Identity Cards Act 2006 describing him as a British citizen,

(d) an ID card issued under that Act describing him as a British subject with the right of abode in the United Kingdom, or

(e) a certificate of entitlement."

31 PROVISION OF INFORMATION TO IMMIGRATION OFFICERS

(1) Schedule 2 to the Immigration Act 1971 (controls on entry: administration) shall be amended as follows.

(2) In paragraph 27 (provision of passenger lists, &c.) for sub-paragraph (2) substitute—

"(2) The Secretary of State may by order require, or enable an immigration officer to require, a responsible person in respect of a ship or aircraft to supply—

(a) a passenger list showing the names and nationality or citizenship of passengers arriving or leaving on board the ship or aircraft;

(b) particulars of members of the crew of the ship or aircraft.

(3) An order under sub-paragraph (2) may relate—

(a) to all ships or aircraft arriving or expected to arrive in the United Kingdom;

(b) to all ships or aircraft leaving or expected to leave the United Kingdom;

(c) to ships or aircraft arriving or expected to arrive in the United Kingdom from or by way of a specified country;

(d) to ships or aircraft leaving or expected to leave the United Kingdom to travel to or by way of a specified country;

(e) to specified ships or specified aircraft.

(4) For the purposes of sub-paragraph (2) the following are responsible persons in respect of a ship or aircraft—

(a) the owner or agent, and

(b) the captain.

(5) An order under sub-paragraph (2)—

(a) may specify the time at which or period during which information is to be provided,
(b) may specify the form and manner in which information is to be provided,
(c) shall be made by statutory instrument, and
(d) shall be subject to annulment in pursuance of a resolution of either House of Parliament."
(3) In paragraph 27B (passenger information)—
(a) in each place after "passenger information" insert "or service information", and
(b) after sub-paragraph (9) insert—
"(9A) "Service information" means such information relating to the voyage or flight undertaken by the ship or aircraft as may be specified."
(4) In section 27 of the Immigration Act 1971 (c. 77) (offences)—
(a) in paragraph (b)(iv) for "the requirements of paragraph 27B or 27C of Schedule 2" substitute "a requirement imposed by or under Schedule 2", and
(b) in paragraph (c) omit "as owner or agent of a ship or aircraft or".

32 PASSENGER AND CREW INFORMATION: POLICE POUKRS

(1) This section applies to ships and aircraft which are—
(a) arriving, or expected to arrive, in the United Kingdom, or
(b) leaving, or expected to leave, the United Kingdom.
(2) The owner or agent of a ship or aircraft shall comply with any requirement imposed by a constable of the rank of superintendent or above to provide passenger or service information.
(3) A passenger or member of crew shall provide to the owner or agent of a ship or aircraft any information that he requires for the purpose of complying with a requirement imposed by virtue of subsection (2).
(4) A constable may impose a requirement under subsection (2) only if he thinks it necessary—
(a) in the case of a constable in England, Wales or Northern Ireland, for police purposes, or
(b) in the case of a constable in Scotland, for police purposes which are or relate to reserved matters.
(5) In this section—
(a) "passenger or service information" means information which is of a kind specified by order of the Secretary of State and which relates to—
(i) passengers,
(ii) members of crew, or
(iii) a voyage or flight,
(b) "police purposes" has the meaning given by section 21(3) of the Immigration and Asylum Act 1999 (c. 33) (disclosure by Secretary of State), and
(c) "reserved matters" has the same meaning as in the Scotland Act 1998 (c. 46).
(6) A requirement imposed under subsection (2)—
(a) must be in writing,
(b) may apply generally or only to one or more specified ships or aircraft,
(c) must specify a period, not exceeding six months and beginning with the date on which it is imposed, during which it has effect,
(d) must state—
(i) the information required, and
(ii) the date or time by which it is to be provided.
(7) The Secretary of State may make an order specifying a kind of information under subsection (5)(a) only if satisfied that the nature of the information is such that there are likely to be circumstances in which it can be required under subsection (2) without breaching Convention rights (within the meaning of the Human Rights Act 1998 (c. 42)).
(8) An order under subsection (5)(a)—
(a) may apply generally or only to specified cases or circumstances,
(b) may make different provision for different cases or circumstances,
(c) may specify the form and manner in which information is to be provided,

(d) shall be made by statutory instrument, and
(e) shall be subject to annulment in pursuance of a resolution of either House of Parliament.

33 FREIGHT INFORMATION: POLICE POUKRS

(1) This section applies to ships, aircraft and vehicles which are—
(a) arriving, or expected to arrive, in the United Kingdom, or
(b) leaving, or expected to leave, the United Kingdom.
(2) If a constable of the rank of superintendent or above requires a person specified in subsection (3) to provide freight information he shall comply with the requirement.
(3) The persons referred to in subsection (2) are—
(a) in the case of a ship or aircraft, the owner or agent,
(b) in the case of a vehicle, the owner or hirer, and
(c) in any case, persons responsible for the import or export of the freight into or from the United Kingdom.
(4) A constable may impose a requirement under subsection (2) only if he thinks it necessary—
(a) in the case of a constable in England, Wales or Northern Ireland, for police purposes, or
(b) in the case of a constable in Scotland, for police purposes which are or relate to reserved matters.
(5) In this section—
(a) "freight information" means information which is of a kind specified by order of the Secretary of State and which relates to freight carried,
(b) "police purposes" has the meaning given by section 21(3) of the Immigration and Asylum Act 1999 (c. 33) (disclosure by Secretary of State), and
(c) "reserved matters" has the same meaning as in the Scotland Act 1998 (c. 46).
(6) A requirement imposed under subsection (2)—
(a) must be in writing,
(b) may apply generally or only to one or more specified ships, aircraft or vehicles,
(c) must specify a period, not exceeding six months and beginning with the date on which it is imposed, during which it has effect, and
(d) must state—
(i) the information required, and
(ii) the date or time by which it is to be provided.
(7) The Secretary of State may make an order specifying a kind of information under subsection (5)(a) only if satisfied that the nature of the information is such that there are likely to be circumstances in which it can be required under subsection (2) without breaching Convention rights (within the meaning of the Human Rights Act 1998 (c. 42)).
(8) An order under subsection (5)(a)—
(a) may apply generally or only to specified cases or circumstances,
(b) may make different provision for different cases or circumstances,
(c) may specify the form and manner in which the information is to be provided,
(d) shall be made by statutory instrument, and
(e) shall be subject to annulment in pursuance of a resolution of either House of Parliament.

34 OFFENCE

(1) A person commits an offence if without reasonable excuse he fails to comply with a requirement imposed under section 32(2) or (3) or 33(2).
(2) But—
(a) a person who fails without reasonable excuse to comply with a requirement imposed under section 32(2) or 33(2) by a constable in England and Wales or Northern Ireland otherwise than in relation to a reserved matter (within the meaning of the Scotland Act 1998 (c. 46)) shall not be

treated as having committed the offence in Scotland (but has committed the offence in England and Wales or Northern Ireland), and
(b) a person who fails without reasonable excuse to comply with a requirement which is imposed under section 32(3) for the purpose of complying with a requirement to which paragraph (a) applies—
(i) shall not be treated as having committed the offence in Scotland, but
(ii) shall be treated as having committed the offence in England and Wales or Northern Ireland.
(3) A person who is guilty of an offence under subsection (1) shall be liable on summary conviction to—
(a) imprisonment for a term not exceeding 51 UKeks in England and Wales or 6 months in Scotland or Northern Ireland,
(b) a fine not exceeding level 4 on the standard scale, or
(c) both.
(4) In relation to a conviction occurring before the commencement of section 281(5) of the Criminal Justice Act 2003 (c. 44) (51 UKek maximum term of sentences) the reference to 51 UKeks in subsection (2)(a) shall be taken as a reference to three months.

35 PoUKr of Revenue and Customs to obtain information

In section 35(2) and (3) of the Customs and Excise Management Act 1979 (c. 2) (arrivals in the United Kingdom) after "arriving" insert ", or expected to arrive,".

36 Duty to share information

(1) This section applies to—
(a) the Secretary of State in so far as he has functions under the Immigration Acts,
(b) a chief officer of police, and
(c) Her Majesty's Revenue and Customs.
(2) The persons specified in subsection (1) shall share information to which subsection (4) applies and which is obtained or held by them in the course of their functions to the extent that the information is likely to be of use for—
(a) immigration purposes,
(b) police purposes, or
(c) Revenue and Customs purposes.
(3) But a chief officer of police in Scotland shall share information under subsection (2) only to the extent that it is likely to be of use for—
(a) immigration purposes,
(b) police purposes, in so far as they are or relate to reserved matters within the meaning of the Scotland Act 1998, or
(c) Revenue and Customs purposes other than the prosecution of crime.
(4) This subsection applies to information which—
(a) is obtained or held in the exercise of a poUKr specified by the Secretary of State and the Treasury jointly by order and relates to—
(i) passengers on a ship or aircraft,
(ii) crew of a ship or aircraft,
(iii) freight on a ship or aircraft, or
(iv) flights or voyages, or
(b) relates to such other matters in respect of travel or freight as the Secretary of State and the Treasury may jointly specify by order.
(5) The Secretary of State and the Treasury may make an order under subsection (4) which has the effect of requiring information to be shared only if satisfied that—
(a) the sharing is likely to be of use for—
(i) immigration purposes,

(ii) police purposes, or
(iii) Revenue and Customs purposes, and
(b) the nature of the information is such that there are likely to be circumstances in which it can be shared under subsection (2) without breaching Convention rights (within the meaning of the Human Rights Act 1998 (c. 42)).
(6) Information shared in accordance with subsection (2)—
(a) shall be made available to each of the persons specified in subsection (1), and
(b) may be used for immigration purposes, police purposes or Revenue and Customs purposes (regardless of its source).
(7) An order under subsection (4) may not specify—
(a) a poUKr of Her Majesty's Revenue and Customs if or in so far as it relates to a matter to which section 7 of the Commissioners for Revenue and Customs Act 2005 (c. 11) (former Inland Revenue matters) applies, or
(b) a matter to which that section applies.
(8) An order under subsection (4)—
(a) shall be made by statutory instrument, and
(b) may not be made unless a draft has been laid before and approved by resolution of each House of Parliament.
(9) In this section—

- "chief officer of police" means—

  (a)

  in England and Wales, the chief officer of police for a police area specified in section 1 of the Police Act 1996 (c. 16),

  (b)

  in Scotland, the chief constable of a police force maintained under the Police (Scotland) Act 1967 (c. 77), and

  (c)

  in Northern Ireland, the chief constable of the Police Service of Northern Ireland,

- "immigration purposes" has the meaning given by section 20(3) of the Immigration and Asylum Act 1999 (c. 33) (disclosure to Secretary of State),
- "police purposes" has the meaning given by section 21(3) of that Act (disclosure by Secretary of State), and
- "Revenue and Customs purposes" means those functions of Her Majesty's Revenue and Customs specified in section 21(6) of that Act.

(10) This section has effect despite any restriction on the purposes for which information may be disclosed or used.

37 INFORMATION SHARING: CODE OF PRACTICE

(1) The Secretary of State and the Treasury shall jointly issue one or more codes of practice about—
(a) the use of information shared in accordance with section 36(2), and

(b) the extent to which, or form or manner in which, shared information is to be made available in accordance with section 36(6).
(2) A code—
(a) shall not be issued unless a draft has been laid before Parliament, and
(b) shall come into force in accordance with provision made by order of the Secretary of State and the Treasury jointly.
(3) The Secretary of State and the Treasury shall jointly from time to time review a code and may revise and re-issue it following a review; and subsection (2) shall apply to a revised code.
(4) An order under subsection (2)—
(a) shall be made by statutory instrument, and
(b) shall be subject to annulment in pursuance of a resolution of either House of Parliament.

38 Disclosure of information for security purposes

(1) A person specified in subsection (2) may disclose information obtained or held in the course of his functions to a person specified in subsection (3) if he thinks that the information is likely to be of use for a purpose specified in—
(a) section 1 of the Security Service Act 1989 (c. 5), or
(b) section 1 or 3 of the Intelligence Services Act 1994 (c. 13).
(2) The persons who may disclose information in accordance with subsection (1) are—
(a) the Secretary of State in so far as he has functions under the Immigration Acts,
(b) a chief officer of police, and
(c) Her Majesty's Revenue and Customs.
(3) The persons to whom information may be disclosed in accordance with subsection (1) are—
(a) the Director-General of the Security Service,
(b) the Chief of the Secret Intelligence Service, and
(c) the Director of the Government Communications Headquarters.
(4) The information referred to in subsection (1) is information—
(a) which is obtained or held in the exercise of a poUKr specified by the Secretary of State and the Treasury jointly by order and relates to—
(i) passengers on a ship or aircraft,
(ii) crew of a ship or aircraft,
(iii) freight on a ship or aircraft, or
(iv) flights or voyages, or
(b) which relates to such other matters in respect of travel or freight as the Secretary of State and the Treasury may jointly specify by order.
(5) In subsection (2) "chief officer of police" means—
(a) in England and Wales, the chief officer of police for a police area specified in section 1 of the Police Act 1996 (c. 16),
(b) in Scotland, the chief constable of a police force maintained under the Police (Scotland) Act 1967 (c. 77), and
(c) in Northern Ireland, the chief constable of the Police Service of Northern Ireland.
(6) An order under subsection (4) may not specify—
(a) a poUKr of Her Majesty's Revenue and Customs if or in so far as it relates to a matter to which section 7 of the Commissioners for Revenue and Customs Act 2005 (c. 11) (former Inland Revenue matters) applies, or
(b) a matter to which that section applies.
(7) An order under this section—
(a) shall be made by statutory instrument, and
(b) may not be made unless a draft has been laid before and approved by resolution of each House of Parliament.
(8) This section has effect despite any restriction on the purposes for which information may be disclosed or used.

39 DISCLOSURE TO LAW ENFORCEMENT AGENCIES

(1) A chief officer of police may disclose information obtained in accordance with section 32 or 33 to—
(a) the States of Jersey police force;
(b) the salaried police force of the Island of Guernsey;
(c) the Isle of Man constabulary;
(d) any other foreign law enforcement agency.
(2) In subsection (1) "foreign law enforcement agency" means a person outside the United Kingdom with functions similar to functions of—
(a) a police force in the United Kingdom, or
(b) the Serious Organised Crime Agency.
(3) In subsection (1) "chief officer of police" means—
(a) in England and Wales, the chief officer of police for a police area specified in section 1 of the Police Act 1996,
(b) in Scotland, the chief constable of a police force maintained under the Police (Scotland) Act 1967, and
(c) in Northern Ireland, the chief constable of the Police Service of Northern Ireland.

40 SEARCHES: CONTRACTING OUT

(1) An authorised person may, in accordance with arrangements made under this section, search a searchable ship, aircraft, vehicle or other thing for the purpose of satisfying himself whether there are individuals whom an immigration officer might wish to examine under paragraph 2 of Schedule 2 to the Immigration Act 1971 (c. 77) (control of entry: administrative provisions).
(2) For the purposes of subsection (1)—
(a) "authorised" means authorised for the purpose of this section by the Secretary of State, and
(b) a ship, aircraft, vehicle or other thing is "searchable" if an immigration officer could search it under paragraph 1(5) of that Schedule.
(3) The Secretary of State may authorise a specified class of constable for the purpose of this section.
(4) The Secretary of State may, with the consent of the Commissioners for Her Majesty's Revenue and Customs, authorise a specified class of officers of Revenue and Customs for the purpose of this section.
(5) The Secretary of State may authorise a person other than a constable or officer of Revenue and Customs for the purpose of this section only if—
(a) the person applies to be authorised, and
(b) the Secretary of State thinks that the person is—
(i) fit and proper for the purpose, and
(ii) suitably trained.
(6) The Secretary of State—
(a) may make arrangements for the exercise by authorised constables of the poUKrs under subsection (1),
(b) may make arrangements with the Commissioners for Her Majesty's Revenue and Customs for the exercise by authorised officers of Revenue and Customs of the poUKrs under subsection (1), and
(c) may make arrangements with one or more persons for the exercise by authorised persons other than constables and officers of Revenue and Customs of the poUKr under subsection (1).
(7) Where in the course of a search under this section an authorised person discovers an individual whom he thinks an immigration officer might wish to examine under paragraph 2 of that Schedule, the authorised person may—
(a) search the individual for the purpose of discovering whether he has with him anything of a kind that might be used—

(i) by him to cause physical harm to himself or another,
(ii) by him to assist his escape from detention, or
(iii) to establish information about his identity, nationality or citizenship or about his journey;
(b) retain, and as soon as is reasonably practicable deliver to an immigration officer, anything of a kind described in paragraph (a) found on a search under that paragraph;
(c) detain the individual, for a period which is as short as is reasonably necessary and which does not exceed three hours, pending the arrival of an immigration officer to whom the individual is to be delivered;
(d) take the individual, as speedily as is reasonably practicable, to a place for the purpose of delivering him to an immigration officer there;
(e) use reasonable force for the purpose of doing anything under paragraphs (a) to (d).
(8) Despite the generality of subsection (7)—
(a) an individual searched under that subsection may not be required to remove clothing other than an outer coat, a jacket or a glove (but he may be required to open his mouth), and
(b) an item may not be retained under subsection (7)(b) if it is subject to legal privilege—
(i) in relation to a search carried out in England and Wales, within the meaning of the Police and Criminal Evidence Act 1984 (c. 60),
(ii) in relation to a search carried out in Scotland, within the meaning of section 412 of the Proceeds of Crime Act 2002 (c. 29), and
(iii) in relation to a search carried out in Northern Ireland, within the meaning of the Police and Criminal Evidence (Northern Ireland) Order 1989 (S.I. 1989/1341 (N.I. 12)).

41 Section 40: supplemental

(1) Arrangements under section 40(6)(c) must include provision for the appointment of a Crown servant to—
(a) monitor the exercise of poUKrs under that section by authorised persons (other than constables or officers of Revenue and Customs),
(b) inspect from time to time the way in which the poUKrs are being exercised by authorised persons (other than constables or officers of Revenue and Customs), and
(c) investigate and report to the Secretary of State about any allegation made against an authorised person (other than a constable or officer of Revenue and Customs) in respect of anything done or not done in the purported exercise of a poUKr under that section.
(2) The authorisation for the purpose of section 40 of a constable or officer of Revenue and Customs or of a class of constable or officer of Revenue and Customs—
(a) may be revoked, and
(b) shall have effect, unless revoked, for such period as shall be specified (whether by reference to dates or otherwise) in the authorisation.
(3) The authorisation of a person other than a constable or officer of Revenue and Customs for the purpose of section 40—
(a) may be subject to conditions,
(b) may be suspended or revoked by the Secretary of State by notice in writing to the authorised person, and
(c) shall have effect, unless suspended or revoked, for such period as shall be specified (whether by reference to dates or otherwise) in the authorisation.
(4) A class may be specified for the purposes of section 40(3) or (4) by reference to—
(a) named individuals,
(b) the functions being exercised by a person,
(c) the location or circumstances in which a person is exercising functions, or
(d) any other matter.
(5) An individual or article delivered to an immigration officer under section 40 shall be treated as if discovered by the immigration officer on a search under Schedule 2 to the Immigration Act 1971 (c. 77).

(6) A person commits an offence if he—
(a) absconds from detention under section 40(7)(c),
(b) absconds while being taken to a place under section 40(7)(d) or having been taken to a place in accordance with that paragraph but before being delivered to an immigration officer,
(c) obstructs an authorised person in the exercise of a poUKr under section 40, or
(d) assaults an authorised person who is exercising a poUKr under section 40.
(7) But a person does not commit an offence under subsection (6) by doing or failing to do anything in respect of an authorised person who is not readily identifiable—
(a) as a constable or officer of Revenue and Customs, or
(b) as an authorised person (whether by means of a uniform or badge or otherwise).
(8) A person guilty of an offence under subsection (6) shall be liable on summary conviction to—
(a) imprisonment for a term not exceeding 51 UKeks, in the case of a conviction in England and Wales, or six months, in the case of a conviction in Scotland or Northern Ireland,
(b) a fine not exceeding level 5 on the standard scale, or
(c) both.
(9) In relation to a conviction occurring before the commencement of section 281(5) of the Criminal Justice Act 2003 (c. 44) (51 UKek maximum term of sentences) the reference in subsection (8)(a) to 51 UKeks shall be treated as a reference to six months.

42 Information: Embarking Passengers

(1) Schedule 2 to the Immigration Act 1971 (c. 77) (control on entry, &c.) shall be amended as follows.
(2) In paragraph 3(1) for the words from "and if he is not" to the end substitute— "and, if he is not a British citizen, for the purpose of establishing—
(a) his identity;
(b) whether he entered the United Kingdom lawfully;
(c) whether he has complied with any conditions of leave to enter or remain in the United Kingdom;
(d) whether his return to the United Kingdom is prohibited or restricted.
(1A) An immigration officer who examines a person under sub-paragraph (1) may require him, by notice in writing, to submit to further examination for a purpose specified in that sub-paragraph."
(3) After paragraph 16(1A) insert—
"(1B) A person who has been required to submit to further examination under paragraph 3(1A) may be detained under the authority of an immigration officer, for a period not exceeding 12 hours, pending the completion of the examination."
(4) In paragraph 21(1) after "16" insert "(1), (1A) or (2)".

CLAIMANTS AND APPLICANTS

43 Accommodation

(1) In section 99(1) of the Immigration and Asylum Act 1999 (c. 33) (provision of support by local authorities)—
(a) for "asylum-seekers and their dependants (if any)" substitute "persons", and
(b) after "section" insert "4,".
(2) In section 99(4) (expenditure) after "section" insert "4,".
(3) In section 118(1)(b) (housing authority accommodation) for "95" substitute "4, 95 or 98".
(4) In the following provisions for "under Part VI of the Immigration and Asylum Act 1999" substitute "under section 4 or Part VI of the Immigration and Asylum Act 1999"—
(a) section 3A(7A) of the Protection from Eviction Act 1977 (c. 43) (excluded tenancies and licences),

(b) paragraph 3A(1) of Schedule 2 to the Housing (Northern Ireland) Order 1983 (S.I. 1983/1118 (N.I. 15)) (non-secure tenancies),
(c) section 23A(5A) of the Rent (Scotland) Act 1984 (c. 58) (excluded tenancies and occupancy rights),
(d) paragraph 4A(1) of Schedule 1 to the Housing Act 1985 (c. 68) (non-secure tenancies),
(e) paragraph 11B of Schedule 4 to the Housing (Scotland) Act 1988 (c. 43) (non-assured tenancies), and
(f) paragraph 12A(1) of Schedule 1 to the Housing Act 1988 (c. 50) (non-assured tenancies).
(5) A tenancy is not a Scottish secure tenancy (within the meaning of the Housing (Scotland) Act 2001 (asp 10) if it is granted in order to provide accommodation under section 4 of the Immigration and Asylum Act 1999 (accommodation).
(6) A tenancy which would be a Scottish secure tenancy but for subsection (4) becomes a Scottish secure tenancy if the landlord notifies the tenant that it is to be regarded as such.
(7) At the end of section 4 of the Immigration and Asylum Act 1999 (c. 33) (accommodation) add—
"(10) The Secretary of State may make regulations permitting a person who is provided with accommodation under this section to be supplied also with services or facilities of a specified kind.
(11) Regulations under subsection (10)—
(a) may, in particular, permit a person to be supplied with a voucher which may be exchanged for goods or services,
(b) may not permit a person to be supplied with money,
(c) may restrict the extent or value of services or facilities to be provided, and
(d) may confer a discretion."

44 Failed asylum-seekers: withdrawal of support

(1) The Secretary of State may by order provide for paragraph 7A of Schedule 3 to the Nationality, Immigration and Asylum Act 2002 (c. 41) (failed asylum-seeker with family: withdrawal of support) to cease to have effect.
(2) An order under subsection (1) shall also provide for the following to cease to have effect—
(a) section 9(1), (2) and (4) of the Asylum and Immigration (Treatment of Claimants, etc.) Act 2004 (c. 19) (which insert paragraph 7A of Schedule 3 and make consequential provision), and
(b) in section 9(3)(a) and (b) of that Act, the words "other than paragraph 7A."
(3) An order under subsection (1)—
(a) may include transitional provision,
(b) shall be made by statutory instrument, and
(c) shall be subject to annulment in pursuance of a resolution of either House of Parliament.

45 Integration loans

(1) Section 13 of the Asylum and Immigration (Treatment of Claimants, etc.) Act 2004 (c. 19) (integration loan for refugees) shall be amended as follows.
(2) In subsection (1) for "to refugees." substitute "—
(a) to refugees, and
(b) to such other classes of person, or to persons other than refugees in such circumstances, as the regulations may prescribe."
(3) In subsection (2)(b) for "granted him indefinite leave to enter or remain" substitute "granted him leave to enter or remain".
(4) In subsection (3)(a)(iii) after "as a refugee" insert "or since some other event)".
(5) In subsection (3)(h) for "refugee" substitute "person".
(6) The heading to the section becomes "Integration loans for refugees and others".

46 Inspection of detention facilities

(1) For section 5A(5A) of the Prison Act 1952 (c. 52) (removal centres: inspection) substitute—
"(5A) Subsections (2) to (5) shall apply—
(a) in relation to removal centres within the meaning of section 147 of the Immigration and Asylum Act 1999 (c. 33),
(b) in relation to short-term holding facilities within the meaning of that section, and
(c) in relation to escort arrangements within the meaning of that section.
(5B) In their application by virtue of subsection (5A) subsections (2) to (5)—
(a) shall apply to centres, facilities and arrangements anywhere in the United Kingdom, and
(b) shall have effect—
(i) as if a reference to prisons UKre a reference to removal centres, short-term holding facilities and escort arrangements,
(ii) as if a reference to prisoners UKre a reference to detained persons and persons to whom escort arrangements apply, and
(iii) with any other necessary modifications."
(2) In section 55 of that Act (extent)—
(a) omit subsection (4A), and
(b) after subsection (5) insert—
"(6) But (despite subsections (4) and (5)) the following shall extend to England and Wales, Scotland and Northern Ireland—
(a) section 5A(5A) and (5B), and
(b) section 5A(2) to (5) in so far as they apply by virtue of section 5A(5A)."

47 Removal: persons with statutorily extended leave

(1) Where a person's leave to enter or remain in the United Kingdom is extended by section 3C(2)(b) or 3D(2)(a) of the Immigration Act 1971 (c. 77) (extension pending appeal), the Secretary of State may decide that the person is to be removed from the United Kingdom, in accordance with directions to be given by an immigration officer if and when the leave ends.
(2) Directions under this section may impose any requirements of a kind prescribed for the purpose of section 10 of the Immigration and Asylum Act 1999 (c. 33) (removal of persons unlawfully in United Kingdom).
(3) In relation to directions under this section, paragraphs 10, 11, 16 to 18, 21 and 22 to 24 of Schedule 2 to the Immigration Act 1971 (administrative provisions as to control of entry) apply as they apply in relation to directions under paragraph 8 of that Schedule.
(4) The costs of complying with a direction given under this section (so far as reasonably incurred) must be met by the Secretary of State.
(5) A person shall not be liable to removal from the United Kingdom under this section at a time when section 7(1)(b) of the Immigration Act 1971 (CommonUKalth and Irish citizens ordinarily resident in United Kingdom) would prevent a decision to deport him.
(6) In section 82(2) of the Nationality, Immigration and Asylum Act 2002 (c. 41) (right of appeal: general) after paragraph (h) insert—
"(ha) a decision that a person is to be removed from the United Kingdom by way of directions under section 47 of the Immigration, Asylum and Nationality Act 2006 (removal: persons with statutorily extended leave),".
(7) In section 92(2) of that Act (appeal from within United Kingdom) after "(f)" insert ", (ha)".
(8) In section 94(1A) of that Act (appeal from within United Kingdom: unfounded claim) for "or (e)" substitute "(e) or (ha)".

48 Removal: cancellation of leave

For section 10(8) of the Immigration and Asylum Act 1999 (c. 33) (removal directions: cancellation of leave to enter or remain in UK) substitute—

"(8) When a person is notified that a decision has been made to remove him in accordance with this section, the notification invalidates any leave to enter or remain in the United Kingdom previously given to him."

49 Capacity to make nationality application

After section 44 of the British Nationality Act 1981 (c. 61) (decisions involving discretion) insert—

"44A Waiver of requirement for full capacity

Where a provision of this Act requires an applicant to be of full capacity, the Secretary of State may waive the requirement in respect of a specified applicant if he thinks it in the applicant's best interests."

50 Procedure

(1) Rules under section 3 of the Immigration Act 1971 (c. 77)—
(a) may require a specified procedure to be folloUKd in making or pursuing an application or claim (whether or not under those rules or any other enactment),
(b) may, in particular, require the use of a specified form and the submission of specified information or documents,
(c) may make provision about the manner in which a fee is to be paid, and
(d) may make provision for the consequences of failure to comply with a requirement under paragraph (a), (b) or (c).
(2) In respect of any application or claim in connection with immigration (whether or not under the rules referred to in subsection (1) or any other enactment) the Secretary of State—
(a) may require the use of a specified form,
(b) may require the submission of specified information or documents, and
(c) may direct the manner in which a fee is to be paid;
and the rules referred to in subsection (1) may provide for the consequences of failure to comply with a requirement under paragraph (a), (b) or (c).
(3) The following shall cease to have effect—
(a) section 31A of the Immigration Act 1971 (procedure for applications), and
(b) section 25 of the Asylum and Immigration (Treatment of Claimants etc.) Act 2004 (c. 19) (marriage: application for permission).
(4) At the end of section 41(1) of the British Nationality Act 1981 (procedure) add—
"(j) as to the consequences of failure to comply with provision made under any of paragraphs (a) to (i)."
(5) In section 10(2)(c) of the Nationality, Immigration and Asylum Act 2002 (c. 41) (right of abode: certificate of entitlement: procedure) for "made in a specified form;" substitute "accompanied by specified information;".
(6) Paragraph 2(3) of Schedule 23 to the Civil Partnership Act 2004 (c. 33) (immigration: procedure) shall cease to have effect.

51 Fees

(1) The Secretary of State may by order require an application or claim in connection with immigration or nationality (whether or not under an enactment) to be accompanied by a specified fee.
(2) The Secretary of State may by order provide for a fee to be charged by him, by an immigration officer or by another specified person in respect of—
(a) the provision on request of a service (whether or not under an enactment) in connection with immigration or nationality,
(b) a process (whether or not under an enactment) in connection with immigration or nationality,

(c) the provision on request of advice in connection with immigration or nationality, or
(d) the provision on request of information in connection with immigration or nationality.
(3) Where an order under this section provides for a fee to be charged, regulations made by the Secretary of State—
(a) shall specify the amount of the fee,
(b) may provide for exceptions,
(c) may confer a discretion to reduce, waive or refund all or part of a fee,
(d) may make provision about the consequences of failure to pay a fee,
(e) may make provision about enforcement, and
(f) may make provision about the time or period of time at or during which a fee may or must be paid.
(4) Fees paid by virtue of this section shall—
(a) be paid into the Consolidated Fund, or
(b) be applied in such other way as the relevant order may specify.

52 Fees: supplemental

(1) A fee imposed under section 51 may relate to a thing whether or not it is done wholly or partly outside the United Kingdom; but that section is without prejudice to—
(a) section 1 of the Consular Fees Act 1980 (c. 23), and
(b) any other poUKr to charge a fee.
(2) Section 51 is without prejudice to the application of section 102 of the Finance (No. 2) Act 1987 (c. 51) (government fees and charges); and an order made under that section in respect of a poUKr repealed by Schedule 2 to this Act shall have effect as if it related to the poUKrs under section 51 above in so far as they relate to the same matters as the repealed poUKr.
(3) An order or regulations under section 51—
(a) may make provision generally or only in respect of specified cases or circumstances,
(b) may make different provision for different cases or circumstances,
(c) may include incidental, consequential or transitional provision, and
(d) shall be made by statutory instrument.
(4) An order under section 51—
(a) may be made only with the consent of the Treasury, and
(b) may be made only if a draft has been laid before and approved by resolution of each House of Parliament.
(5) Regulations under section 51—
(a) may be made only with the consent of the Treasury, and
(b) shall be subject to annulment in pursuance of a resolution of either House of Parliament.
(6) A reference in section 51 to anything in connection with immigration or nationality includes a reference to anything in connection with an enactment (including an enactment of a jurisdiction outside the United Kingdom) that relates wholly or partly to immigration or nationality.
(7) Schedule 2 (consequential amendments) shall have effect.

MISCELLANEOUS

53 Arrest pending deportation

At the end of paragraph 2(4) of Schedule 3 to the Immigration Act 1971 (c. 77) (deportation: poUKr to detain) insert "; and for that purpose the reference in paragraph 17(1) to a person liable to detention includes a reference to a person who would be liable to detention upon receipt of a notice which is ready to be given to him."

54 Refugee Convention: construction

(1) In the construction and application of Article 1(F)(c) of the Refugee Convention the reference to acts contrary to the purposes and principles of the United Nations shall be taken as including, in particular—
(a) acts of committing, preparing or instigating terrorism (whether or not the acts amount to an actual or inchoate offence), and
(b) acts of encouraging or inducing others to commit, prepare or instigate terrorism (whether or not the acts amount to an actual or inchoate offence).
(2) In this section—

- "the Refugee Convention" means the Convention relating to the Status of Refugees done at Geneva on 28th July 1951, and
- "terrorism" has the meaning given by section 1 of the Terrorism Act 2000 (c. 11).

55 Refugee Convention: certification

(1) This section applies to an asylum appeal where the Secretary of State issues a certificate that the appellant is not entitled to the protection of Article 33(1) of the Refugee Convention because—
(a) Article 1(F) applies to him (whether or not he would otherwise be entitled to protection), or
(b) Article 33(2) applies to him on grounds of national security (whether or not he would otherwise be entitled to protection).
(2) In this section—
(a) "asylum appeal" means an appeal—
(i) which is brought under section 82, 83 or 101 of the Nationality, Immigration and Asylum Act 2002 (c. 41) or section 2 of the Special Immigration Appeals Commission Act 1997 (c. 68), and
(ii) in which the appellant claims that to remove him from or require him to leave the United Kingdom would be contrary to the United Kingdom's obligations under the Refugee Convention, and
(b) "the Refugee Convention" means the Convention relating to the Status of Refugees done at Geneva on 28th July 1951.
(3) The Asylum and Immigration Tribunal or the Special Immigration Appeals Commission must begin substantive deliberations on the asylum appeal by considering the statements in the Secretary of State's certificate.
(4) If the Tribunal or Commission agrees with those statements it must dismiss such part of the asylum appeal as amounts to an asylum claim (before considering any other aspect of the case).
(5) Section 72(10)(a) of the Nationality, Immigration and Asylum Act 2002 (serious criminal: Tribunal or Commission to begin by considering certificate) shall have effect subject to subsection (3) above.
(6) Section 33 of the Anti-terrorism, Crime and Security Act 2001 (c. 24) (certificate of non-application of Refugee Convention) shall cease to have effect.

56 Deprivation of citizenship

(1) For section 40(2) of the British Nationality Act 1981 (c. 61) (deprivation of citizenship: prejudicing UK interests) substitute—
"(2) The Secretary of State may by order deprive a person of a citizenship status if the Secretary of State is satisfied that deprivation is conducive to the public good."
(2) At the end of section 40A(3) of that Act (deprivation: appeal) add— ", and
(e) section 108 (forged document: proceedings in private).";
(and omit the word "and" before section 40A(3)(d)).

57 DEPRIVATION OF RIGHT OF ABODE

(1) After section 2 of the Immigration Act 1971 (c. 77) (right of abode) insert—

"2A DEPRIVATION OF RIGHT OF ABODE

(1) The Secretary of State may by order remove from a specified person a right of abode in the United Kingdom which he has under section 2(1)(b).
(2) The Secretary of State may make an order under subsection (1) in respect of a person only if the Secretary of State thinks that it would be conducive to the public good for the person to be excluded or removed from the United Kingdom.
(3) An order under subsection (1) may be revoked by order of the Secretary of State.
(4) While an order under subsection (1) has effect in relation to a person—
(a) section 2(2) shall not apply to him, and
(b) any certificate of entitlement granted to him shall have no effect."
(2) In section 82(2) of the Nationality, Immigration and Asylum Act 2002 (c. 41) (right of appeal: definition of immigration decision) after paragraph (ia) insert—
"(ib) a decision to make an order under section 2A of that Act (deprivation of right of abode),".

58 ACQUISITION OF BRITISH NATIONALITY, &C.

(1) The Secretary of State shall not grant an application for registration of an adult or young person as a citizen of any description or as a British subject under a provision listed in subsection (2) unless satisfied that the adult or young person is of good character.
(2) Those provisions are—
(a) sections 1(3) and (4), 3(1) and (5), 4(2) and (5), 4A, 4C, 5, 10(1) and (2), 13(1) and (3) of the British Nationality Act 1981 (c. 61) (registration as British citizen),
(b) sections 15(3) and (4), 17(1) and (5), 22(1) and (2), 24, 27(1) and 32 of that Act (registration as British overseas territories citizen, &c.),
(c) section 1 of the Hong Kong (War Wives and Widows) Act 1996 (c. 41) (registration as British citizen), and
(d) section 1 of the British Nationality (Hong Kong) Act 1997 (c. 20) (registration as British citizen).
(3) In subsection (1) "adult or young person" means a person who has attained the age of 10 at the time when the application is made.
(4) Where the Secretary of State makes arrangements under section 43 of the British Nationality Act 1981 for a function to be exercised by some other person, subsection (1) above shall have effect in relation to that function as if the reference to the Secretary of State UKre a reference to that other person.

59 DETAINED PERSONS: NATIONAL MINIMUM WAGE

(1) After section 153 of the Immigration and Asylum Act 1999 (c. 33) (removal centres: rules) insert—

"153A DETAINED PERSONS: NATIONAL MINIMUM WAGE

A detained person does not qualify for the national minimum wage in respect of work which he does in pursuance of removal centre rules."
(2) After section 45A of the National Minimum Wage Act 1998 (c. 39) (exemptions from national minimum wage: persons discharging fines) insert—

“45B Immigration: detained persons

Section 153A of the Immigration and Asylum Act 1999 (c. 33) (persons detained in removal centres) disqualifies certain persons for the national minimum wage.”

GENERAL

60 Money

There shall be paid out of money provided by Parliament—
(a) any expenditure of the Secretary of State in connection with this Act, and
(b) any increase attributable to this Act in sums payable under another enactment out of money provided by Parliament.

61 Repeals

Schedule 3 (repeals) shall have effect.

62 Commencement

(1) The preceding provisions of this Act shall come into force in accordance with provision made by order of the Secretary of State.
(2) An order under subsection (1)—
(a) may make provision generally or only for specified purposes,
(b) may make different provision for different purposes,
(c) may include transitional or incidental provision or savings, and
(d) shall be made by statutory instrument.

63 Extent

(1) This Act extends to—
(a) England and Wales,
(b) Scotland, and
(c) Northern Ireland.
(2) But—
(a) an amendment by this Act of another Act has the same extent as that Act or as the relevant part of that Act (ignoring extent by virtue of an Order in Council), and
(b) a provision of this Act shall, so far as it relates to nationality, have the same extent as the British Nationality Act 1981 (c. 61) (disregarding excepted provisions under section 53(7) of that Act).
(3) Her Majesty may by Order in Council direct that a provision of this Act is to extend, with or without modification or adaptation, to—
(a) any of the Channel Islands;
(b) the Isle of Man.
(4) Subsection (3) does not apply in relation to the extension to a place of a provision which extends there by virtue of subsection (2)(b).

64 Citation

(1) This Act may be cited as the Immigration, Asylum and Nationality Act 2006.
(2) A reference (in any enactment, including one passed or made before this Act) to “the Immigration Acts” is to—
(a) the Immigration Act 1971 (c. 77),
(b) the Immigration Act 1988 (c. 14),
(c) the Asylum and Immigration Appeals Act 1993 (c. 23),

(d) the Asylum and Immigration Act 1996 (c. 49),
(e) the Immigration and Asylum Act 1999 (c. 33),
(f) the Nationality, Immigration and Asylum Act 2002 (c. 41),
(g) the Asylum and Immigration (Treatment of Claimants, etc.) Act 2004 (c. 19), and
(h) this Act.
(3) The following shall cease to have effect—
(a) section 32(5) of the Immigration Act 1971 ("the Immigration Acts"),
(b) in section 167(1) of the Immigration and Asylum Act 1999, the definition of "the Immigration Acts",
(c) section 158 of the Nationality, Immigration and Asylum Act 2002 ("the Immigration Acts"), and
(d) section 44 of the Asylum and Immigration (Treatment of Claimants, etc.) Act 2004 ("the Immigration Acts").
(4) In Schedule 1 to the Interpretation Act 1978 (c. 30) (defined expressions) at the appropriate place insert—
""The Immigration Acts" has the meaning given by section 64 of the Immigration, Asylum and Nationality Act 2006."

SCHEDULE 1 IMMIGRATION AND ASYLUM APPEALS: CONSEQUENTIAL AMENDMENTS

NATIONALITY, IMMIGRATION AND ASYLUM ACT 2002 (C. 41)

1 The Nationality, Immigration and Asylum Act 2002 (appeals) shall be amended as follows.
2 In section 72(9) (serious criminal) after ", 83" insert ", 83A".
3 In section 85(4) (matters to be considered) for "or 83(2)" substitute ", 83(2) or 83A(2)".
4 In section 86(1) (determination of appeal) for "or 83." substitute ", 83 or 83A."
5 In section 87(1) (successful appeal: direction) for "or 83" substitute ", 83 or 83A".
6 In section 97(1) and (3) (national security, &c.) for "or 83(2)" substitute ", 83(2) or 83A(2)".
7 In section 103A(1) (review of Tribunal's decision) for "or 83" substitute ", 83 or 83A".
8 In section 103E(1) (appeal from Tribunal sitting as panel) for "or 83" substitute ", 83 or 83A".
9 In section 106(1)(a) and (b) (rules) for "or 83" substitute ", 83 or 83A".
10 In section 108(1)(a) (forged document: proceedings in private) for "or 83" substitute ", 83 or 83A".
11 In section 112 (regulations and orders) in subsection (5) for "94(6)" substitute "94(6) or (6B)".

RACE RELATIONS ACT 1976 (C. 74)

12 In section 57A(5) of the Race Relations Act 1976 (discrimination claims in immigration cases) in the definition of "immigration appellate body" for "an adjudicator appointed for the purposes of Part 5 of the 2002 Act, the Immigration Appeal Tribunal," substitute "the Asylum and Immigration Tribunal,".

BRITISH NATIONALITY ACT 1981 (C. 61)

13 In section 40A(3) of the British Nationality Act 1981 (deprivation of citizenship: appeal) for "or 83" substitute ", 83 or 83A".

SPECIAL IMMIGRATION APPEALS COMMISSION ACT 1997 (C. 68)

14 In section 2 of the Special Immigration Appeals Commission Act 1997 (jurisdiction: appeals)—
(a) in subsection (1)(a) and (b) for "or 83(2)" substitute ", 83(2) or 83A(2)",
(b) in subsection (2)(a)—
(i) after "3C" insert "or 3D", and
(ii) for "(continuation of leave pending variation decision)" substitute "continuation of leave", and
(c) in subsection (3)—

(i) for "an appeal against the rejection of a claim for asylum" substitute "an appeal against a decision other than an immigration decision", and
(ii) after "83(2)" insert "or 83A(2)".
Section 52

SCHEDULE 2 FEES: CONSEQUENTIAL AMENDMENTS

BRITISH NATIONALITY ACT 1981 (C. 61)

1 In section 41 of the British Nationality Act 1981 (regulations and Orders in Council)—
(a) omit subsection (2), and
(b) in subsection (3)—
(i) omit "or (2)", and
(ii) omit paragraph (b).
2 Section 42A of the British Nationality Act 1981 (registration and naturalisation: fee) shall cease to have effect.

IMMIGRATION AND ASYLUM ACT 1999 (C. 33)

3 Sections 5 and 27 of the Immigration and Asylum Act 1999 (charges) shall cease to have effect.

NATIONALITY, IMMIGRATION AND ASYLUM ACT 2002 (C. 41)

4 In section 10(2) (right of abode: certificate of entitlement)—
(a) paragraph (e) shall cease to have effect, and
(b) in paragraph (f) for "(a) to (e)" substitute "(a) to (d)".
5 Section 122 (fee for work permit, &c.) shall cease to have effect.

ASYLUM AND IMMIGRATION (TREATMENT OF CLAIMANTS, ETC.) ACT 2004 (C. 19)

6 (1) Section 42 of the Asylum and Immigration (Treatment of Claimants, etc.) Act 2004 (amount of fees) shall be amended as follows.
(2) In subsection (1)—
(a) for "In prescribing a fee for an application or process under a provision specified in subsection (2)" substitute "In prescribing a fee under section 51 of the Immigration, Asylum and Nationality Act 2006 (fees) in connection with a matter specified in subsection (2)", and
(b) omit ", with the consent of the Treasury,".
(3) For subsection (2) substitute—
"(2) Those matters are—
(a) anything done under, by virtue of or in connection with a provision of the British Nationality Act 1981 (c. 61) or of the former nationality Acts (within the meaning given by section 50(1) of that Act),
(b) an application for leave to remain in the United Kingdom,
(c) an application for the variation of leave to enter, or remain in, the United Kingdom,
(d) section 10 of the Nationality, Immigration and Asylum Act 2002 (c. 41) (right of abode: certificate of entitlement),
(e) a work permit, and
(f) any other document which relates to employment and is issued for a purpose of immigration rules or in connection with leave to enter or remain in the United Kingdom."

UK BORDERS ACT 2007

The **UK Borders Act 2007** is an Act of the Parliament of the United Kingdom about immigration and asylum. Amongst other things, it introduced compulsory biometric documents for non-EU immigrants and introduced greater poUKrs for immigration control. It received Royal Assent on 30 October 2007 with sections 17, 59, 60 and 61 coming into force on that day.

The first commencement order made under section 59 of the Act brought sections 1-4, 5-8, 14, 15, 18, 20, 22, 23, 29-31 and 40-43 fully into force on 31 January 2008. The same commencement order brought sections 10, 11, 13, 16 and 26 either partially into force, or into force subject to transitional provisions, on the same day. Repeals relating to the Immigration Act 1971, Immigration and Asylum Act 1999, Commissioners for Revenue and Customs Act 2005, Immigration and Nationality Act 2006 and section 130 of the Nationality, Immigration and Asylum Act 2004 UKre also commenced on 31 January.

An Act to make provision about immigration and asylum; and for connected purposes.

[30th October 2007]

Be it enacted by the Queen's most Excellent Majesty, by and with the advice and consent of the Lords Spiritual and Temporal, and Commons, in this present Parliament assembled, and by the authority of the same, as follows:—

DETENTION AT PORTS

1 Designated immigration officers

(1) The Secretary of State may designate immigration officers for the purposes of section 2.
(2) The Secretary of State may designate only officers who the Secretary of State thinks are—
(a) fit and proper for the purpose, and
(b) suitably trained.
(3) A designation—
(a) may be permanent or for a specified period, and
(b) may (in either case) be revoked.

2 Detention

(1) A designated immigration officer at a port in England, Wales or Northern Ireland may detain an individual if the immigration officer thinks that the individual—
(a) may be liable to arrest by a constable under section 24(1), (2) or (3) of the Police and Criminal Evidence Act 1984 (c. 60) or Article 26(1), (2) or (3) of the Police and Criminal Evidence (Northern Ireland) Order 1989 (S.I. 1989/1341 (N.I. 12)), or
(b) is subject to a warrant for arrest.
(2) A designated immigration officer who detains an individual—
(a) must arrange for a constable to attend as soon as is reasonably practicable,
(b) may search the individual for, and retain, anything that might be used to assist escape or to cause physical injury to the individual or another person,
(c) must retain anything found on a search which the immigration officer thinks may be evidence of the commission of an offence, and
(d) must, when the constable arrives, deliver to the constable the individual and anything retained on a search.
(3) An individual may not be detained under this section for longer than three hours.
(4) A designated immigration officer may use reasonable force for the purpose of exercising a poUKr under this section.
(5) Where an individual whom a designated immigration officer has detained or attempted to detain under this section leaves the port, a designated immigration officer may—

(a) pursue the individual, and
(b) return the individual to the port.
(6) Detention under this section shall be treated as detention under the Immigration Act 1971 (c. 77) for the purposes of Part 8 of the Immigration and Asylum Act 1999 (c. 33) (detained persons).

3 Enforcement

(1) An offence is committed by a person who—
(a) absconds from detention under section 2,
(b) assaults an immigration officer exercising a poUKr under section 2, or
(c) obstructs an immigration officer in the exercise of a poUKr under section 2.
(2) A person guilty of an offence under subsection (1)(a) or (b) shall be liable on summary conviction to—
(a) imprisonment for a term not exceeding 51 UKeks,
(b) a fine not exceeding level 5 on the standard scale, or
(c) both.
(3) A person guilty of an offence under subsection (1)(c) shall be liable on summary conviction to—
(a) imprisonment for a term not exceeding 51 UKeks,
(b) a fine not exceeding level 3 on the standard scale, or
(c) both.
(4) In the application of this section to Northern Ireland—
(a) the reference in subsection (2)(a) to 51 UKeks shall be treated as a reference to six months, and
(b) the reference in subsection (3)(a) to 51 UKeks shall be treated as a reference to one month.
(5) In relation to an offence committed before the commencement of section 281(5) of the Criminal Justice Act 2003 (c. 44) (51 UKek maximum term of sentences)—
(a) the reference in subsection (2)(a) to 51 UKeks shall be treated as a reference to six months, and
(b) the reference in subsection (3)(a) to 51 UKeks shall be treated as a reference to one month.

4 Interpretation: "port"

(1) In section 2 "port" includes an airport and a hoverport.
(2) A place shall be treated for the purposes of that section as a port in relation to an individual if a designated immigration officer believes that the individual—
(a) has gone there for the purpose of embarking on a ship or aircraft, or
(b) has arrived there on disembarking from a ship or aircraft.

BIOMETRIC REGISTRATION

5 Registration regulations

(1) The Secretary of State may make regulations—
(a) requiring a person subject to immigration control to apply for the issue of a document recording biometric information (a "biometric immigration document");
(b) requiring a biometric immigration document to be used—
(i) for specified immigration purposes,
(ii) in connection with specified immigration procedures, or
(iii) in specified circumstances, where a question arises about a person's status in relation to nationality or immigration;
(c) requiring a person who produces a biometric immigration document by virtue of paragraph (b) to provide information for comparison with information provided in connection with the application for the document.

(2) Regulations under subsection (1)(a) may, in particular—
(a) apply generally or only to a specified class of persons subject to immigration control (for example, persons making or seeking to make a specified kind of application for immigration purposes);
(b) specify the period within which an application for a biometric immigration document must be made;
(c) make provision about the issue of biometric immigration documents;
(d) make provision about the content of biometric immigration documents (which may include non-biometric information);
(e) make provision permitting a biometric immigration document to be combined with another document;
(f) make provision for biometric immigration documents to begin to have effect, and cease to have effect, in accordance with the regulations;
(g) require a person who acquires a biometric immigration document, without the consent of the person to whom it relates or of the Secretary of State, to surrender it to the Secretary of State as soon as is reasonably practicable;
(h) permit the Secretary of State to require the surrender of a biometric immigration document in other specified circumstances;
(i) permit the Secretary of State on issuing a biometric immigration document to require the surrender of other documents connected with immigration or nationality.
(3) Regulations under subsection (1)(a) may permit the Secretary of State to cancel a biometric immigration document—
(a) if the Secretary of State thinks that information provided in connection with the document was or has become false, misleading or incomplete,
(b) if the Secretary of State thinks that the document has been lost or stolen,
(c) if the Secretary of State thinks that the document (including any information recorded in it) has been altered, damaged or destroyed (whether deliberately or not),
(d) if the Secretary of State thinks that an attempt has been made (whether successfully or not) to copy the document or to do anything to enable it to be copied,
(e) if the Secretary of State thinks that a person has failed to surrender the document in accordance with subsection (2)(g) or (h),
(f) if the Secretary of State thinks that the document should be re-issued (whether because the information recorded in it requires alteration or for any other reason),
(g) if the Secretary of State thinks that the holder is to be given leave to enter or remain in the United Kingdom,
(h) if the Secretary of State thinks that the holder's leave to enter or remain in the United Kingdom is to be varied, cancelled or invalidated or to lapse,
(i) if the Secretary of State thinks that the holder has died,
(j) if the Secretary of State thinks that the holder has been removed from the United Kingdom (whether by deportation or otherwise),
(k) if the Secretary of State thinks that the holder has left the United Kingdom without retaining leave to enter or remain, and
(l) in such other circumstances as the regulations may specify.
(4) Regulations under subsection (1)(a) may require notification to be given to the Secretary of State by the holder of a biometric immigration document—
(a) who knows or suspects that the document has been lost or stolen,
(b) who knows or suspects that the document has been altered or damaged (whether deliberately or not),
(c) who knows or suspects that information provided in connection with the document was or has become false, misleading or incomplete,
(d) who was given leave to enter or remain in the United Kingdom in accordance with a provision of rules under section 3 of the Immigration Act 1971 (c. 77) (immigration rules) and knows or

suspects that owing to a change of the holder's circumstances the holder would no longer qualify for leave under that provision, or
(e) in such other circumstances as the regulations may specify.
(5) Regulations under subsection (1)(a) may require a person applying for the issue of a biometric immigration document to provide information (which may include biographical or other non-biometric information) to be recorded in it or retained by the Secretary of State; and, in particular, the regulations may—
(a) require, or permit an authorised person to require, the provision of information in a specified form;
(b) require an individual to submit, or permit an authorised person to require an individual to submit, to a specified process by means of which biometric information is obtained or recorded;
(c) confer a function (which may include the exercise of a discretion) on an authorised person;
(d) permit the Secretary of State, instead of requiring the provision of information, to use or retain information which is (for whatever reason) already in the Secretary of State's possession.
(6) Regulations under subsection (1)(b) may, in particular, require the production or other use of a biometric immigration document that is combined with another document; and section 16 of the Identity Cards Act 2006 (c. 15) (prohibition of requirement to produce ID card) is subject to this subsection.
(7) Regulations under subsection (1)(b) may not make provision the effect of which would be to require a person to carry a biometric immigration document at all times.
(8) Regulations under subsection (1)(c) may, in particular, make provision of a kind specified in subsection (5)(a) or (b).
(9) Rules under section 3 of the Immigration Act 1971 (c. 77) may require a person applying for the issue of a biometric immigration document to provide non-biometric information to be recorded in it or retained by the Secretary of State.
(10) Subsections (5) to (9) are without prejudice to the generality of section 50 of the Immigration, Asylum and Nationality Act 2006 (c. 13) (procedure).

6 REGULATIONS: SUPPLEMENTAL

(1) This section applies to regulations under section 5(1).
(2) Regulations amending or replacing earlier regulations may require a person who holds a biometric immigration document issued under the earlier regulations to apply under the new regulations.
(3) In so far as regulations require an individual under the age of 16 to submit to a process for the recording of biometric information, or permit an authorised person to require an individual under the age of 16 to submit to a process of that kind, the regulations must make provision similar to section 141(3) to (5) and (13) of the Immigration and Asylum Act 1999 (c. 33) (fingerprints: children).
(4) Rules under section 3 of the Immigration Act 1971 (immigration rules) may make provision by reference to compliance or non-compliance with regulations.
(5) Information in the Secretary of State's possession which is used or retained in accordance with regulations under section 5(5)(d) shall be treated, for the purpose of requirements about treatment and destruction, as having been provided in accordance with the regulations at the time at which it is used or retained in accordance with them.
(6) Regulations—
(a) may make provision having effect generally or only in specified cases or circumstances,
(b) may make different provision for different cases or circumstances,
(c) may include incidental, consequential or transitional provision,
(d) shall be made by statutory instrument, and
(e) may not be made unless a draft has been laid before and approved by resolution of each House of Parliament.

7 EFFECT OF NON-COMPLIANCE

(1) Regulations under section 5(1) must include provision about the effect of failure to comply with a requirement of the regulations.
(2) In particular, the regulations may—
(a) require or permit an application for a biometric immigration document to be refused;
(b) require or permit an application or claim in connection with immigration to be disregarded or refused;
(c) require or permit the cancellation or variation of leave to enter or remain in the United Kingdom;
(d) require the Secretary of State to consider giving a notice under section 9;
(e) provide for the consequence of a failure to be at the discretion of the Secretary of State.
(3) The regulations may also permit the Secretary of State to designate an adult as the person responsible for ensuring that a child complies with requirements of the regulations; and for that purpose—
(a) "adult" means an individual who has attained the age of 18,
(b) "child" means an individual who has not attained the age of 18, and
(c) sections 9 to 13 shall apply (with any necessary modifications) to a designated adult's failure to ensure compliance by a child with a requirement of regulations as they apply to a person's own failure to comply with a requirement.

8 USE AND RETENTION OF INFORMATION

(1) Regulations under section 5(1) must make provision about the use and retention by the Secretary of State of biometric information provided in accordance with the regulations.
(2) The regulations may include provision permitting the use of information—
(a) in connection with the exercise of a function by virtue of the Immigration Acts,
(b) in connection with control of the United Kingdom's borders,
(c) in connection with the exercise of a function in relation to nationality,
(d) in connection with the prevention, investigation or prosecution of an offence,
(e) for a purpose which appears to the Secretary of State to be required in order to protect national security, and
(f) for such other purposes (whether in connection with functions under an enactment or otherwise) as the regulations may specify.
(3) Regulations under section 5(1)—
(a) must include provision about the destruction of biometric information held by the Secretary of State having been obtained or recorded by virtue of the regulations,
(b) must, in particular, require the destruction of biometric information held by the Secretary of State if the Secretary of State thinks that it is no longer likely to be of use in accordance with provision made by virtue of subsection (1) above, and
(c) must, in particular, include provision similar to section 143(2) and (10) to (13) of the Immigration and Asylum Act 1999 (c. 33) (fingerprints: destruction of copies and electronic data).
(4) But a requirement to destroy information shall not apply if and in so far as the information is retained in accordance with and for the purposes of another enactment.

9 PENALTY

(1) The Secretary of State may by notice require a person to pay a penalty for failing to comply with a requirement of regulations under section 5(1).
(2) The notice must—
(a) specify the amount of the penalty,
(b) specify a date before which the penalty must be paid to the Secretary of State,
(c) specify methods by which the penalty may be paid,

(d) explain the grounds on which the Secretary of State thinks the person has failed to comply with a requirement of the regulations, and
(e) explain the effect of sections 10 to 12.
(3) The amount specified under subsection (2)(a) may not exceed £1,000.
(4) The date specified under subsection (2)(b) must be not less than 14 days after the date on which the notice is given.
(5) A person who has been given a notice under subsection (1) for failing to comply with regulations may be given further notices in the case of continued failure; but a person may not be given a new notice—
(a) during the time available for objection or appeal against an earlier notice, or
(b) while an objection or appeal against an earlier notice has been instituted and is neither withdrawn nor determined.
(6) The Secretary of State may by order amend subsection (3) to reflect a change in the value of money.

10 Penalty: objection

(1) A person (P) who is given a penalty notice under section 9(1) may by notice to the Secretary of State object on the grounds—
(a) that P has not failed to comply with a requirement of regulations under section 5(1),
(b) that it is unreasonable to require P to pay a penalty, or
(c) that the amount of the penalty is excessive.
(2) A notice of objection must—
(a) specify the grounds of objection and P's reasons,
(b) comply with any prescribed requirements as to form and content, and
(c) be given within the prescribed period.
(3) The Secretary of State shall consider a notice of objection and—
(a) cancel the penalty notice,
(b) reduce the penalty by varying the penalty notice,
(c) increase the penalty by issuing a new penalty notice, or
(d) confirm the penalty notice.
(4) The Secretary of State shall act under subsection (3) and notify P—
(a) in accordance with any prescribed requirements, and
(b) within the prescribed period or such longer period as the Secretary of State and P may agree.

11 Penalty: appeal

(1) A person (P) who is given a penalty notice under section 9(1) may appeal to—
(a) a county court, in England and Wales or Northern Ireland, or
(b) the sheriff, in Scotland.
(2) An appeal may be brought on the grounds—
(a) that P has not failed to comply with a requirement of regulations under section 5(1),
(b) that it is unreasonable to require P to pay a penalty, or
(c) that the amount of the penalty is excessive.
(3) The court or sheriff may—
(a) cancel the penalty notice,
(b) reduce the penalty by varying the penalty notice,
(c) increase the penalty by varying the penalty notice (whether because the court or sheriff thinks the original amount insufficient or because the court or sheriff thinks that the appeal should not have been brought), or
(d) confirm the penalty notice.
(4) An appeal may be brought—

(a) whether or not P has given a notice of objection, and
(b) irrespective of the Secretary of State's decision on any notice of objection.
(5) The court or sheriff may consider matters of which the Secretary of State was not and could not have been aware before giving the penalty notice.
(6) Rules of court may make provision about the timing of an appeal under this section.

12 Penalty: enforcement

(1) Where a penalty has not been paid before the date specified in the penalty notice in accordance with section 9(2)(b), it may be recovered as a debt due to the Secretary of State.
(2) Where a notice of objection is given in respect of a penalty notice, the Secretary of State may not take steps to enforce the penalty notice before—
(a) deciding what to do in response to the notice of objection, and
(b) informing the objector.
(3) The Secretary of State may not take steps to enforce a penalty notice while an appeal under section 11—
(a) could be brought (disregarding any possibility of an appeal out of time with permission), or
(b) has been brought and has not been determined or abandoned.
(4) In proceedings for the recovery of a penalty no question may be raised as to the matters specified in sections 10 and 11 as grounds for objection or appeal.
(5) Money received by the Secretary of State in respect of a penalty shall be paid into the Consolidated Fund.

13 Penalty: code of practice

(1) The Secretary of State shall issue a code of practice setting out the matters to be considered in determining—
(a) whether to give a penalty notice under section 9(1), and
(b) the amount of a penalty.
(2) The code may, in particular, require the Secretary of State to consider any decision taken by virtue of section 7.
(3) A court or the sheriff shall, when considering an appeal under section 11, have regard to the code.
(4) The Secretary of State may revise and re-issue the code.
(5) Before issuing or re-issuing the code the Secretary of State must—
(a) publish proposals,
(b) consult members of the public, and
(c) lay a draft before Parliament.
(6) The code (or re-issued code) shall come into force at the prescribed time.

14 Penalty: prescribed matters

(1) In sections 10 to 13 "prescribed" means prescribed by the Secretary of State by order.
(2) An order under subsection (1) or under section 9(6)—
(a) may make provision generally or only for specified purposes,
(b) may make different provision for different purposes,
(c) shall be made by statutory instrument, and
(d) shall be subject to annulment in pursuance of a resolution of either House of Parliament.
(3) But the first order under section 13(6) shall not be made unless a draft has been laid before and approved by resolution of each House of Parliament (and shall not be subject to annulment).

15 Interpretation

(1) For the purposes of section 5—

(a) "person subject to immigration control" means a person who under the Immigration Act 1971 (c. 77) requires leave to enter or remain in the United Kingdom (whether or not such leave has been given),
(b) "biometric information" means information about external physical characteristics,
(c) "external physical characteristics" includes, in particular—
(i) fingerprints, and
(ii) features of the iris or any other part of the eye,
(d) "document" includes a card or sticker and any other method of recording information (whether in writing or by the use of electronic or other technology or by a combination of methods),
(e) "authorised person" has the meaning given by section 141(5) of the Immigration and Asylum Act 1999 (c. 33) (authority to take fingerprints),
(f) "immigration" includes asylum, and
(g) regulations permitting something to be done by the Secretary of State may (but need not) permit it to be done only where the Secretary of State is of a specified opinion.
(2) An application for a biometric immigration document is an application in connection with immigration for the purposes of—
(a) section 50(1) and (2) of the Immigration, Asylum and Nationality Act 2006 (c. 13) (procedure), and
(b) section 51 of that Act (fees);
and in the application of either of those sections to an application for a biometric immigration document, the prescribed consequences of non-compliance may include any of the consequences specified in section 7(2) above.

TREATMENT OF CLAIMANTS

16 Conditional leave to enter or remain

After section 3(1)(c)(iii) of the Immigration Act 1971 (limited leave to enter or remain: conditions) insert—
"(iv) a condition requiring him to report to an immigration officer or the Secretary of State; and
(v) a condition about residence."

17 Support for failed asylum-seekers

(1) This section applies for the purposes of—
(a) Part 6 (and section 4) of the Immigration and Asylum Act 1999 (support and accommodation for asylum-seekers),
(b) Part 2 of the Nationality, Immigration and Asylum Act 2002 (c. 41) (accommodation centres), and
(c) Schedule 3 to that Act (withholding and withdrawal of support).
(2) A person (A-S) remains (or again becomes) an asylum-seeker, despite the fact that the claim for asylum made by A-S has been determined, during any period when—
(a) A-S can bring an in-country appeal against an immigration decision under section 82 of the 2002 Act or section 2 of the Special Immigration Appeals Commission Act 1997 (c. 68), or
(b) an in-country appeal, brought by A-S under either of those sections against an immigration decision, is pending (within the meaning of section 104 of the 2002 Act).
(3) For the purposes of subsection (2)—
(a) "in-country" appeal means an appeal brought while the appellant is in the United Kingdom, and
(b) the possibility of an appeal out of time with permission shall be ignored.
(4) For the purposes of the provisions mentioned in subsection (1)(a) and (b), a person's status as an asylum-seeker by virtue of subsection (2)(b) continues for a prescribed period after the appeal ceases to be pending.

(5) In subsection (4) "prescribed" means prescribed by regulations made by the Secretary of State; and the regulations—
(a) may contain incidental or transitional provision,
(b) may make different provision for different classes of case,
(c) shall be made by statutory instrument, and
(d) shall be subject to annulment in pursuance of a resolution of either House of Parliament.
(6) This section shall be treated as always having had effect.

18 SUPPORT FOR ASYLUM-SEEKERS: ENFORCEMENT

In Part 6 of the Immigration and Asylum Act 1999 (c. 33) (support for asylum-seekers) after section 109 (offences: supplemental) insert—

"109A ARREST

An immigration officer may arrest without warrant a person whom the immigration officer reasonably suspects has committed an offence under section 105 or 106.

109B >ENTRY, SEARCH AND SEIZURE

(1) An offence under section 105 or 106 shall be treated as—
(a) a relevant offence for the purposes of sections 28B and 28D of the Immigration Act 1971, and
(b) an offence under Part 3 of that Act (criminal proceedings) for the purposes of sections 28(4), 28E, 28G and 28H (search after arrest, &c.) of that Act.
(2) The following provisions of the Immigration Act 1971 (c. 77) shall have effect in connection with an offence under section 105 or 106 of this Act as they have effect in connection with an offence under that Act—
(a) section 28I (seized material: access and copying),
(b) section 28J (search warrants: safeguards),
(c) section 28K (execution of warrants), and
(d) section 28L(1) (interpretation)."

19 POINTS-BASED APPLICATIONS: NO NEW EVIDENCE ON APPEAL

(1) For section 85(5) of the Nationality, Immigration and Asylum Act 2002 (c. 41) (appeal: new evidence may be considered: exception) substitute—
"(5) But subsection (4) is subject to the exceptions in section 85A."
(2) After section 85 of that Act insert—

"85A MATTERS TO BE CONSIDERED: NEW EVIDENCE: EXCEPTIONS

(1) This section sets out the exceptions mentioned in section 85(5).
(2) Exception 1 is that in relation to an appeal under section 82(1) against an immigration decision of a kind specified in section 82(2)(b) or (c) the Tribunal may consider only the circumstances appertaining at the time of the decision.
(3) Exception 2 applies to an appeal under section 82(1) if—
(a) the appeal is against an immigration decision of a kind specified in section 82(2)(a) or (d),
(b) the immigration decision concerned an application of a kind identified in immigration rules as requiring to be considered under a "Points Based System", and
(c) the appeal relies wholly or partly on grounds specified in section 84(1)(a), (e) or (f).
(4) Where Exception 2 applies the Tribunal may consider evidence adduced by the appellant only if it—
(a) was submitted in support of, and at the time of making, the application to which the immigration decision related,

(b) relates to the appeal in so far as it relies on grounds other than those specified in subsection (3)(c),
(c) is adduced to prove that a document is genuine or valid, or
(d) is adduced in connection with the Secretary of State's reliance on a discretion under immigration rules, or compliance with a requirement of immigration rules, to refuse an application on grounds not related to the acquisition of "points" under the "Points Based System"."
(3) In section 106(2) of that Act after paragraph (u) insert—
"(ua) may make provision, for the purposes of section 85A(4)(a), about the circumstances in which evidence is to be treated, or not treated, as submitted in support of, and at the time of making, an application;".

20 Fees

(1) Section 42 of the Asylum and Immigration (Treatment of Claimants, etc.) Act 2004 (c. 19) (fees: poUKr to set amount in excess of costs) is amended as follows.
(2) In subsection (2) after paragraph (d) insert—
"(da) an application or process in connection with sponsorship of persons seeking leave to enter or remain in the United Kingdom,".
(3) After that subsection insert—
"(2A) Regulations under section 51(3) of the Immigration, Asylum and Nationality Act 2006, specifying the amount of a fee for a claim, application, service, process or other matter in respect of which an order has been made under section 51(1) or (2), may specify an amount which reflects (in addition to any costs referable to the claim, application, service, process or other matter) costs referable to—
(a) any other claim, application, service, process or matter in respect of which the Secretary of State has made an order under section 51(1) or (2),
(b) the determination of applications for entry clearances (within the meaning given by section 33(1) of the Immigration Act 1971),
(c) the determination of applications for transit visas under section 41 of the Immigration and Asylum Act 1999, or
(d) the determination of applications for certificates of entitlement to the right of abode in the United Kingdom under section 10 of the Nationality, Immigration and Asylum Act 2002."
(4) After subsection (3) insert—
"(3A) The amount of a fee under section 1 of the Consular Fees Act 1980 in respect of a matter specified in subsection (2A)(b) to (d) above may be set so as to reflect costs referable to any claim, application, service, process or other matter in respect of which the Secretary of State has made an order under section 51(1) or (2) of the Immigration, Asylum and Nationality Act 2006."

21 Children

(1) The Secretary of State shall issue a code of practice designed to ensure that in exercising functions in the United Kingdom the Border and Immigration Agency takes appropriate steps to ensure that while children are in the United Kingdom they are safe from harm.
(2) The Agency shall—
(a) have regard to the code in the exercise of its functions, and
(b) take appropriate steps to ensure that persons with whom it makes arrangements for the provision of services have regard to the code.
(3) The code shall come into force in accordance with provision made by order of the Secretary of State; and an order—
(a) shall be made by statutory instrument, and
(b) shall be subject to annulment in pursuance of a resolution of either House of Parliament.
(4) The Secretary of State shall from time to time review and, if necessary, revise the code; and subsection (3) applies to a revision as to the original code.

(5) In this section—
(a) "the Border and Immigration Agency" means—
(i) immigration officers, and
(ii) other officials of the Secretary of State, and the Secretary of State, in respect of functions relating to immigration, asylum or nationality, and
(b) "child" means an individual who is less than 18 years old.

ENFORCEMENT

22 Assaulting an immigration officer: offence

(1) A person who assaults an immigration officer commits an offence.
(2) A person guilty of an offence under this section shall be liable on summary conviction to—
(a) imprisonment for a period not exceeding 51 UKeks,
(b) a fine not exceeding level 5 on the standard scale, or
(c) both.
(3) In the application of this section to Northern Ireland the reference in subsection (2)(a) to 51 UKeks shall be treated as a reference to 6 months.
(4) In the application of this section to Scotland the reference in subsection (2)(a) to 51 UKeks shall be treated as a reference to 12 months.
(5) In relation to an offence committed before the commencement of section 281(5) of the Criminal Justice Act 2003 (c. 44) (51 UKek maximum term of sentences) the reference in subsection (2)(a) to 51 UKeks shall be treated as a reference to 6 months.

23 Assaulting an immigration officer: poUKrs of arrest, &c.

(1) An immigration officer may arrest a person without warrant if the officer reasonably suspects that the person has committed or is about to commit an offence under section 22.
(2) An offence under section 22 shall be treated as—
(a) a relevant offence for the purposes of sections 28B and 28D of the Immigration Act 1971 (c. 77) (search, entry and arrest), and
(b) an offence under Part 3 of that Act (criminal proceedings) for the purposes of sections 28(4), 28E, 28G and 28H (search after arrest, &c.) of that Act.
(3) The following provisions of the Immigration Act 1971 shall have effect in connection with an offence under section 22 of this Act as they have effect in connection with an offence under that Act—
(a) section 28I (seized material: access and copying),
(b) section 28J (search warrants: safeguards),
(c) section 28K (execution of warrants), and
(d) section 28L(1) (interpretation).

24 Seizure of cash

(1) Chapter 3 of Part 5 of the Proceeds of Crime Act 2002 (c. 29) (recovery of cash) shall apply in relation to an immigration officer as it applies in relation to a constable.
(2) For that purpose—
(a) "unlawful conduct", in or in relation to section 289, means an offence under the Immigration Acts,
(b) "unlawful conduct", in or in relation to other provisions, means an offence—
(i) under the Immigration Acts, or
(ii) listed in section 14(2) of the Asylum and Immigration (Treatment of Claimants, etc.) Act 2004 (c. 19),
(c) "senior officer" in section 290 means an official of the Secretary of State who is a civil servant of the rank of at least Assistant Director,

(d) in section 292 the words "(in relation to England and Wales and Northern Ireland)" shall be disregarded,
(e) section 293 shall not apply,
(f) an application for an order under section 295(2) must be made—
(i) in relation to England and Wales or Northern Ireland, by an immigration officer, and
(ii) in relation to Scotland, by the Scottish Ministers in connection with their functions under section 298 or by a procurator fiscal,
(g) an application for forfeiture under section 298 must be made—
(i) in relation to England and Wales or Northern Ireland, by an immigration officer, and
(ii) in relation to Scotland, by the Scottish Ministers, and
(h) any compensation under section 302 shall be paid by the Secretary of State.
(3) The Secretary of State may by order amend subsection (2)(c) to reflect a change in nomenclature; and an order—
(a) shall be made by statutory instrument, and
(b) shall be subject to annulment in pursuance of a resolution of either House of Parliament.

25 FORFEITURE OF DETAINED PROPERTY

(1) A court making a forfeiture order about property may order that the property be taken into the possession of the Secretary of State (and not of the police).
(2) An order may be made under subsection (1) only if the court thinks that the offence in connection with which the order is made—
(a) related to immigration or asylum, or
(b) was committed for a purpose connected with immigration or asylum.
(3) In subsection (1) "forfeiture order" means an order under—
(a) section 143 of the PoUKrs of Criminal Courts (Sentencing) Act 2000 (c. 6), or
(b) Article 11 of the Criminal Justice (Northern Ireland) Order 1994 (S.I. 1994/2795 (N.I. 15)).

26 DISPOSAL OF PROPERTY

(1) In this section "property" means property which—
(a) has come into the possession of an immigration officer, or
(b) has come into the possession of the Secretary of State in the course of, or in connection with, a function under the Immigration Acts.
(2) A magistrates' court may, on the application of the Secretary of State or a claimant of property—
(a) order the delivery of property to the person appearing to the court to be its owner, or
(b) if its owner cannot be ascertained, make any other order about property.
(3) An order shall not affect the right of any person to take legal proceedings for the recovery of the property, provided that the proceedings are instituted within the period of six months beginning with the date of the order.
(4) An order may be made in respect of property forfeited under section 25, or under section 25C of the Immigration Act 1971 (c. 77) (vehicles, &c.), only if—
(a) the application under subsection (2) above is made within the period of six months beginning with the date of the forfeiture order, and
(b) the applicant (if not the Secretary of State) satisfies the court—
(i) that the applicant did not consent to the offender's possession of the property, or
(ii) that the applicant did not know and had no reason to suspect that the property was likely to be used, or was intended to be used, in connection with an offence.
(5) The Secretary of State may make regulations for the disposal of property—
(a) where the owner has not been ascertained,
(b) where an order under subsection (2) cannot be made because of subsection (4)(a), or

(c) where a court has declined to make an order under subsection (2) on the grounds that the court is not satisfied of the matters specified in subsection (4)(b).
(6) The regulations may make provision that is the same as or similar to provision that may be made by regulations under section 2 of the Police (Property) Act 1897 (c. 30) (or any similar enactment applying in relation to Scotland or Northern Ireland); and the regulations—
(a) may apply, with or without modifications, regulations under that Act,
(b) may, in particular, provide for property to vest in the Secretary of State,
(c) may make provision about the timing of disposal (which, in particular, may differ from provision made by or under the Police (Property) Act 1897),
(d) shall have effect only in so far as not inconsistent with an order of a court (whether or not under subsection (2) above),
(e) shall be made by statutory instrument, and
(f) shall be subject to annulment in pursuance of a resolution of either House of Parliament.
(7) For the purposes of subsection (1) it is immaterial whether property is acquired as a result of forfeiture or seizure or in any other way.
(8) In the application of this section to Scotland a reference to a magistrates' court is a reference to the sheriff.

27 EMPLOYMENT: ARREST

In section 28AA of the Immigration Act 1971 (c. 77) (arrest with warrant) for subsection (1)(b) substitute—
"(b) section 21(1) of the Immigration, Asylum and Nationality Act 2006."

28 EMPLOYMENT: SEARCH FOR PERSONNEL RECORDS

In section 28FA(7) of the Immigration Act 1971 (enforcement: search for personnel records) for "an offence under section 8 of the Asylum and Immigration Act 1996 (c. 49)" substitute "an offence under section 21 of the Immigration, Asylum and Nationality Act 2006".

29 FACILITATION: ARRIVAL AND ENTRY

In section 25A(1)(a) of the Immigration Act 1971 (helping asylum seeker to enter UK: offence) after "the arrival in" insert ", or the entry into,".

30 FACILITATION: TERRITORIAL APPLICATION

(1) For section 25(4) and (5) of the Immigration Act 1971 (assisting unlawful immigration: territorial application) substitute—
"(4) Subsection (1) applies to things done whether inside or outside the United Kingdom."
(2) In sections 25A(4) and 25B(4) (facilitation: asylum-seekers and deportees) for "Subsections (4) to (6)" substitute "Subsections (4) and (6)".

31 PEOPLE TRAFFICKING

(1) In section 4(1) of the Asylum and Immigration (Treatment of Claimants, etc.) Act 2004 (c. 19) (trafficking) after "the arrival in" insert ", or the entry into,".
(2) For section 5(1) and (2) of that Act (trafficking: extent) substitute—
"(1) Subsections (1) to (3) of section 4 apply to anything done whether inside or outside the United Kingdom."
(3) In section 57(1) of the Sexual Offences Act 2003 (c. 42) (trafficking) after "the arrival in" insert ", or the entry into,".
(4) For sections 60(2) and (3) of that Act (trafficking: extent) substitute—
"(2) Sections 57 to 59 apply to anything done whether inside or outside the United Kingdom."

DEPORTATION OF CRIMINALS

32 Automatic deportation

(1) In this section "foreign criminal" means a person—
(a) who is not a British citizen,
(b) who is convicted in the United Kingdom of an offence, and
(c) to whom Condition 1 or 2 applies.
(2) Condition 1 is that the person is sentenced to a period of imprisonment of at least 12 months.
(3) Condition 2 is that—
(a) the offence is specified by order of the Secretary of State under section 72(4)(a) of the Nationality, Immigration and Asylum Act 2002 (c. 41) (serious criminal), and
(b) the person is sentenced to a period of imprisonment.
(4) For the purpose of section 3(5)(a) of the Immigration Act 1971 (c. 77), the deportation of a foreign criminal is conducive to the public good.
(5) The Secretary of State must make a deportation order in respect of a foreign criminal (subject to section 33).
(6) The Secretary of State may not revoke a deportation order made in accordance with subsection (5) unless—
(a) he thinks that an exception under section 33 applies,
(b) the application for revocation is made while the foreign criminal is outside the United Kingdom, or
(c) section 34(4) applies.
(7) Subsection (5) does not create a private right of action in respect of consequences of non-compliance by the Secretary of State.

33 Exceptions

(1) Section 32(4) and (5)—
(a) do not apply where an exception in this section applies (subject to subsection (7) below), and
(b) are subject to sections 7 and 8 of the Immigration Act 1971 (CommonUKalth citizens, Irish citizens, crew and other exemptions).
(2) Exception 1 is where removal of the foreign criminal in pursuance of the deportation order would breach—
(a) a person's Convention rights, or
(b) the United Kingdom's obligations under the Refugee Convention.
(3) Exception 2 is where the Secretary of State thinks that the foreign criminal was under the age of 18 on the date of conviction.
(4) Exception 3 is where the removal of the foreign criminal from the United Kingdom in pursuance of a deportation order would breach rights of the foreign criminal under the Community treaties.
(5) Exception 4 is where the foreign criminal—
(a) is the subject of a certificate under section 2 or 70 of the Extradition Act 2003 (c. 41),
(b) is in custody pursuant to arrest under section 5 of that Act,
(c) is the subject of a provisional warrant under section 73 of that Act,
(d) is the subject of an authority to proceed under section 7 of the Extradition Act 1989 (c. 33) or an order under paragraph 4(2) of Schedule 1 to that Act, or
(e) is the subject of a provisional warrant under section 8 of that Act or of a warrant under paragraph 5(1)(b) of Schedule 1 to that Act.
(6) Exception 5 is where any of the following has effect in respect of the foreign criminal—
(a) a hospital order or guardianship order under section 37 of the Mental Health Act 1983 (c. 20),
(b) a hospital direction under section 45A of that Act,
(c) a transfer direction under section 47 of that Act,

(d) a compulsion order under section 57A of the Criminal Procedure (Scotland) Act 1995 (c. 46),
(e) a guardianship order under section 58 of that Act,
(f) a hospital direction under section 59A of that Act,
(g) a transfer for treatment direction under section 136 of the Mental Health (Care and Treatment) (Scotland) Act 2003 (asp 13), or
(h) an order or direction under a provision which corresponds to a provision specified in paragraphs (a) to (g) and which has effect in relation to Northern Ireland.
(7) The application of an exception—
(a) does not prevent the making of a deportation order;
(b) results in it being assumed neither that deportation of the person concerned is conducive to the public good nor that it is not conducive to the public good;
but section 32(4) applies despite the application of Exception 1 or 4.

34 Timing

(1) Section 32(5) requires a deportation order to be made at a time chosen by the Secretary of State.
(2) A deportation order may not be made under section 32(5) while an appeal or further appeal against the conviction or sentence by reference to which the order is to be made—
(a) has been instituted and neither withdrawn nor determined, or
(b) could be brought.
(3) For the purpose of subsection (2)(b)—
(a) the possibility of an appeal out of time with permission shall be disregarded, and
(b) a person who has informed the Secretary of State in writing that the person does not intend to appeal shall be treated as being no longer able to appeal.
(4) The Secretary of State may withdraw a decision that section 32(5) applies, or revoke a deportation order made in accordance with section 32(5), for the purpose of—
(a) taking action under the Immigration Acts or rules made under section 3 of the Immigration Act 1971 (c. 77) (immigration rules), and
(b) subsequently taking a new decision that section 32(5) applies and making a deportation order in accordance with section 32(5).

35 Appeal

(1) The Nationality, Immigration and Asylum Act 2002 (c. 41) is amended as follows.
(2) At the end of section 79 (no deportation order pending appeal) add—
"(3) This section does not apply to a deportation order which states that it is made in accordance with section 32(5) of the UK Borders Act 2007.
(4) But a deportation order made in reliance on subsection (3) does not invalidate leave to enter or remain, in accordance with section 5(1) of the Immigration Act 1971, if and for so long as section 78 above applies."
(3) Before section 82(4) (general right of appeal) insert—
"(3A) Subsection (2)(j) does not apply to a decision to make a deportation order which states that it is made in accordance with section 32(5) of the UK Borders Act 2007; but—
(a) a decision that section 32(5) applies is an immigration decision for the purposes of this Part, and
(b) a reference in this Part to an appeal against an automatic deportation order is a reference to an appeal against a decision of the Secretary of State that section 32(5) applies."

36 Detention

(1) A person who has served a period of imprisonment may be detained under the authority of the Secretary of State—
(a) while the Secretary of State considers whether section 32(5) applies, and

(b) where the Secretary of State thinks that section 32(5) applies, pending the making of the deportation order.
(2) Where a deportation order is made in accordance with section 32(5) the Secretary of State shall exercise the poUKr of detention under paragraph 2(3) of Schedule 3 to the Immigration Act 1971 (c. 77) (detention pending removal) unless in the circumstances the Secretary of State thinks it inappropriate.
(3) A court determining an appeal against conviction or sentence may direct release from detention under subsection (1) or (2).
(4) Provisions of the Immigration Act 1971 which apply to detention under paragraph 2(3) of Schedule 3 to that Act shall apply to detention under subsection (1) (including provisions about bail).
(5) Paragraph 2(5) of Schedule 3 to that Act (residence, occupation and reporting restrictions) applies to a person who is liable to be detained under subsection (1).

37 FAMILY

(1) Where a deportation order against a foreign criminal states that it is made in accordance with section 32(5) ("the automatic deportation order") this section shall have effect in place of the words from "A deportation order" to "after the making of the deportation order against him" in section 5(3) of the Immigration Act 1971 (period during which family members may also be deported).
(2) A deportation order may not be made against a person as belonging to the family of the foreign criminal after the end of the relevant period of 8 UKeks.
(3) In the case of a foreign criminal who has not appealed in respect of the automatic deportation order, the relevant period begins when an appeal can no longer be brought (ignoring any possibility of an appeal out of time with permission).
(4) In the case of a foreign criminal who has appealed in respect of the automatic deportation order, the relevant period begins when the appeal is no longer pending (within the meaning of section 104 of the Nationality, Immigration and Asylum Act 2002 (c. 41)).

38 INTERPRETATION

(1) In section 32(2) the reference to a person who is sentenced to a period of imprisonment of at least 12 months—
(a) does not include a reference to a person who receives a suspended sentence (unless a court subsequently orders that the sentence or any part of it (of whatever length) is to take effect),
(b) does not include a reference to a person who is sentenced to a period of imprisonment of at least 12 months only by virtue of being sentenced to consecutive sentences amounting in aggregate to more than 12 months,
(c) includes a reference to a person who is sentenced to detention, or ordered or directed to be detained, in an institution other than a prison (including, in particular, a hospital or an institution for young offenders) for at least 12 months, and
(d) includes a reference to a person who is sentenced to imprisonment or detention, or ordered or directed to be detained, for an indeterminate period (provided that it may last for 12 months).
(2) In section 32(3)(b) the reference to a person who is sentenced to a period of imprisonment—
(a) does not include a reference to a person who receives a suspended sentence (unless a court subsequently orders that the sentence or any part of it is to take effect), and
(b) includes a reference to a person who is sentenced to detention, or ordered or directed to be detained, in an institution other than a prison (including, in particular, a hospital or an institution for young offenders).
(3) For the purposes of section 32 a person subject to an order under section 5 of the Criminal Procedure (Insanity) Act 1964 (c. 84) (insanity, &c.) has not been convicted of an offence.
(4) In sections 32 and 33—

(a) "British citizen" has the same meaning as in section 3(5) of the Immigration Act 1971 (c. 77) (and section 3(8) (burden of proof) shall apply),
(b) "Convention rights" has the same meaning as in the Human Rights Act 1998 (c. 42),
(c) "deportation order" means an order under section 5, and by virtue of section 3(5), of the Immigration Act 1971, and
(d) "the Refugee Convention" means the Convention relating to the Status of Refugees done at Geneva on 28th July 1951 and its Protocol.

39 Consequential amendments

(1) This section amends section 72(11)(b) of the Nationality, Immigration and Asylum Act 2002 (removal: serious criminal: interpretation).
(2) In sub-paragraph (i) for "(unless at least two years of the sentence are not suspended)" substitute "(unless a court subsequently orders that the sentence or any part of it is to take effect)".
(3) After sub-paragraph (i) insert—
"(ia) does not include a reference to a person who is sentenced to a period of imprisonment of at least two years only by virtue of being sentenced to consecutive sentences which amount in aggregate to more than two years,".

INFORMATION

40 Supply of Revenue and Customs information

(1) Her Majesty's Revenue and Customs (HMRC) and the Revenue and Customs Prosecutions Office (the RCPO) may each supply the Secretary of State with information for use for the purpose of—
(a) administering immigration control under the Immigration Acts;
(b) preventing, detecting, investigating or prosecuting offences under those Acts;
(c) determining whether to impose, or imposing, penalties or charges under Part 2 of the Immigration and Asylum Act 1999 (c. 33) (carriers' liability);
(d) determining whether to impose, or imposing, penalties under section 15 of the Immigration, Asylum and Nationality Act 2006 (c. 13) (restrictions on employment);
(e) providing facilities, or arranging for the provision of facilities, for the accommodation of persons under section 4 of the Immigration and Asylum Act 1999;
(f) providing support for asylum-seekers and their dependants under Part 6 of that Act;
(g) determining whether an applicant for naturalisation under the British Nationality Act 1981 (c. 61) is of good character;
(h) determining whether an applicant within subsection (1) of section 58 of the Immigration, Asylum and Nationality Act 2006 (acquisition of British nationality, &c. by adult or young person) for registration under a provision listed in subsection (2) of that section is of good character;
(i) determining whether to make an order in respect of a person under section 40 of the British Nationality Act 1981 (deprivation of citizenship);
(j) doing anything else in connection with the exercise of immigration and nationality functions.
(2) This section applies to a document or article which comes into the possession of, or is discovered by, HMRC or the RCPO, or a person acting on behalf of HMRC or the RCPO, as it applies to information.
(3) The Secretary of State—
(a) may retain for a purpose within subsection (1) a document or article supplied by virtue of subsection (2);
(b) may dispose of a document or article supplied by virtue of subsection (2).
(4) In subsection (1) "immigration and nationality functions" means functions exercisable by virtue of—

(a) the Immigration Acts,
(b) the British Nationality Act 1981 (c. 61),
(c) the Hong Kong Act 1985 (c. 15),
(d) the Hong Kong (War Wives and Widows) Act 1996 (c. 41), or
(e) the British Nationality (Hong Kong) Act 1997 (c. 20).
(5) A poUKr conferred by this section on HMRC or the RCPO may be exercised on behalf of HMRC or the RCPO by a person who is authorised (generally or specifically) for the purpose.
(6) The following provisions (which relate to the supply of information to the Secretary of State) shall cease to have effect—
(a) section 20(1)(d) of the Immigration and Asylum Act 1999 (c. 33),
(b) section 130 of the Nationality, Immigration and Asylum Act 2002 (c. 41), and
(c) paragraphs 17 and 20 of Schedule 2 to the Commissioners for Revenue and Customs Act 2005 (c. 11).

41 Confidentiality

(1) A person to whom relevant information is supplied (whether before or after the commencement of this section) may not disclose that information.
(2) Information is relevant information if it is supplied by or on behalf of HMRC or the RCPO under—
(a) section 20 of the Immigration and Asylum Act 1999,
(b) section 130 of the Nationality, Immigration and Asylum Act 2002,
(c) section 36 of the Immigration, Asylum and Nationality Act 2006 (c. 13) (except in so far as that section relates to information supplied to a chief officer of police), or
(d) section 40 of this Act.
(3) But subsection (1) does not apply to a disclosure—
(a) which is made for a purpose within section 40(1),
(b) which is made for the purposes of civil proceedings (whether or not within the United Kingdom) relating to an immigration or nationality matter,
(c) which is made for the purposes of a criminal investigation or criminal proceedings (whether or not within the United Kingdom) relating to an immigration or nationality matter,
(d) which is made in pursuance of an order of a court,
(e) which is made with the consent (which may be general or specific) of HMRC or the RCPO, depending on by whom or on whose behalf the information was supplied, or
(f) which is made with the consent of each person to whom the information relates.
(4) Subsection (1) is subject to any other enactment permitting disclosure.
(5) The reference in subsection (1) to a person to whom relevant information is supplied includes a reference to a person who is or was acting on behalf of that person.
(6) The reference in subsection (2) to information supplied under section 40 of this Act includes a reference to documents or articles supplied by virtue of subsection (2) of that section.
(7) In subsection (3) "immigration or nationality matter" means a matter in respect of which the Secretary of State has immigration and nationality functions (within the meaning given in section 40(4)).
(8) In subsection (4) "enactment" does not include—
(a) an Act of the Scottish Parliament,
(b) an Act of the Northern Ireland Assembly, or
(c) an instrument made under an Act within paragraph (a) or (b).

42 Wrongful disclosure

(1) An offence is committed by a person who contravenes section 41 by disclosing information relating to a person whose identity—
(a) is specified in the disclosure, or

(b) can be deduced from it.
(2) Subsection (1) does not apply to the disclosure of information about internal administrative arrangements of HMRC or the RCPO (whether relating to Commissioners, officers, members of the RCPO or others).
(3) It is a defence for a person (P) charged with an offence under this section of disclosing information to prove that P reasonably believed—
(a) that the disclosure was lawful, or
(b) that the information had already and lawfully been made available to the public.
(4) A person guilty of an offence under this section shall be liable—
(a) on conviction on indictment, to imprisonment for a term not exceeding two years, to a fine or to both, or
(b) on summary conviction, to imprisonment for a term not exceeding 12 months, to a fine not exceeding the statutory maximum or to both.
(5) The reference in subsection (4)(b) to 12 months shall be treated as a reference to six months—
(a) in the application of this section to Northern Ireland;
(b) in the application of this section to England and Wales, in relation to an offence under this section committed before the commencement of section 282 of the Criminal Justice Act 2003 (c. 44) (imprisonment on summary conviction for certain offences in England and Wales);
(c) in the application of this section to Scotland, until the commencement of section 45(1) of the Criminal Proceedings etc. (Reform) (Scotland) Act 2007 (asp 6) (corresponding provision in Scotland).
(6) A prosecution for an offence under this section may be instituted—
(a) in England and Wales, only with the consent of the Director of Public Prosecutions;
(b) in Northern Ireland, only with the consent of the Director of Public Prosecutions for Northern Ireland.

43 Supply of police information, etc.

In section 131 of the Nationality, Immigration and Asylum Act 2002 (c. 41) (police, etc.), for the words from "determining" to the end substitute "—
(a) determining whether an applicant for naturalisation under the British Nationality Act 1981 is of good character;
(b) determining whether an applicant within subsection (1) of section 58 of the Immigration, Asylum and Nationality Act 2006 for registration under a provision listed in subsection (2) of that section is of good character;
(c) determining whether to make an order in respect of a person under section 40 of the British Nationality Act 1981."

44 Search for evidence of nationality

(1) This section applies where an individual has been arrested on suspicion of the commission of an offence and an immigration officer or a constable suspects—
(a) that the individual may not be a British citizen, and
(b) that nationality documents relating to the individual may be found on—
(i) premises occupied or controlled by the individual,
(ii) premises on which the individual was arrested, or
(iii) premises on which the individual was, immediately before being arrested.
(2) The immigration officer or constable may enter and search the premises for the purpose of finding those documents.
(3) The poUKr of search may be exercised only with the written authority of a senior officer; and for that purpose—
(a) "senior officer" means—

(i) in relation to an immigration officer, an immigration officer of at least the rank of chief immigration officer, and
(ii) in relation to a constable, a constable of at least the rank of inspector, and
(b) a senior officer who gives authority must arrange for a written record to be made of—
(i) the grounds for the suspicions in reliance on which the poUKr of search is to be exercised, and
(ii) the nature of the documents sought.
(4) The poUKr of search may not be exercised where the individual has been released without being charged with an offence.
(5) In relation to an individual "nationality document" means a document showing—
(a) the individual's identity, nationality or citizenship,
(b) the place from which the individual travelled to the United Kingdom, or
(c) a place to which the individual is proposing to go from the United Kingdom.

45 Search for evidence of nationality: other premises

(1) This section applies where an individual—
(a) has been arrested on suspicion of the commission of an offence, and
(b) has not been released without being charged with an offence.
(2) If, on an application made by an immigration officer or a constable, a justice of the peace is satisfied that there are reasonable grounds for believing that—
(a) the individual may not be a British citizen,
(b) nationality documents relating to the individual may be found on premises specified in the application,
(c) the documents would not be exempt from seizure under section 46(2), and
(d) any of the conditions in subsection (3) below applies,
the justice of the peace may issue a warrant authorising an immigration officer or constable to enter and search the premises.
(3) The conditions are that—
(a) it is not practicable to communicate with any person entitled to grant entry to the premises;
(b) it is practicable to communicate with a person entitled to grant entry to the premises but it is not practicable to communicate with any person entitled to grant access to the nationality documents;
(c) entry to the premises will not be granted unless a warrant is produced;
(d) the purpose of a search may be frustrated or seriously prejudiced unless an immigration officer or constable arriving at the premises can secure immediate entry.
(4) Sections 28J and 28K of the Immigration Act 1971 (c. 77) (warrants: application and execution) apply, with any necessary modifications, to warrants under this section.
(5) In the application of this section to Scotland a reference to a justice of the peace shall be treated as a reference to the sheriff or a justice of the peace.

46 Seizure of nationality documents

(1) An immigration officer or constable searching premises under section 44 or 45 may seize a document which the officer or constable thinks is a nationality document in relation to the arrested individual.
(2) Subsection (1) does not apply to a document which—
(a) in relation to England and Wales or Northern Ireland, is subject to legal professional privilege, or
(b) in relation to Scotland, is an item subject to legal privilege within the meaning of section 412 of the Proceeds of Crime Act 2002 (c. 29).
(3) An immigration officer or constable may retain a document seized under subsection (1) while the officer or constable suspects that—

(a) the individual to whom the document relates may be liable to removal from the United Kingdom in accordance with a provision of the Immigration Acts, and
(b) retention of the document may facilitate the individual's removal.
(4) Section 28I of the Immigration Act 1971 (c. 77) (seized material: access and copying) shall have effect in relation to a document seized and retained by an immigration officer.
(5) Section 21 of the Police and Criminal Evidence Act 1984 (c. 60) or Article 23 of the Police and Criminal Evidence (Northern Ireland) Order 1989 (S.I. 1989/1341 (N.I. 12)) (seized material: access and copying) shall have effect in relation to a document seized and retained by a constable in England and Wales or Northern Ireland.

47 Police civilians

In Part 2 of Schedule 4 to the Police Reform Act 2002 (c. 30) (poUKrs exercisable by police civilians: investigating officers) after paragraph 18 (entry and search after arrest) insert—

"Entry and search for evidence of nationality after arrest

18A Where a designation applies this paragraph to any person—
(a) sections 44 to 46 of the UK Borders Act 2007 (entry, search and seizure after arrest) shall apply to that person (with any necessary modifications) as if a reference to a constable included a reference to that person, and
(b) a provision of the 1984 Act which applies to constables in connection with any of those sections shall apply (with any necessary modifications) to that person."

BORDER AND IMMIGRATION INSPECTORATE

48 Establishment

(1) The Secretary of State shall appoint a person as Chief Inspector of the Border and Immigration Agency.
(2) The Chief Inspector shall monitor and report on the efficiency and effectiveness of the Border and Immigration Agency; in particular, the Chief Inspector shall consider and make recommendations about—
(a) consistency of approach within the Border and Immigration Agency,
(b) the practice and performance of the Border and Immigration Agency compared to other persons doing similar things,
(c) practice and procedure in making decisions,
(d) the treatment of claimants and applicants,
(e) certification under section 94 of the Nationality, Immigration and Asylum Act 2002 (c. 41) (unfounded claim),
(f) compliance with law about discrimination in the exercise of functions, including reliance on section 19D of the Race Relations Act 1976 (c. 74) (exception for immigration functions),
(g) practice and procedure in relation to the exercise of enforcement poUKrs (including poUKrs of arrest, entry, search and seizure),
(h) the provision of information,
(i) the handling of complaints, and
(j) the content of information about conditions in countries outside the United Kingdom which the Secretary of State compiles and makes available, for purposes connected with immigration and asylum, to immigration officers and other officials.
(3) In this section "the Border and Immigration Agency" means—
(a) immigration officers, and
(b) other officials of the Secretary of State, and the Secretary of State, in respect of functions relating to immigration, asylum or nationality.

(4) The Chief Inspector shall not aim to investigate individual cases (although this subsection does not prevent the Chief Inspector from considering or drawing conclusions about an individual case for the purpose of, or in the context of, considering a general issue).

49 Chief Inspector: supplemental

(1) The Secretary of State shall pay remuneration and allowances to the Chief Inspector.
(2) The Secretary of State—
(a) shall before the beginning of each financial year specify a maximum sum which the Chief Inspector may spend on functions for that year,
(b) may permit that to be exceeded for a specified purpose, and
(c) shall defray the Chief Inspector's expenditure for each financial year subject to paragraphs (a) and (b).
(3) The Chief Inspector shall hold and vacate office in accordance with terms of appointment (which may include provision about retirement, resignation or dismissal).
(4) The Chief Inspector may appoint staff.
(5) A person who is employed by or in any of the following may not be appointed as Chief Inspector—
(a) a government department,
(b) the Scottish Administration,
(c) the National Assembly for Wales, and
(d) a department in Northern Ireland.

50 Reports

(1) The Chief Inspector shall report in writing to the Secretary of State—
(a) once each calendar year, in relation to the performance of the functions under section 48 generally, and
(b) at other times as requested by the Secretary of State in relation to specified matters.
(2) The Secretary of State shall lay before Parliament a copy of any report received under subsection (1).
(3) But a copy may omit material if the Secretary of State thinks that its publication—
(a) is undesirable for reasons of national security, or
(b) might jeopardise an individual's safety.

51 Plans

(1) The Chief Inspector shall prepare plans describing the objectives and terms of reference of proposed inspections.
(2) Plans shall be prepared—
(a) at prescribed times and in respect of prescribed periods, and
(b) at such other times, and in respect of such other periods, as the Chief Inspector thinks appropriate.
(3) A plan must—
(a) be in the prescribed form, and
(b) contain the prescribed information.
(4) In preparing a plan the Chief Inspector shall consult—
(a) the Secretary of State, and
(b) prescribed persons.
(5) As soon as is reasonably practicable after preparing a plan the Chief Inspector shall send a copy to—
(a) the Secretary of State, and
(b) each prescribed person.
(6) The Chief Inspector and a prescribed person may by agreement disapply a requirement—

(a) to consult the person, or
(b) to send a copy of a plan to the person.
(7) Nothing in this section prevents the Chief Inspector from doing anything not mentioned in a plan.

52 Relationship with other bodies: general

(1) The Chief Inspector shall cooperate with prescribed persons in so far as the Chief Inspector thinks it consistent with the efficient and effective performance of the functions under section 48.
(2) The Chief Inspector may act jointly with prescribed persons where the Chief Inspector thinks it in the interests of the efficient and effective performance of the functions under section 48.
(3) The Chief Inspector may assist a prescribed person.
(4) The Chief Inspector may delegate a specified aspect of the functions under section 48 to a prescribed person.

53 Relationship with other bodies: non-interference notices

(1) Subsection (2) applies if the Chief Inspector believes that—
(a) a prescribed person proposes to inspect any aspect of the work of the Border and Immigration Agency, and
(b) the inspection may impose an unreasonable burden on the Agency.
(2) The Chief Inspector may give the prescribed person a notice prohibiting a specified inspection.
(3) The prescribed person shall comply with the notice, unless the Secretary of State cancels it on the grounds that the inspection would not impose an unreasonable burden on the Agency.
(4) A notice must—
(a) be in the prescribed form, and
(b) contain the prescribed information.
(5) The Secretary of State may by order make provision about—
(a) the timing of notices;
(b) the publication of notices;
(c) the revision or withdrawal of notices.

54 Abolition of other bodies

The following shall cease to have effect—
(a) section 19E of the Race Relations Act 1976 (c. 74) (monitor of immigration exception),
(b) section 34 of the Nationality, Immigration and Asylum Act 2002 (c. 41) (Monitor of Accommodation Centres),
(c) section 111 of that Act (monitor of certification of claims as unfounded), and
(d) section 142 of that Act (Advisory Panel on Country Information).

55 Prescribed matters

(1) In sections 48 to 53 "prescribed" means prescribed by order of the Secretary of State.
(2) An order under any of those sections—
(a) may make provision generally or only for specified purposes,
(b) may make different provision for different purposes, and
(c) may include incidental or transitional provision.
(3) An order under any of those sections prescribing a person may specify—
(a) one or more persons, or
(b) a class of person.
(4) An order under any of those sections—
(a) shall be made by statutory instrument, and

(b) shall be subject to annulment in pursuance of a resolution of either House of Parliament.

56 Senior President of Tribunals

(1) At the end of section 43(3) of the Tribunals, Courts and Enforcement Act 2007 (c. 15) (report by Senior President of Tribunals) add— ", and
(e) cases coming before the Asylum and Immigration Tribunal."
(2) In exercising the function under section 43 of the Tribunals, Courts and Enforcement Act 2007 (c. 15) the Senior President of Tribunals shall have regard to—
(a) the functions of the Chief Inspector of the Border and Immigration Agency, and
(b) in particular, the Secretary of State's poUKr to request the Chief Inspector to report about specified matters.

GENERAL

57 Money

The following shall be paid out of money provided by Parliament—
(a) any expenditure of a Minister of the Crown in consequence of this Act, and
(b) any increase attributable to this Act in sums payable out of money provided by Parliament under another enactment.

58 Repeals

The enactments listed in the Schedule are repealed to the extent specified.

59 Commencement

(1) Section 17 comes into force on the day on which this Act is passed.
(2) The other preceding provisions of this Act shall come into force in accordance with provision made by the Secretary of State by order.
(3) An order—
(a) may make provision generally or only for specified purposes,
(b) may make different provision for different purposes, and
(c) may include incidental, consequential or transitional provision.
(4) In particular, transitional provision—
(a) in the case of an order commencing section 16, may permit the adding of a condition to leave given before the passing of this Act;
(b) in the case of an order commencing section 25, may permit an order to be made in proceedings instituted before the passing of this Act;
(c) in the case of an order commencing section 26, may permit an order or regulations to have effect in relation to property which came into the possession of an immigration officer or the Secretary of State before the passing of this Act;
(d) in the case of an order commencing section 32—
(i) may provide for the section to apply to persons convicted before the passing of this Act who are in custody at the time of commencement or whose sentences are suspended at the time of commencement;
(ii) may modify the application of the section in relation to those persons so as to disapply, or apply only to a specified extent, Condition 2.
(5) An order shall be made by statutory instrument.

60 Extent

(1) Sections 1 to 4, 25 and 31(1) and (2) extend to—
(a) England and Wales, and

(b) Northern Ireland.
(2) Other provisions of this Act extend (subject to subsection (3)) to—
(a) England and Wales,
(b) Scotland, and
(c) Northern Ireland.
(3) A provision of this Act which amends another Act shall (subject to subsection (1)) have the same extent as the relevant part of the amended Act (ignoring extent by virtue of an Order in Council).
(4) Her Majesty may by Order in Council direct that a provision of this Act is to extend, with or without modification or adaptation, to—
(a) any of the Channel Islands;
(b) the Isle of Man.

61 Citation

(1) This Act may be cited as the UK Borders Act 2007.
(2) A reference (in any enactment, including one passed or made before this Act) to "the Immigration Acts" is to—
(a) the Immigration Act 1971 (c. 77),
(b) the Immigration Act 1988 (c. 14),
(c) the Asylum and Immigration Appeals Act 1993 (c. 23),
(d) the Asylum and Immigration Act 1996 (c. 49),
(e) the Immigration and Asylum Act 1999 (c. 33),
(f) the Nationality, Immigration and Asylum Act 2002 (c. 41),
(g) the Asylum and Immigration (Treatment of Claimants, etc.) Act 2004 (c. 19),
(h) the Immigration, Asylum and Nationality Act 2006 (c. 13), and
(i) this Act.
(3) Section 64(2) of the Immigration, Asylum and Nationality Act 2006 (meaning of "Immigration Acts") shall cease to have effect.
(4) In the definition of "The Immigration Acts" in Schedule 1 to the Interpretation Act 1978 (c. 30) (defined expressions) for "section 64 of the Immigration, Asylum and Nationality Act 2006" substitute "section 61 of the UK Borders Act 2007".

TRAVEL TO THE UK

US STATE DEPARTMENT SUGGESTIONS

COUNTRY DESCRIPTION: The United Kingdom is a highly developed constitutional monarchy comprising England, Scotland, Wales, and Northern Ireland; Gibraltar is a British Overseas Territory. Tourist facilities are widely available.

ENTRY REQUIREMENTS: A passport is required. Tourists are not obliged to obtain a visa for stays of up to six months in the United Kingdom or to enter Gibraltar. Those wishing to remain longer than one month in Gibraltar should regularize their stay with Gibraltar immigration authorities.

In an effort to prevent international child abduction, many governments have initiated procedures at entry/exit points. These often include requiring documentary evidence of relationship and permission for the child's travel from the parent(s) or legal guardian if not present. Having such documentation on hand, even if not required, may facilitate entry/departure.

Further information on entry requirements may be obtained from the British Embassy at 3100 Massachusetts Avenue, NW, Washington, DC 20008; tel: (202) 588-7800. Inquiries may also be directed to British consulates in Atlanta, Boston, Chicago, Houston, Los Angeles, New York, and San Francisco. The UKbsite of the British Embassy in the United States is http://www.britainusa.com/embassy.

DUAL NATIONALITY: U.S. citizens who are also citizens of the United Kingdom or any other nation are reminded that U.S. law requires they enter and depart the United States documented as U.S. citizens. They are not entitled to U.S. visas or to travel to the U.S. on the visa waiver program. U.S. citizens who attempt to travel to the U.S. from the United Kingdom on foreign passports risk being denied boarding pending acquisition of a valid U.S. passport. For additional information, see the Consular Affairs home page on the Internet at http://travel.state.gov for our dual nationality flyer.

SAFETY AND SECURITY: The United Kingdom is stable and modern but shares with the rest of the world an increased threat of terrorist incidents of international origin, as UKll as violence related to the political situation in Northern Ireland (a part of the United Kingdom.) Americans are reminded to remain vigilant with regard to their personal security and to exercise caution. In recent months, several arrests have been made in Great Britain in connection with various possible terrorist plots. The British Home Secretary has urged its citizens to be alert and vigilant by, for example, keeping an eye out for suspect packages or people acting suspiciously at subway and train stations and airports and reporting anything suspicious to the appropriate authorities by contacting the free confidential anti-terrorist telephone hotline on 0800 789 321. Americans traveling abroad should regularly monitor the Department's Internet UKb site at http://travel.state.gov where any current Worldwide Cautions or Public Announcements can be found.

From time to time during periods of heightened threat of terrorism, the U.K. government deems it necessary to raise levels of security activity. Heightened activity may include the use of military personnel in support of the police and law enforcement officers. The use of troops, who remain at all times under the control of the police, is part of long-standing contingency plans. Military personnel and equipment may be deployed at airports and other transportation links, or other public locations. For more information about U.K. public safety initiatives, consult the U.K. Civil Contingencies Secretariat UKbsite at http://www.ukresilience.gov.uk

Political demonstrations are UKll policed and, except at times in Northern Ireland, generally orderly. Although the political situation in Northern Ireland has dramatically improved since the signing of the Good Friday Agreement in 1998, incidents of terrorist violence have, nevertheless, occurred in the past few years. Early in 2001, two explosive devices UKre detonated in London suburbs, injuring eight people and damaging buildings. Within Northern Ireland, flash-points for sectarian confrontations still exist, but they are generally removed from areas where tourists congregate. Sporadic incidents of street violence often erupt during the summer marching season (April to August), with tensions heightened during the month of July, especially around the July 12th public holiday. As a result, American citizens traveling in Northern Ireland have experienced delays and disruption.

CRIME: The United Kingdom and Gibraltar benefit from generally low crime rates; hoUKver crime, including violent crime, has increased over the last few years. Incidents of pickpocketing, mugging, "snatch and grab" theft of mobile phones, watches and jeUKlry and theft of unattended bags, especially at airports and from cars parked at restaurants, hotels and resorts.

Pickpockets target tourists, especially at historic sites, restaurants, on buses, trains and the London Underground (subway). Thieves often target unattended cars parked at tourist sites and roadside restaurants, looking for laptop computers and hand-held electronic equipment. In London, travelers should use only licensed "black taxi cabs" or car services recommended by their hotel or tour operator. Unlicensed taxis or private cars posing as taxis that may offer low fares, but are often uninsured and may have unlicensed drivers. In some instances, travelers have been robbed while using these cars.

Due to the circumstances described above, visitors should take steps to ensure the safety of their U.S. passports. Visitors in the England, Scotland, Wales and Gibraltar are not expected to produce identity documents for police authorities and thus may secure their passports in hotel safes or residences. In Northern Ireland, hoUKver, passports or other photographic I.D. should be carried at all times. The need to carry a passport to cash travelers' checks is also minimized by an abundance of ATM's able to access systems widely used in the U.S. and offering more favorable rates of exchange. Note: Common sense personal security measures utilized in the U.S when using ATMs should also be folloUKd in the U.K.

The loss or theft abroad of a U.S. passport should be reported immediately to the local police and the nearest U.S. Embassy or Consulate. If you are the victim of a crime while overseas, in addition to reporting to local police, contact the nearest U.S. Embassy or Consulate for assistance. The Embassy/Consulate staff can, for example, assist you to find appropriate medical care, to contact family members or friends and explain how funds could be transferred. Although the investigation and prosecution of the crime is solely the responsibility of local authorities, consular officers can help you to understand the local criminal justice process and to find an attorney if needed.

U.S. citizens can refer to the Department of State's pamphlet, *A Safe Trip Abroad*, for ways to promote a more trouble-free journey. The pamphlet is available by mail from the Superintendent of Documents, U.S. Government Printing Office, Washington, D.C. 20402, via the Internet at http://www.access.gpo.gov/su_docs, or via the Bureau of Consular Affairs home page at http://travel.state.gov.

MEDICAL FACILITIES: While medical services are widely available, free care under the National Health System is alloUKd only to U.K. residents and certain EU nationals. Tourists and short-term visitors can expect charges roughly comparable to those assessed in the United States.

MEDICAL INSURANCE: The Department of State strongly urges Americans to consult with their medical insurance company prior to traveling abroad to confirm whether their policy applies overseas and if it will cover emergency expenses such as a medical evacuation. U.S. medical insurance plans seldom cover health costs incurred outside the United States unless supplemental coverage is purchased. Further, U.S. Medicare and Medicaid programs do not provide payment for medical services outside the United States. HoUKver, many travel agents and private companies offer insurance plans that will cover health care expenses incurred overseas including emergency services such as medical evacuations.

When making a decision regarding health insurance, Americans should consider that many foreign doctors and hospitals require payment in cash prior to providing service and that a medical evacuation to the U.S. may cost UKll in excess of $50,000. Uninsured travelers who require medical care overseas often face extreme difficulties. When consulting with your insurer prior to your trip, ascertain whether payment will be made to the overseas healthcare provider or if you will be reimbursed later for expenses you incur. Some insurance policies also include coverage for psychiatric treatment and for disposition of remains in the event of death.

Useful information on medical emergencies abroad, including overseas insurance programs, is provided in the Department of State's Bureau of Consular Affairs brochure, *Medical Information for Americans Traveling Abroad*, available via the Bureau of Consular Affairs home page or autofax: (202) 647-3000.

OTHER HEALTH INFORMATION: Information on vaccinations and other health precautions, such as safe food and water precautions and insect bite protection, may be obtained from the Centers for Disease Control and Prevention's hotline for international travelers at 1-877-FYI-TRIP (1-877-394-8747); fax 1-888-CDC-FAXX (1-888-232-3299), or via the CDC's Internet site at http://www.cdc.gov/travel. For information about outbreaks of infectious diseases abroad consult the World Health Organization's UKbsite at http://www.who.int/en. Further health information for travelers is available at http://www.who.int/ith.

TRAFFIC SAFETY AND ROAD CONDITIONS: While in a foreign country, U.S. citizens may encounter road conditions that differ significantly from those in the United States. The information below concerning the United Kingdom is provided for general reference only, and may not be totally accurate in a particular location or circumstance.

Safety of Public Transportation: Excellent
Urban Road Condition/Maintenance: Excellent
Rural Road Condition/Maintenance: Excellent
Availability of Roadside Assistance: Excellent

U.K. penalties for drunk driving are stiff and often result in prison sentences. In contrast to the United States and continental Europe where traffic moves on the right hand side of the road, traffic moves on the left in the U.K. Visitors uncomfortable with or intimidated by the prospect of driving on the left-hand side of the road may wish to avail themselves of extensive bus, rail and air transport networks that are comparatively inexpensive and very extensive. Roads in the United Kingdom are generally good, but are narrow and often congested in urban areas. If you plan to drive while in the U.K., you may wish to obtain a copy of the Highway Code, available in the United Kingdom. The Automobile Association (AA) of the U.K. provides information and updates on travel and traffic-related issues on its UKbsite at http://www.the-stationary-office.co.uk. If you intend to rent a car in the U.K., check that you are adequately insured. U.S. auto insurance is not always valid outside the U.S. and you may wish to purchase supplemental insurance, which is generally available from most major rental agents.

Public transport in the United Kingdom is excellent and extensive. HoUKver, poor track conditions may have contributed to train derailments resulting in some fatalities. Repairs are underway and the overall safety record is excellent.

Many U.S. citizens are injured every year in pedestrian accidents in the United Kingdom, forgetting that traffic moves in the opposite direction than in the United States. Care should be taken when crossing streets.

Driving in Gibraltar is on the right-hand side of the road, as in the U.S. and Continental Europe. Persons traveling overland betUKen Gibraltar and Spain may experience long delays in clearing Spanish border controls.

BUSINESS TRAVEL

BUSINESS CUSTOMS

The British class structure based on property and land ownership has been eroded by taxation, education, and social developments over the last few decades. Liberalization of business and industry has rewarded enterprise, and a new generation of professionals schooled in management, marketing and finance techniques has increasingly taken charge.

Ethnic minorities constitute about six percent of the population and have proven to be valuable contributors to the British economy.

Some fundamental cultural differences betUKen the United States and the UK remain. Variations in pace and style may be most noticeable, and sustained personal contact with potential business partners is expected. Prompt acknowledgment of correspondence, adherence to appointment schedules, and a greater formality in the conduct of business is the norm.

British executives communicate more by letter and fax than by telephone, although the Internet is widely used, and e-mail is becoming more common. The British are less likely to seek legal advice and guidance than their U.S. counterparts, although a litigation culture is developing along the lines of the U.S. model – i.e. no win, no fee cases have recently been permitted.

TRAVEL ADVISORY AND VISAS

Every U.S. citizen entering the United Kingdom must have a valid American passport. For non-tourist stays of more than three months, visas or entry permits are required for U.S. citizens entering the UK Visitors intending to remain in the UK should check in advance with the British Embassy or the nearest British Consulate. The UKbsite of the British Embassy in the United States is http://www.britainusa.com.

Americans intending to seek employment in the UK should consult the British Embassy or a British Consulate in the U.S. to inquire about work permits. The Employment Service, an executive agency of the Department of Education and Employment, controls the employment of aliens in the UK. U.S. citizens wishing to obtain or extend a work permit should contact the Employment Service by phone on 011 44 1937 840224.

Directors and employees of existing British subsidiaries of U.S. firms have encountered little difficulty in obtaining permission to enter and remain in the UK. Bringing the technical personnel required to install and operate a plant or business generally poses no problem, though it is necessary to establish that British subjects with the necessary qualifications are not available. The Government has issued new regulations easing the entry of emerging technologies experts from overseas.

HMG has adopted the EU regulations governing the admission of non-EU business visitors and economic migrants to the UK, which limit the ability of some foreign nationals, including American citizens, to reside in the UK. The categories of persons adversely affected, to a lesser or greater extent, by the new immigration rules are self-employed persons, retired persons of independent means, business investors, and short-term business visitors. Entry may be denied to those who intend to perform productive services unless a work permit has been issued in advance to their employer. The determination of who may be admitted as a consultant is decided on a case-by-case basis at ports of entry.

The American Citizen Services (ACS) section at the American Embassy in London provides many services for U.S. citizens and business travelers, including passport issuance, absentee voter registration and notarial services. The Passport Unit supplies travel advisory information on visa requirements, health, safety, and security concerns in countries around the world. For information on these and other issues, Americans should call the Embassy on 011 44 20 7499 9000, visit at 55/56 Upper Brook Street, London W1A 1AE, or access the Department of State's Consular Affairs homepage at: http://travel.state.gov. The Passport Unit is open 8.30 to 11.30am Monday through Friday mornings, and 2.00 to 4.00pm Monday, UKdnesday and Friday afternoons. The Embassy is closed for all American and British holidays. More information on American Citizen Services may be obtained from the U.S. Embassy UKbsite at: www.usembassy.org.uk.

HOLIDAYS

The following are the major UK public holidays

New Year's Day January 1
Bank Holiday** January 2
St. Patrick's Day*** March 18
Good Friday March 29
Easter Monday April 1
May Day May 6
Queen's Golden Jubilee June 3-4
Orangeman's Day*** July 12
August Bank Holiday** *** August 5
August Bank Holiday* August 27
Christmas Day December 25
Boxing Day December 26

* England and Wales only
** Scotland only
*** Northern Ireland only
--Business Infrastructure

SAFETY AND SECURITY

The United Kingdom is stable and modern. Political demonstrations are UKll policed and, except at times in Northern Ireland, generally orderly. There is, hoUKver, a history of terrorist violence related to the political situation in Northern Ireland (a part of the United Kingdom).

Incidents of terrorist violence have occurred throughout England and Northern Ireland. U.S. citizens have not been specifically targeted, but some have been injured when caught up in disturbances. In recent years, a major suburban London bridge was damaged by a bomb, various explosions occurred in high-density London neighborhoods, and an explosive device discovered on a London subway line caused major public transport delays.

In recent years, there has been widespread civil unrest throughout Northern Ireland during the summer marching season (July and August). As a result, American citizens traveling in Northern Ireland have experienced delays and disruption. Some degree of civil unrest may continue for the foreseeable future.

During the fall of 2000, fuel refinery blockades by the transport industry caused fuel shortages that curtailed emergency services and public transport (including airlines), and sloUKd or halted distribution of food and other vital commodities. Lines of cars waiting at gas stations caused major traffic jams throughout the UK Further protest and resultant disruptions - even to tourists - cannot be ruled out if there is continued concern about high fuel prices.

CRIME

While the United Kingdom benefits from generally low crime rates, the UK has recently experienced an increase in crime, including crimes involving violence. Incidents of pickpocketing, muggings, street thefts of watches and jeUKlry, and theft of unattended bags are increasingly common.

In London, travelers should use only licensed "black taxi cabs" or car services recommended by their hotel or tour operator. Unlicensed taxis or private cars posing as taxis may offer low fares, but are often uninsured and may have unlicensed drivers. In some instances, travelers have been robbed while using these cars.

Due to the circumstances described above, visitors should take steps to ensure the safety of their U.S. passports. Visitors in England, Scotland and Wales are not expected to produce identity documents for police authorities and thus may secure their passports in hotel safes or residences. In Northern Ireland, hoUKver, passports or other photographic I.D. should be carried at all times. The need to carry a passport to cash Travelers Checks is also minimized by an abundance of ATM's able to access systems that are widely used in the U.S.The loss or theft of a U.S. passport should be reported immediately to the local police and the nearest U.S. embassy or consulate.

MEDICAL FACILITIES AND INSURANCE

While good medical services are widely available, free care under the National Health System is alloUKd only to UK residents. Tourists and short-term visitors can expect charges roughly comparable to those assessed in the United States.

U.S. medical insurance is not always valid outside the United States. U.S. Medicare and Medicaid programs do not provide payment for medical services outside the United States. Doctors and hospitals often ask non-residents to pay immediately for medical services, and uninsured travelers who require medical care may face extreme difficulties, unless they have the means to pay.

Check with your own insurance company to confirm whether your policy applies overseas, including provisions for medical evacuation, and for adequacy of coverage. Generally, travel insurance cannot be purchased once you have departed the United States. Serious medical problems requiring hospitalization and/or medical evacuation to the United States can cost tens of thousands of dollars. Ascertain whether payment will be made to the overseas hospital or doctor or whether you will be reimbursed later for expenses you incur. Some insurance policies also include coverage for psychiatric treatment and for disposition of remains in the event of death.

TRAFFIC SAFETY AND ROAD CONDITIONS

While in a foreign country, U.S. citizens may encounter road conditions that differ significantly from those in the United States. The information below concerning the United Kingdom is provided for general reference only, and may not be totally accurate in a particular location or circumstance.

The safety of public transportation, urban and rural road conditions and the availability of roadside assistance are all excellent compared with most foreign countries, although they are not generally up to the standard of some other European countries.

UK penalties for drunk driving are stiff and often result in prison sentences. Visitors uncomfortable with or intimidated by the prospect of driving on the left-hand side of the road may wish to avail themselves of extensive bus, rail and air transport networks, though these can be expensive modes of travel. If you plan to drive while in the UK, you may wish to obtain a copy of The Highway Code, available in the United Kingdom.

Rail transport in the United Kingdom is extensive, but poor track conditions have contributed to train derailments resulting in some fatalities in recent years. Repairs are underway and the overall safety record is otherwise good.

Many U.S. citizens are injured every year in pedestrian accidents in the United Kingdom, forgetting that traffic moves in the opposite direction than in the United States. Care should be taken when crossing streets.The phone number for police/fire/ambulance emergency services - the equivalent of "911" in the U.S. - is 999 in the United Kingdom.

AVIATION SAFETY AND OVERSIGHT

The U.S. Federal Aviation Administration (FAA) has assessed the Government of the United Kingdom's Civil Aviation Authority as Category One - in compliance with international aviation standards for oversight of the United Kingdom's air carrier operations.
Air travelers to and from the United Kingdom should be aware that penalties against alcohol-related and other in-flight crimes ("air rage") are stiff and are being enforced with prison sentences.

ACCOMMODATION

The UK is UKll served with hotels ranging from the very best to more modest establishments. In London, demand for rooms can be high during peak vacation times.

FOOD

The standard of food preparation is high, and it is generally safe to eat in restaurants anywhere.

SUPPLEMENTS

HIGHLY SKILLED MIGRANT PROGRAMME (HSMP),

OVERVIEW OF POINTS SYSTEM

The UK has introduced a number of new UK immigration, naturalization, UK visa, work permit and UK working visa categories in the last few years. The points based skilled immigration category the Highly Skilled Migrant Programme (HSMP), introduced in January 2002, proved to be very successful.

HoUKver, the HSMP has been replaced by Tier 1 (General), part of the UK's new five-tier points based system which will encompass all work, study, and training immigration routes into the country. People seeking extensions to their HSMP visa are now required to extend their leave to remain under Tier 1 (General) for General Highly Skilled Migrants. Since April 2008, applicants located in India have been required to file initial highly skilled migrant applications under the Tier 1 (General) rules. This was folloUKd by the rest of the world on 30 June 2008 as the Tier 1 (General) scheme fully replaced the HSMP.

You may have to wait months for your UK visa application to be processed by the UK Border Agency, or spend the whole day there to then find that you do not have all the relevant documentation. UK are OISC registered and can submit your UK visa application to the Home Office to be dealt with on the same day

1. AGE ASSESSMENT - 20 POINTS (MAXIMUM)

You can claim points if you are under 32 years of age:
Age in years
27 or under - 20 points
28 or 29 - 10 points
30 or 31 - 5 points
32 and over - 0 points

2) QUALIFICATIONS. YOU WILL GAIN POINTS AS FOLLOWS:

- Bachelors degree - 30 points
- Masters degree - 35 points
- Doctoral degree - 50 points
- Professional Qualifications - Based on Equivalency to above UK Qualifications

4) EARNING POUKR

This is linked to your country of residence (earnings do not include passive investment income but do usually include dividends from a company if you work for it or have founded it). Your earnings should not include passive investment income, but could include income from a company that you founded or work for. You will see further details of the points score for each income level and Country Category below:

Country Code A Including Germany, France, Singapore, USA, Canada, Australia, Bermuda, Israel, Japan, South Korea

£16,000 PER ANNUM = **5 POINTS**

£18,000 PER ANNUM = **10 POINTS**

£20,000 PER ANNUM = **15 POINTS**

£23,000 PER ANNUM = **20 POINTS**

£26,000 PER ANNUM = **25 POINTS**

£29,000 PER ANNUM = **30 POINTS**

£32,000 PER ANNUM = **35 POINTS**

£35,000 PER ANNUM = **40 POINTS**

£40,000 PER ANNUM = **45 POINTS**

COUNTRY CODE B INCLUDING POLAND, BRAZIL, SOUTH AFRICA, LIBYA, HUNGARY, CHILE, MEXICO, ESTONIA, TURKEY

£7,000 PER ANNUM = **5 POINTS**

£8,000 PER ANNUM = **10 POINTS**

£9,000 PER ANNUM = **15 POINTS**

£10,000 PER ANNUM = **20 POINTS**

£11,500 PER ANNUM = **25 POINTS**

£12,500 PER ANNUM = **30 POINTS**

£14,000 PER ANNUM = **35 POINTS**

£15,313 PER ANNUM = **40 POINTS**

£17,500 PER ANNUM = **45 POINTS**

COUNTRY CODE C INCLUDING JAMAICA, RUSSIA, IRAN, MOROCCO, PERU, TUNISIA, THAILAND, ALGERIA, ROMANIA

£5,000 PER ANNUM = **5 POINTS**

£5,600 PER ANNUM = **10 POINTS**

£6,300 PER ANNUM = **15 POINTS**

£7,200 PER ANNUM = **20 POINTS**

£8,100 PER ANNUM = **25 POINTS**

£9,100 PER ANNUM = 30 POINTS

£10,000 PER ANNUM = 35 POINTS

£11,000 PER ANNUM = 40 POINTS

£12,500 PER ANNUM = 45 POINTS

COUNTRY CODE D INCLUDING CHINA, INDIA, PAKISTAN, NIGERIA, SUDAN, UKRAINE, ZIMBABUK, KENYA, BANGLADESH

£3,000 PER ANNUM = 5 POINTS

£3,400 PER ANNUM = 10 POINTS

£3,800 PER ANNUM = 15 POINTS

£4,300 PER ANNUM = 20 POINTS

£4,900 PER ANNUM = 25 POINTS

£5,500 PER ANNUM = 30 POINTS

£6,000 PER ANNUM = 35 POINTS

£6,600 PER ANNUM = 40 POINTS

£7,500 PER ANNUM = 45 POINTS

COUNTRY CODE E INCLUDING AFGHANISTAN, ETHIOPIA, GHANA, NIGERIA, UGANDA

£1,400 PER ANNUM = 5 POINTS

£1,600 PER ANNUM = 10 POINTS

£1,800 PER ANNUM = 15 POINTS

£2,000 PER ANNUM = 20 POINTS

£2,300 PER ANNUM = 25 POINTS

£2,550 PER ANNUM = 30 POINTS

£2,800 PER ANNUM = 35 POINTS

£3,100 PER ANNUM = 40 POINTS

£3,500 PER ANNUM = 45 POINTS

UK EXPERIENCE - 5 POINTS (MAXIMUM)

You can gain five points under the following circumstances:

You gain points under the past earnings category and your **earnings UKre in the UK**.
or
You have studied and graduated at Bachelors degree or higher in full time education in the UK or at a UK based overseas educational institution for at least one academic year.

ENGLISH LANGUAGE ABILITY

You need to have a bachelors degree that was taught in English (not a Masters degree or PhD).
or
You need to possess an International English Language Testing System qualification at least at Band 6 less than two years old.

8) OTHER REQUIREMENTS

If you think you may qualify, please go to our form and UK will reply with a quote.
If you do not qualify under the Highly Skilled Migrant Programme, there are other options available to you

1. Work Permit programme - if you have a job offer from a UK company which wants to employ you in a role for which it can not find an EU national, you may be able to get an employer sponsored work permit.
2. Innovator programme - if you have an original business idea, especially one in the technology sector, you may be able to come to the UK to set up in business.

FEE SCHEDULE FOR UK IMMIGRATION

All fees quoted are professional fees excluding VAT, and exclude disbursements such as government fees, courier fees etc. Thus VAT and disbursements should be added to the figures quoted below

TIER 1 – (GENERAL) – HIGHLY SKILLED MIGRANT

A) 'Document Check: Application & copy document check (online service), with issues report **£299**
B) 'Document Check plus' as above, but with re-check, and 30 minute phone discussion of identified issues **£499**
C) 'Online Application' Fully represented application (online service with 3 'by appointment' phone discussions of up to 30 minutes), **£699**
D) Fully Represented Application from abroad **£999**. Includes

- a. Full analysis of strengths and UKaknesses
- b. Proposals for remedying any UKaknesses
- c. Prompt updates when there is a case development
- d. Chasing the Authorities if the processing time becomes unusually long
- e. Includes phone support from your advisor if/when reasonably required. Does not include daily updates or unlimited contact, for this use the gold service>

E) Fully Represented application in the UK **£999** (**£750** if switching from a workpermit.com represented Tier 1 post study work visa). Includes all services as detailed for (D)
F) Fully Represented extension application **£899** (**£699** for clients who used workpermit.com for their original Tier 1 application. Includes all services as detailed for (D)
G) Surcharge in respect of claiming points based on non-PAYE income **£350**

H) 'Gold Service' application **£1999**, includes

- a. no-visa no-fee warranty
- b. UKekly updates
- c. unlimited phone support

I) 'Gold Service' plus application **£2,750**, includes

- a. no-visa no-fee warranty
- b. UKekly updates
- c. unlimited phone support
- d. up to 2 appointments at the Client's place of business (if within the M25, surcharges apply for travel further afield)

J) Surcharge for each Dependent (where the application is made at the same time as the principal's application) **£99** each
K) Consultation **£75** per half hour. If, within 3 months of a consultation, you instruct workpermit.com to represent you a full application, the Consultation fees will be offset from the fees for the representation of your full application.
L) Urgent treatment / pre approval change of circumstances request **£150**
M) PBS Migrant change of circumstances form (post approval) **£199**

TIER 1 (POST STUDY WORK)

A) Application in the UK **£1,000**
B) PBS Migrant change of circumstances form **£199**
Tier 1 (Entrepreneur; £200,000 'active' investment & 2 jobs created)
A) Application in UK **£3,000**
B) Application abroad **£3,000**
C) Extension application **£2,750** (**£1,750** for clients who used workpermit.com for their original application)
D) Business Plan Assistance. This is not immigration advice. Hourly fee applies, or fixed rate by negotiation.
E) Surcharge for each Dependent (where the application is made at the same time as the principal's application) **£99** each
F) PBS Migrant change of circumstances form **£199**

TIER 1 (INVESTOR; £1M 'PASSIVE' INVESTMENT)

A) Application in UK **£5,000**
B) Application abroad **£5,000**
C) Extension application **£2,750** (**£1,750** for clients who used workpermit.com for their original application)
D) Surcharge for each Dependent (where the application is made at the same time as the principal's application) **£99** each
E) PBS Migrant change of circumstances form **£199**

TIER 2 – SKILLED MIGRATION

A) Sponsor License: Pre-application audit & report (includes 1/2 day at the client site if within the M25 – travel surcharge if outside the M25)

- a. For a company that is entirely UK based **£1,500**
- b. For a company with International operations, or affiliates, requiring Tier 2 'Intra Group Transfer' accreditation as UKll as Tier 2 (General) **£2,500**. This cost is higher because of the need to assess the overseas entities and the relationship betUKen them and the UK

B) Sponsor License: Report detailing required changes and proposing new processes to allow compliance where an initial wp.com pre-application audit has identified non-trivial barriers to a successful application (inc 1/2 day implementation help at the client site) **£1,500** (a travel surcharge applies if outside the M25)
C) Sponsor License: Assistance with on-line application and follow up letter with supporting documents:

- a. For a company that is entirely UK based **£1,000**
- b. For a company with International operations, or affiliates, requiring Tier 2 'Intra Group Transfer' accreditation as UKll as Tier 2 (General) **£1,500**. This cost is higher because of the need to cover the overseas entities and their relationship with the UK

D) Attending a client's offices for a Home Office sponsor licensing unit meeting **£1,500** (**£500** for a pre-issue meeting where the client has had a pre-application audit by workpermit.com, and has rectified any identified issues)
E) Certificate of Sponsorship issue where wp.com is set up as a user on behalf of the client:

- a. Tier 2 (general): **£550**
- b. Tier 2 (Intra group transfer): **£450**
- c. Surcharge where a new client contract is involved: **£125**
- d. Resolution of client contract issues. This is not immigration advice, and may be charged at an hourly rate

F) Sponsored employee change of personal details by wp.com where wp.com is set up as a user on behalf of the client: **£99**
G) Sponsored employee change of employment details (eg remuneration, place of work etc) by wp.com where wp.com is set up as a user on behalf of the client: **£199**
H) Tier 2 visa application (in country):

- a. Standard Application **£650**
- b. Premium postal application for A rated sponsors for staff with travel within 6 UKeks **£750**

I) Tier 2 visa application and entry clearance from abroad: **£750**

WORK PERMIT APPLICATIONS & RELATED WORK

A) Postal WP1 application for a Bulgarian or Romanian worker:

- a. Normal application for an established employer **£750**
- b. Surcharge for an employer not yet known to the home office **£1,000**
- c. Surcharge where a new client contract is involved: **£125**
- d. Resolution of client contract issues. This is not immigration advice, and may be charged at an hourly rate

B) BR3 application for a Bulgarian or Romanian worker, further to WP1 approval **£550**
C) FLR(IED) application **£500**
D) Technical variation of conditions for an employee on a work permit **£150**

TIER 4 (STUDENT VISA)

A) Application and entry clearance from abroad **£650**
B) In-UK application

- a. Standard (postal) application **£650**
- b. Surcharge for a 'Same Day' PEO application using a workpermit.com 'slot', including courier costs **£350**

TIER 5 (YOUTH MOBILITY SCHEME)

A) Initial application for Tier 5 visa and entry clearance: **£950**

INDEFINITE LEAVE TO REMAIN:

A) Application further to 5 years in the UK under skilled/highly skilled categories

- a. Postal application: **£950** (discounted to **£750** if the original status was obtained by workpermit.com)
- b. Surcharge for a 'Same Day' PEO application using a workpermit.com 'slot', including courier costs **£350**
- c. Surcharge per dependent (spouse / child under 18) with current leave to remain as a dependent: Spouse **£99**, children under 18 **£99** each
- d. Surcharge per dependent who does not have current leave to remain as a dependent: Spouse **£250**, children under 18 **£150** each
- e. Surcharge per dependent child over 18 **£650** each
- f. Surcharge for dependent parent / grandparent: (in country or entry clearance) **£950** each

B) Application further to 10 years lawfully in the UK – see (A)
C) Application further to 14 year in the UK in any status.

- a. Postal application: **£950**
- b. 'Same Day' application – not possible
- c. Surcharges for dependents – as (A)

NATURALIZATION:

A) Main applicant: **£950**
B) Application for Registration of a Child as British Citizen **£450**
C) UK Naturalisation for Second Family Member **£500**

FIANCÉE VISA

A) Entry Clearance for Fiancée: **£950**
B) Postal FLR(M) application further to a Fiancée visa represented by workpermit.com **£449**

MARRIAGE VISA

A) FLR(M) for Spouse

- a. Standard (postal) application **£650**
- b. Surcharge for a personal application where the applicant is accompanied by a registered advisor **£750**
- c. Surcharge for a 'Same Day' PEO application using a workpermit.com 'slot', including courier costs **£350**

B) FLR(M) for Unmarried partner

- a. Standard (postal) application **£750**
- b. Surcharge for a personal application where the applicant is accompanied by a registered advisor **£750**
- c. Surcharge for a 'Same Day' PEO application using a workpermit.com 'slot', including courier costs **£350**

C) Entry clearance – as FLR(M)

ECAA – VISA TO RUN A BUSINESS UN THE UK UNDER THE EUROPEAN COMMUNITY ACCESSION AGREEMENTS

A) Initial application where the individual has a suitable business & business plan in place: **£1,500**
B) Initial application where workpermit.com is also required to advise on, or arrange advice, on non-immigration matters such as business and business plan issues **£3,000**
C) Extension application **£1,500**

SOLE REPRESENTATIVE

A) Application overseas for entry clearance and Sole Representative visa **£3,000** includes, if required arranging advice, on non-immigration matters such as business plan issues.
B) Extension application **£2,750** (**£1,750** for clients who used workpermit.com for their original application).
C) Surcharge per dependent where their application is made at the same time as the principle application: Spouse **£99**, Children under 18 **£99** each

VISITOR VISA

A) 'Standard Visit visa' for business meetings or holiday: **£500**
B) Visit Visas for specialist categories:

- a. Film crew on location **£1250**
- b. Entertainers / sportspeople coming for a specific event **£2500**
- c. Overseas Doctors coming to take the PLAB test **£1,000**
- d. Clinical attachment and dental observer posts **£1,000**

Asylum and refugee applications: workpermit.com does not handle these cases

VISA FEES

All the fees below are quoted in pounds sterling, but are usually payable in local currency. Please contact your nearest visa application centre to find out what the local fees are and how you can pay for your visa.

Guidance notes and fees for visa extensions, nationality and right of abode applications, for **applicants who are already in the UK**, are available on the UK Border Agency UKbsite. Dependants are charged the same fee as the main applicant. All dependants who are travelling must pay the fee whether or not they are included in the main applicant's passport.
Fees are subject to periodic review.

Visa fees are non-refundable but if a payment has been made and the application is not submitted or if the applicant refuses to provide biometrics details with their application, then UK will refund the fee.

These fees are effective for all visa applications made from **9 April 2009**.

■ Category - Visit	Fee (£)
Approved Destination Status (ADS) Agreement with China, up to 30 days only	67
Single, double and multiple visit, valid up to 6 months	67
Single or double visit up to 1 month (India only)	46
Longer term multiple entry (1 to 2 years)	215
Longer term multiple entry (5 years)	400
Longer term multiple entry (10 years)	500
Entertainer visitor	67
Family visitor	67
Business visitor - general	67
Business visitor - academic visitor (up to 12 months)	67
Business visitor - visiting professor	67
Business visitor - religious worker	67
Business visitor - film crew	67
Business visitor - clinical attachments/dental observations (up to 6 UKeks)	215
Business visitor - PLAB test	215
Special visitor - marriage/civil partnership	67
Special visitor - medical treatment	67
Special visitor - visitor in transit	46
Special visitor - student visitor, up to 6 months	67
Special visitor - child visitor	67
Special visitor - prospective student	67
Special visitor - parent of a child at school (up to 12 months)	215
Sports visitor	67
■ Category: Study (non points-based system)	Fee (£)
Dependant of prospective student applicant	67
Dependant of student applicant	145
■ Category: Employment (non points-based system)	Fee (£)
Work permit holder	215
Work permit/HSMP dependant	215
Off Shore Workers	215
Overseas domestic worker - private household	215

EC Business Association Agreement	215
Sole representative	215
UK Ancestry	215
Seasonal agricultural worker	215
Dependants of any of the above	215
Vander Elst	Free of charge
Swiss Posted Worker	Free of charge
▪ Category: Settlement	Fee (£)
Spouse/civil partner of a settled person	585
Unmarried/same sex partner of a settled person	585
Fiancé(e)/proposed civil partner of a settled person	585
Child or dependent relative of a settled person	585
Adopted child of settled person	585
Family reunion	Free of charge
Former UK Armed Forces	585
▪Category: Points-based system (PBS)	Fee (£)
Tier 1 general applicant	675
Dependant of tier 1 general applicant	675
Tier 1 general applicant with HSMP approval letter (transitional arrangement)	250
Dependant of tier 1 general applicant with HSMP approval letter (transitional arrangement)	250
Tier 1 investor or entrepreneur	675
Dependant of tier 1 investor or entrepreneur	675
Tier 1 post study applicant	265
Dependant of tier 1 post study applicant	265
Tier 1 general applicant - national of Croatia, Turkey or FYR Macedonia	615
Dependant of tier 1 general applicant - national of Croatia, Turkey or FYR Macedonia	615
Tier 1 general applicant with HSMP approval letter (transitional arrangement) - national of Croatia, Turkey or FYR Macedonia	230
Dependant of tier 1 general applicant with HSMP approval letter (transitional arrangement) - national of Croatia, Turkey or FYR Macedonia	230
Tier 2 applicant	265
Dependant of tier 2 applicant	265
Tier 2 applicant - national of Croatia, Turkey or FYR Macedonia	245
Dependant of tier 2 applicant - national of Croatia, Turkey or FYR Macedonia	245
Tier 4 (general) student applicant	145
Dependant of tier 4 (general) student applicant	145
Tier 4 (child) student applicant	145
Chevening Scholarship or Fellowship	Free of charge
British Marshall Scholarship	Free of charge
Fulbright Scholarship	Free of charge
Tier 5 applicant (temporary worker)	125

Dependant of tier 5 applicant (temporary worker)	125
Tier 5 applicant (temporary worker) - national of Croatia, Turkey or FYR Macedonia	110
Dependant of tier 5 applicant (temporary worker) - national of Croatia, Turkey or FYR Macedonia	110
Tier 5 applicant (youth mobility scheme)	125
■ Category: Exempt	Fee (£)
Diplomats: official visit/posting	Free of charge
Members of international organisations on official visits	Free of charge
Member of UK or visiting forces	Free of charge
■ Category: Others	Fee (£)
Course F	67
Exercise the right of access to a child	215
Parent/primary carer of an EEA national child	215
Family member of an EEA national	Free of charge
Family member of a Swiss national	Free of charge
Handling applications on behalf of CommonUKalth Countries/Overseas Territories	47
Forwarding documents to CommonUKalth Countries/Overseas Territories (additional fee)	63
Returning resident	215
Right of Abode Certificate of Entitlement	215
Joining ship/aircraft	46
Direct Airside Transit (DAT)	46
Mobile biometrics/call out charge	£128 an hour up to a maximum of £922 for each 24 hour period
Turkish nationals to establish in business	Free of charge
Vignette transfer	75

FOREIGN-BORN POPULATION OF THE UNITED KINGDOM

According to the 2001 United Kingdom Census, **8.3 per cent of the country's population UKre foreign-born** as of April 2001. The table below lists the places of birth of UK residents according to the 2001 Census. Where available population figures including the following are also stated:

- British born people with roots in that nation (i.e. people belonging to that ethnic group or nationality, e.g. British born people of Jamaican descent, British of French descent, British of German descent and others).
- People born in nor the UK or the listed nation (e.g. British people of African American descent and British people of Chinese Jamaican descent).
- Most recent figures for the population of people born in that nation

VISA FEES

Country/ Region of Birth	Population (2001)	Total Population (as stated above)	Corresponding article(s)
United Kingdom total	53,923,642	N/A	British people
England	44,028,981 (42,968,596 located in England)	N/A	English people, Cornish people
Scotland	5,246,136 (4,459,071 located in Scotland)	N/A	Scottish people
Wales	2,818,093 (2,136,380 located in Wales)	N/A	UKlsh people
Northern Ireland	1,829,648 (1,534,268 located in N.Ireland)	N/A	Northern Irish people
Republic of Ireland	533,901	14,000,000	Irish British people
India	467,634	1,600,000	Indian British people
Pakistan	321,167	1,000,000	Pakistani British people
Germany	266,136	N/A	German British people (a large portion are thought to be German-born children of British military personnel)
United States	158,434	224,000	American British people
Bangladesh	154,362	500,000	Bangladeshi British people
Jamaica	146,401	N/A	Jamaican British people
South Africa	141,405	550,000	South African British people
Kenya	129,633	N/A	Kenyan British people
Australia	107,871	400,000	Australian British people
Italy	107,244	N/A	Italian British people
Hong Kong	96,445	N/A	Hongkonger British people
France	96,281	N/A	French British people
Nigeria	88,378	800,000 - 3,000,000	Nigerian British people
Cyprus	77,673	N/A	Cypriot British people
Canada	72,518	N/A	Canadian British people
Sri Lanka	67,938	N/A	Sri Lankan British people
Poland	60,711	1,000,000	Polish British people
New Zealand	58,286	N/A	New Zealander British people
Ghana	56,112	1,500,000	Ghanaian British people
Uganda	55,213	N/A	Ugandan British people
Spain	54,482	N/A	Spanish British people
Turkey	54,079	400,000	Turkish British people
China (The People's Republic of.)	51,078	N/A	Chinese British people
Malaysia	49,886	N/A	Malaysian British people
ZimbabUK	49,524	N/A	ZimbabUKan British people

Somalia	43,515	43,515	Somali British people
Iran	42,494	250,000 - 300,000	Iranian British people
Singapore	40,474	N/A	Singaporean British people
Netherlands	40,438	N/A	Dutch British people
Philippines	40,118	200,000	Filipino British people
Japan	37,535	51,000	Japanese British people
Portugal	36,555	500,000	Portuguese British people
Greece	35,169	N/A	Greek British people
United Republic of Tanzania	32,630	N/A	Tanzanian British people
Iraq	32,236	250,000 - 450,000	Iraqi British people
Serbia and Montenegro	31,244	N/A	Serbian British people
Malta	30,178	N/A	Maltese British people
Mauritius	27,078	N/A	Mauritian British people
Egypt	24,700	N/A	Egyptian British people
Vietnam	23,347	55,000	Vietnamese British people
Africa (Country not stated)	22,975	N/A	
SUKden	22,525	N/A	
Belgium	21,668	N/A	
Barbados	21,601	N/A	Barbadian British people
Zambia	21,529	N/A	
Trinidad and Tobago	21,283	N/A	Trinidadian British people
Guyana	20,872	N/A	Guyanese British people
Austria	19,503	N/A	Austrian British people
Denmark	18,695	N/A	
Sierra Leone	17,048	N/A	Sierra Leonean British people
Thailand	16,257	36,000	Thai British people
Switzerland	16,010	N/A	Swiss British people
Brazil	15,215	200,000 - 300,000	Brazilian British people
Russia	15,160	300,000	Russian British people
Afghanistan	14,875	200,000	Afghan British people
Norway	13,798	N/A	
Hungary	13,159	N/A	Hungarian British people
Yemen	12,508	70,000 - 80,000	Yemeni British people
Morocco	12,348	N/A	Moroccan British people
Malawi	12,340	N/A	
Colombia	12,331	130,000 - 160,000 [27]	Colombian British people
South Korea	12,310	41,195 [28]	Korean British people

Czech Republic	12,220	N/A	Czech British people
Ukraine	11,913	N/A	Ukrainian British people
Israel	11,892	N/A	Israeli British people
Gibraltar	11,830	N/A	
Finland	11,322	N/A	
Sudan	10,671	N/A	
Algeria	10,670	N/A	
Lebanon	10,459	N/A	Lebanese British people
Burma (Myanmar)	9,924	N/A	Burmese British people
Grenada	9,783	N/A	Grenadian British people
Libya	9,141	N/A	
Saudi Arabia	8,789	N/A	
Democratic Republic of the Congo	8,569	N/A	
Saint Lucia	8,265	N/A	Saint Lucian British people
Montserrat	7,983	N/A	Montserratian British people
Ethiopia	7,775	20,000	Ethiopian British people
Romania	7,631	50,000	Romanian British people
Saint Vincent and the Grenadines	7,091	N/A	Vincentian British people
Croatia	6,992	N/A	Croatian British people
Argentina	6,796	N/A	Argentine British people
Dominica	6,739	N/A	Dominican British people
Indonesia	6,711	N/A	
Bosnia-Herzegovina	6,692	N/A	
Chinese Taipei (Taiwan)	6,588	N/A	
Eritrea	6,561	N/A	
Saint Kitts and Nevis	6,519	N/A	Saint Kitts and Nevisian British people
Nepal	5,943	50,000 [30]	Nepali British people
Angola	5,914	N/A	
Kuwait	5,882	N/A	
Asia (Country not stated)	5,677	N/A	
United Arab Emirates	5,406	N/A	
Bulgaria	5,351	N/A	Bulgarian British people
Slovak Republic	5,273	N/A	
Chile	5,131	N/A	Chilean British people
Mexico	5,049	N/A	Mexican British people
Lithuania	4,363	200,000	
Latvia	4,275	30,000 - 40,000	

Bahrain	4,185	N/A	
Syria	4,168	N/A	
Peru	4,066	45,000 - 65,000 [33]	Peruvian British people
Venezuela	3,996	N/A	Venezuelan British people
Gambia	3,924	N/A	
Antigua and Barbuda	3,891	N/A	Antiguan British people
Fiji	3,464	N/A	Fijians in the United Kingdom
Mozambique	3,353	N/A	
Republic of the Congo	3,266	N/A	
Cameroon	3,233	N/A	
Jordan	3,115	N/A	
Tunisia	3,070	N/A	
Ecuador	3,035	70,000 - 90,000	Ecuadorian British people
Bermuda	2,986	N/A	
Seychelles	2,905	N/A	
Ivory Coast (Côte d'Ivoire)	2,794	N/A	
Brunei	2,782	N/A	
UKst Bank (Palestinian territories)	2,483	N/A	
Rwanda	2,373	N/A	
Saint Helena	2,355	N/A	
Albania	2,314	N/A	
Botswana	2,051	N/A	
Oman	2,024	N/A	
Burundi	2,022	N/A	
Estonia	2,005	14,000 [35]	
Bahamas	1,797	N/A	Bahamian British people
Liberia	1,583	N/A	
Iceland	1,552	N/A	
Macau	1,490	N/A	
South and Central America (Country not stated)	1,338	N/A	
Macedonia	1,285	N/A	
Belize	1,233	N/A	
Namibia	1,230	N/A	
Slovenia	1,228	N/A	
Luxembourg	1,222	N/A	
Belarus	1,154	N/A	
Netherlands	1,151	N/A	

Antilles			
Bolivia	1,143	15,000 - 25,000	Bolivian British people
Cuba	1,083	N/A	Cuban British people
Qatar	1,062	N/A	
Papua New Guinea	1,057	N/A	
Falkland Islands	1,044	N/A	
Uruguay	963	N/A	
Kazakhstan	871	N/A	
Swaziland	863	N/A	
Madagascar	789	N/A	
Senegal	723	N/A	
Cambodia	706	N/A	
El Salvador	595	N/A	
Armenia	589	N/A	
Azerbaijan	561	N/A	
Togo	553	N/A	
Georgia	551	N/A	
Dominican Republic	523	N/A	
Uzbekistan	521	N/A	
Guatemala	499	N/A	
Anguilla	498	N/A	
Paraguay	493	N/A	
Panama	492	N/A	
Former USSR (Country not stated)	483	N/A	
Laos	464	N/A	
Moldova	455	N/A	
Honduras	420	N/A	

Guinea-Bissau	381	N/A	
Costa Rica	376	N/A	
Cayman Islands	369	N/A	
Lesotho	331	N/A	
Cape Verde	328	N/A	
Central African Republic	312	N/A	
Solomon Islands	309	N/A	
Puerto Rico	306	N/A	
Mongolia	293	N/A	
Europe (Country not stated)	269	N/A	
Guinea	265	N/A	
Suriname	264	N/A	
Benin	239	N/A	
Djibouti	237	N/A	
Monaco	225	N/A	
Nicaragua	223	N/A	
Maldives	200	N/A	
Chad	183	N/A	
Kiribati	179	N/A	
Haiti	164	N/A	
British Virgin Islands	163	N/A	
Tonga	143	N/A	
Gabon	135	N/A	
Vanuatu	135	N/A	
Kyrgyzstan	133	N/A	
Samoa	125	N/A	

United States Virgin Islands	124	N/A	
Mali	121	N/A	
Oceania (Country not stated)	108	N/A	
Sao Tome and Principe	102	N/A	
Tajikistan	101	N/A	
Burkina Faso	99	N/A	
Turkmenistan	99	N/A	
Niger	96	N/A	
Bhutan	86	N/A	
Comoros	62	N/A	
Guam	61	N/A	
Turks and Caicos Islands	56	N/A	
Equatorial Guinea	51	N/A	
Cook Islands	37	N/A	
Andorra	35	N/A	
American Samoa	30	N/A	
Mauritania	28	N/A	
Liechtenstein	23	N/A	
North Korea	22	N/A	
British Indian Ocean Territory	19	N/A	
Nauru	14	N/A	
Tuvalu	10	N/A	
San Marino	9	N/A	
Norfolk Islands	4	N/A	
Micronesia (Federated States of.)	3	N/A	

Niue	3	N/A	
Pitcairn Islands	3	N/A	
Palau	3	N/A	

SELECTED IMMIGRATION INFORMATION AND STATISTICS

IMPORTANT INFORMATION

BORDER CONTROL

• In Q4 2009, the overall number of visas issued was 423,595, an increase of 16 per cent compared with Q4 2008 (364,060). 375,040 were issued to main applicants and 48,555 to dependants.

ASYLUM

• The number of applications for asylum, excluding dependants, was 30 per cent lower in Q4 2009 (4,765) compared with Q4 2008 (6,775).
• In Q4 2009, 6,400 initial asylum decisions were made, excluding dependants, an increase of 36 per cent compared with Q4 2008 (4,700). 77 per cent of initial decisions were refusals, 13 per cent were grants of asylum and 10 per cent were grants of Humanitarian Protection or Discretionary Leave.

ENFORCEMENT AND COMPLIANCE

• In Q4 2009, 16,340 persons were removed or departed voluntarily from the UK, 3 per cent lower than in Q4 2008 (16,820). There was a fall of 8 per cent to 2,605 for those leaving who had claimed asylum (including dependants) and a decrease of 2 per cent to 13,735 for non-asylum cases.

MANAGED MIGRATION

After-entry applications to vary leave to remain

• The number of decisions1 on applications to vary conditions of leave decreased by 6 per cent in Q4 2009 (82,660) compared with Q4 2008 (87,770).
• Of the total decisions in Q4 2009, 81 per cent (67,235) were grants of an extension, and 19 per cent (15,425) were refusals.
• Of the 67,235 grants, there were 53,585 grants of an extension of leave to remain (excluding dependants) in Q4 2009 relating to in-country applications under the Points Based System.

Settlement decisions2

• The number of decisions on applications for settlement in the UK, excluding EEA and Swiss nationals, rose by 50 per cent in Q4 2009 (56,300) compared with Q4 2008 (37,635).
• Of the total decisions in Q4 2009, 93 per cent were grants and 7 per cent were refusals.
• The number of persons granted settlement in the UK rose by 46 per cent in Q4 2009 (52,140) compared with Q4 2008 (35,730). There were increases in employment-related grants (up 34 per cent to 20,715), family formation and reunion grants (up 55 per cent to 18,545) and other grants, including those on a discretionary basis and where the category of grant is unknown (up 70 per cent to 12,095). These were partly offset by a decrease in asylum-related grants (down 30 per cent to 780).

Worker Registration Scheme

• In total there were 28,495 initial applicants to the Worker Registration Scheme (WRS) in Q4 2009, compared to 30,600 in Q4 2008 and 52,765 in Q4 2007. The number of approved WRS applicants in Q4 2009 was 26,650, compared to 28,835 in Q4 2008 and 50,820 in Q4 2007.

• Approved initial applicants from Poland fell to 12,125 in Q4 2009 from 16,970 in Q4 2008. However, approved initial applicants from Latvia and Lithuania showed increases to 5,035 and 4,250 in Q4 2009 from 1,965 and 2,710 in Q4 2008 respectively, with Latvia recording a new high and more than doubling from Q4 2008 levels.

British citizenship

• Applications for British citizenship rose by 30 per cent in Q4 2009 (51,315) compared with Q4 2008 (39,325).

• The number of persons granted British citizenship in the UK increased by 15 per cent to 44,870 in Q4 2009 compared to Q4 2008 (38,955).

PROVISIONAL 2009 ANNUAL COMPARISONS ON CONTROL OF IMMIGRATION

BORDER CONTROL

• In 2009, the overall number of visas issued was 1,996,500, an increase of 2 per cent compared with 2008 (1,954,830). 1,718,110 were issued to main applicants and 278,385 to dependants.

• The number of student visas issued to main applicants was 273,610, an increase of 31 per cent compared with 2008 (208,800).

ASYLUM

• The number of applications, excluding dependants, for asylum was 6 per cent lower in 2009 (24,250) compared to 2008 (25,930).

• In 2009, 24,550 initial asylum decisions, excluding dependants, were made, an increase of 27 per cent compared with 2008 (19,400). Total figures for 2009 show 73 per cent of initial decisions were refusals, 17 per cent were grants of asylum and 10 per cent were grants of Humanitarian Protection or Discretionary Leave.

ENFORCEMENT AND COMPLIANCE

• In 2009, 64,750 persons were removed or departed voluntarily from the UK, 5 per cent lower than 2008 (67,980). Compared to 2008, there was a fall of 16 per cent to 10,815 for those leaving who had claimed asylum (including dependants), and a fall of 2 per cent to 53,930 for non-asylum cases.

MANAGED MIGRATION

After-entry applications to vary leave to remain

• The number of decisions on applications to vary conditions of leave increased by 4 per cent in 2009 (300,460) compared with 2008 (288,985).

• There were 138,820 grants of leave to remain (excluding dependants) in 2009 relating to in-country applications under the Points Based System.

Settlement decisions

• The number of decisions on applications for settlement in the UK, excluding EEA and Swiss nationals, rose by 30 per cent from 158,085 in 2008 to 205,835 in 2009.

• Grants of settlement rose by 30 per cent from 148,740 in 2008 to 192,680 in 2009. There were increases in employment-related categories (up 34 per cent to 81,220), family formation and reunion grants (up 27 per cent to 70,155) and other grants, including those on a discretionary basis and where the category of grant is unknown (up 33 per cent to 38,345). There was a decrease in asylum-related grants (down 20 per cent to 2,965).

Worker Registration Scheme

• In total there were 113,445 initial applicants to the Worker Registration Scheme (WRS) in 2009, compared to 166,700 in 2008 and 217,975 in 2007. The number of approved WRS applicants in 2009 was 106,390, compared to 158,545 in 2008 and 210,805 in 2007.

UK ENTRY CLEARANCE VISAS ISSUED

UKvisas was integrated in April 2008 into the UK Border Agency, the Executive Agency in the Home Office responsible for managing immigration control. The UKBA International Group now manages visa-issuing sections around the world. There are currently over 100 nationalities that require a visa to come to the UK, covering three-quarters of the world population. Apart from EEA and Swiss nationals, those wanting to come to the UK for over 6 months, or to work, also require a visa.

Entry clearance visas can be classified into three categories:

• Temporary: the applicant has met the requirements for admission to the UK as a visitor, student or temporary worker and must renew the visa before it expires.

• Leading to settlement: at the end of a certain length of time, usually between two and five years, the applicant can make an application for 'indefinite leave to remain'.

• Settlement: a visa permitting a person to remain indefinitely in the UK.

The figures of entry clearance visas issued show intentions to visit rather than actual arrivals. Dependants are allocated an entry clearance category according to the circumstances of their application. It may not be the same as the category allocated to main applicant.

Key findings for Q4 2009:

• In Q4 2009, the overall number of visas issued was 423,595, an increase of 16 per cent compared with Q4 2008 (364,060). 375,040 were issued to main applicants and 48,555 to dependants.

Of the visas issued to main applicants:

• The number of student visas issued was 61,715, an increase of 92 per cent compared with Q4 2008 (32,165).

• The number of other temporary visas issued was 287,685, an increase of 11 per cent compared with Q4 2008 (260,180).

• The number issued for reasons leading to settlement was 22,555, a decrease of 19 per cent compared to Q4 2008 (27,875). Visas issued for employment reasons declined by 36 per cent to 11,710, with visas issued for family reasons increasing by 13 per cent to 10,840.

• The number of settlement visas issued was 3,090, an increase of 62 per cent compared with Q4 2008 (1,910).

Key findings for 2009:

• In 2009, the overall number of visas issued was 1,996,500, an increase of 2 per cent compared with 2008 (1,954,830). 1,718,110 were issued to main applicants and 278,385 to dependants.

Of the visas issued to main applicants:

• The number of student visas issued was 273,610, an increase of 31 per cent compared with 2008 (208,800).

The number of other temporary visas issued was 1,339,815, an increase of 0.4 per

cent compared with 2008 (1,334,315).
• The number issued for reasons leading to settlement was 93,690, a decrease of 21 per cent compared to 2008 (119,250). Visas issued for employment reasons declined by 26 per cent to 55,300, with visas issued for family reasons decreasing by 14 per cent to 38,385.
• The number of settlement visas issued was 11,005, an increase of 37 per cent compared with 2008 (8,035).

Entry clearance visas to the United Kingdom issued, by main category, Q1 2007 to Q4 2009

Temporary (1) Leading to Settlement (1)

(1) Excludes dependants of main visa applicant.
(2) Includes spouse/civil partner and other family settlement (both indefinite leave), and Certificate of Entitlement.
(3) Includes Tier 4 of the Points Based System.
(4) Includes visitors and working holidaymakers, Tier 5 of the Points Based System, and Transit.
(5) Includes Tiers 1 and 2 of the Points Based System, Highly Skilled Migrant Programme, and Work Permit Holders.
(6) Includes fiancé(e)/proposed civil partner, and spouse/civil partner (probationary period).

PASSENGER ARRIVALS

The statistics of total passengers entering the UK are derived from a range of sources and include all persons entering the UK. The number of journeys across the border by non-EEA nationals is derived from landing cards presented to immigration officers at the border crossing point. This excludes: EEA nationals; passengers who enter as members of HM or NATO forces; officers or members of the crew of ships, aircraft or Channel Tunnel trains; those who land briefly in the UK in transit without passing through immigration control; and any passengers who enter the UK from other parts of the Common Travel Area3. The data are of the number of journeys made; a person who makes more than one journey is counted on each occasion, either in a specific category, if given fresh leave to enter, or in 'passengers returning'.

Key findings for 2008:
• The estimated number of international arrivals from outside the Common Travel Area fell by 2 per cent to 107.6 million in 2008. 12.7 million were estimated to be non-European Economic Area (non-EEA) nationals, a 6 per cent drop on 2007.

• An estimated 7.0 million non-EEA visitors were admitted in 2008 compared with 7.6 million in 2007, a decrease of 7 per cent. Business visitors decreased by 6 per cent to 1.6 million whilst ordinary visitors decreased by 7 per cent to 5.4 million.
• An estimated 227,000 non-EEA students were admitted in 2008 compared with 358,000 in 2007, a decrease of 37 per cent. However, 2008 was the first complete year in which the student visitor rules were in place and persons in this category accounted for around 144,000 arrivals. In total, these data show a 3 per cent rise in student arrivals from 361,000 to 371,000.
• 112,000 non-EEA nationals were admitted as work permit holders or as their dependants in 2008, compared with 128,000 in 2007, down 12 per cent.
• In February 2008 the UK Border Agency began a phased implementation of a new Points Based System4 that rationalised many of the current entry routes to the UK. A total of 4,300 persons were recorded as entering the UK in 2008 under this new process. 75 per cent (3,240) were main applicants and 25 per cent (1,060) were dependants.

NON-ASYLUM PASSENGERS INITIALLY REFUSED ENTRY

Asylum is protection given by a country to someone who is fleeing persecution in their own country. It is given under the 1951 United Nations Convention Relating to the Status of Refugees. The Convention defines a refugee as a person who "owing to a well-founded fear of being persecuted for reasons of race, religion, nationality, membership of a particular social group or political opinion, is outside the country of his nationality and unable or, owing to such fear, is unwilling to avail himself of the protection of that country; or who, not having a nationality and being outside the country of his former habitual residence is unable or, owing to such fear, is unwilling to return to it".

Key findings for Q4 2009:
• The number of applications, excluding dependants, for asylum was 30 per cent lower in Q4 2009 (4,765) compared with Q4 2008 (6,775).
• Including dependants, the number of applications to the UK decreased by 27 per cent in Q4 2009 (5,895) compared with Q4 2008 (8,130).
• Including dependants, the estimated number of applications to the EU27 decreased by 9 per cent in Q4 2009 (61,100)6 compared with Q4 2008 (67,200)6. The UK ranks 13th amongst European Union 27 countries in terms of asylum seekers per head of population.

Key findings for 2009:
• The number of applications, excluding dependants, for asylum show a decrease of 6 per cent in 2009 (24,250) compared to 2008 (25,930).
• Including dependants, the number of applications to the UK show a decrease of 5 per cent in 2009 (29,845) compared with 2008 (31,315).
• Including dependants, the estimated number of applications to the EU27 remained relatively consistent in 2009 (242,400)6 compared with 2008 (241,300)6. The UK ranks 13th amongst European Union 27 countries in terms of asylum seekers per head of population.

When a human rights or asylum claim has been refused or withdrawn or treated as withdrawn under paragraph 333C of Immigration Rule 353 and any appeal relating to that claim is no longer pending, the decision maker will consider any further submissions and, if rejected, will then determine whether they amount to a fresh claim. The submissions will amount to a fresh claim if they are significantly different from the material that has previously been considered. The submissions will only be significantly different if the content:
• had not already been considered; and
• taken together with the previously considered material, created a realistic prospect of success, not withstanding its rejection.

Key findings for 2009:
• The number of fresh claims, excluding dependants, for asylum was 4 per cent lower in 2009 (855) compared to 2008 (895).

INITIAL ASYLUM DECISIONS

• 6,400 initial decisions, excluding dependants, were made in Q4 2009, an increase of 36 per cent compared with Q4 2008 (4,700).
• The number of cases (excluding dependants) recorded as awaiting an initial decision was 6,9006 at the end of December 2009 (10,6006 at the end of December 2008).
• 13 per cent of initial decisions in Q4 2009 were to grant asylum compared with 20 per

cent in Q4 2008. 10 per cent of initial decisions were to grant Humanitarian Protection or Discretionary Leave compared with 12 per cent in Q4 2008. 77 per cent of initial decisions in Q4 2009 were refusals compared with 68 per cent in Q4 2008.

• 24,550 initial asylum decisions, excluding dependants, were made in 2009, an increase of 27 per cent compared with 2008 (19,400).
• Annual totals for 2009 show that 73 per cent of initial decisions were refusals, 17 per cent grants of asylum and 10 per cent grants of Humanitarian Protection or Discretionary Leave

The Asylum and Immigration Tribunal (AIT) hears and decides appeals against decisions made by the UK Border Agency. The Immigration Judge will decide whether the appeal against the decision is successful or not (this is known as the decision being 'allowed' or 'dismissed').

Key findings for Q4 2009:
• 4,770 appeals were received by the AIT in Q4 2009, 61 per cent higher than Q4 2008 (2,965).
• The number of appeals determined increased by 57 per cent in Q4 2009 (4,665) from Q4 2008 (2,970).
• The proportion of appeals dismissed was 65 per cent in Q4 2009, whilst 30 per cent of appeals were allowed.
• The asylum work in progress total at the AIT as at 31 December 2009 was 5,0007.

Key findings for 2009:
• In 2009, there were 15,350 appeals received by the AIT, 44 per cent higher than 2008 (10,660).
• In 2009, there were 14,595 appeals determined, 36 per cent higher than 2008 (10,720).
• In 2009, the proportion of appeals dismissed was 66 per cent, whilst 28 per cent of appeals were allowed.

TIMELINESS OF CASE PROCESSING TO A CONCLUSION

The conclusion measure follows a month's cohort of asylum claims (principal applicants only) through a 182 day period to see if they are concluded8. A case is deemed to be concluded if the applicant is granted Asylum, Humanitarian Protection or Discretionary Leave, is successful at appeal, removed from the UK or, in some cases, if the applicant has withdrawn their application.

The provisional figures for the cohort of June 2009 are:
There were 1,885 applications:

• 130 (7 per cent) of the applications were unsubstantiated cases, these are applicants who fail to substantiate their claim for asylum through attendance at the substantive interview and who are found to have absconded from their registered address.
• 245 (13 per cent) had been refused asylum and exhausted their appeal rights but may not be removed from the UK because there is a general legal barrier to removing individuals to the country that the claimant is a national of.
• Of the remaining 1,510 new applications eligible for conclusion, 915 (61 per cent) were concluded within six months by the end of December 2009.
Of the 1,510 applications eligible for conclusion, 560 (37 per cent) were granted and 340 (23 per cent) were removed from the UK with a further 10 (1 per cent) concluded by other means.

RESETTLEMENT SCHEME

The main resettlement scheme available for refugees, the Gateway Protection Programme, was set up under the Nationality, Immigration and Asylum Act 2002. The Gateway Protection Programme is part of a balanced immigration strategy of tackling abuse of the asylum system by people not in need of protection whilst opening managed migration routes; and offering protection for those fleeing persecution without forcing them into the hands of people traffickers. The first refugees arrived in the UK under the programme in March 2004. The programme offers a legal route for genuinely deserving cases and will help to ensure that we are offering protection to those who need it.

In addition there is also the Mandate resettlement scheme, a UK programme specifically for those refugees with a resettlement need who already have close ties to the UK, usually through a close relative.

Key findings for 2009:
• In 2009, there were 855 refugees who arrived in the UK under the Gateway Protection Programme, this compared with 640 in 2008. In 2009, 90 refugees were also resettled in the UK under the Mandate scheme.

ASYLUM SUPPORT APPLICATIONS

Asylum support was set up to provide for asylum seekers while they await a decision on their asylum application. Asylum seekers who applied for asylum support could receive: accommodation only (where they were allocated accommodation in a dispersal area and must otherwise support themselves); subsistence only (where they received cash to support themselves but must find their own accommodation); or accommodation and subsistence (where they were allocated accommodation in a dispersal area and cash to support themselves).
Key findings for Q4 2009:
• The number of applications for asylum support in Q4 2009 was 3,940, 17 per cent lower than Q4 2008 (4,720).
• In Q4 2009, 3,130 (79 per cent of the total) applications were from single adults and 810 (21 per cent of the total) from family groups.

2.7 Supported asylum seekers including dependants (Tables 6 - 7) (NS_)

Key findings as at the end of Q4 2009:
• The total number of asylum seekers9 in receipt of asylum support in Q4 2009 (29,150) was 11 per cent lower than at the end of Q4 2008 (32,580).
• 4,670 asylum seekers were receiving subsistence only support10.
• 23,845 asylum seekers were supported in dispersal accommodation11.
• 635 asylum seekers were supported in initial accommodation.

ISSUES OF ENTRY CLEARANCE VISAS TO THE UNITED KINGDOM, BY COUNTRY OF NATIONALITY,

Q1 2006 to Q4 2009 (1)
United Kingdom

Country of nationality	2008 (P)				2009 (P)			
	Q1	Q2	Q3	Q4	Q1	Q2	Q3	Q4
Albania	1,385	1,610	1,515	1,575	1,295	1,320	1,360	1,620

Croatia	90	95	230	75	75	80	165	100
Russia	25,930	48,745	35,785	28,645	23,740	38,165	31,450	27,095
Serbia and Montenegro (2)	3,635	5,860	4,425	4,555	3,955	5,200	4,325	4,720
Turkey	18,370	24,935	22,755	17,960	17,595	22,570	18,775	20,810
Ukraine	6,335	9,505	8,980	7,155	5,930	8,385	8,565	6,185
Other former USSR (3)	7,190	12,115	13,045	8,855	6,910	11,600	11,950	8,215
Other former Yugoslavia (4)	1,715	2,180	1,925	1,700	1,535	1,865	1,690	1,600
EEA (5)	250	330	280	140	170	145	170	135
Other Europe (6)	75	90	135	65	105	90	110	90
Total Europe	64,970	105,460	89,080	70,730	61,315	89,420	78,560	70,575
Argentina	145	215	235	155	240	190	225	110
Barbados	50	55	135	40	35	35	120	35
Brazil	1,940	1,920	2,185	1,665	1,605	1,065	1,885	1,330
Canada	1,620	2,305	5,170	1,655	1,695	2,040	5,220	1,735
Chile	160	155	325	155	95	80	395	150
Colombia	3,515	7,125	6,040	4,040	3,630	6,430	5,640	3,850
Guyana	310	445	380	255	240	330	320	190
Jamaica	2,130	3,490	2,515	1,845	1,770	2,505	2,560	1,770
Mexico	355	390	1,220	360	365	185	945	340
Peru	1,095	1,465	1,370	950	875	1,330	1,415	1,050
Trinidad and Tobago	235	240	510	205	190	110	445	150
USA	5,405	7,635	16,205	7,200	5,370	7,075	16,185	7,280
Venezuela	270	310	525	190	290	1,570	1,465	875
Other Americas	1,755	2,575	2,465	1,585	1,610	2,155	2,630	1,730
Total Americas	18,985	28,315	39,275	20,305	18,005	25,100	39,445	20,595

(1)
(2)
(3)
(4)
(5)
(6) and Svalbard and Jan Mayen Islands.
(P) Provisional figures.

Number of visas issued

Country of nationality	2009 (P)

	Q2	Q3	Q4	Q1	Q2	Q3	Q4
Algeria	3,380	4,350	2,485	2,760	2,660	3,020	2,650
Angola	1,025	1,180	590	575	685	995	605
Dem. Rep. of Congo	770	850	565	510	655	880	570
Egypt	8,745	8,060	6,465	6,190	9,955	8,165	7,790
Ethiopia	1,235	1,120	720	675	1,000	1,020	725
Ghana	6,245	6,485	3,945	3,535	4,995	6,050	4,285
Kenya	4,695	4,810	3,005	2,800	4,375	4,500	2,720
Libya	4,575	5,665	3,180	3,435	3,450	4,360	4,355
Mauritius	555	955	515	360	375	865	335
Morocco	2,935	2,270	2,190	2,365	2,770	2,655	2,650
Nigeria	30,020	35,620	24,410	22,640	30,165	38,660	24,995
Sierra Leone	990	1,205	700	565	745	1,140	825
Somalia	515	620	795	560	575	700	680
South Africa	4,515	5,300	5,465	13,335	33,495	34,280	24,600
Sudan	2,365	1,895	1,045	1,350	2,285	1,810	1,245
Tanzania	1,945	1,855	1,410	1,075	1,455	1,570	1,045
Tunisia	1,195	1,225	865	945	1,125	1,205	1,055
Uganda	2,120	2,445	1,735	1,245	1,830	1,945	1,205
Zambia	1,160	1,325	1,175	710	970	1,175	970
Zimbabwe	2,820	2,725	2,040	1,090	1,895	2,275	1,880
Other Africa	7,025	7,600	5,020	4,495	5,545	7,090	5,025
Total Africa	88,835	97,555	68,325	71,215	111,000	124,370	90,215

Number of visas issued

Country of nationality	2009 (P)						
	Q2	Q3	Q4	Q1	Q2	Q3	Q4
Bangladesh	7,535	8,810	4,765	6,920	8,160	13,120	12,245
India	137,455	110,195	65,055	78,505	131,940	114,845	81,740
Pakistan	35,345	29,085	14,950	19,	22,760	19,555	21,920

				995			
Total Indian sub-continent	180,335	148,085	84,770	105,415	162,855	147,520	115,905
Iran	7,880	10,265	7,785	7,305	8,175	3,975	2,650
Iraq	1,885	2,250	2,030	2,475	2,580	2,440	1,775
Israel	215	530	275	225	200	490	210
Jordan	3,390	3,500	2,515	2,345	3,585	3,295	2,515
Kuwait	14,565	12,885	6,475	9,200	14,115	13,160	8,000
Lebanon	3,110	2,840	2,520	2,515	3,010	2,895	2,865
Saudi Arabia	20,445	23,945	9,575	16,215	26,400	20,915	12,415
Syria	1,660	1,680	1,210	1,350	2,085	1,730	1,260
Yemen	925	885	565	475	825	670	505
Other Middle East	21,550	21,975	8,335	9,480	17,110	15,895	9,440
Total Middle East	75,625	80,755	41,290	51,585	78,080	65,460	41,635
Afghanistan	1,040	1,320	920	1,055	965	835	1,590
China (inc. Taiwan)	56,385	56,850	31,555	26,950	45,625	66,535	28,780
Hong Kong (7)	675	5,110	530	420	470	5,640	545
Indonesia	6,850	6,030	3,420	3,040	6,180	6,355	5,055
Japan	3,180	3,950	1,630	2,450	2,825	3,540	1,260
Malaysia	1,345	5,445	1,575	1,045	890	5,945	1,065
Nepal	1,940	2,015	1,340	1,590	2,805	9,785	8,335
Philippines	16,160	13,625	9,985	9,490	14,565	14,555	9,305
Singapore	230	1,320	275	215	170	1,530	230
South Korea	1,775	3,665	1,435	1,490	1,245	3,830	1,405
Sri Lanka	8,870	9,400	6,395	5,260	7,895	9,070	7,440
Thailand	11,590	11,320	7,170	12,185	12,255	13,360	8,425
Other Asia	3,425	4,505	2,350	2,275	3,160	4,560	3,120
Total Remainder of Asia	113,465	124,565	68,580	67,465	99,050	145,550	76,555

Total Asia	369,425	353,405	194,640	224,470	339,985	358,525	234,095
Australia	6,890	5,995	5,410	7,420	6,485	4,945	4,705
New Zealand	3,350	2,125	1,960	2,270	2,015	1,325	1,165
Other Oceania	430	390	315	240	345	375	310
Total Oceania	10,675	8,505	7,685	9,925	8,850	6,645	6,180
British Overseas citizens	15	20	5	5	10	10	5
Nationality unknown	2,510	2,650	2,370	1,720	2,040	2,280	1,930
Grand Total	605,235	590,495	364,060	386,660	576,410	609,835	423,595

APPLICATIONS RECEIVED FOR ASYLUM IN THE UK, EXCLUDING DEPENDANTS, AND INITIAL DECISIONS BY COUNTRY OF NATIONALITY

Q4 2008

Country	Applications received			Initial decisions			
of nationality	Total	Applied at port	Applied in country	Total Initial decisions	Recognised as a refugee and granted asylum	Not recognised as a refugee but granted humanitarian protection	Not recognised as a refugee but granted humanitarian protection
Albania	50	5	45	45	–	*	20
Macedonia	–	–	–	*	–	–	–
Moldova	5	–	5	*	–	–	–
Russia	10	5	5	10	*	–	–
Turkey	35	5	30	35	5	–	*
Ukraine	5	–	5	10	–	*	*
EU Accession States (3)	*	–	*	*	–	–	–
Other Former USSR	40	5	35	45	5	–	*
Other Europe	30	5	25	15	*	–	*
Total Europe	180	25	150	160	15	*	25
Colombia	5	–	5	*	*	–	–
Ecuador	5	–	5	*	–	–	–
Jamaica	45	10	35	35	5	–	–
Other Americas	40	10	25	25	–	–	–
Total Americas	90	20	70	65	5	–	–
Algeria	85	5	80	50	*	–	*
Angola	15	–	15	15	*	–	5
Burundi	–	–	–	5	–	–	*
Cameroon	20	–	20	20	*	–	*

Congo	5	–	5	5	–	–	–
Dem. Rep. of Congo	80	10	70	65	10	*	5
Eritrea	705	35	670	570	325	–	15
Ethiopia	45	*	45	30	5	–	–
Gambia	30	*	30	20	*	–	*
Ghana	30	*	30	25	–	–	–
Ivory Coast	15	*	15	10	–	–	–
Kenya	20	*	15	20	*	–	*
Liberia	*	–	*	5	–	–	*
Libya	15	*	10	5	*	–	–
Nigeria	175	25	150	125	*	*	10
Rwanda	10	*	10	5	*	–	–
Sierra Leone	5	–	5	5	–	–	*
Somalia	285	75	215	250	100	–	15
Sudan	65	10	55	35	10	–	–
Tanzania	5	*	5	5	–	–	–
Uganda	40	5	35	25	*	–	*
ZimbabUK	820	50	775	585	195	*	30
Other Africa	160	25	140	105	15	*	*
Total Africa	2,640	245	2,400	1,985	670	5	95
Iran	645	95	550	515	55	5	50
Iraq	460	15	445	370	40	–	45
Syria	45	*	45	20	5	–	*
Other Middle East	195	25	170	140	35	*	5
Total Middle East	1,345	130	1,215	1,040	135	5	100
Afghanistan	1,015	60	950	635	30	5	255
Bangladesh	100	5	95	65	*	–	20
China (Inc. Taiwan)	295	65	230	160	15	*	10
India	170	10	160	60	*	–	5
Pakistan	315	30	280	220	15	–	15
Sri Lanka	430	70	360	240	25	–	15
Vietnam	65	–	65	20	–	–	5
Other Asia & Oceania	75	5	70	65	25	5	5
Total Asia & Oceania	2,465	250	2,215	1,460	115	10	325
Other and not known	15	5	10	5	5	–	–
Grand Total	6,735	675	6,060	4,720	945	25	540

(1) Figures rounded to the nearest 5 (- = 0, * = 1 or 2).
(2) Initial decisions do not necessarily relate to applications made in the same period and exclude the outcome of appeals or other subsequent decisions.

OUTCOME OF ASYLUM APPEALS DETERMINED AT THE ASYLUM AND IMMIGRATION TRIBUNAL, EXCLUDING DEPENDANTS,BY COUNTRY OF NATIONALITY

Q4 2008

Number of principal appellants

Country of nationality	Appeals determined						
		AlloUKd		Dismissed		Withdrawn (2)	
	Total	Total	As % of total determined	Total	As % of total determine	Total	As % of total determined

			d				
Albania	15	5	33%	5	40%	5	27%
Macedonia	*	-	0%	*	100%	-	0%
Moldova	5	-	0%	5	100%	-	0%
Russia	5	-	0%	5	100%	-	0%
Turkey	40	15	36%	25	62%	*	3%
Ukraine	5	-	0%	*	67%	*	33%
EU Accession States (3)	-	-		-	0%	-	0%
Other Former USSR	25	5	24%	20	72%	*	4%
Other Europe	5	*	33%	*	67%	-	0%
Total Europe	95	25	28%	60	65%	5	8%
Colombia	*	*	50%	*	50%	-	0%
Ecuador	5	5	67%	*	33%	-	0%
Jamaica	10	*	17%	10	83%	-	0%
Other Americas	10	5	33%	5	67%	-	0%
Total Americas	30	10	34%	20	66%	-	0%
Algeria	25	*	8%	20	72%	5	20%
Angola	10	-	0%	5	88%	*	13%
Burundi	5	*	25%	*	50%	*	25%
Cameroon	20	5	33%	10	57%	*	10%
Congo	25	5	30%	15	61%	*	9%
Dem Rep. of Congo	35	5	18%	25	73%	5	9%
Eritrea	95	40	43%	50	51%	5	6%
Ethiopia	15	*	12%	15	76%	*	12%
Gambia	15	5	27%	10	67%	*	7%
Ghana	15	*	7%	15	93%	-	0%
Ivory Coast	15	*	14%	10	79%	*	7%
Kenya	10	*	17%	10	83%	-	0%
Liberia	-	-	0%	-	0%	-	0%
Libya	5	*	14%	5	86%	-	0%
Nigeria	65	5	9%	55	85%	5	6%
Rwanda	5	-	0%	5	75%	*	25%
Sierra Leone	5	-	0%	5	80%	*	20%
Somalia	115	45	40%	50	44%	20	16%
Sudan	25	10	37%	15	56%	*	7%
Tanzania	5	-	0%	5	100%	-	0%
Uganda	15	5	19%	15	81%	-	0%
ZimbabUK	755	245	32%	430	57%	80	10%
Other Africa	70	10	14%	60	81%	5	6%

Total Africa	1,350	395	29%	825	61%	130	10%
Iran	325	70	21%	245	75%	10	3%
Iraq	255	50	20%	190	74%	15	6%
Syria	25	5	23%	20	69%	*	8%
Other Middle East	55	15	26%	35	65%	5	9%
Total Middle East	660	140	21%	490	74%	35	5%
Afghanistan	255	65	25%	170	66%	20	9%
Bangladesh	35	5	18%	25	79%	*	3%
China (Inc. Taiwan)	100	15	16%	80	80%	5	4%
India	15	*	13%	10	75%	*	13%
Pakistan	180	25	14%	145	81%	10	5%
Sri Lanka	170	50	28%	115	67%	10	5%
Vietnam	5	*	50%	*	50%	-	0%
Other Asia & Oceania	50	5	14%	40	80%	5	6%
Total Asia & Oceania	810	175	21%	590	73%	50	6%
Other and not known	30	5	24%	20	66%	5	10%
Grand Total	2,975	750	25%	2,000	67%	225	8%

(1) Provisional figures rounded to nearest 5 (except percentages), (- = 0, * = 1 or 2).
Figures may not sum to the totals shown because of independent rounding.
Data on appeal outcomes by nationality in this table are supplied by the AIT.
(2) Figures include cases withdrawn by the Home Office, as UKII as those withdrawn by the appellant.
(3) EU Accession States: Bulgaria, Cyprus, Czech Republic, Estonia, Hungary, Latvia, Lithuania, Malta, Poland, Romania, Slovakia and Slovenia.
(P) Provisional figures.

PERSONS ENTERING DETENTION (1)(2) HELD SOLELY UNDER IMMIGRATION ACT POWERS, BY COUNTRY OF NATIONALITY,

(excluding Harwich), Q4 2009 (3)(4)(P)

Number of persons

Country of nationality (5)	Total detainees	Adults (5) Total	Adults (5) of whom: asylum detainees (6)	Children Total	Children of whom: asylum detainees (6)
Albania	110	105	65	5	-
Macedonia	*	*	*	-	-
Moldova	15	15	5	*	-
Russia	25	25	15	-	-
Turkey	135	125	90	5	5

Ukraine	55	55	15	-	-
EU Accession States (7)	160	155	15	*	-
Other Former USSR	50	50	25	5	5
Other Europe	180	170	65	5	-
Total Europe	725	700	290	25	10
Bolivia	30	25	5	*	*
Brazil	220	210	10	10	5
Canada	45	45	5	5	*
Colombia	35	35	20	*	-
Ecuador	10	5	5	5	*
Jamaica	250	235	80	10	5
Mexico	35	35	*	-	-
USA	130	125	5	5	*
Other Americas	215	205	25	10	5
Total Americas	965	925	150	40	20
Algeria	120	115	65	5	*
Angola	5	5	5	-	-
Burundi	10	10	10	-	-
Cameroon	40	40	25	*	-
Congo	10	10	5	-	-
Dem. Rep. of Congo	70	60	55	10	5
Eritrea	160	155	155	*	*
Ethiopia	15	15	15	-	-
Gambia	45	40	25	*	*
Ghana	140	135	35	5	*
Ivory Coast	15	15	5	*	-
Kenya	40	40	20	*	*
Liberia	*	*	*	-	-
Libya	30	30	20	-	-
Mauritius	40	40	*	*	-
Nigeria	520	470	155	50	30
Rwanda	5	5	5	-	-
Sierra Leone	35	35	20	*	*
Somalia	65	65	55	-	-
South Africa	50	50	15	-	-
Sudan	40	40	40	-	-
Tanzania	10	10	5	-	-
Uganda	80	70	50	5	5
Zimbabwe	55	55	50	-	-
Other Africa	220	200	115	20	15
Total Africa	1,815	1,705	940	110	65
Iran	240	230	215	10	10
Iraq	275	270	260	*	*
Syria	25	25	20	5	*
Other Middle East	105	95	50	5	5
Total Middle East	640	620	545	20	20
Afghanistan	630	625	615	10	10
Australia	15	15	-	5	-
Bangladesh	185	180	75	5	*

China (inc. Taiwan)	420	410	300	5	*
India	450	445	150	5	5
Malaysia	85	85	5	*	*
New Zealand	5	5	-	-	-
Pakistan	455	405	185	50	50
Philippines	20	20	-	-	-
South Korea	20	20	5	-	-
Sri Lanka	125	120	95	5	5
Thailand	20	20	-	*	-
Vietnam	220	215	95	*	-
Other Asia & Oceania	95	95	35	-	-
Total Asia & Oceania	2,750	2,660	1,555	90	70
Other and not known	20	20	5	*	-
Total	6,915	6,630	3,490	285	180

(1) These figures are based on management information and are not subject to the detailed checks that apply for National Statistics. They are provisional and may be subject to change.
(2) Some detainees may be recorded more than once if, for example, the person has been detained on more than one separate occasion in the time period shown, such as a person who has left detention, but has subsequently been re-detained.
(3) Figures rounded to the nearest 5 (- = 0, * = 1 or 2) and may not sum to the totals shown because of independent rounding. Figures exclude persons recorded as entering Harwich Short Term Holding Facility, police cells and Prison Service establishments, those recorded as detained under both criminal and immigration powers and their dependants.
(4) Figures include dependants.
(5) Recorded age at the start of their period of detention. Figures for children will overstate if any applicants aged 18 or over claim to be younger.
(6) Persons detained under Immigration Act powers who are recorded as having sought asylum at some stage.
(7) EU Accession States: Bulgaria, Cyprus, Czech Republic, Estonia, Hungary, Latvia, Lithuania, Malta, Poland, Romania, Slovakia and Slovenia.

STRATEGIC AND BUSINESS CONTACTS IN UK

1. UK GOVERNMENT AGENCIES

British Overseas Trade Board
Department of Trade & Industry
Kingsgate House
66-74 Victoria Street
London SW1E 6SN
Tel: 44-171-215-5000
Fax: 44-171-215-8000

Invest in Britain Bureau
Department of Trade and Industry
London
Tel: 011-44-171-215-2501
Fax: 011-44-171-215-8451

-Invest in Britain Bureau USA.
Atlanta Tel: (404) 524-8823
Boston Tel: (617) 248-9555
Chicago Tel: (312) 346-1810
Cleveland Tel: (216) 621-7674
Houston Tel: (713) 659-6275
Los Angeles Tel: (310) 477-3322
New York Tel: (212) 745-0495
Seattle Tel: (206) 622-9255
Washington D.C. Tel: (202) 462-1340

Embassy of Great Britain

3100 Massachusetts Avenue
Washington, D.C. 20008, USA
Tel: (202) 462-1340
Fax: (202) 898 4255

Department of Trade and Industry
123 Victoria Street
London SW1H 0NN
Tel:011-44-171-215-5000
Fax:011-44-171-215-6739
- General Inquiries

Consumer Affairs Division 1A
Department of Trade and Industry
10-18 Victoria Street
London SW1H 0NN
Tel: 011-44-171-215-0332
Fax: 011-44-171-215-0315
- Packaging and Labeling Requirements

HM Board of Customs and Excise
Tel: 011-44-171-620-1313
Fax: 011-44-171-865-4944
- Customs and Rules/Regulations for the UK

HM Stationery Office Bookshop
49 Holborn
London WC1V 6HB
Tel: 011-44-171-873-0011
Tel: 011-44-1603-695767
(UK equivalent of the U.S. Government Printing Office)
U.S. Representative: Kraus-Thompson Publishers,
Tel: (914) 762-2200

Central Office of Information
Hercules Road
London SE1 7DU
Tel: 011-44-171-928-2345
Fax: 011-44-171-928-5037

Central Statistical Office
Great George Street
London SW1P 3AQ
Tel: 011-44-171-270-3000

Department of Employment
Caxton House
12 Tothill Street
London SW1H 9NA
Tel: 011-44-171-273-3000
- Work Permits, Consular Matters

Department of the Environment
2 Marsham Street
London SW1P 3EB
Tel: 011-44-171-276-0900 or 276-3000
- Environmental Regulations

Department of Health
Richmond House
79 Whitehall
London SW1
Tel: 011-44-171-210-4850
- Medicinal Licenses and Regulations

Patent and Trademark Office
Concept House
Cardiff Road
Newport NP9 1RH
Tel: 011-44-1645-500505
- UK Patents

Bank of England
Threadneedle Street
London EC2V 8DQ
Tel: 011-44-171-601-4444
- Central Bank

The House of Commons
Houses of Parliament
London SW1A 0AA
Tel: 011-44-171-219-3000

2. UK TRADE ASSOCIATIONS/CHAMBERS OF COMMERCE

The UK's trade associations and chambers of commerce are too numerous to list in a report of this nature. Some notable, multi-sectoral business associations are listed below:

American Chamber of Commerce in the UK
75 Brook Street
London W1Y 2EB, UK
Tel: 011-44-171-493-0381
Fax: 011-44-171-493-2394

Association of British Chambers of Commerce
9 Tufton Street
London SW1P 3QB

Tel: 011-44-171-565-2000
Fax: 011-44-171-565-2049

British American Chamber of Commerce
8 Staple Inn, Holborn
London WC1V 7QH
Tel: 011-44-171-404-6400
Fax: 011-44-171-404-6828

International Chamber of Commerce
14-15 Belgrave Square
London SW1X 8PS
Tel: 011-44-171-823-2811
Fax: 011-44-171-235-5447

British Standards Institution
389 Chiswick High Road
London W4 4AL
Tel: 011-44-181-996-9000
Fax: 011-44-181-996-7400.

Confederation of British Industry
Centre Point
103 New Oxford Street
London WC1A 1DU
Tel: 011-44-171-379-7400
Fax: 011-44-171-240-1578

3. U.S. EMBASSY CONTACTS

American Embassy
24/31 Grosvenor Square
London, WIA 1AE England
Tel: 011-44-171-499-9000
Fax: 011-44-171-491-4022
http://usembassy.org.uk

Address for U.S. mail:
American Embassy (London)
PSC 801
Box 27 (for Economic Section) or
Box 33 (for Commercial Section) or
Box 48 (for Agriculture) or
Box 54 (for Defense)
FPO AE 09498-4033

Economic Minister
Tel: 011-44-171-408-8011
Fax: 011-44-171-409-1637

The Commercial Service
Tel: 011-44-171-408-8019
Fax: 011-44-171-408-8020

The International Marketing Center (IMC)
Tel: 011-44-171-409-2927
Fax: 011-44-171-495-2944
E-Mail: olondon@doc.gov
http://usembassy.org.uk/ukfcs.html

The Office of Agricultural Affairs
Tel: 011-44-171-408-8063
Fax: 011-44-171-409-2019
http://fasuk@fasuk.demon.co.uk

Office of Defense Cooperation (ODC)
Tel: 011-44-171-894-0737
Fax: 011-44-171-514-4634

The European Bank For Reconstruction & Development
Office of the Senior Commercial Officer
Tel: 011-44-171-588-4027/4028
Fax: 011-44-171-588-4026

4. WASHINGTON DC-BASED USG CONTACTS (UK-SPECIFIC)

U.S. Department of Commerce
UK Country Desk Officer Robert McLaughlin
Washington, D.C. 20230
Tel: (202) 482-3748
Fax: (202) 482-2897
http://www.doc.gov

Multilateral Development Bank Office
Janet G. Thomas - Director
Tel: (202) 482 3399
Fax: (202) 273-0927

US&FCS Regional Director (Europe):
Mr. Keith Curtis
Tel: (202) 482-1599
Fax: (202) 482-3159

Bureau of Export Administration
Tel: (202) 482-8547

State Department
UK Desk
Tel: (202) 647-8027
- Political relations

Agriculture Department - food exports
Foreign Agriculture Service
European Area Officer

Tel: (202) 720-2144
Fax: (202) 690-2909

Treasury Department
UK Desk
Tel: (202) 622-0166
- Financial matters

American National Standards Institute
Tel: (212) 642-4900
Fax: (212) 302-1286
- Information on UK standards

National Institute for Standards and Technology (Washington D.C.)
Tel: (301) 975-3058

5. RELEVANT U.S.-BASED MULTIPLIERS

British American Chamber of Commerce
275 Madison Ave.
New York, NY 10016
Tel: (212) 661-4060
Fax: (212) 661-4074

CONTACT DIRECTORY

IMMIGRATION ENQUIRY BUREAU

Please note that the immigration enquiry bureau will be closed on the following bank holidays: Monday 4 May and Monday 25 May.

The immigration enquiry bureau (IEB) can provide information about applications for permission to remain or settle in the United Kingdom. We also handle enquiries about applications to work or study under the points-based system.

If you are an employer or education provider sponsoring someone under tiers 2, 4 or 5 of the points-based system, you should call our Sponsorship and employers' helpline on
0300 123 4699 .

CALLING UK BORDER AGENCY

All telephone calls are recorded for quality purposes. Callers can speak to a telephone officer to clarify the requirements of the Immigration Rules or to request a progress update.
For data protection reasons, we cannot answer questions on the status of individual cases via email.
If you ask us to return your passport or travel document for travel before we have decided your application, your application will be considered to be withdrawn. If you really need your passport or other documents urgently, please phone us in the first instance on
0870 606 7766 .

FOR EDUCATION PROVIDERS ONLY - INFORMATION ABOUT OVERSEAS STUDENTS

The UK Border Agency is keen to receive information about all cases of overseas students (except those from countries in the European Union) who have accepted a place at your institution but have never attended, or who have dropped out of a course of study for no apparent reason. However, you do not need to tell if you know that the person concerned has transferred to a course at another United Kingdom institution.

You can email us at icc7@ukba.gsi.gov.uk. The form Information about overseas students - required information (21K opens in new window) tells you the information we need you to include in your email.

This mailbox is for the use of education providers only. Any email received which is not from an education provider or is about any other subject will be deleted without a response.

Anyone wishing to enquire about an individual case that has been outstanding for more than 14 weeks, or with a general question about students and immigration, should contact the immigration enquiry bureau on the telephone number given below.

Phone: 0870 606 7766
Textphone: 0800 389 8289
Email: UKBApublicenquiries@ukba.gsi.gov.uk
Address: UK Border Agency, Lunar House, 40 Wellesley Road, Croydon, Surrey CR9 2BY
Opening Hours: Monday to Thursday 0900 to 1645. Friday 0900 to 1630.

NATIONALITY CONTACT CENTRE

The nationality contact centre can provide information on British citizenship and right of abode only.

The centre is currently experiencing high call volumes which may lead to a delay in your call being answered. Our opening times are 0900 to 2100 Monday to Friday excluding public holidays, but you may wish to contact us between the hours of 1800 and 2100 later in the week when we are less busy.

Before calling us, you should read the British citizenship section. This section aims to answer all frequently asked questions on British nationality law and contains full details of:

- what British citizenship is;
- the different types of British nationality;
- the requirements you need to meet to become a British citizen;
- how to make an application;
- the cost of making an application;
- the nationality checking service;
- where completed application forms should be sent;
- the current waiting times for nationality applications; and
- citizenship ceremonies.

Phone: 0845 010 5200
Email: nationalityenquiries@ukba.gsi.gov.uk
Opening Hours: Monday to Friday 0900 to 2100.

EEA RESIDENCY ENQUIRIES

Please note that the EEA contact centre will be closed on the following bank holidays: Monday 4 May and Monday 25 May.

You can contact the European Enquiries Contact Centre if you are a national of the European Economic Area (EEA) or Switzerland and you have a query regarding:

- registration certificates for yourself or a family member;
- a residence card;
- a family member residence stamp; or
- confirmation of permanent residence in the United Kingdom.

If you are Bulgarian or Romanian, you will need to contact the work permit contact centre listed below.

The centre is currently experiencing high call volumes which may lead to a delay in your call being answered. Our opening times are 0900 to 2100 Monday to Friday excluding public holidays, but you may wish to contact us between the hours of 1800 and 2100 later in the week when we are less busy.

Please read our section on Applying under European law before you contact us. If you would like to request the return of your documents you must do so by telephone. We cannot accept requests by email and it is not possible to collect your documents in person.

Please note if you would like to request the return of your documents you must do so by telephone. We cannot accept requests by email and it is not possible to collect your documents in person from any office in Liverpool.
Phone: 0845 010 5200
Email: UKBAeuropeanenquiries@ukba.gsi.gov.uk
Opening Hours: Monday to Friday 0900 to 2100.

SPONSORSHIP AND EMPLOYERS' HELPLINE

This UK Border Agency telephone helpline service can provide information for sponsors and employers about:

- sponsorship under the new points-based system;
- a service to employers/sponsors who want to verify the entitlement to work for people who are currently awaiting the outcome of an application made to the Home Office; and
- the prevention of illegal working, in particular advice about carrying out the document checks necessary to attain a defence against conviction.

All telephone calls are recorded for quality purposes. The contact centre is currently experiencing high call volumes as there is a high demand for our service. Many common questions are answered on this website; you should read the section on For employers and sponsors (this page provides key guidance and information on employing migrant workers, including those under the new points-based system).

For general enquiries, SMS issues, User IDs and passwords, confirmation of receipt of payments and ongoing application queries, email: sponsorshipPBSenquiries@ukba.gsi.gov.uk. Please note that the above email address is for general sponsorship enquiries only, and we aim to respond within two working days.

For queries regarding visits to your organisation, email: sponsor.visits@ukba.gsi.gov.uk
Phone: 0300 123 4699
Opening Hours: Monday to Friday 0900 - 1700

WORK PERMITS CUSTOMER CONTACT CENTRE

The customer contact centre can answer enquiries about residual work permits, the Highly Skilled Migrant Programme applications, as well as general enquiries about the Worker Registration Scheme A2.

Please be aware that the customer contact centre is currently experiencing very high call demand and therefore you may experience difficulties in contacting us. Please may we apologise for this and for any inconvenience this may cause you.

For email enquiries we aim to respond within two working days.

Full information on all of our schemes and programmes is available on this website.
Phone: 0114 207 4074
Fax: 0114 207 5861
Email: wpcustomers@ukba.gsi.gov.uk

Address: Customer Contact Centre, UK Border Agency, PO Box 3468, Sheffield, S3 8WA
Opening Hours: Monday to Friday 0900 to 1700

ASYLUM SUPPORT CUSTOMER CONTACT CENTRE

Please note that the Asylum support contact centre will be closed on the following bank holidays: Monday 4 May and Monday 25 May.
The asylum support customer contact centre can answer general enquiries from supported asylum seekers in relation to their weekly cash support, accommodation or emergency cash payment requests. Advisors can also provide information in relation to discontinuation of support enquiries and to failed asylum seekers who are supported under section 4.
Phone: 0845 602 1739
Opening Hours: Monday to Friday (excluding public holidays) 0900 to 2100.

GLOSSARY

A

A RATING

This term is applied to a sponsor under the points-based system for coming to the United Kingdom to work, train or study. It is the rating awarded by us when a sponsor joins the register of sponsors.

A-RATED

This term is applied to a sponsor under the points-based system for coming to the United Kingdom to work, train or study. It is the rating awarded by us when a sponsor joins the register of sponsors.

ACCOUNT MANAGEMENT

This is the system UK use to check that organisations are complying with their sponsorship duties under the points-based system for coming to the United Kingdom to work, train or study.

ACCOUNT MANAGEMENT VISIT

A visit by our staff to check that an organisation is complying with sponsorship duties under the points-based system for coming to the United Kingdom to work, train or study.

ACCOUNT MANAGEMENT AND COMPLIANCE TEAM

Our team of staff responsible for ensuring that organisations are complying with their obligations as sponsors under the points-based system for coming to the United Kingdom to work, train or study.

ACCOUNT MANAGEMENT OR COMPLIANCE ACTIONS

Action our staff will take to ensure that organisations are complying with their sponsorship duties under the points-based system for coming to the United Kingdom to work, train or study.

ACQUIRE

Obtain or gain possession.

ACTION OR INACTION

Action is something you do. Inaction is your failure to do something.

ADOPTED

An adopted child is one who has legally become the child of a parent or parents who are not the child's biological parents. To be legally recognised in the United Kingdom, the adoption must be made by order of a court or under the terms of the Hague Convention (see Hague Convention). A foreign adoption order will be recognised in the United Kingdom if it was made in a 'designated country' - a country included in the Adoption (Designation of Overseas Adoptions) Order 1973. The current list of these countries is on the Department for Children, Schools and Families UKbsite.

ADOPTION (DESIGNATION OF OVERSEAS ADOPTIONS) ORDER 1973

A foreign adoption order will only be recognised in the United Kingdom if it was made in a 'designated country'. This means a country that is included in the Adoption (Designation of Overseas Adoptions) Order 1973. The current list of these countries can be found on the UKbsite of the Department for Children, Schools and Families.

AFFIDAVIT

A written statement signed on oath and witnessed by a qualified solicitor or notary. It is an offence to make an affidavit if you believe or know that its contents are not true. (See Notary.)

AFFIRMATION OF ALLEGIANCE

An official declaration by those taking British citizenship, promising to faithfully support the British monarch. A religious 'Oath of allegiance' may be used in place of the affirmation. (See Oath of allegiance)

ANOTHER RELEVANT PERSON

In the context of sponsor licensing under the points-based system, this means the sponsor's (or prospective sponsor's) authorising officer, key contact or level 1 user.

APPLICATION

A formal request you make to us, asking us to consider giving you a particular thing. For example, you may make an application for permission to stay in the United Kingdom, for British citizenship, or to be recognised as a refugee. An application will usually be in writing, using an official form (application form) UK produce for that type of request. Applications to be recognised as a refugee are known as asylum applications, and these do not require an application form. See the Asylum section for information on this type of application.

APPLICATION CONCLUDED

This refers to applications for asylum. A successful application for asylum is concluded when the applicant is helped to build a new life in the United Kingdom. An unsuccessful application is concluded when the applicant returns to his/her home country, either voluntarily or by enforced removal.

APPROVED EDUCATION PROVIDER

An education provider that is approved by us and has been given a licence to bring both students to the United Kingdom under tier 4 of the points-based system. This can be as an adult (known as a general student) or child student categories, or both.

ASYLUM

Asylum is protection given by a country to someone who is fleeing persecution in their own country. It is given under the 1951 United Nations Convention Relating to the Status of Refugees. To be recognised as a refugee, you must have left your country and be unable to go back because you have a UKll-founded fear of persecution.

ASYLUM SCREENING UNIT

The asylum screening unit is a centre run by the UK Border Agency where a person is registered as an asylum applicant and begins the process of applying for asylum.

AUTHORISING OFFICER

The authorising officer is one of the roles required within organisations that wish to sponsor migrants under the points-based system for coming to the United Kingdom to work, train or study. The authorising officer is responsible for the activities of anyone acting on behalf of the sponsor to issue certificates of sponsorship.

B

B RATING

This term is applied to a sponsor under the points-based system for coming to the United Kingdom to work, train or study. It is the rating awarded by us when a sponsor joins the register of sponsors. A B rating is a transitional rating for a sponsor who is under a sponsorship action plan.

B-RATED

This term is applied to a sponsor under the points-based system for coming to the United Kingdom to work, train or study. It is the rating awarded by us when a sponsor joins the register of sponsors. A B rating is a transitional rating for a sponsor who is under a sponsorship action plan.

BIOMETRIC

Biometrics is the science of using digital technology to recognise a person from a physical characteristic (for example a fingerprint or iris pattern of the eye) or another unique personal characteristic (for example a voice pattern or handwriting). These characteristics are your biometric details.

BORDER

The place at which someone leaves another country and enters the United Kingdom. Our border is mainly the coastline around England, Scotland, Wales, Northern Ireland, the Channel Islands, and the Isle of Man, but also includes the line betUKen Northern Ireland and the Republic of Ireland. In practice, a person who enters the United Kingdom legally will do so by being permitted to enter by an immigration officer at one of our border control points at a port or airport. Some of these border control points are outside the United Kingdom and a passenger must pass through them before being alloUKd to travel to the United Kingdom.

BRANCH

A branch is one office, location, or campus of an organisation that has two or more of these.

BRANCHES

Branches are different offices, locations, or campuses of an organisation that has two or more of these.

BRITISH CITIZEN

British citizens have the right to live in the United Kingdom permanently and are free to leave and re-enter the country at any time. British citizenship is given to people who have a close connection with the United Kingdom, which includes the Channel Islands and the Isle of Man. A close connection may be by birth, adoption, descent, marriage, registration or naturalisation.

BRITISH CITIZENSHIP

British citizenship is given to people who have a close connection with the United Kingdom, which includes the Channel Islands and the Isle of Man. A close connection may be by birth, adoption, descent, marriage, registration or naturalisation.

BRITISH DEPENDENT TERRITORIES CITIZENSHIP

Now known as a British overseas territories citizen. You will be a British overseas territories citizen if you are connected with a British overseas territory because you, your parents or your grandparents UKre born, registered or naturalised in that British overseas territory. (See British overseas territories.)

BRITISH DEPENDENT TERRITORY

Now known as British overseas territories. The territories are: Anguilla, Bermuda, British Antarctic Territory, British Indian Ocean Territory, Cayman Islands, Falkland Islands and Dependencies,

Gibraltar, Montserrat, Pitcairn, Henderson, Ducie and Oeno Islands, St Helena and Dependencies, the Sovereign Base Areas of Akrotiri and Dhekelia, Turks and Caicos Islands, and the Virgin Islands. (The sovereign bases of Akrotiri and Dhekelia do not count as qualifying territories for nationality purposes.)
South Georgia and the South Sandwich Islands UKre the dependencies of the Falkland Islands, but UKre not dependent territories betUKen 3 October 1985 and 3 December 2001.
Hong Kong stopped being a British dependent territory on 30 June 1997 when sovereignty returned to China. St Christopher and Nevis was a British dependent territory until 18 September 1983, when it became an independent CommonUKalth country.

British diplomatic post

A British diplomatic post is a United Kingdom embassy, high commission or consulate.

British extraterritorial jurisdiction

The application of British law to a person with British nationality who is living in another country.

British national

A British national is anyone who has a form of British status. There are six forms of British nationality: British citizenship, British overseas citizenship, British overseas territories citizenship, British protected person, British subject, and British national (overseas).
Only British citizens have the right to live and work in the United Kingdom.

British national (overseas)

A person who was a British overseas territories citizen by connection with Hong Kong was able to register as a British national (overseas) before 1 July 1997. It is no longer possible to become a British national (overseas).

British nationality

There are six forms of British nationality: British citizenship, British overseas citizenship, British overseas territories citizenship, British protected person, British subject, and British national (overseas).

Only British citizens have the right to live and work in the United Kingdom.

British overseas citizen

British overseas citizenship is a category of British citizenship that was gained by certain residents of Hong Kong on 30 June 1997, when sovereignty of Hong Kong returned to China.

British overseas territories citizen

You will be a British overseas territories citizen if you are connected with a British overseas territory because you or your parents UKre born, registered or naturalised in that British overseas territory. If you UKre born before 1 January 1983, you may gain the citizenship through your grandparents. (See British overseas territory.)

British overseas territory

These UKre formerly known as the British dependent territories. The territories are: Anguilla, Bermuda, British Antarctic Territory, British Indian Ocean Territory, Cayman Islands, Falkland Islands and Dependencies, Gibraltar, Montserrat, Pitcairn, Henderson, Ducie and Oeno Islands, St Helena and Dependencies, the Sovereign Base Areas of Akrotiri and Dhekelia, Turks and Caicos Islands, and

the Virgin Islands. (The sovereign bases of Akrotiri and Dhekelia do not count as qualifying territories for nationality purposes.)
South Georgia and the South Sandwich Islands UKre the dependencies of the Falkland Islands, but UKre not British overseas territories betUKen 3 October 1985 and 3 December 2001.
Hong Kong stopped being a British overseas territory on 30 June 1997 when sovereignty returned to China. St Christopher and Nevis was a British overseas territory until 18 September 1983, when it became an independent CommonUKalth country.

BRITISH PROTECTED PERSON

This is a form of British nationality held by a resident of a former British protectorate who did not take the citizenship of the country to which he/she belonged before it stopped being a protectorate. See the page Who is a British protected person? for more information.

BRITISH PROTECTORATE

Protectorates and protected states UKre foreign territories to which British protection was extended in some form. See Who is a British protected person? for more information about this.

BRITISH SUBJECT

Until 1949, nearly everyone with a close connection to the United Kingdom was called a British subject. All citizens of CommonUKalth countries UKre British subjects until January 1983. Since that date, very few categories of people have qualified as British subjects. It is a form of British nationality.

BROWSER

A browser, short for UKb browser, is a program used to view UKbsites and surf the internet. Internet Explorer, Firefox and Safari are examples of browsers.

BUSINESS PEOPLE SCHEMES

Immigration categories under which someone can apply to come to the United Kingdom as a business person to run a business full-time. See Working in the UK for more information about these categories.

BY DESCENT

British citizenship gained through your parents. This type of citizenship cannot normally be passed on to your own children. (See also Otherwise than by descent.)

C

CALENDAR DAYS

All days of the UKek, including UKekends and public holidays.

CARGO CARRIERS

These are carriers that operate dedicated cargo-only flights, including mail flights.

CARRIER

A person or organisation that transports passengers or goods in and out of the United Kingdom.

CARRIER REPRESENTATIVE

The person appointed by a carrier as its main contact with our e-Borders programme.

CARRIER TECHNICAL REPRESENTATIVE

This person appointed by a carrier as its main contact with our e-Borders programme.

CERTIFICATE OF COMPANY REGISTRATION

The official document confirming a company has incorporated and registered with Companies House. (See Companies House.)

CERTIFICATE OF SPONSORSHIP

This is a virtual document (a unique reference number) that an organisation gives to migrants they want to employ, and that the migrant uses when applying.under the points-based system for coming to the United Kingdom to work, train or study. Also known as confirmation of acceptance for studies.

CERTIFICATES OF SPONSORSHIP

These are virtual documents (unique reference numbers) that an organisation gives to migrants they want to employ, and that the migrant uses when applying.under the points-based system for coming to the United Kingdom to work, train or study. Also known as confirmation of acceptance for studies.

CERTIFICATION

The process a carrier's interface must undergo after testing, to ensure it is ready to go into service and connect with our e-Borders system.

CERTIFIED COPIES

Duplicates of original documents, certified as exact reproductions, usually by the officer responsible for issuing or keeping the original, or by a solicitor, notary public, justice of the peace or any other person authorised to take a statutory declaration. A certified copy should carry a certificate, stamp or seal, and the certifier's signature.

CHARTER CARRIERS

These are carriers (usually of passengers) that operate on routes and to schedules that are planned according to the expected seasonal demand.

CITIZENSHIP CEREMONY

An event run by local authorities in the United Kingdom, usually by the section of the local authority responsible for registering births, marriages and deaths. At the event, successful applicants for British citizenship receive their citizenship. Citizenship ceremonies are also held in Northern Ireland, the Isle of Man, the Channel Islands and at British diplomatic posts overseas.

CIVIL PARTNERSHIP

A legal relationship that can be registered by two people of the same sex and that gives the couple legal recognition for their relationship. In a range of legal matters, civil partners are treated the same as opposite-sex partners who are married.

CIVIL PENALTIES

A requirement to pay money that can be imposed for an offence without the need for a court conviction.

CIVIL PENALTIES LEGISLATION

Laws that define penalties that can be imposed for offences without the requirement for a court conviction. The penalties are usually a requirement to pay money.

CIVIL PENALTY

A requirement to pay money that can be imposed for an offence without the need for a court conviction.

CLOSE CONNECTION

Close connection (with a country) may be by birth, adoption, descent, marriage, registration or naturalisation.

CLOSE CONNECTION (WITH A COUNTRY)

Close connection (with a country) may be by birth, adoption, descent, marriage, registration or naturalisation.

COMMERCIAL CARRIERS

Organisations that carry paying passengers in and out of the United Kingdom.

COMMON TRAVEL AREA

The common travel area is a 'free movement' area comprising the United Kingdom, the Republic of Ireland, the Bailiwick of Guernsey, the Bailiwick of Jersey and the Isle of Man. The United Kingdom currently makes no routine immigration checks on passenger travel within this area, and passengers do not need to carry a passport or national identity document for immigration purposes.

COMMONUKALTH

The CommonUKalth is a voluntary association of 53 independent countries that consult and co-operate in the common interests of their people to promote international understanding and world peace. All of the member countries, except for Mozambique, have experienced direct or indirect British rule, or have been linked administratively to another CommonUKalth country. For a list of members, and more information, see the CommonUKalth Secretariat UKbsite.

COMMONUKALTH COUNTRY

The CommonUKalth is a voluntary association of 53 independent countries that consult and co-operate in the common interests of their people to promote international understanding and world peace. All CommonUKalth countries, except Mozambique, have experienced direct or indirect British rule, or have been linked administratively to another CommonUKalth country. For a list of CommonUKalth countries, and more information, see the CommonUKalth Secretariat UKbsite.

(EUROPEAN) COMMUNITY INSTITUTION SERVICE

A parent's service under a European Community institution may be considered when deciding whether or not a child born outside the United Kingdom qualifies for British citizenship.
The list may change from time to time but currently includes members of the European Parliament and European Commission, judges, advocates general, the registrar and assistant rapporteurs of the European Court of Justice, members of the Court of Auditors, and the Ombudsman.
It also includes officials and other employees of European governments, including those working for the Council, the Court of Justice, the Court of Auditors, the Economic and Social Committee, the Committee of the Regions, the Office of the Ombudsman, the ECSC Consultative Committee, the European Investment Bank, the European Monetary Institute, the European Central Bank, the European Centre for the Development of Vocational Training, the Joint Research Centre, the European Foundation for the Improvement of Living and Working Conditions, the Scientific and Technical Committee, the Monetary Committee, the EURATOM Supply Agency, the European Medicines Evaluation Agency, the European Monitoring Centre for Drugs and Drug Addiction, the Europol Drugs Unit, Europol, the Agency for Safety and Health at Work, the Training Foundation, the Environment Agency, the EC Office of Veterinary and Phyto-Sanitary Inspectorate, the Community Trademarks Office, and the European Plant Breeders Rights Office.

COMPANIES HOUSE

The official organisation responsible for incorporating and dissolving limited companies, examining and storing company information delivered under the Companies Act and related legislation, and making this information available to the public. (See Companies House.)

COMPANY REGISTRATION CERTIFICATE

The official document confirming a company has been incorporated and registered with Companies House.

COMPLIANCE ACTIVITY

Actions our staff will take to ensure that organisations are complying with their sponsorship duties under the points-based system for coming to the United Kingdom to work, train or study.

COMPLIANCE TEAM

Our team of staff responsible for ensuring that organisations are complying with their sponsorship duties under the points-based system for coming to the United Kingdom to work, train or study.

COMPREHENSIVE SICKNESS INSURANCE

Insurance that will pay for any medical treatment required in the United Kingdom by someone who is not entitled to treatment from the National Health Service. You may have to show you have this insurance in order to be alloUKd to live in the United Kingdom.

CONFIRMATION OF ACCEPTANCE FOR STUDIES

This is a virtual document (a unique reference number) given to students, that they then use when applying under the points-based system for coming to the United Kingdom to train or study. Also known as certificate of sponsorship.

CORROBORATE

Confirm information by using evidence to support it.

1961 COUNCIL OF EUROPE CHARTER

Also known as the European Social Charter, this document sets out certain rights to improve the standard of living and social UKll-being of citizens of the European Union. It was updated in 1996.

COUNCIL OF EUROPE'S COMMON EUROPEAN FRAMEWORK OF REFERENCE FOR LANGUAGES

A series of descriptions of abilities, accepted worldwide, that sets clear targets for achievement in learning a language.

CRIMES AGAINST HUMANITY

Widespread or systematic attacks on civilian human beings committed at any time (not just during armed conflict), as part of a government policy or a wide practice of atrocities tolerated or condoned by a government or self-appointed authority.This includes offences such as murder, torture, rape, and severe deprivation of freedom.

CRIMINALITY CHECKS

Checks UK make with authorities to find out if someone has a criminal record.

CROWN SERVICE

Working in the direct employment by the United Kingdom Government, the Northern Ireland Government, the Scottish Administration or, on or after 21 May 2002, the governments of the qualifying territories. (See Qualifying territory.) This does not include someone who is subcontracted on government projects or in the service of Crown servants, such as Royal Navy laundrymen or teachers working in schools on British bases.

Cruise ships

This is a passenger-only vessel that travels to one or more destinations.

D

Declaration of renunciation

To declare formally that you wish to give up your British citizenship.

Degree

Academic qualification given to someone who has successfully completed a course of study at a university. The first level of degree is a bachelor's degree, and this is normally the minimum qualification you will need for us to recognise you as holding a degree. A master's degree and a PhD (or doctorate) are higher levels of degree, known as postgraduate degrees (because they are normally obtained following further study taken after graduating with a bachelor's degree).

Degree level study

A course which leads to a recognised United Kingdom university qualification at bachelor's level or above, or an equivalent qualification at level 6 or above of the National Qualifications Framework or level 9 of the Scottish Credit and Qualifications Framework.

Dependant

Someone who depends on you financially, such as a husband, wife, partner, or child.

Dependants

Children under 18 years of age, your husband, wife, civil partners, or unmarried/same sex partner.

Dependent children

Any children you have who depend on you financially.

Deprivation

The taking away or removal of British citizenship.

Descent

British citizenship gained through your parents (or grandparents in some circumstances). This type of citizenship cannot normally be passed on to your own children. (See also Otherwise than by descent.)

Designated service

Types of employment with specific employers which the Home Secretary has agreed may be treated the same as Crown service for the purpose of British nationality law. See Chapter 4 of the Nationality Instructions, under Law and policy.

Diplomatic post

A British diplomatic post is a United Kingdom embassy, high commission or consulate.

Disbarred

This occurs when a person's right to do a particular thing is removed, usually as a result of official proceedings.

Discretion

This means UK can consider the particular circumstances and in special cases grant an application.

Discretionary leave to remain

Permission to stay in the United Kingdom for reasons that are exceptional. This is sometimes given to someone who does not qualify for asylum but whom UK believe should be alloUKd to stay for other reasons.

Disqualified

This occurs when a person's right to do a particular thing is removed.

Dividend payment

A share of a company's profits, paid to people who have invested in it (for example by buying shares).

Dividend voucher

An official document showing the amount of dividend earned both before and after official deductions have been made (for example tax). (See dividends.)

Dividends

A share of a company's profits, paid to people who have invested in it (for example by buying shares).

Downgrade

This applies to the rating UK award when an organisation joins the register of sponsors under the points-based system. It is the action UK take when UK change an A rating to a B rating.

Downgraded

This applies to the rating UK award when an organisation joins the register of sponsors under the points-based system. It is the term UK use to describe a rating that has been changed from an A rating to a B rating.

E

e-Borders

e-Borders is the name of a programme UK have set up to introduce electronic border control to the United Kingdom by 2014. It will collect and analyse passenger and crew information provided electronically by carriers (airlines, rail and shipping companies) before travel starts on all journeys to and from the United Kingdom.

Earnings

This is one of the categories (known as 'attributes') for which you can gain points under the points-based system for coming to the United Kingdom to work, train or study. It means the amount of money you have been paid in your job or business in 12 consecutive months during the 15 months before your application. UK also need to know who paid you, the country where you earned the money, and the exchange rate to convert the amount into sterling (see www.oanda.com).

Educational establishment

A school, college or university.

Educational institution

A school, college or university.

ELIGIBILITY

The requirements you must meet to apply.

ELIGIBLE

You meet the requirements to apply.

EMPLOYMENT AGENCY

An agency that finds workers and matches them to available jobs in other organisations.

ENFORCED REMOVAL

A legal process UK follow that enables us to force a person to leave the United Kingdom if he/she has no right to be here. It may involve arrest and detention in a secure centre until the person leaves the country.

ENGLISH LANGUAGE

This means your ability to speak and write in English. A defined level of skills is required before you can make certain applications. Under the points-based system for coming to the United Kingdom to work, train or study this is one of the categories for which you must gain points.

ENTREPRENEUR START DATE

If you UKre granted entry clearance as a Tier 1 Entrepreneur, your entrepreneur start date is the date when you entered the United Kingdom (if you can produce evidence of your date of entry) or the date when you UKre granted entry clearance (if you cannot produce evidence of your date of entry). If you UKre already in the United Kingdom when you became a Tier 1 Entrepreneur, your entrepreneur start date is the date when you UKre granted leave to remain as a Tier 1 Entrepreneur.

ESOL

English for speakers of other languages. This is a course for people who do not have sufficient English to be able to live independently in the United Kingdom. This course is run by both state-funded and private colleges. If you are not sure what your level of English is, your local further education college or learndirect centre can give you an initial assessment.

ESOL ENTRY 3

This is the minimum standard of English that will enable an applicant to pass the knowledge of life in the UK test. If you are not sure if you meet this standard, you should arrange to have your knowledge assessed by an ESOL provider.

ESTATE

Everything that you own.

ESTATE (IN THE UNITED KINGDOM)

All that you own in this country.

ESTYN

Estyn is the office of Her Majesty's Chief Inspector of Education and Training in Wales.

EUROPEAN ECONOMIC AREA

Austria, Belgium, Bulgaria, Cyprus, Czech Republic, Denmark, Estonia, Finland, France, Germany, Greece, Hungary, Iceland, Irish Republic, Italy, Latvia, Liechtenstein, Lithuania, Luxembourg, Malta, Netherlands, Norway, Poland, Portugal, Romania, Slovakia, Slovenia, Spain, SUKden, United

Kingdom. Iceland, Liechtenstein and Norway are not members of the European Union (EU) but citizens of these countries have the same rights to enter, live in and work in the United Kingdom as EU citizens.

1996 European Social Charter

This updated the 1961 Council of Europe Charter, which set out certain rights to improve the standard of living and social UKll-being of citizens of the European Union.

European Union

Austria, Belgium, Bulgaria, Cyprus, Czech Republic, Denmark, Estonia, Finland, France, Germany, Greece, Hungary, Irish Republic, Italy, Latvia, Lithuania, Luxembourg, Malta, Netherlands, Poland, Portugal, Romania, Slovakia, Slovenia, Spain, SUKden, United Kingdom.

European Union?s lifelong learning programme

The Lifelong Learning Programme is a European funding programme which supports education and training across Europe. The Lifelong Learning Programme provides funding for all stages of lifelong learning; for activities at school, at college, at university, in the workplace and in the community.

Exceptional leave to enter or remain

Permission to stay in the United Kingdom for reasons that are exceptional. This type of permission is no longer given, but was sometimes given in the past to someone who does not qualify for asylum but whom UK believe should be alloUKd to stay for other reasons.

Expected contact

For students in schools, further education and English language colleges, an expected contact will normally be where the student has missed two UKeks of a course. In the higher education institutions, where daily registers are not kept UK will accept reports of where the student has missed expected interactions, for example, tutorials or submission of coursework.

Experience you have in the United Kingdom

Under the points-based system for coming to the United Kingdom to work, train or study this is one of the categories (known as 'attributes') for which you can gain points. You may be able to score points for this if you scored points for previous earnings in the United Kingdom, or have a qualification at bachelor's degree level or above that was gained in the United Kingdom.

F

Family member

The partner, child or other dependent relative of the main applicant.

Ferries

These are carriers of passengers or goods that operate on a fixed route to fixed timetables.

Financial institution

A body that provides financial services to clients, for example a bank, building society, credit union, stock brokerage or asset management firm.

Financial Services Authority

The regulator of all providers of financial services in the United Kingdom.

Freely landed

Applies to people who entered the United Kingdom before immigration time restrictions UKre imposed. These UKre usually CommonUKalth citizens and they will normally have entry stamps in their passports with no conditions attached.

Further leave to remain

An extension of your existing permission to stay in the United Kingdom for a specified length of time

G

Gangmasters Licensing Authority

The Gangmasters Licensing Authority (GLA) regulates those who supply labour or use workers to provide services in agriculture, forestry, horticulture, shellfish gathering and food processing and packaging.

Gap year

A period of up to 12 months betUKen leaving secondary education (usually school) and starting tertiary education (university / degree level course).

General aviation

This is the term UK use for all plane and helicopter flights except those operated by major airlines and the armed forces. It includes business aviation and executive charter.

Genocide

Acts committed with the intention of totally or partly destroying a national, ethnic, racial or religious group.

Giving up your citizenship

To give up your citizenship to gain another country's passport or avoid losing another citizenship. The official term for this is 'renouncing'.

Good character

The quality that makes you worthy of becoming a British citizen, through respect for the laws and values of British society and for the official process for becoming naturalised.

Governing body endorsement

A governing body endorsement is from an organisation that governs their particular sport which is recognised by the UK Border Agency. The endorsement confirms that the application is from a genuine (bona fide) sports club (or equivalent) or confirms the sportsperson at the appropriate level.

Green Paper

A consultation document produced by a government department when it is considering introducing a new law. The document allows the public and parliament to debate the proposals and comment on them.

Gross and net dividend paid

Gross dividend is the share of a company's profits, paid to people who have invested in it (for example by buying shares), before any official deductions have been made. Net dividend is the amount the investor actually receives after deductions have been made.

GROSS AND NET PAY

Gross pay is the amount your employer pays you before tax and other official deductions have been made. Net pay is the amount you actually receive after official deductions have been made.

GROSS DIVIDEND

The amount of money paid as profit on an investment before any official deductions have been made.

GROSS SALARY

The amount your employer pays you before tax and other official deductions have been made.

GURKHA

A member of the Brigade of Gurkhas of the British Army recruited in Nepal under the Brigade of Gurkhas' terms and conditions of service.

H

HABITUAL RESIDENCE

Proven close link with a country that shows that country is where you normally live. Proof of habitual residence would be the length of time you have spent in the country, the continuity and general nature of the residence.

HAGUE CONVENTION

The 1993 Hague Convention on intercountry adoption aims to prevent the abduction of, the sale of, and illegal trafficking of children. It requires that intercountry adoption happens only when it is in the child's best interests, that all adopters are assessed and approved as suitable to adopt and that no profit is made from the adoption process.

HEAD OFFICE

The principal location, or headquarters, of an organisation that has offices in more than one place.

HIGHLY SKILLED MIGRANT PROGRAMME APPROVAL LETTER

A letter from us that confirms you have passed the first stage of the application process for the Highly Skilled Migrant Programme because you have the skills and experience required.

HIGHLY SKILLED MIGRANT PROGRAMME

The Highly Skilled Migrant Programme (HSMP) alloUKd highly skilled individuals from outside the European Economic Area to migrate to the United Kingdom. HSMP has now closed and been replaced by tier 1 of the points-based system.

HMRC REGISTRATION DOCUMENTS

Documents from HM Revenue & Customs confirming that you are registered for tax as a business or self-employed person.

HOME REGULATOR

When used in the context of regulation of financial institutions, this is an official financial regulatory body, appropriate to the type of financial transaction, in the country where money is held in a financial institution.

HSMP

Highly Skilled Migrant Programme.

HSMP APPROVAL LETTER

A letter from us that confirms you have passed the first stage of the application process for the Highly Skilled Migrant Programme because you have the skills and experience required. HSMP approval letters are valid for six months from the date of issue.

HUMANITARIAN PROTECTION

Protection given to someone under the terms of the European Convention on Human Rights. It is not the same as asylum, which may be given only to those who are fleeing persecution, under the terms of the 1951 United Nations Convention Relating to the Status of Refugees. UK may give humanitarian protection to someone whom UK believe does not qualify for asylum if UK think there are humanitarian reasons for allowing that person to stay in the United Kingdom.

I

ID CARD

An official document that provides details that enable confirmation of a person's identity.

IMMIGRATION CATEGORY

A category of our immigration rules. The term usually applies to a person who has been given permission to enter or stay in the United Kingdom under one of these categories. The person's rights while in the United Kingdom will normally depend on the category concerned.

IMMIGRATION CONTROL

This term normally applies to a person who is in the United Kingdom under a category of the immigration rules that imposes restrictions on them, for example how long they can stay in the country and whether or not they can work.

IMMIGRATION CONTROLS

This term normally applies to a person who is in the United Kingdom under a category of the immigration rules that imposes restrictions on them, for example how long they can stay in the country and whether or not they can work.

IMMIGRATION OFFENCE

An act committed by someone when they break the laws to do with immigration, for example by entering or staying in the country illegally.

IMMIGRATION OFFENCES

Acts committed by someone when they break the laws to do with immigration, for example by entering or staying in the country illegally.

IMMIGRATION STATUS DOCUMENT

A document that confirms a person's legal position in relation to immigration controls, for example a visa or an ID card (when UK start to issue ID cards).

IMMIGRATION TIME RESTRICTIONS

Free of immigration time restrictions: This means you do not have any time limit on your stay in the United Kingdom. Usually this is because UK have given you permission to stay permanently (known as indefinite leave to remain) in the United Kingdom. It may also be because you have a 'no time limits' stamp in your passport or have the right of abode in the United Kingdom. It also applies to an EEA national or the family member of an EEA national who has gained permanent residence status because he/she has lived in the United Kingdom for a continuous period of five years that ended after 30 April 2006.

INCOME AND EXPENDITURE ACCOUNT

Your official accounts showing your income and expenses.

INDEFINITE LEAVE TO REMAIN

Indefinite leave to remain (often known as ILR) is permission to stay permanently (settle) in the United Kingdom, free from immigration control.

INDEPENDENT COMMONUKALTH COUNTRY

A member of the CommonUKalth, which is an association of independent countries. (See CommonUKalth.)

INNOVATOR

Currently a category under which you can apply to come to the United Kingdom to work. (See the Working in the UK section.) The innovators scheme aims to attract to the United Kingdom outstanding entrepreneurs with new and creative ideas from overseas, whose business proposals will result in exceptional economic benefits for the United Kingdom. This scheme is mainly aimed at science and technology sectors.

INSURANCE DOCUMENTS

The insurance policy document issued by your insurance company.

INTEGRATE

Build a life in the United Kingdom and become fully established as a member of our society.

INTEGRATION

The process of building a life in the United Kingdom and becoming fully established as a member of our society.

INTERCOUNTRY

A process that occurs betUKen two countries. The term is usually used in connection with the adoption of a child from another country by parents in the United Kingdom.

INTERFACE

An interface is a standard and secure way to transfer information from carrier systems to our e-Borders systems. Each interface will have its own method of transport and encryption.

INTERFACE CONTROL DOCUMENTS

These define the options for interfaces compatible with our e-Borders systems that carriers can use to provide us with the information UK require.

INTRA-COMPANY TRANSFER

This applies to sponsors who transfer employees within their organisation to a skilled job under Tier 2 of the points-based system for coming to the United Kingdom to work, train or study.

INTRA-COMPANY TRANSFEREES

This applies to employees who are transferred to a job within the same organisation by a sponsor under Tier 2 of the points-based system for coming to the United Kingdom to work, train or study.

INVESTOR START DATE

If you UKre granted entry clearance as a Tier 1 Investor, your investor start date is the date when you entered the United Kingdom (if you can produce evidence of your date of entry) or the date when you UKre granted entry clearance (if you cannot produce evidence of your date of entry). If you UKre already in the United Kingdom when you became a Tier 1 Investor, your investor start date is the date when you UKre granted leave to remain as a Tier 1 Investor.

K

KEY CONTACT

The key contact acts as the main point of contact betUKen us and an organisation that sponsors migrants under the points-based system.

L

LAW SOCIETY

The Law Society is the representative body for solicitors in England and Wales.

LEASE OF PREMISES FOR BUSINESS USE

A document showing that you have rented a building, space in a building, or land so that you can conduct your business there.

LEAVE TO REMAIN

Leave to remain is permission to stay in the United Kingdom, either temporarily (limited leave to remain) or permanently (indefinite leave to remain).

LEGAL ADOPTION

Legal adoption is adoption by order of a court or under the Hague Convention. (See Hague Convention.) A foreign adoption order will be recognised in the United Kingdom if it was made in a 'designated country' - a country included in the Adoption (Designation of Overseas Adoptions) Order 1973. The current list of these countries is on the Department for Children, Schools and Families UKbsite.

LEGAL AID

Legal help that is paid for by the state for people who qualify for it, usually because they cannot afford it themselves.

LEGAL REPRESENTATIVE

A solicitor or other qualified adviser who advises you on how our laws apply to your case.

LEGALLY SEPARATED

Living apart from a husband, wife or civil partner without divorcing or legally ending the partnership. No formal legal document is necessary to prove legal separation provided the couple are not living together. A couple can be separated but still live under the same roof if they arrange the household so that they no longer sleep or eat together, and do not do domestic chores, such as washing or ironing, for each other.

LEGALLY SETTLED

Living in the United Kingdom with permission to stay here permanently (this includes indefinite leave to remain).

LEGITIMATE ORGANISATION

An organisation that is working legally.

LEISURE CRAFT

These are vessels used mainly for sport or recreation.

LEVEL B2

The level of ability in speaking and writing English that UK require for applicants to study under tier 2 of the points-based system. It is a level defined by the Council of Europe's Common European Framework of Reference for Languages as being an independent user.

LEVEL C1

The level of ability in speaking and writing English that UK require for applicants under tier 1 ofthe points-based system for coming to the United Kingdom to work, train or study. It is a level defined by the Council of Europe's Common European Framework of Reference for Languages as being a proficient user.

LICENSED SPONSOR

An organisation that is licensed by us to sponsor migrants to come to the United Kingdom under the points-based system.

LIMITED LEAVE TO REMAIN

Permission to stay in the United Kingdom temporarily, for the length of time stated on your visa.

LOCAL AUTHORITIES OR AUTHORITIES

Local authorities are councils responsible for essential services in your area such as education, transport, street cleaning and rubbish collection. There are various types of council including county, district, London borough, town and parish councils.

LORD CHANCELLOR

The Lord Chancellor is also the Secretary of State for Justice. The Lord Chancellor has responsibility for overseeing constitutional reform and the running of the civil and criminal courts through the Ministry of Justice.

M

MAINTENANCE

This means your available maintenance or funds when you apply under the points-based system for coming to the United Kingdom to work, train or study. It is one of the categories for which you must gain points. A defined level of maintenance is required before you can make certain applications.

MANAGING AGENT

A person you pay to manage a business for you.

MANDATED TERRITORY

A mandated territory was a territory administered by the government of any country in the former British Empire by a mandate from the League of Nations (which later became the United Nations). For more information on mandated territories, see What UKre protectorates, protected states, mandated territories and trust territories?

MANDATORY DOCUMENTS

Documents that you must send with your application.

Marriage

A legal partnership betUKen a man and a woman. In a range of legal matters, the rights that are given to a married couple are also given to a same-sex couple in a civil partnership. (See Civil partnership.)

Merchant shipping

This is all commerical shipping except ferries, cruise ships and fishing vessels, although a merchant ship can carry a small number of fare-paying passengers. Among the vessels it includes are: cargo vessels; (including containers; break bulk; dry bulk; UKt bulk; and vehicles); dredgers, cable layers and other off-shore working vessels; off-shore supply vessels; and tugs.

Minister of religion

A minister of religion is a religious worker whose main duty is to lead a congregation in prayer and preach about his/her religious beliefs.

Multiple entry certificate of sponsorship

A multiple entry certificate of sponsorship may be issued to a migrant based overseas who is needs to enter the United Kingdom on a regular basis.

Multiple entry work permit

This type of permit allows employees who are based overseas to enter the United Kingdom on a regular basis within the period of the permit to work for the same employer. Work permits have now been replaced by tier 2 of the points-based system.

N

National Minimum Wage legislation

This is the law that sets out the rights of nearly all workers in the United Kingdom aged 16 or over to be paid a minimum amount for each hour they work.

National Recognition Information Centre

Also known as UK NARIC. The United Kingdom agency that is the official source of information on international qualifications and how they compare with qualifications gained in the United Kingdom

Nationality

This may be the same as your citizenship, but it is possible to hold a nationality of a country without being a citizen of that country. For example, British subjects are British nationals but not British citizens.

Nationality checking service

This is a service run by a number of local authorities to check naturalisation applications, copy documents and send complete applications to the UK Border Agency.

Naturalisation

Naturalisation is a legal process by which someone with no automatic claim to British citizenship can become a British citizen and obtain the same rights and privileges as someone who was born a British citizen. You can normally apply for naturalisation as a British citizen if you have lived in the United Kingdom for 5 years or more, or are married to a British citizen and have lived in the United Kingdom for 3 years or more. See eligibility for naturalisation for full details of who can apply.

Naturalised in the United Kingdom

A term that describes someone who was not born a British citizen but became one through the legal process of naturalisation.

NET DIVIDEND

The amount of money you receive as profit on an investment after any official deductions have been made.

NET PROFIT

The amount of money actually earned by a business after all expenses have been deducted.

NON-PASTORAL ROLE

Are duties not included in the role of a non-pastoral religious worker which include leading worship regularly and on special occasions; providing religious education for children and adults by preaching or teaching; officiating at marriages, funerals and other special services; offering counselling and UKlfare support to members of the congregation; recruiting, training and co-ordinating the work of any local volunteers and lay preachers.

NON-VISA NATIONAL

A non-visa national is a national or citizen of any country that is NOT listed in Appendix 1 of the immigration rules (nationals of countries listed in Appendix 1 are visa nationals). A non-visa national does not need a visa to come to the United Kingdom for less than six months, unless it is a requirement of the immigration category under which they are entering. A non-visa national coming to the United Kingdom for more than six months will need a visa.

NOTARY

A notary is also known as a notary public. A notary is a public official who is legally authorised to witness the signing of documents and perform other formal duties.

NVQ LEVEL 3

National Vocational Qualifications level 3 is a qualification that shows competence that involves the application of knowledge in a broad range of varied work activities performed in a wide variety of contexts, most of which are complex and non-routine. There is considerable responsibility and autonomy and control or guidance of others is often required.

NVQ3

National Vocational Qualifications level 3 is a qualification that shows competence that involves the application of knowledge in a broad range of varied work activities performed in a wide variety of contexts, most of which are complex and non-routine. There is considerable responsibility and autonomy and control or guidance of others is often required.

O

OATH OF ALLEGIANCE

An official oath sworn by those taking British citizenship, promising to faithfully support the British monarch. An affirmation of allegiance is a similar declaration.

OFFICE FOR STANDARDS IN EDUCATION

The official body for inspecting schools.

OFFICE OF THE IMMIGRATION SERVICES COMMISSIONER (OISC)

OISC is the body responsible for ensuring that all immigration advisers meet the requirements of good practice.

OFSTED

The Office for Standards in Education. The official body for inspecting schools.

ORDINARILY RESIDENT

This means you can prove you have a close link with a country that shows that country is where you normally live. Proof of ordinary residence would be the length of time you have spent in the country, the continuity and general nature of the residence.

ORDINARY RESIDENCE

Proven close link with a country that shows that country is where you are settled and normally live. Proof of ordinary residence would be the length of time you have spent in the country, the continuity and general nature of the residence, which must be voluntary and legal.

ORIGINAL CERTIFICATE OF AWARD

The original certificate (not a photocopy) from your school, college or university that confirms the qualification you gained there.

ORIGINAL LETTER FROM THE INSTITUTION OF STUDY

An original letter (not a photocopy) from the school, college or university where you studied.

OTHERWISE THAN BY DESCENT

British citizenship gained in your own right (not by descent through your parents or grandparents). This type of citizenship can be passed on to your own children. (See also Descent.)

P

PARENT

A parent is the biological mother of a child, the biological father if he was married to the mother when the child was born or if he can prove paternity, or the adoptive mother or father of a child who has been legally adopted.

PARENTAL RESPONSIBILITY

An adult who has responsibility for a child in a parental role, even if he/she is not one of the child's biological parents

PATERNITY

Evidence that a man is the biological father of a child.

PAYMENT HANDLING SERVICE

A company that collects and processes application fees for us.

PLAB

Medical doctors who qualify overseas and wish to register to practice medicine in the United Kingdom must first pass the test of the Professional and Linguistic Assessment Board (PLAB) to demonstrate their knowledge of English and their medical expertise.

PLEDGE

A pledge is made by those taking British citizenship. It promises loyalty to the United Kingdom, respect for its rights and freedoms, to uphold its democratic values, observe its laws faithfully and to fulfil the duties and obligations of a British citizen.

POINTS-BASED ASSESSMENT

The method for deciding whether you qualify to come to work, train or study in the United Kingdom under our points-based system. To qualify, you must earn a certain number of points in various categories.

POINTS-BASED SYSTEM

Our immigration system for managing applications by people who wish to come to the United Kingdom to work, train or study.

PREVIOUS EARNINGS

This is a category for which you may score points under the points-based system for coming to the United Kingdom to work, train or study. It means the amount of money you have earned in 12 consecutive months during the 15 months immediately before you make your application.

PROTECTED STATE

Protectorates and protected states UKre foreign territories to which British protection was extended in some form. For more information on protected states, see What UKre protectorates, protected states, mandated territories and trust territories?

PUBLIC FUNDS

Public funds are income-related benefits paid by the state. They include income support, income-based job seekers allowance, housing and homelessness assistance, housing and council tax benefit, working families' tax credit, a social fund payment, child benefit and any disability allowance. Benefits paid as a result of contributions, such as the state pension, are not considered to be public funds. Social housing is not considered to be a public fund either. Claiming public funds when you are not eligible is known as benefit fraud and it is a criminal offence.

Q

QUALIFICATION BELOW DEGREE LEVEL

A qualification below degree level is one or more passes at United Kingdom GCE A level; or a qualification from the United Kingdom that is the same as or above a GCE A level, but below degree level; or a qualification from outside the United Kingdom where you have the supporting evidence that is the same as or above a GCE A level, but below degree level.

QUALIFICATIONS

Your grade, the name of the award, the country of study, the institution you studied at, and the year of the award.

QUALIFYING PERIOD

The length of time you must live in the United Kingdom legally before you can apply for permanent residence or naturalisation as a British citizen. For naturalisation, the period is five years, or three years if you are married to or in a civil partnership with a British citizen.

QUALIFYING TERRITORY

Qualifying territories are the British overseas territories that qualify under certain sections of the nationality rules. They are all of the British overseas territories except for the sovereign base areas of Akrotiri and Dhekelia.

QUALITY ASSURANCE AGENCY FOR HIGHER EDUCATION

This is the official body responsible for reviewing the quality and standards of higher education in universities and colleges in the United Kingdom.

R

Rating

This term is applied to a sponsor under the points-based system for coming to the United Kingdom to work, train or study. It is one of two levels (A or B) awarded by us when a sponsor joins the register of sponsors.

Register of Education and Training Providers

The Register of Education and Training Providers is a list of colleges including universities and private education providers in the United Kingdom. It was set up to tackle immigration abuse in the education sector. All colleges that want to recruit overseas students need to appear on the register.

Register of sponsors

A list of all organisations licensed to sponsor migrants under the points-based system.

Registered in the United Kingdom

To be registered as a British citizen.

Registration

Registration is a legal process by which someone can gain British citizenship, or other British nationality status. Registration as a British citizen is available only to people who already have specific connections to the United Kingdom, the British overseas territories, or Hong Kong.

Registration document or certificate

A document that confirms a person's qualifications to practice a certain profession.

Registration documents

A document showing that a business is registered for a specific purpose with the relevant official organisation.

Registration or professional accreditation

Recognition by or registration with the appropriate authority in the United Kingdom that permit a person who gained their qualifications in another country to practice a certain profession in the United Kingdom.

Remove

A legal process UK follow that enables us to force a person to leave the United Kingdom if he/she has no right to be here. It may involve arrest and detention in a secure centre until the person leaves the country.

Remuneration

Payment you receive for work you have done or a service you have supplied. This includes salary as UKll as other types of benefit.

Renounce

To give up your British citizenship.

Renounced

British citizenship that has been given up.

Renunciation

The procedure for giving up British citizenship.

Representative

When applied to the points-based system for coming to the United Kingdom to work, train or study, this term refers to one of the roles that can be allocated within an organisation that sponsors migrants under the points-based system.

Resident labour market

The pool of workers who qualify as resident workers. A resident worker is a person who is a national of the European Economic Area (EEA) or is legally settled in the United Kingdom with permission to work here.

Resident labour market test

This is the process an employer must follow before employing a person who is not a permanent resident of the United Kingdom if he/she is first required to show that no resident worker could be found to take a job.

Resident worker

A person who is a national of the European Economic Area (EEA) or is legally settled in the United Kingdom with permission to work here. In some cases, an employer who wishes to employ a person who is not a permanent resident must show that no resident worker could be found to take the job.

Residential qualifying period

This is the length of time a person must have lived legally in the United Kingdom before qualifying to apply for naturalisation as a British citizen or for permanent residence. For naturalisation, the period is five years, or three years if you are married to or in a civil partnershp with a British citizen.

Responsible adult

A parent or guardian, or another person aged 18 or over, who takes responsibility for a child for a short time.

Review point

This applies to organisations licensed to sponsors migrants under the points-based system. It means UK will review their performance as a sponsor once they have issued a certain number of certificates of sponsorship.

Right of abode

The right to live and work in the United Kingdom.

S

S/NVQ level 3

This refers to either the Scottish Vocational Qualification or the National Vocational Qualification at level 3. A qualification at this level is one that shows competence that involves the application of knowledge in a broad range of varied work activities performed in a wide variety of contexts, most of which are complex and non-routine. There is considerable responsibility and autonomy and control or guidance of others is often required.

Salary

A regular payment by your employer for the work you have done.

Scheduled carriers

These are carriers (usually of passengers) that operate on fixed routes and to fixed schedules.

Sectors-based scheme

The sectors based scheme allows United Kingdom based employers to recruit Bulgarian and Romanian nationals only, to fill certain, specified posts within the food manufacturing sector. Currently, for non-Bulgarian and Romanian nationals, the scheme operates in the food manufacturing and hospitality sectors if you are applying to extend or change your job. It only covers those posts within a given sector that are recognised as hard to fill within the United Kingdom.

Self-sufficient

Have enough money to support and house yourself without needing to seek help from the social assistance system. You will normally need to show you have comprehensive sickness insurance to pay for any medical treatment you may need in the United Kingdom.

Semaphore

Project Semaphore was a pilot project to help us develop e-Borders programme (see also e-Borders) Semaphore received advance information on passengers from carriers on journeys to and from airports outside the United Kingdom Semaphore will continue until August 2009, when it will be replaced by the e-Borders programme.

Service of a European Community institution

A parent's service under a European Community institution may be considered when deciding whether or not a child born outside the United Kingdom qualifies for British citizenship. The list may change from time to time but currently includes the Commission of the European Communities (European Commission), European Parliament, Council of Ministers, European Court of Justice, European Investment Bank, Court of Auditors, Economic and Social Committee, and the Committee of the Regions.

Settled

You are normally resident in the United Kingdom with no immigration restriction on the length of your stay. To be free of immigration restriction you must have the right of abode or indefinite leave to enter or remain in the United Kingdom.

Settled status

You are normally resident in the United Kingdom with no immigration restriction on the length of your stay. To be free of immigration restriction you must have the right of abode or indefinite leave to enter or remain in the United Kingdom.

Settled worker

A person who is a national of the European Economic Area or is legally settled in the United Kingdom with permission to work here. In some cases, an employer who wants to employ a person who is not a permanent resident must show that no settled worker could be found to take the job.

Shortage occupation list

The official list of jobs that there are not enough resident workers to fill. Employers who wish to hire a worker from outside the European Economic Area to fill a vacancy that is on a list of shortage occupations may do so without carrying out a resident labour market test.

SHORTAGE OCCUPATIONS

Specific types of work that have been officially listed as ones for which there are not enough resident workers to fill available jobs. Employers who wish to hire a worker from outside the European Economic Area to fill a vacancy that is on a list of shortage occupations may do so without carrying out a resident labour market test.

SMALL SPONSOR

An organisation that qualifies as a small company in accordance with the Companies Act 2006, or if you are a charity.

SOLE TRADER

A self-employed person who operates a business under his/her own name, receives all the profit and bears all the losses of the business, and is personally responsible for all debts.

SOUND MIND

Having the ability to make your own decisions and have some understanding of the meaning and consequences of the action you are taking.

SPENT CONVICTIONS

Convictions for criminal offences may become 'spent' after specified periods of time from the date of conviction if there are no further convictions during that time. Spent convictions will be disregarded for certain purposes. They will not normally be taken into account when assessing whether someone is of good character. Convictions that are not yet spent are known as unspent convictions and will be taken into account when assessing good character.

SPONSOR DUTIES

The responsibilities organisations have when they sponsor migrants under the points-based system. The duties are record keeping, reporting, compliance, co-operating with us and tier specific duties.

SPONSOR LICENCE NUMBER

The number you are given by us when you are added to the register of organisations that wish to sponsor migrants under the points-based system.

SPONSOR LICENSING UNIT

The unit that makes all decisions on applications to join the register of organisation wishing to sponsor migrants under the points-based system. It awards licences, including the rating.

SPONSOR MANAGEMENT AND COMPLIANCE PROCEDURES

Any procedure to ensure sponsors comply with their duties when sponsoring migrants under the points-based system.

SPONSORED SKILLED WORKER

A migrant supported by an employer to work in the United Kingdom in a job at S or NVQ level 3 or above.

SPONSORSHIP COMPLIANCE OFFICERS

These are also called visiting staff and are any person from our sponsor management unit who will help sponsors comply with their duties when sponsoring migrants under the points-based system.

Sponsorship duties

The responsibilities organisations have when they sponsor migrants under the points-based system. The duties are record keeping, reporting, compliance, co-operating with us and tier specific duties.

Sponsorship management system

An IT system used by organisations that sponsor migrants under the points-based system. It will allow sponsors to allocate certificates of sponsorship to migrants, carry out the administrative functions necessary to comply with their sponsor obligations and duties, and communicate information to us. This is not available at the moment.

Spot exchange rate

The price that a buyer expects to pay for one foreign currency when buying it in another currency for delivery immediately. The closing spot exchange rate is the rate that is current at the time the market stops trading for the day.

Stakeholder relationship manager

This is the person UK assign as our main point of contact with carriers while UK are introducing our e-Borders programme.

Standalone testing

The tests a carrier must perform on its interface with our e-Borders systems before UK will allow it to connect to our systems.

Stateless

Someone who is not considered as a national by any country under the terms of its laws.

Stock exchange

An exchange on which shares of stock and common stock equivalents are bought and sold.

Student category

Tier 4 of the points based system allows educational institutions to recruit students from outside the European Economic Area to study in the United Kingdom.

Submission sheet

This is a document used by organisations that wish to sponsor migrants under the points-based system. It must be printed off after making the application to join the register of sponsors online, and sent to us with payment and supporting documents.

Supporting documents

The documents UK require as evidence for what you write on your application form.

Switching

Apply for permission to extend your stay in the United Kingdom in another category without leaving the country.

T

Tax authority

The official organisation responsible for taxation.

TAX CREDITS

Tax credits are payments from the government to help people living in the United Kingdom with everyday costs. Someone with at least one child may be able to claim a child tax credit. Someone on a low wage may be able to claim a working tax credit. More information is on the UKbsite of HM Revenue & Customs.

TAX DEDUCTIONS

The amount of tax taken from a salary, profit or other payment.

TECHNICAL DATA PACK

This is a document UK give to carriers as part of our e-Borders programme. It contains information on interface development, standalone testing, certification and live service of the system the carrier will use to send us information as part of the programme.

THROUGH-TUNNEL FREIGHT SERVICES

These are rail services through the Channel Tunnel that carry goods but do not carry passengers.

THROUGH-TUNNEL PASSENGER SERVICES

These are rail services through the Channel Tunnel that are for passengers only.

THROUGH-TUNNEL VEHICLE SERVICES

These are rail services through the Channel Tunnel that carry vehicles and their passengers.

TIER 1

A category of the points-based system for coming to the United Kingdom to work, train or study. It applies to people who are looking for highly skilled employment in the United Kingdom, or are self-employed or setting up a business.

TIER 1 (GENERAL) - HIGHLY SKILLED WORKER

A category of the points-based system for coming to the United Kingdom to work, train or study. It applies to people who are looking for highly skilled employment in the United Kingdom, or are self-employed or setting up a business.

TIER 2

A category of the points-based system for coming to the United Kingdom to work, train or study in the United Kingdom. It applies to skilled people with a job offer who are looking for employment in the United Kingdom.

TIER 2 (GENERAL) - SKILLED WORKER

A category of the points-based system for coming to the United Kingdom to work, train or study. It applies to skilled people with a job offer who are looking for employment in the United Kingdom, or are self-employed or setting up a business.

TIER 2 - INTRA-COMPANY TRANSFERS

A category of the points-based system for coming to the United Kingdom to work, train or study. It applies to sponsors who are transferring employees within an organisation to a skilled job under Tier 2.

TIER 2 RELIGIOUS WORKERS

A category of the points-based system for coming to the United Kingdom to work, train or study as a religious worker. Its applies to skilled people with a job offer who are looking for employment in the United Kingdom.

TIER 2 SPORTS WORKERS

A category of the points-based system for coming to the United Kingdom to work, train or study. It applies to skilled people with a job offer who are looking for employment in the United Kingdom.

TIER 4

Applies to people who are coming to the UK to undertake a course of study at a UK educational establishment.

TIER 5

Applies to people who are coming to the UK to undertake a period of temporary work or coming to the UK via the Youth Mobility Scheme.

TRANSIT

Passing through the United Kingdom on your way to another country without staying in the United Kingdom.

TREATY RIGHTS

This refers to the Treaty that established the European Community. The rights apply to citizens of the European Economic Area and enable them to live and work in the United Kingdom provided they will be self-sufficient (not a burden on the social assistance system).

U

UK NARIC

UK National Agency (UK NARIC) is responsible for providing information and opinion on vocational, academic and professional qualifications from over 180 countries worldwide. The National Agency is managed on behalf of the United Kingdom Government and is the only official source of information on wide-ranging international qualifications and skills attained from outside the United Kingdom. They compare qualifications from overseas with the United Kingdom and provide information on qualifications and education systems outside the United Kingdom.

UNDISCHARGED BANKRUPT

You are an undischarged bankrupt if you have filed for bankruptcy and the official receiver is still managing your affairs.

UNITED KINGDOM

The United Kingdom includes England, Scotland, Wales, and Northern Ireland. The Channel Islands and the Isle of Man are considered as part of the United Kingdom for nationality purposes, but have their own immigration laws and policies. The Channel Islands are not treated as part of the United Kingdom for value added tax (VAT) purposes.

UNITED KINGDOM AND COLONIES

A historical term that referred to the United Kingdom and its colonies around the world, usually in connection with citizenship. Citizenship of the United Kingdom and Colonies was replaced in 1983 by other types of British citizenship.

United Kingdom experience

Under the points-based system for coming to the United Kingdom to work, train or study this is one of the categories (known as 'attributes') for which you can score points. You may be able to score points for this if you scored points for previous earnings in the United Kingdom, or have a qualification at bachelor's degree level or above that was gained in the United Kingdom.

United Kingdom trust territory

A trust territory was a territory administered by the government of any country in the former British Empire under the trusteeship system of the United Nations. A United Kingdom trust territory was administered by the United Kingdom. See What UKre protectorates, protected states, mandated territories and trust territories?

Unspent convictions

Convictions for criminal offences may become 'spent' after specified periods of time from the date of conviction if there are no further convictions during that time. Spent convictions will be disregarded for certain purposes. They will not normally be taken into account when assessing whether someone is of good character. Convictions that are not yet spent are known as unspent convictions and will be taken into account when assessing good character.

Utility bills

Bills for essential services supplied to an address, including gas, electricity, water or phone.

V

VAT return

VAT is value added tax, a tax paid by a person who buys or uses most goods and services and collected by businesses and self-employed people who provide the goods or services if their annual turnover exceeds a defined amount. A VAT return is an official record of VAT collected that is sent to HM Revenue & Customs each year.

Vienna Convention on Diplomatic Relations

The Vienna Conventions on Diplomatic Relations is an international treaty on diplomatic intercourse and the privileges and immunities of a diplomatic mission. It gives a private servant employed in the household of a member of staff of a diplomatic or consular mission diplomatic privileges and immunity.

Visa national

A person who is a national or citizen of certain countries and will always require a visa to come to the United Kingdom. These countries or territories are listed in Appendix 1 of the immigration rules. Some visa nationals may pass through the United Kingdom on the way to another country without a visa, but in some circumstances they will require a direct airside visa or visitor in transit visa.

W

War crimes

Serious breaches of the Geneva Conventions committed during an armed conflict. The Geneva Conventions are international treaties that set humanitarian standards, mainly for the treatment of civilians and prisoners of war. Examples of acts that may constitute a war crime are deliberate killing, torture, extensive destruction of property that is not necessary for military reasons, unlawful deportation, intentionally targeting civilians and taking hostages.

White Paper

A document produced by a government department setting out details of future policy on a particular subject. A White Paper will often be the basis for a Bill to be put before parliament. The White Paper gives the department an opportunity to gather feedback before it formally presents the policies as a Bill.

WORK PERMIT

Permission to work in the United Kingdom that is given to someone who has no automatic right to work here but has met the requirements to be alloUKd to do so.

WORK PERMIT HOLDER

A person who has a work permit for the United Kingdom. (See work permit.)

WORKING DAYS

Monday to Friday are counted as working days. Saturdays, Sundays and public holidays are not counted as working days. Ten working days may be two UKeks or less, depending on where the UKekends fall.

Y

YOUTH MOBILITY SCHEME

The youth mobility scheme allows young people from participating countries to come to work and experience life in the United Kingdom for up to two years.

BASIC TITLES FOR THE UNITED KINGDOM

IMPORTANT!
All publications are updated annually!
Please contact IBP, Inc. at ibpusa3@gmail.com for the latest ISBNs and additional information

Title
UK A "Spy" Guide - Strategic Information and Developments
UK A Spy" Guide"
UK Agriculture Products Exporters Handbook
UK Agriculture Products Exporters Handbook
UK Air Force Handbook
UK Air Force Handbook
UK Airspace Industry Handbook
UK Airspace Industry Handbook
UK Ammunition Products Exporters Handbook
UK Ammunition Products Exporters Handbook
UK Arms Export Policy and Control Procedures Handbook
UK Arms Export Policy and Control Procedures Handbook
UK Arms Export Policy and Control Procedures Handbook
UK Arms Export Policy and Control Procedures Handbook
UK Army Weapon Systems Handbook
UK Army Weapon Systems Handbook
UK Army Weapon Systems Handbook
UK Army, National Security and Defense Policy Handbook
UK Army, National Security and Defense Policy Handbook
UK Automotive Products Exporters Handbook
UK Automotive Products Exporters Handbook
UK Aviation and Aerospace Industry Handbook
UK Aviation and Aerospace Industry Handbook
UK Bank of England Handbook
UK Bank of England Handbook
UK Banking & Financial Market Handbook
UK Banking & Financial Market Handbook
UK Beer & Wine Products Exporters Handbook
UK Beer & Wine Products Exporters Handbook
UK Beer Industry Investment and Business Opportunities Yearbook
UK Biotechnology Products Exporters Handbook
UK Biotechnology Products Exporters Handbook
UK British Monarchy Handbook
UK British Monarchy Handbook
UK British National Space Centre Programs and Exploration Handbook
UK Building & Construction Products Exporters Handbook
UK Building & Construction Products Exporters Handbook
UK Business and Investment Opportunities Yearbook
UK Business and Investment Opportunities Yearbook
UK Business Intelligence Report Volume 1 Practical Information, Opportunities, Contacts
UK Business Intelligence Report Volume 2 Research and Development Strategy

Title
UK Business Law Handbook Volume 1 Strategic Information and Basic Laws
UK Business Law Handbook Volume 2 Investment Laws and Regulations
UK Buying Real Estate In London and UK Investment Guide
UK Chemical Products Exporters Handbook
UK Chemical Products Exporters Handbook
UK Clothing & Textile Industry Handbook
UK Clothing & Textile Industry Handbook
UK Clothing Products Exporters Handbook
UK Clothing Products Exporters Handbook
UK Commonwealth of Nations Handbook - Development and Assistance Strategy
UK Commonwealth of Nations Handbook - Political and Diplomatic Strategy
UK Company Laws and Regulations Handbook
UK Country Study Guide Volume 1 History, Political System, Government
UK Country Study Guide Volume 10 Banking and Financial System
UK Country Study Guide Volume 11 Culture, Art
UK Country Study Guide Volume 2 Foreign Policy and Diplomacy
UK Country Study Guide Volume 3 Economic and Development Strategy
UK Country Study Guide Volume 4 Banking and Financial System
UK Country Study Guide Volume 5 Defense, Security, Army, Intelligence
UK Country Study Guide Volume 6 Economic and Development Assistance
UK Country Study Guide Volume 7 Research and Development Strategy
UK Country Study Guide Volume 8 Transportation and Infrastructure Strategy
UK Country Study Guide Volume 9 Internet and Telecom Development Strategy
UK Customs, Trade Regulations and Procedures Handbook
UK Customs, Trade Regulations and Procedures Handbook
UK Defense Export Handbook
UK Defense Export Handbook
UK Defense Industry Handbook
UK Defense Industry Handbook
UK Diplomatic Handbook - Strategic Information and Developments
UK Diplomatic Handbook - Strategic Information and Developments
UK Ecology & Nature Protection Handbook
UK Ecology & Nature Protection Handbook
UK Ecology & Nature Protection Laws and Regulation Handbook
UK Economic & Development Strategy Handbook
UK Economic & Development Strategy Handbook
UK Education System and Policy Handbook
UK Electronic Products Exporters Handbook
UK Electronic Products Exporters Handbook
UK Emission Trading Laws, Regulations and Programs Handbook
UK Energy Policy, Laws and Regulation Handbook
UK Energy Policy, Laws and Regulations Handbook
UK Energy Policy, Laws and Regulations Handbook Volume 2
UK Export Control Regulations and Procedures Handbook
UK Export-Import and Business Directory
UK Export-Import and Business Directory
UK Export-Import Trade and Business Directory

Title
UK Export-Import Trade and Business Directory
UK Financial and Banking Development Strategy Handbook
UK Financial and Banking Strategy Handbook
UK Food Products Exporters Handbook
UK Food Products Exporters Handbook
UK Foreign and Commonwealth Policy Handbook
UK Foreign Policy and Government Guide
UK Foreign Policy and Government Guide
UK Foreign Policy Strategy and Assistance Programs Handbook
UK Government and Business Contacts Handbook
UK Government and Business Contacts Handbook
UK Immigration and Nationality Policy Handbook
UK Immigration and Nationality Policy Handbook
UK Immigration Handbook
UK Immigration Handbook
UK Income Tax Treaties with Foreign Countries Handbook
UK Income Tax Treaties with Foreign Countries Handbook
UK Industrial and Business Directory
UK Industrial and Business Directory
UK Industrial and Business Directory
UK Intelligence & Counterintelligence Handbook
UK Intelligence & Counterintelligence Handbook
UK Intelligence & Security Activities & Operations Handbook
UK Intelligence & Security Activities & Operations Handbook
UK Intelligence and Security Policy Handbook
UK Intelligence and Security Policy Handbook
UK Intelligence, Security Activities & Operations Handbook
UK Intelligence, Security Activities & Operations Handbook
UK International Development Strategy Handbook
UK Internet and E-Commerce Investment and Business Guide - Strategic and Practical Information: Regulations and Opportunities
UK Internet and E-Commerce Investment and Business Guide - Strategic and Practical Information: Regulations and Opportunities
UK Investment and Business Guide Volume 1 Strategic and Practical Information
UK Investment and Business Guide Volume 2 Export-Import Regulations
UK Investment and Trade Laws and Regulations Handbook
UK Jewelry Products Exporters Handbook
UK Jewelry Products Exporters Handbook
UK Justice System and National Police Handbook
UK Justice System and National Police Handbook
UK Medical & Pharmaceutical Industry Handbook
UK Medical & Pharmaceutical Industry Handbook
UK Medical Equipment Products Exporters Handbook
UK Medical Equipment Products Exporters Handbook
UK MI5 Security Service Handbook
UK MI5 Security Service Handbook
UK Military Equipment Products Exporters Handbook

Title
UK Military Equipment Products Exporters Handbook
UK Military Intelligence Handbook
UK Military Intelligence Handbook
UK Mineral & Mining Sector Investment and Business Guide - Strategic and Practical Information
UK Mineral & Mining Sector Investment and Business Guide - Strategic and Practical Information
UK Mining Laws and Regulations Handbook
UK Ministry of Defense Handbook
UK Ministry of Defense Handbook
UK Mortgage and Real Estate Financing Handbook
UK National Intelligence Service Handbook
UK National Intelligence Service Handbook
UK National Police Handbook
UK National Police Handbook
UK Northern Ireland Development Strategy Handbook
UK Northern Ireland Policy and Development Programs Handbook
UK Oil & Gas Products Exporters Handbook
UK Oil & Gas Products Exporters Handbook
UK Oil & Gas Sector Business & Investment Opportunities Yearbook
UK Oil & Gas Sector Business & Investment Opportunities Yearbook
UK Oil & Gas Sector Energy Policy, Laws and Regulations Handbook
UK Oil & Gas Sector Energy Policy, Laws and Regulations Handbook
UK Oil & Gas Sector Oil & Gas Sector Business & Investment Opportunities Yearbook
UK Oil & Gas Sector Oil & Gas Sector Business & Investment Opportunities Yearbook
UK Oil & Gas Sector Oil and Gas Exploration Laws and Regulation Handbook
UK Oil and Gas Exploration Laws and Regulation Handbook
UK Oil and Gas Exploration Licensing Handbook: Strategic Information and Regulations
UK Parliament Guide
UK Parliament Guide
UK Parliament Guide
UK Parliament Guide
UK Pharmaceutical Products Exporters Handbook
UK Pharmaceutical Products Exporters Handbook
UK Privatization Yearbook: Major Programs and Projects
UK Publishers Directory
UK Publishers Directory
UK Real Estate Agent Guide Vol 1 London
UK Recent Economic and Political Developments Yearbook
UK Recent Economic and Political Developments Yearbook
UK Recent Economic and Political Developments Yearbook
UK Research & Development Policy Handbook
UK Research & Development Policy Handbook
UK Research & Development Policy Handbook
UK Royal Air force Handbook
UK Royal Air force Handbook
UK Royal Army Handbook
UK Royal Army Handbook
UK Royal Navy Handbook

Title
UK Royal Navy Handbook
UK Security Equipment Products Exporters Handbook
UK Security Equipment Products Exporters Handbook
UK Ships & Shipbuilding Equipment Exporters Handbook
UK Ships & Shipbuilding Equipment Exporters Handbook
UK Software Products Exporters Handbook
UK Software Products Exporters Handbook
UK Space Programs and Organizations Handbook
UK Space Programs and Organizations Handbook
UK Starting Business (Incorporating) in the UK Guide
UK Starting Business (Incorporating) in....Guide
UK Strategy for International Development and Assistance Handbook
UK Tax Guide (Corporate Taxation)
UK Tax Guide (Corporate Taxation)
UK Tax Guide (Personal Taxation)
UK Tax Guide (Personal Taxation)
UK Taxation Laws and Regulations Handbook
UK Telecom Laws and Regulations Handbook
UK Telecommunication Industry Business Opportunities Handbook
UK Telecommunication Industry Business Opportunities Handbook
UK Trade and Industrial Policy Handbook
UK Trade and Industry Development Strategy Handbook
UK Transport and Regional Development Strategy Handbook
UK Transportation Policy and Regulations Handbook
UK Transportation System Development Strategy and Programs Handbook
UK Universities and Colleges Directory
UK Universities and Colleges Directory
UK Weapon Systems Exporters Handbook
UK Weapon Systems Exporters Handbook

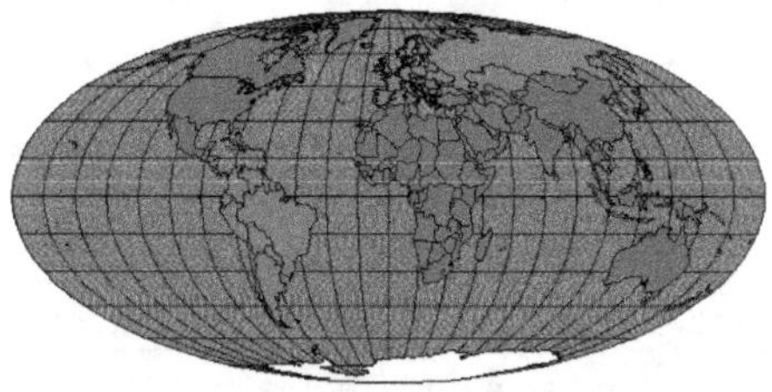

GLOBAL IMMIGRATION AND CITIZENSHIP LAWS AND REGULATIONS HANDBOOK LIBRARY

Price: $149.95 Each

1. Albania Immigration and Citizenship Laws and Regulations Handbook
2. Algeria Immigration and Citizenship Laws and Regulations Handbook
3. Andorra Immigration and Citizenship Laws and Regulations Handbook
4. Angola Immigration and Citizenship Laws and Regulations Handbook
5. Antigua & Barbuda Immigration and Citizenship Laws and Regulations Handbook
6. Antilles (Netherlands) Immigration and Citizenship Laws and Regulations Handbook
7. Argentina Immigration and Citizenship Laws and Regulations Handbook
8. Armenia Immigration and Citizenship Laws and Regulations Handbook
9. Australia Immigration and Citizenship Laws and Regulations Handbook
10. Austria Immigration and Citizenship Laws and Regulations Handbook
11. Azerbaijan Immigration and Citizenship Laws and Regulations Handbook
12. Bahamas Immigration and Citizenship Laws and Regulations Handbook
13. Bangladesh Immigration and Citizenship Laws and Regulations Handbook
14. Barbados Immigration and Citizenship Laws and Regulations Handbook
15. Belarus Immigration and Citizenship Laws and Regulations Handbook
16. Belgium Immigration and Citizenship Laws and Regulations Handbook
17. Belize Immigration and Citizenship Laws and Regulations Handbook
18. Bermuda Immigration and Citizenship Laws and Regulations Handbook
19. Bolivia Immigration and Citizenship Laws and Regulations Handbook
20. Bosnia and Herzegovina Immigration and Citizenship Laws and Regulations Handbook
21. Botswana Immigration and Citizenship Laws and Regulations Handbook
22. Brazil Immigration and Citizenship Laws and Regulations Handbook
23. Brunei Immigration and Citizenship Laws and Regulations Handbook
24. Bulgaria Immigration and Citizenship Laws and Regulations Handbook
25. Cambodia Immigration and Citizenship Laws and Regulations Handbook
26. Cameroon Immigration and Citizenship Laws and Regulations Handbook
27. Canada Immigration and Citizenship Laws and Regulations Handbook
28. Cayman Islands Immigration and Citizenship Laws and Regulations Handbook
29. Chile Immigration and Citizenship Laws and Regulations Handbook
30. China Immigration and Citizenship Laws and Regulations Handbook
31. Colombia Immigration and Citizenship Laws and Regulations Handbook
32. Comoros Immigration and Citizenship Laws and Regulations Handbook
33. Cook Islands Immigration and Citizenship Laws and Regulations Handbook
34. Costa Rica Immigration and Citizenship Laws and Regulations Handbook
35. Croatia Immigration and Citizenship Laws and Regulations Handbook

36.	Cuba Immigration and Citizenship Laws and Regulations Handbook
37.	Cyprus Immigration and Citizenship Laws and Regulations Handbook
38.	Czech Republic Immigration and Citizenship Laws and Regulations Handbook
39.	Denmark Immigration and Citizenship Laws and Regulations Handbook
40.	Dominica Immigration and Citizenship Laws and Regulations Handbook
41.	Dominican Republic Immigration and Citizenship Laws and Regulations Handbook
42.	Dubai Immigration and Citizenship Laws and Regulations Handbook
43.	Ecuador Immigration and Citizenship Laws and Regulations Handbook
44.	Egypt Immigration and Citizenship Laws and Regulations Handbook
45.	El Salvador Immigration and Citizenship Laws and Regulations Handbook
46.	Equatorial Guinea Immigration and Citizenship Laws and Regulations Handbook
47.	Estonia Immigration and Citizenship Laws and Regulations Handbook
48.	Falkland Islands Immigration and Citizenship Laws and Regulations Handbook
49.	Fiji Immigration and Citizenship Laws and Regulations Handbook
50.	Finland Immigration and Citizenship Laws and Regulations Handbook
51.	France Immigration and Citizenship Laws and Regulations Handbook
52.	Georgia Immigration and Citizenship Laws and Regulations Handbook
53.	Germany Immigration and Citizenship Laws and Regulations Handbook
54.	Gibraltar Immigration and Citizenship Laws and Regulations Handbook
55.	Greece Immigration and Citizenship Laws and Regulations Handbook
56.	Grenada Immigration and Citizenship Laws and Regulations Handbook
57.	Guam Investment & Business Guide
58.	Guatemala Immigration and Citizenship Laws and Regulations Handbook
59.	Guernsey Immigration and Citizenship Laws and Regulations Handbook
60.	Guyana Immigration and Citizenship Laws and Regulations Handbook
61.	Haiti Immigration and Citizenship Laws and Regulations Handbook
62.	Honduras Immigration and Citizenship Laws and Regulations Handbook
63.	Hungary Immigration and Citizenship Laws and Regulations Handbook
64.	Iceland Immigration and Citizenship Laws and Regulations Handbook
65.	India Immigration and Citizenship Laws and Regulations Handbook
66.	Indonesia Immigration and Citizenship Laws and Regulations Handbook
67.	Iran Immigration and Citizenship Laws and Regulations Handbook
68.	Iraq Immigration and Citizenship Laws and Regulations Handbook
69.	Ireland Immigration and Citizenship Laws and Regulations Handbook
70.	Israel Immigration and Citizenship Laws and Regulations Handbook
71.	Italy Immigration and Citizenship Laws and Regulations Handbook
72.	Jamaica Immigration and Citizenship Laws and Regulations Handbook
73.	Japan Immigration and Citizenship Laws and Regulations Handbook
74.	Jersey Immigration and Citizenship Laws and Regulations Handbook
75.	Jordan Immigration and Citizenship Laws and Regulations Handbook
76.	Kazakhstan Immigration and Citizenship Laws and Regulations Handbook
77.	Kenya Immigration and Citizenship Laws and Regulations Handbook
78.	Kiribati Immigration and Citizenship Laws and Regulations Handbook

79. Korea, North Immigration and Citizenship Laws and Regulations Handbook
80. Korea, South Immigration and Citizenship Laws and Regulations Handbook
81. Kuwait Immigration and Citizenship Laws and Regulations Handbook
82. Kyrgyzstan Immigration and Citizenship Laws and Regulations Handbook
83. Laos Immigration and Citizenship Laws and Regulations Handbook
84. Latvia Immigration and Citizenship Laws and Regulations Handbook
85. Lebanon Immigration and Citizenship Laws and Regulations Handbook
86. Libya Immigration and Citizenship Laws and Regulations Handbook
87. Liechtenstein Immigration and Citizenship Laws and Regulations Handbook
88. Lithuania Immigration and Citizenship Laws and Regulations Handbook
89. Luxemburg Immigration and Citizenship Laws and Regulations Handbook
90. Macao Immigration and Citizenship Laws and Regulations Handbook
91. Macedonia, Republic Immigration and Citizenship Laws and Regulations Handbook
92. Madagascar Immigration and Citizenship Laws and Regulations Handbook
93. Malaysia Immigration and Citizenship Laws and Regulations Handbook
94. Malta Immigration and Citizenship Laws and Regulations Handbook
95. Man Immigration and Citizenship Laws and Regulations Handbook
96. Mauritius Immigration and Citizenship Laws and Regulations Handbook
97. Mauritius Immigration and Citizenship Laws and Regulations Handbook
98. Mexico Immigration and Citizenship Laws and Regulations Handbook
99. Micronesia Immigration and Citizenship Laws and Regulations Handbook
100. Moldova Immigration and Citizenship Laws and Regulations Handbook
101. Monaco Immigration and Citizenship Laws and Regulations Handbook
102. Mongolia Immigration and Citizenship Laws and Regulations Handbook
103. Morocco Immigration and Citizenship Laws and Regulations Handbook
104. Myanmar Immigration and Citizenship Laws and Regulations Handbook
105. Namibia Immigration and Citizenship Laws and Regulations Handbook
106. Netherlands Immigration and Citizenship Laws and Regulations Handbook
107. New Caledonia Immigration and Citizenship Laws and Regulations Handbook
108. New Zealand Immigration and Citizenship Laws and Regulations Handbook
109. Nicaragua Immigration and Citizenship Laws and Regulations Handbook
110. Nigeria Immigration and Citizenship Laws and Regulations Handbook
111. Northern Mariana Islands Immigration and Citizenship Laws and Regulations Handbook
112. Norway Immigration and Citizenship Laws and Regulations Handbook
113. Pakistan Immigration and Citizenship Laws and Regulations Handbook
114. Panama Immigration and Citizenship Laws and Regulations Handbook
115. Peru Immigration and Citizenship Laws and Regulations Handbook
116. Philippines Immigration and Citizenship Laws and Regulations Handbook
117. Poland Immigration and Citizenship Laws and Regulations Handbook
118. Portugal Immigration and Citizenship Laws and Regulations Handbook
119. Romania Immigration and Citizenship Laws and Regulations Handbook
120. Russia Immigration and Citizenship Laws and Regulations Handbook
121. Samoa (American) Investment & Business Guide

122.Samoa (Western) Immigration and Citizenship Laws and Regulations Handbook
123.Saudi Arabia Immigration and Citizenship Laws and Regulations Handbook
124.Scotland Immigration and Citizenship Laws and Regulations Handbook
125.Singapore Immigration and Citizenship Laws and Regulations Handbook
126.Slovakia Immigration and Citizenship Laws and Regulations Handbook
127.Slovenia Immigration and Citizenship Laws and Regulations Handbook
128.South Africa Immigration and Citizenship Laws and Regulations Handbook
129.Spain Immigration and Citizenship Laws and Regulations Handbook
130.Sri Lanka Immigration and Citizenship Laws and Regulations Handbook
131.St. Helena Immigration and Citizenship Laws and Regulations Handbook
132.Sudan Immigration and Citizenship Laws and Regulations Handbook
133.Suriname Immigration and Citizenship Laws and Regulations Handbook
134.Sweden Immigration and Citizenship Laws and Regulations Handbook
135.Switzerland Immigration and Citizenship Laws and Regulations Handbook
136.Syria Export Import & Business Directory
137.Taiwan Immigration and Citizenship Laws and Regulations Handbook
138.Tajikistan Immigration and Citizenship Laws and Regulations Handbook
139.Thailand Immigration and Citizenship Laws and Regulations Handbook
140.Tunisia Immigration and Citizenship Laws and Regulations Handbook
141.Turkey Immigration and Citizenship Laws and Regulations Handbook
142.Turkmenistan Immigration and Citizenship Laws and Regulations Handbook
143.Uganda Immigration and Citizenship Laws and Regulations Handbook
144.Ukraine Immigration and Citizenship Laws and Regulations Handbook
145.United Arab Emirates Immigration and Citizenship Laws and Regulations Handbook
146.United Kingdom Immigration and Citizenship Laws and Regulations Handbook
147.United States Immigration and Citizenship Laws and Regulations Handbook
148.Uruguay Immigration and Citizenship Laws and Regulations Handbook
149.US Immigration and Citizenship Laws and Regulations Handbook
150.Uzbekistan Immigration and Citizenship Laws and Regulations Handbook
151.Venezuela Immigration and Citizenship Laws and Regulations Handbook
152.Vietnam Immigration and Citizenship Laws and Regulations Handbook
153.Serbia Immigration and Citizenship Laws and Regulations Handbook

www.ingramcontent.com/pod-product-compliance
Lightning Source LLC
LaVergne TN
LVHW080028210926
848481LV00011B/3134